DEVELOPMENTAL DISABILITIES:

A HANDBOOK FOR INTERDISCIPLINARY PRACTICE

Developmental Disabilities

A Handbook for Interdisciplinary Practice

Bruce A. Thyer, Ph.D.
Nancy P. Kropf, Ph.D.
University of Georgia
Editors

BROOKLINE BOOKS

Cover design by Erica Schultz.

Library of Congress Cataloging-in-Publication Data
Developmental disabilities: a handbook for interdisciplinary practice
 / Bruce A. Thyer, Nancy P. Kropf, editors.
        p.   cm.
     Includes bibiographical references and index.
     ISBN 1-57129-003-6 (pbk.)
     1. Developmentally disabled children–Services for.
   2. Developmentally disabled children–Rehabilitation.
   3.Developmentally disabled–Services for. 4. Developmentally
   disabled–Rehabilitation.   I. Thyer, Bruce A.   II. Kropf, Nancy P.
   RJ135.D4756   1995
   362.4'088–dc20   95-23149
                                                        CIP

ISBN 1-57129-003-6

Second printing, 1996.

Published by
Brookline Books
P.O. Box 1047 • Cambridge, Massachusetts 02238-1047

Contents

Preface

Bruce A. Thyer, Ph.D., & Nancy P. Kropf, Ph.D.,

University of Georgia

INTERDISCIPLINARY: involving, or joining, two or more disciplines.

Over the life course of the current cohort of elderly people with developmental disabilities, services and programs have changed dramatically. It is incredible to think that an older person of today was born into a society that offered two primary lifestyle choices for people with developmental disabilities: institutionalization, or unsupported (and often unappreciated) family care. Today the array of possible service options for persons with developmental disabilities is large and continues to expand. Likewise, a growing number of professionals in numerous disciplines touch the lives of people with developmental disabilities and their families.

This book is a response to one current model of developmental disability services, that of practice in the context of Interdisciplinary Teams. Often, one consumer will have interaction with multiple service professionals, all of whom have a certain responsibility to help in achieving specific goals. The effective planning and coordination of such services requires more than a "Case Manager" who serves as the *maestro* of an orchestra of independent players. The players (disciplinary service providers) must work collaboratively from the beginning of providing care, in full awareness of each other's capabilities and activities, and taking into account multiple dimensions of the consumer's life; e.g. physical, social, economic, health, etc. In order to be effective service providers, we all must become skilled in our own profession but also have some understanding about the role of other professionals as part of interdisciplinary and multidisciplinary teams.

The best preparation to practice in such interdisciplinary environments is to have received interdisciplinary training during one's schooling, a type of program described thusly:

> Interdisciplinary training means an integrated educational process involving the interdependent contributions of several relevant disciplines to enhance professional growth as it relates to training, service and research. The interdisciplinary process promotes the development and use of a basic language, core body of knowledge, relevant skills and an understanding of the attitudes, values, and methods of participating disciplines (U.S. Dept. of Health, Education &Welfare, 1976, p. 9).

Heretofore, acquiring this basic language, core body of knowledge, and understanding of other disciplines has been a difficult undertaking due to the lack of a central resource which brought much of this content together. This book arose from our recognition of this fact. By carefully selecting qualified representatives of the major disciplines usually involved in interdisciplinary care, persons with considerable practice experience within University Affiliated Programs and other interdisciplinary contexts, we hope to have compiled a major educational and training resource for students and graduate professionals. A facetious subtitle for this volume could be "Everything You Need to Know about Every Discipline Involved in Helping Persons with Developmental Disabilities".

As the debate about health care reform wages, this volume is especially pertinent. Interdisciplinary practice stresses functional relevance in services. The current cohort of older people with developmental disabilities began their life under a model of practice which often sought to isolate people with disabilities from their communities. If people could not be "cured", then they would at least be "contained." With the advent of the contemporary philosophy of inclusion of people with developmental disabilities, a wider array of professionals are involved in providing interventions to support individuals in their own family homes and communities. One single professional (or discipline) cannot possibly achieve that goal. Collaboration, consultation, and coordination between service providers from various professional backgrounds are needed—which forms the basis for interdisciplinary team practice.

The major goals of interdisciplinary training include the following (H.E.W., 1976, p. 10):

1. To train professionals to gain compe-

tency in their own field.
2. To train professionals to work with multi-handicapped individuals, their families and with the community, in the provision of preventive, ameliorative and supportive services.
3. To increase knowledge of professionals about each other's skills and activities.
4. To aid trainees in each discipline to develop skills from other disciplines that are applicable to their own functioning.
5. To train professionals to effectively collaborate with each other in an interdisciplinary process to promote maximum health care and social functioning of the handicapped individual and his family.
6. To develop professional leaders who can stimulate and develop national policies toward the multiply handicapped and further interdisciplinary service and academic training programs.
7. To encourage and support the accumulation of information generated by interdisciplinary and other activities, experiences, and research.

This book is targeted to goals 3-7. To some extent, it assumes a thorough familiarity with one's home discipline and professional services. Given that foundation, here is additional content on the skills and activities of *other* professionals, from which one can enhance personal practice and learn to work effectively with colleagues, in an atmosphere of mutual respect.

The chapters in this book were selected to help students and current service professionals in developmental disabilities become more knowledgeable about the background and service provided by colleagues in other disciplines. Family members and other caregivers of persons with developmental disabilities may also find it useful to become oriented about the differing contributions of professionals in various disciplines. We are aware that a number of important disciplines are not included in this first edition, a regrettable circumstance required by space limitations.

Cecilia Rokusek, Dean of the College of Health Professions at Governor's State University at University Park, Illinois, starts the book with an introduction to the nature of interdisciplinary practice, and in the concluding chapter Drs. Zolinda Stoneman and Michael Malone at the University of Georgia provide us with a look towards the future of such care. Each of the intervening sixteen chapters explores a specific discipline and describes its professional services for people with developmental disabilities. Each chapter should increase the reader's familiarity with the educational background, licensing and certification requirements, and practice approaches of a specific discipline. Finally, a case example concludes each chapter, integrating conceptual content into actual practice applications with consumers and families, within the interdisciplinary team context.

The editors are grateful to many people who made this book a reality. Among these are the developers of the philosophy and practice of interdisciplinary teams, and also those academics, professionals, and government personnel involved in the establishment of the nationwide network of University Affiliated Facilities (now known as University Affiliated Programs), whose programs were among the earliest exemplars of interdisciplinary services, a tradition of excellence in professional care for persons with developmental disabilities which continues into the present. We are particularly grateful to the chapter authors who share their particular areas of expertise and experience. We deeply appreciate their willingness to lend their time and talent towards making this long-needed book a reality, and

their patience in seeing it brought to completion. Additionally, we wish to thank those of you who will read this book and join us in our efforts to insure that all people with developmental disabilities will be treated with dignity and respect in our professional practice, and to promote the principle that such persons have a *right* to empirically supported services.

Several individuals have provided an inordinate degree of support, and therefore deserve individual acknowledgment. Professor Zolinda Stoneman, Director of the Georgia University Affiliated Program, provided the editors with considerable support for several years which has in part made our editing of this book possible. The support and encouragement of various members of the Interdisciplinary Committee of the American Association of University Affiliated Programs is also gratefully acknowledged. Back in 1978, Virginia Insley, M.S.W., and Juanita Evans, M.S.W., of the Maternal and Child Health Branch of the Bureau of Community Health Services with the then-named Department of Health, Education and Welfare introduced the first editor to the world of UAP's and of interdisciplinary practice in the provision of service to persons with developmental disabilities. As such they deserve credit for the possible merits of this work. Its shortcomings are the responsibility of the editors.

References

U.S. Department of Health, Education and Welfare (1976). *Graduate social work education in the University-affiliated facility: Instruction manual and evaluation guide*. Rockville, MD: Author (DHEW Publication No. HSA 778-5226).

Foreword

I. Leslie Rubin, M.D., Chair (1991-1994), Interdisciplinary Council,

American Association of University Affiliated Programs

The survival of *Homo sapiens sapiens* is quite a success story. After all, this species is rather small compared to its predatory competitors, the big cats or the big bears. It is not as fast as the ungulates who need to escape the big cats. It is not readily able to climb trees to escape danger like its prehensile primate relatives. It does not have large claws like the bear or large teeth like the baboon, or both like the sabre tooth tiger.

What has happened, then, that in so brief a span of the history of life on earth *Homo sapiens sapiens* has been able to dominate almost every other species of animal life, to protect itself from almost every other species, to increase its population by exceedingly large proportions, and to live in almost every part of the Earth, even escaping its confines to explore the mysteries of space?

The answer to that question is obviously complex and has challenged, troubled and excited members of the species for as long as there is any record of thought. The domains of thought around this topic may have a scientific, a philosophic, and even a religious set of considerations. It would be presumptuous to suggest that anyone can provide all the answers, but in the scope of this preface and in the context of the subject matter of this book, I will attempt to provide some personal perceptions and offer a perspective.

Biologically, the members of the species have some uniquely well-developed abilities:

- to learn from experience
- to adapt their behavior in keeping with the learned experiences
- to use their hands to make tools and other artifacts that enhance their limited powers to hunt—or escape from—larger, stronger, or swifter animals
- to adapt to changing conditions, and to make things that enable them to survive in almost any environment.

These skills are further enhanced by the increasingly sophisticated means of communication between individual members of the species. Communication by voice and gesture between individual members of the species has evolved to a degree that enables great clarity of communication and precision of information. This powerful tool has allowed experience to become collective and not merely personal. For example, an individual who experiences a danger or discovers a source of food can transmit this learned experience to other members of the species; thus, they have the benefit of the vital information without necessarily having the experience personally. This ability has enabled the species collectively to accumulate additional survival skills in increasingly difficult, complex, and varied situations.

Increasing sophistication in communication, coupled with an ability to create tools, has enabled the species to communicate with members separated by space or time. The development of writing as a means of communication allowed for the expansion of knowledge and collective experience over successive generations across broad reaches of time. Likewise, it has become possible to communicate with members of the same species who may be living at the same time but many miles away. This communication at a distance helped to develop specific skills and domains of creativity in thought as well as manual dexterity.

Thus, individuals could develop skills in specific areas of activity that had evolved across great distances in regional location as well as time. The development of tools—for domestic use, for hunting, for warfare, for defense, for entertainment, for other social and religious purposes—has continued to be modified and refined by the same basic principles of skill development, through learning and communication. Since the industrial revolution and, in our day, the technological revolution, the process itself has seen a dramatic surge as a result of the development of products that aid communication. This has led to the development of increasingly sophisticated and specialized areas of knowledge and expertise. In addition, there has been a proliferation of these specialized areas of knowledge and expertise. Currently, therefore, there exist a number of disciplines with highly specialized expertise in a variety of areas that are vital to the survival of the individual within the species as well as for the species as a whole.

The explanation above for the successful survival of *Homo sapiens sapiens*, however, tells only part of the story. The narrative above has clearly focused on the development of sophisticated skills as a result of the application of intelligence, dexterity and communication that apply predominantly to individuals within the species. In truth, the development of these sophisticated skills, which allowed this relatively small and weak species to triumph against all odds, would not have been possible without social organization.

Social organization is not unique to humans; it is a common phenomenon in animal life from the hives of bees, flocks of birds, prides of lions, to the troops of baboons. The field of sociobiology has given us insights into the critical interrelationship between the individuals within the collective units of each species. The defensive quality of herds of ungulates, the migratory practices of flocks of birds, the hunting practices of a pride of lions, the survival of the whole of the bee or ant society in their common purpose of assuring the survival of their common 'organism,' all illustrate the natural fact of survival of the individual through the collective of the species 'community,' and the survival of the community of the species through the individual.

Sociobiologically, each species has a characteristic structure function and size to its 'community.' Within the community, individuals or groups of individuals have specific functional roles and responsibilities. There is a minimum number of individuals as well as a maximum, below and above which the community will not survive or will splinter.

The human community has similarities and some unique differences. The similarities are that it is exceedingly difficult for the individual to live outside of the community. The survival of the individual and the community are interdependent, and the roles and responsibilities of individuals or groups of individuals are specified. The major differences lie in the unique biological characteristics of humans, as described above: the sophistication of their ability to learn, to communicate, to create thoughts and objects, and to develop skills.

These abilities have enabled the human species to develop a variety of sophisticated skills embodied in individuals within the community. The sociobiological imperatives have created the situation where these sets of skills have become increasingly important and increasingly integrated into the fabric of the community. In addition, the interdependence of the members of the community on one another's skills and expertise has fostered the development of such social attributes as cooperation, collaboration, and consideration and respect for others. These elements, coupled with advances in technology, have been instrumental to the growth and elaboration of communities that make up societies of the human species.

It is within this context that individuals with certain specialized expertise cooperate and collaborate with one another to address the issues that challenge societies or individuals within the societies. The individuals in whom certain skills reside represent the knowledge 'disciplines,' and the process whereby they collectively and cooperatively collaborate becomes the *interdisciplinary* process.

In the 1960's when the President's Commission on Mental Retardation reviewed the understanding of and approach to mental retardation in the country, they came to the conclusion that:

- There needed to be more services for people with mental retardation and their families
- There needed to be more research done into the understanding, prevention, and treatment of mental retardation
- There needed to be centers for the training of professionals in mental retardation
- The services, research, and training had to be done with an *interdisciplinary* approach.

University Affiliated Programs (UAP's) were established around the country in order to fulfill this need. These facilities became united through the development of a central office which has since become known as the American Association of University Affiliated Programs, or AAUAP. The formation of the AAUAP had, as part of its functional operation, a council comprised of representatives from the array of professional disciplines who met on interdisciplinary issues. It was this Interdisciplinary Council that helped to guide the approach to interdisciplinary conceptualization, philosophy, practice, and training within the network of University Affiliated Programs in the early years.

Indeed, through the passage of time, the focus of the UAP's on interdisciplinary approach to providing services and supports to children and adults with developmental disabilities and their families has become the established mode of practice and training. In a sense, the goal in the establishment of the UAP's has been met. But there is still much to be done in all areas mentioned above, especially in improving on training and services through appropriate research, but also in making sure that the interdisciplinary approach becomes more widespread. This latter goal can only be achieved through a process of demystification and dissemination.

What better way to do this than to have a clear and concise text, readily available and accessible, that outlines the ideas behind interdisciplinary philosophy, and an approach to interdisciplinary practice—as well as providing an outline on the identity and roles of some of the common professional disciplines involved in the process?

This book was conceived during a meeting of the Interdisciplinary Council of the AAUAP in Austin, Texas. We had been reviewing disciplinary training and cross-disciplinary training in interdisciplinary practice when it became clear that there were no real guidelines that could be used for this purpose. Thus the present volume was conceived.

In this book, the editors have assembled an impressive collection of contributions towards meeting the need of providing a reference text for individuals who are involved in interdisciplinary training and practice for children and adults with developmental disabilities and their families. This book is also an important reference for centers that are in the process of developing interdisciplinary programs.

Many years ago, conductor Arthur Fiedler appeared in a television commercial where he said, *"Orange juice is not just for breakfast anymore."* Well, the truth of the matter is that interdisciplinary practice is not just for mental retardation or developmental disabilities anymore. It has become clear that the philosophy and practice embodied in the interdisciplinary approach extend very broadly to almost all areas of human endeavor where experts from different skill areas work together to achieve a common goal. To address this issue, some universities have developed programs that deal with the academics of what 'interdisciplinary' is and does.

If you think about it, almost all bodies of knowledge come from diverse sources, and the categorizing of certain specific areas of specific knowledge and expertise comes from a focus on that topic. Thomas S. Kuhn, in his book *The Structure of Scientific Revolutions*, comments that the establishment of a specific discipline of discussion or speculation represents the beginning of the science in that particular area. While it is quite reasonable to isolate any aspect of knowledge for detailed scientific study or investigation, it becomes necessary to combine areas of knowledge to appreciate the understanding of its application. In truth, one cannot exist without the other. The enhancement of knowledge and understanding must focus on specific, well-delineated concepts, while the application of that knowledge and understanding requires a broader perspective and conceptual framework that almost invariably incorporates knowledge and understanding from a variety of disciplines.

In this context, then, the interdisciplinary concept is not new, merely the articulation of the concept and the establishment of the framework of the process so that the goal is accomplished. Bruce Thyer has helped us to articulate the framework as well as to look at some of the elements involved in fine detail. For this we are grateful, and we know that those who use this book will have no trouble in finding its conceptual and practical value.

1

An Introduction to the Concept of Interdisciplinary Practice

Cecilia Rokusek, Ed.D., R.D., C.H.E.

The term *interdisciplinary* often evokes the idealistic and lofty idea that a group of persons will come together to synthesize *all* the available knowledge, resources, skills, and techniques to solve *all* problems. Although this image is always there, interdisciplinary team process should actually evoke the idea of individuals coming together to identify the course of action that is most effective and reasonable for the challenge(s) presented. It means equal input and respect from *all* persons to reach a goal—or scores of goals. Not all the resources, knowledge, skills, and techniques may be available or even reasonable to present. There is a solid reality to the interdisciplinary team process that is family-centered and community-based.

As society moves from a highly specialized, individualized, and competitive model of care delivery to a more collaborative, interactive, multi-skilled model, the practice of interdisciplinary care delivery will grow significantly. The interdisciplinary team model can already be seen in the field of primary care, particularly for special needs populations. Team members representing professionals, parents, consumers, paraprofessionals, and community resources can view the individual consumer from a lifespan approach in assessment and planning. A team function is usually not a one-time arrangement.

Interdisciplinary teams are agents of change whose impact is the result of collective collaboration, not the strengths or abilities of the individual team members. The focus is on the individual consumer, who is often a *member* of the team assessing and planning for his or her future.

The history of the interdisciplinary team process and its impact on persons with disabilities is often confused with, and clouded by, *multi*disciplinary efforts. There is a clear need, first, to establish a conceptual framework from which to build interdisciplinary team practice, and secondly, to put it into the context of society's changing health-care delivery system. Finally, institutions of higher education must incorporate interdisciplinary theory and practice into their academic training programs at all levels, including continuing education, enabling both professionals and consumers to participate.

This chapter will outline the history of the interdisciplinary process and will present a conceptualization of the theory and practice of the interdisciplinary process. The challenges of a changing care-delivery system are highlighted. Finally, the challenges to educators are presented, to insure (a) that interdisciplinary theory and practice will be a substantial part of the curriculum for all disciplines involved with persons who have disabilities, and (b) that opportunities will be available for interdisciplinary process education for parents and consumers.

The History of Interdisciplinary Practice: Past, Present and Future

Interdisciplinary teams (IDTs), under various labels, have been used in the medical, educational, and social service disciplines since the 1920s. Although the term *IDT* and a better understanding of it did not gain momentum until World War II, interdisciplinary rehabilitation centers grew across the country. The home-care model was established in the late 1940s as a way to provide medical services in the home to patients whose problems had already been treated and stabilized in the hospital but no longer required hospital care (Wise, Berkhard, Rubin, & Kyte, 1974). In the mid- and late 1950s the interdisciplinary team concept was not often found in the literature, primarily because the practice of interdisciplinary teaming was not used extensively.

An early example of the application of interdisciplinary practice outside of the rehabilitation setting was developed in the state of Washington in the 1950s. Interdisciplinary clinics for children with developmental disabilities were established jointly by the Washington School of Medicine and the Washington State Department of Health. These clinics have spread throughout the state and continue up to the present time (1995) to be a model for interdisciplinary care for exceptional children and their families. The 1960s and 1970s gave rise to the conceptualization and development of interdisciplinary teams, which led to an understanding of interdisciplinary team practice, particularly as it relates to University Affiliated Programs (UAPs) for children with special needs, abused children, or children in need of rehabilitation services.

The successful development of interdisciplinary teams for delivering primary health care began in Latin America in the early 1980s (Reisman & Duran, 1983). The multidisciplinary team was the most common functionary in primary health care in the United States during this time and up to the early 1990s. In 1986, the American Academy of Pediatrics developed *Project Bridge—Decision Making for Early Services: A Team Approach* (American Academy of Pediatrics, 1986) in an attempt to train pediatricians and other health, educational and social service professionals to work together with families to plan for infants and children with special needs. The effectiveness of the Latin American model was partially due to the initial planning and task delineation for each professional. Detailed job descriptions, job evaluations, and a developed curriculum for training provided the foundation for the overall success of the team development.

Interdisciplinary Theory and Practice

Disciplinary professionals, working within the context of interdisciplinary teams, will make significant contributions in health care reform, particularly in the delivery of primary care throughout the entire community. The interdisciplinary actions of these team members—their contributions to the consumer with special needs and his or her family—are important. Significant paradigm shifts are occurring in society that increase the need for interdisciplinary team development in the care of persons with disabilities in the home, the community, the school, the health-care setting, and the whole of society. The demographic shift toward an increasingly older population, combined with the continued movement of persons with special needs into community-based programs, will also increase the need for interdisciplinary professionals working in the community, most especially in the area of home-care. In addition, it is estimated that interdisciplinary professionals will eventually make up as much as two-thirds of the primary health care force in the community.

Interdisciplinary professionals have a unique role in health-care reform and the delivery of services, and in providing care from the home to the school and to the work environment. The roles of interdisciplinary professionals will be expanded and challenged in the areas of case coordination and comprehensive care throughout the lifespan. All allied health professionals, human service professionals, and education professionals in the care of people with disabilities will have to look at the context of their interdisciplinary care in terms of first contact (which often deals with accessibility), longitudinal care (which is continuous), comprehensive care (the diagnostic and assessment components, therapeutics and interventions, and ongoing prevention), and finally coordinated care, in the context of each person's environment.

The day of the therapeutic practitioner is passing. No single provider/professional has all the knowledge and skills necessary to meet contemporary care needs, particularly for individuals with disabilities living fully integrated, independent, and productive lives within individual communities. In addition, interdisciplinary teams can no longer be made up only of specialized disciplinary professionals. Teams must include the consumer, and family or family members, if appropriate. In addition, teams will vary in size and make-up according to the needs and desires of the consumer. Interdisciplinary teams may include community planners, clergy, architects, engineers, attorneys, chamber of commerce representatives, business managers, fundraisers, policemen, hospital aids, multi-skilled technicians, human resource leaders, and city housing, labor and transportation representatives.

A community-based philosophy and interdisciplinary education has helped health-care delivery to be more patient/client-focused. This focus on the patient/consumer in the interdisciplinary team will expand. Community-based health-care teams will be the norm of the future. The traditional barriers confronting the practice of interdisciplinary care are likely to decrease as managed care offered through corporate and institutional health care delivery entities—particularly those focused on primary care—expands. The definition of the primary care team will be broader than the current conceptualization and will consist of varying combinations of providers which reflect the individual needs of the patient/consumer, which might include education and certainly social services.

Teams will look very different from one another. In the scope of primary care, team composition will depend on the needs of the individual, the community, and more specifically on community-defined needs in relationship to the individual. The major challenge for professionals working in the developmental disability field, within the context of changing demographics and shifts in health care delivery, is to develop both an understanding of interdisciplinary theory and working skills in the delivery and practice of interdisciplinary team care. Although the literature on interdisciplinary team development and process appears substantial, there is actually a severe paucity of basic theoretical and outcome research on interdisciplinary team process and practice.

One of the best definitions of interdisciplinary practice comes from the social work literature. Interdisciplinary practice is the ability to practice one's own profession while linking into the work of others (cf. Falck, 1977). Interdisciplinary practice requires knowledge and skill that differentiates one's work from that of others within a single frame of reference. Consumers/patients gain from the numerous advantages of interdependent practice in that various (and often numerous) needs are met, continuity of service is likely, and professionals/practitioners are open to several approaches and options.

The theory and practice of the interdisciplinary team process has been difficult to articulate, because of the paucity of research —particularly outcomes reasearch—and because of the difficulty in higher education of integrating the theory, techniques, and skills for interdisciplinary practice while also teaching the basic disciplinary knowledge, principles, and theories of an entire profession. With the changing environment of the care delivery system, it will become essential to include and integrate interdisciplinary theory and practice in professional education.

It is important first to distinguish between the models of team practice. Figure 1-1 illustrates the models of team practice that are most usually observed from an actual environmental and practice perspective. The *interdisciplinary* team is also identified in

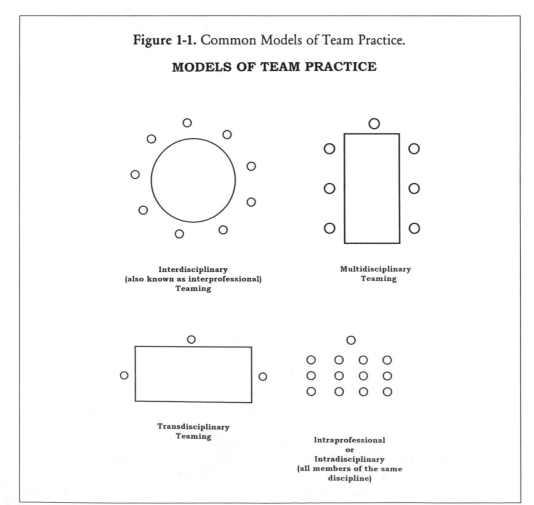

Figure 1-1. Common Models of Team Practice.

MODELS OF TEAM PRACTICE

Interdisciplinary
(also known as interprofessional)
Teaming

Multidisciplinary
Teaming

Transdisciplinary
Teaming

Intraprofessional
or
Intradisciplinary
(all members of the same
discipline)

some settings as the *interprofessional* team. Most often this setting includes a round table where each member is viewed as an equal in all decision-making and consensus-building. If a round table is not available, other table arrangements can be made, but most commonly no one would be seated at the head of the arrangement.

In the *multidisciplinary* team environment, an elongated rectangular table is most often used. There is a clearly identified arrangement for the team leader or chair. This arrangement, from a more traditional medical model, identifies the team leader as the person in charge and ultimately responsible for the final decision-making of the team. Team members may not always be viewed as equal in the process.

The *transdisciplinary* team process is the most recent of all models to be developed. It is an environmental model developed as an offspring from the interdisciplinary team process. It is often used in pediatric practice for specific physical disabilities. The model defines a group of professionals (most usually 3 to 5) who come together to plan for and work with an individual who has an identifiable need or set of needs for which all disciplines need not be involved. This transdisciplinary team can bring in other team members as necessary and bridge to appropriate services as needed. Effective transdisciplinary teams work with, and are part of, larger interdisciplinary teams. The transdisciplinary environment is one of equal team membership including decision-making and consensus-building. As with the interdisciplinary team model, there must be a high level of discipline comfort and cross-discipline understanding.

The final model is that of the *unidisciplinary* or *intradisciplinary* team. In this environment, all members are of the same discipline, although various specialties within that discipline could exist within one team. Discipline professionals need to

be comfortable in that environment before a comfort level is usually achieved in the other team environments. The same principles of equal recognition and participation in decision-making and consensus-building need to be followed.

Interdisciplinary practice is always group practice (Falck, 1977). Dominance, control, superiority, and extreme individualism do not mix well with interdisciplinary practice. *Interdisciplinary practice* means three or more practitioners working in an interdependent work relationship, working for a common end, and spanning three or more fields of learning and professional activity. *Multidisciplinary practice* is professional activity by three or more practitioners, directed by a common problem, with a designated leader who assumes the responsibility for the direction and final decision-making of the group. The focus is not on the interdependent working relationship of the team members, but rather on the input of the team members to the team leader, who assimilates and directs the final outcome/recommendations.

Interactive collaboration, as opposed to directed one-way input, is another important distinguishing point between interdisciplinary and multidisciplinary team practice. Interdisciplinary team practice requires that members be well-grounded in the professions and able to share common work goals, yet know enough of the knowledge and functions of the other team members and their disciplines to interact openly and meaningfully to benefit the consumer/patient.

All members of an interdisciplinary team must share the ability to:

1. understand a common professional language
2. decrease control of all work boundaries
3. understand the delivery system(s) available and remain open to all available

resources
4. communicate openly and effectively to peers and others in and outside of the professional work environment
5. integrate their professional abilities and unique personal qualities into the team, and recognize the specialized culture, values, traditions, knowledge, training, personal emotions, and experiences that the other members bring to the team
6. work well in teams and contribute towards consensus building

The basic conceptual foundations of interdisciplinary practice include:

1. a commitment to one's individual discipline or experiential background, to recognizing the value of others' disciplines and backgrounds, and to integrating the work of others with one's own
2. an ability to look at the "whole" in the delivery of services that focus on a consumer in a holistic fashion while operating in numerous personal and professional environments
3. recognition of the interdependency of disciplinary practice and other environmental input from paraprofessionals, families and consumers
4. respect for the expertise of all disciplinary professionals, paraprofessionals, families and consumers
5. recognition of the ultimate benefit to consumers and their families through increased knowledge and skills and cross-disciplined assessment, problem-solving, intervention, prevention, and short- and long-term planning

The foundation is the commitment professionals have to their individual discipline or experiential background and the recognition and integration of other team members with their disciplinary or experiential

backgrounds. The experiential background is an important area for team members to recognize. As interdisciplinary teams develop and assume greater roles in health care delivery and educational planning, consumers, parents, and community members at large become even more significant members of the team. This first principle lays the foundation from which the other four theoretical principles are built.

Interdisciplinary Team Function in a Changing Delivery System

With shifting demographics and changing paradigms of health-care delivery, IDTs serving individuals with developmental disabilities must deal with new environments and challenging barriers. As a result, composition of the team will vary according to the community or environment from which it comes. These teams will often deal with expanded roles in primary care delivery. Teams in the next decade will need to deal with:

1) serving the medically needy in both rural and urban areas (possibly using interactive telecommunications to access team members)
2) developing community health plans that may determine team composition
3) assuring adequate time for the interdisciplinary team process to work at all levels within the community and throughout the lifespans of the individuals with special needs
4) advocating for patient-focused care
5) establishing interdisciplinary practice in community-bused managed care
6) using a triage approach to lifelong care planning for all individuals, including determining problems and needs, planning, and ongoing follow-up

Interdisciplinary teams working with

special-needs populations can have a major impact in providing high-quality and effective case coordination. The significant factors are adequate funding, potential regulatory barriers that could inhibit direct access to various health professionals, capitations, and uncertainties as to the outcomes in health care reform.

Figure 1-2 illustrates the interdisciplinary service delivery model focusing on the environments which the consumer lives in and is impacted by. This conceptualization puts the consumer and family at the center and recognizes them as part of the interdisciplinary team environment that includes the professionals, paraprofessionals, and community members at large with whom they most directly interact and live day-to-day. This family and community environment working together assesses the additional needs of the consumer to be served and works with the outside environment to obtain services or individual assistance. There is ongoing coordination between all environments to avoid duplication and to assure that whatever is being provided is most appropriate and effective for the individual and family. The process is interactive, comprehensive, and coordinated throughout the span of need.

Interdisciplinary practice results in the creation of an interdependent and common work environment incorporating a systems approach, including all the environments (physical, social, etc.) which a consumer lives in or is impacted by. Interdisciplinary practice is grounded in disciplinary professionals who are able to collaborate equally with other discipline professionals, paraprofessionals, and consumers. Professionals practicing in the context of interdisciplinary teams should possess:

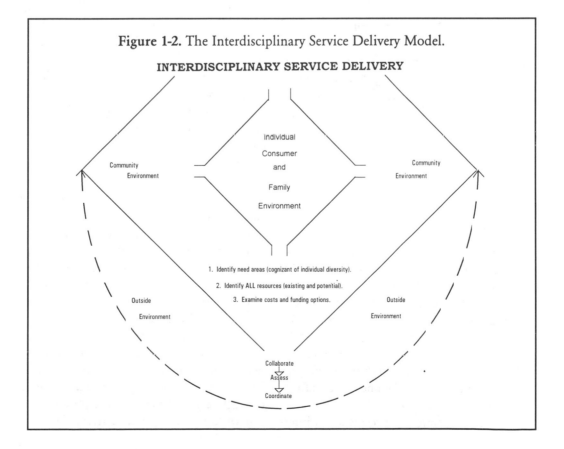

Figure 1-2. The Interdisciplinary Service Delivery Model.

INTERDISCIPLINARY SERVICE DELIVERY

Individual
Consumer
and
Family
Environment

Community
Environment

Community
Environment

1. Identify need areas (cognizant of individual diversity).
2. Identify ALL resources (existing and potential).
3. Examine costs and funding options.

Outside
Environment

Outside
Environment

Collaborate
Assess
Coordinate

1. knowledge and skill in interdisciplinary theory and service delivery
2. knowledge and skill in group dynamics and practice
3. the ability to create an interdependent and common work environment incorporating a systems approach, including relevant physical and social environments
4. the ability to collaborate equally with other disciplines, professionals, paraprofessionals, consumers and families
5. knowledge of and skill in policy making and service delivery issues
6. knowledge of and skill in consumer-focused case-coordination of care
7. skill in team development and consensus-building

Individuals involved in interdisciplinary practice need to assess and define these skills throughout their career. With each new or added team member, the components of interdisciplinary practice are challenged. In addition, administrative changes, reorganization, fiscal restructuring, policy changes, and local, state, or national reform as related to education, health, or social services, can all significantly impact—and many times put stress on—the team members involved in interdisciplinary practice.

Challenges for Professional Education

Health care, social service, and educational professionals, as well as those involved in educating the public, will have to examine and identify the most effective ways of educating individuals who will serve on the IDTs of the future. (See Moseley, 1992.) Team members must be knowledgeable and skillful in interdisciplinary theory and process, and they must feel empowered to function effectively as a team.

There is a paucity of research on inter-disciplinary theory and process as well as interdisciplinary education. The research that has been done in education demonstrates that shared learning experiences, in the classroom and in a clinical setting, will help students at the college and university level to develop the understanding, appreciation, respect, and skill necessary to work with others on the health care team (Sutlive, 1989). There is also a significant need to enhance students' knowledge of and trust in members of other health professions, social services professions, and education professions, as well as other service providers, parents, and consumers themselves. This is particularly true in the allied health professions, since such professionals often view health care from one narrow disciplinary perspective.

If professional isolation and fragmentation continue, interdisciplinary teams will never work, and health care reform, too, will probably fail. Continued fragmentation, service duplication, and expanded costs will be the result. The consumer cannot be overlooked as a team member. This includes both the individuals with disabilities and their families. To get their expectations met, consumers will also have to become advocates of their own health care and to be educated about what questions to ask and how to work with team members as an equal. The public will have to be educated about the responsibility for their health, not only in times of need for acute care, but also with emphasis on prevention and healthy living. They must also learn what role they can play if asked to be on a health team for the community or for an individual with a special need.

The paraprofessional or technician-level practitioner will also be an important member of the team and so must be educated. Education must be on patient care, patient care delivery, and the interdisciplinary process within that care and delivery. Primary care will be the norm. The physician assistant, physical therapist, occupational therapist, nutritionist, teacher, and social worker will need to acquire a more comprehensive understanding of the capabilities of other professions. They will have to develop professional trust and respect which will serve as the basis for referral. With a referral, the focal point of the health-care professions—and educational and social services as well—will have to be the consumer of health care, rather than the profession itself. This may result in a change in the professional socialization of students. The challenge of educational institutions will be to develop and devise learning situations and learning strategies that provide the greatest opportunities for students to collaborate in learning and to teach each other about the professions. (See Szasz, 1970.)

Arranging for foundation courses (e.g., anatomy, physiology, biochemistry, etc.) to include students from a variety of disciplines establishes a baseline knowledge of such topics, but may not inculcate the values of interdisciplinary practice. Disciplinary students may pay little attention to material or examples that refer to the activities of other professions. It may be that students need to acquire a sound professional identity and become comfortable with it *before* they are ready to engage in significant interdisciplinary learning activities.

It is essential that students be brought together for certain interdisciplinary coursework after they have developed such a sense of professional identity. However, interdisciplinary coursework in IDT development (theory and practice), teaching and learning processes, health systems, and political systems are courses the students may value very little—not because they are interdisciplinary, but because students may not see the direct clinical application of the content while these courses are being taught.

What is needed are structured learning activities such as actual patient care simulations or clinical experiences that model sound interdisciplinary involvement. Courses in history taking and physical diagnosis and team development that are shared by all the disciplines have some relevance. Classroom teaching should reinforce the clinical experience, and faculty should actually convey in their classroom examples the clinical interdisciplinary philosophy in their work. Partnerships between community-based providers and academic institutions whereby students can work on interdisciplinary teams are important. These teams should be working effectively and should exemplify for the students what interdisciplinary team functioning is all about.

Students also need to become knowledgeable about primary care. Primary care consists of all facets of health care and other care throughout the lifespan, including diagnosis of acute and chronic illnesses, management of illness, rehabilitation, and patient education activities. The focus is not only on care during illness but care during wellness as well.

Institutions of higher education need to examine interdisciplinary education as an overarching core component in their professional education. In addition, opportunities for continuing education in interdisciplinary theory and practice should be made available to paraprofessionals, parents, consumers, and community leaders. Cross-teaching needs to be included in the curriculum, and methods to establish cross-faculty appointments should be established and encouraged. The following integrated curricular sections are recommended:

1. group dynamics
2. team development
3. interdisciplinary theory and practice
4. communication for the professional and lay person, focusing on interper-

sonal communication
5. introduction to the professions
6. ethics
7. community-based care

Interdisciplinary practice is a variant of disciplinary practice. Students must be knowledgeable and skillful in their own professions first. Institutions of higher education must build an environment that demonstrates and builds students' knowledge of and skill in interdisciplinary practice.

Figure 1-3 illustrates the educational core from which to build a knowledge base and skill level for students to work in an interdisciplinary environment. The model is

built on three interacting and enhancing student cores: (1) discipline-specific required courses, (2) interdisciplinary set of courses, and (3) supporting or elective courses selected by the student or recommended by a specfic discipline.

Disciplines involved in interdisciplinary team practice assist in developing the interdisciplinary core focused on team development and process in a variety of practice environments. Supporting student courses provide students with an opportunity to interact with other disciplines and students outside of a major or related area. The challenge remains that students in many discipline courses of study (majors) often do not

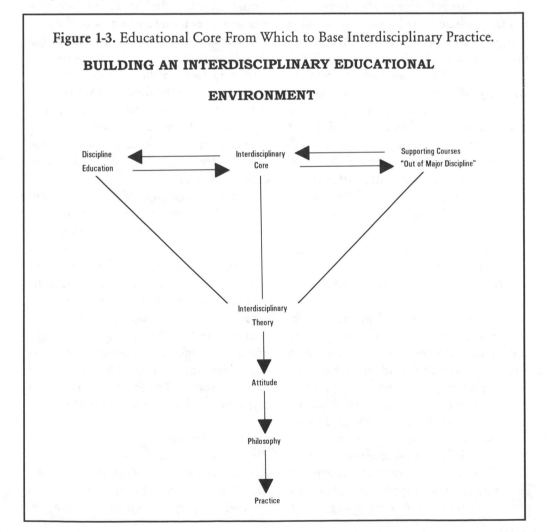

Figure 1-3. Educational Core From Which to Base Interdisciplinary Practice.

BUILDING AN INTERDISCIPLINARY EDUCATIONAL

ENVIRONMENT

Discipline Education

Interdisciplinary Core

Supporting Courses "Out of Major Discipline"

Interdisciplinary Theory

Attitude

Philosophy

Practice

have an opportunity to take elective courses. Curricula should be examined to enable students to take two or three elective courses. The course work, along with faculty who support and believe in the interdisciplinary process, can help to create an environment that will help students develop an understanding of what interdisciplinary theory and practice truly are. These students need to have the attitudes and philosophy necessary to create other interdisciplinary environments in their practice.

There are constraints to interdisciplinary practice (Falck, 1977), for example:

1. *role blurring*—to an extent that everyone does what everyone else does, thus depriving clients the benefits of different approaches to their problems
2. *role specialization*—to an extreme degree, thus depriving clients of consistent, integrated treatment
3. *professional expansionism*—the wish to gain total control (An example of this might be the physician who presumes to be able to "integrate" the bio-psycho-social aspects of patient treatment.)
4) *the wish for indispensability*—leading to an increase in professional territoriality, with attendant social recognition, power, grants, and prestige
5) *enhancement*—of personal status, income, and influence

Students should be made aware of these constraints, and others, and discuss them openly in an interdisciplinary environment.

The major attitudes necessary for successful interdisciplinary practice are:

1. thorough commitment to the disciplinary profession's values and ethics, and belief in the usefulness of one's own profession
2. belief in a holistic approach to client problems

3. recognition of the interdependency of practice
4. recognition of the expertise of colleagues and others

In 1993, the Pew Health Professions Commission stated that local community health needs must be well integrated with the mission of health-profession schools. Critical guidelines will have to be set that divide critical standards of care developed by interdisciplinary teams. Issues such as functional assessment, prevention, counseling, and home and long-term care will have to be addressed as the standards of care. This involves not only a change in the present idea of the system, but the total integration of the interdisciplinary system of health care, most significantly as it affects individuals with disabilities.

The twenty-first century offers significant opportunities and challenges for interdisciplinary professionals. Such professionals will have the opportunity to develop the practice of interdependent collaboration into more patient-focused care in which the consumer is involved.

The development of interdisciplinary teams must be fostered in academic institutions and must be clearly understood by faculty so that the theory and practice can be fostered among students. Interdisciplinary team development can be done well or poorly. It is clearly unfortunate that students often have their first experience in IDTs only after they graduate.

Development of interdisciplinary education is critically important. Students need experience in the interdisciplinary process in order to work more with the individual, as well as with the colleagues or discipline professionals who will be involved in the individual's total care. Students need to learn, within the balance of their profession and their talents, how to be a positive interpersonal and interdependent force in the total care of an individual throughout the life span. Negativity between professionals can clearly disrupt and overwhelm the patient/consumer and provide negative care. Team professionals must no longer be confronted with an authoritarian view that any one discipline is "in charge" of the team. They must support a shared leadership responsibility that follows patient/consumer needs rather than the needs of a given discipline. The theory and practice of interdisciplinary education means that professionals understand each other's terminology and do not hesitate to ask for clarification of what they do not understand. The relevance of each professional and paraprofessional must also be emphasized. Academic programs in health professions, social work, education, and other disciplines involved in the care of people with disabilities must include opportunities for students to interact with and learn from each other concerning their respective disciplines and their roles in the care of people with disabilities. Patient-focused interdisciplinary outcome research is needed, as well as expanded research in interdisciplinary education and further conceptualization of theory and practice, particularly as related to primary care.

References

Falck, H. S. (1977). Interdisciplinary education and implications for social work practice. *Journal of Education for Social Work, 13*(2), 30-37.

Moseley, M. (1992). Educating faculty for teaching in an interdisciplinary general education sequence. *Journal of General Education, 41*, 8-17.

Reisman, A., & Duran, L. (1983). Designing primary health care teams for developing countries. *Public Health Reports, 98*, 184-189.

Sutlive, V. H. Jr. (1989). Breakthrough or babel: Communication or confusion in interdisciplinary education. *Urban Anthropology, 18*, 95-109.

Szasz, G. (1970). Educating for the health team. *Canadian Journal of Public Health, 61*, 345-350.

Wise, H., Beckhard, R., Rubin, I., & Kyte, A. L. (1974). *Making health teams work*. Cambridge, MA: Ballinger.

2

Administration

Mary Richardson, Ph.D., M.H.A., & Vic Keeran, M.S., M.S.W.

Administration is the discipline which is dedicated to the organization, management, and delivery of services to individuals with disabilities on an equitable and cost-effective basis (Kazuk, 1987). Different titles are used to denote individuals in these job positions, such as administrator, manager, or director. Despite the diversity of titles, administration can be defined functionally. Administrators assume the responsibility for managing the human, financial and informational resources of the organization; planning, implementing and monitoring the programs and activities of the organization; and evaluating the quality and cost-effectiveness of these programs and activities.

In the United States, professional administration surfaced in the early 1900s during an era of growth of enterprise and entrepreneurship (Ross, 1992). Scientific approaches to administration at that time were aimed at "rationalizing" the work process and making it as efficient as possible (Quinn, Faerman & McGrath, 1990). With the shifts in societal values and rapid technological advances during this century, the nature of administration has changed dramatically. Moving beyond the scientific approach to administration, the human relations model emerged, placing

on the values of commitment, cohesion, and morale within an organization. More recently, the complexity of society and the tremendous competition for scarce resources throughout both the public and private sectors of the economy have placed greater demands upon the organization to be adaptable and flexible.

A great deal of literature has been devoted to the changes which have occurred in administration and the characteristics that are identified with well-functioning organizations. Alvin Toffler, the futurologist, has characterized many of the changes in the practice of administration in his book *Third Wave* (1980). As the title implies, there has been a movement away from the past routine of mass production toward high levels of specialization in products and professionalism. Peters and Waterman (1987) analyzed the characteristics of successful firms. Their findings focused for a clear three critical factors: (a) on's mission (b) awareness of the thinking by small the need to for need for an organization groups, th speed and flexibility. Others, tior scribed the increased awareness need for congruence of individu organizational needs (Bennis & Na

1985; Covey, 1990; Drucker, 1985; Maslow, 1971).

With the trend toward specialization came a demand for higher levels of skills and competence. However, specialization also emphasized and created boundaries in organizations. As efforts required the contributions of different types of specialists, the structure and nature of organizations changed. The importance shifted away from the individuals who performed the tasks (workers) to the outcomes of their work (products). One result of these shifts has been in the formation of multi- or interdisciplinary teams. Frequently, organizations join together to establish networks, alliances, and joint ventures which form linkages that promote their common objectives.

The complexity of the administrative environment has changed dramatically and has affected many service organizations that serve individuals with disabilities and their families. In some cases, health, education, and social services are included within a single organization. In other situations, the organization may develop a loose referral network or formal alliance with other organizations who offer complementary services. Effective service delivery in this type of service system is dependent upon integrating the knowledge of all the professionals from various disciplines and backgrounds into a coherent and functioning interdisciplinary team.

Organizations must be responsive to a public environment which includes multiple constituencies. Groups that have an include organizational functioning in sources, regular advocates, funding responsibility for policy makers. The organization (or a network between the and the environment organizations) to the administrator, in organizations the clinical staff. Effective primarily has become increasingly important with

organization seeking to survive and thrive under these complex conditions.

In interdisciplinary organizations, such as those which serve persons with developmental disabilities and their families, it is helpful to understand the total functioning of the organization. Organizational practice encompasses both clinical and administrative practices (see Table 1). Both elements are important, and together they create a total system for the client.

Effective administrative practice requires a strategic blend of leadership, analytical, and technical skills. Leadership, sometimes referred to as "the art" of administrative practice, is defined as a process in which one person influences others in their attainment of common goals (Fiedler, 1971). Effectiveness in a leadership position is associated with the degree of success with which a group performs the primary assigned task; it includes those areas by which the administrator influences both the behavior of other individuals in the organization and the interaction between the organization and its environment. Examples of skills required in an administrative position are influencing, motivating, communicating, delegating, networking, negotiating, consensus building, conflict management, and other interpersonal and human management skills.

In addition to leadership qualities, an administrator must possess technical and analytical skills. These skill areas are aimed at organizational planning and evaluation, promoting efficiency in the allocation of resources, and reducing variability and promoting quality in the production of services. Examples include systems assessment and analysis, the application and use of information technology, implementing quality assurance systems, budgeting, financial analysis and management, community/consumer needs assessment and technical planning, risk assessment and management, pro-

2

Administration

Mary Richardson, Ph.D., M.H.A., & Vic Keeran, M.S., M.S.W.

Administration is the discipline which is dedicated to the organization, management, and delivery of services to individuals with disabilities on an equitable and cost-effective basis (Kazuk, 1987). Different titles are used to denote individuals in these job positions, such as administrator, manager, or director. Despite the diversity of titles, administration can be defined functionally. Administrators assume the responsibility for managing the human, financial and informational resources of the organization; planning, implementing and monitoring the programs and activities of the organization; and evaluating the quality and cost-effectiveness of these programs and activities.

In the United States, professional administration surfaced in the early 1900s during an era of growth of enterprise and entrepreneurship (Ross, 1992). Scientific approaches to administration at that time were aimed at "rationalizing" the work process and making it as efficient as possible (Quinn, Faerman & McGrath, 1990). With the shifts in societal values and rapid technological advances during this century, the nature of administration has changed dramatically. Moving beyond the scientific approach to administration, the human relations model emerged, placing emphasis on the values of commitment, cohesion, and morale within an organization. More recently, the complexity of society and the tremendous competition for scarce resources throughout both the public and private sectors of the economy have placed greater demands upon the organization to be adaptable and flexible.

A great deal of literature has been devoted to the changes which have occurred in administration and the characteristics that are identified with well-functioning organizations. Alvin Toffler, the futurologist, has characterized many of the changes in the practice of administration in his book *Third Wave* (1980). As the title implies, there has been a movement away from the past routine of mass production toward high levels of specialization in products and professionalism. Peters and Waterman (1987) analyzed the characteristics of successful firms. Their findings focused attention on three critical factors: (a) the need for a clear awareness of the organization's mission (b) the need to foster creative thinking by small groups, and (c) the need for an organization to be able to respond to changing requirements with speed and flexibility. Others have described the increased awareness of the need for congruence of individual and organizational needs (Bennis & Nanus,

1985; Covey, 1990; Drucker, 1985; Maslow, 1971).

With the trend toward specialization came a demand for higher levels of skills and competence. However, specialization also emphasized and created boundaries in organizations. As efforts required the contributions of different types of specialists, the structure and nature of organizations changed. The importance shifted away from the individuals who performed the tasks (workers) to the outcomes of their work (products). One result of these shifts has been in the formation of multi- or interdisciplinary teams. Frequently, organizations join together to establish networks, alliances, and joint ventures which form linkages that promote their common objectives.

The complexity of the administrative environment has changed dramatically and has affected many service organizations that serve individuals with disabilities and their families. In some cases, health, education, and social services are included within a single organization. In other situations, the organization may develop a loose referral network or formal alliance with other organizations who offer complementary services. Effective service delivery in this type of service system is dependent upon integrating the knowledge of all the professionals from various disciplines and backgrounds into a coherent and functioning interdisciplinary team.

Organizations must be responsive to a public environment which includes multiple constituencies. Groups that have an interest in organizational functioning include consumers, advocates, funding sources, regulators, and policy makers. The responsibility for the interface between the organization (or a network of organizations) and the environment often falls primarily to the administrator, in consultation with the clinical staff. Effective administration has become increasingly important to the organization seeking to survive and thrive under these complex conditions.

In interdisciplinary organizations, such as those which serve persons with developmental disabilities and their families, it is helpful to understand the total functioning of the organization. Organizational practice encompasses both clinical and administrative practices (see Table 1). Both elements are important, and together they create a total system for the client.

Effective administrative practice requires a strategic blend of leadership, analytical, and technical skills. Leadership, sometimes referred to as "the art" of administrative practice, is defined as a process in which one person influences others in their attainment of common goals (Fiedler, 1971). Effectiveness in a leadership position is associated with the degree of success with which a group performs the primary assigned task; it includes those areas by which the administrator influences both the behavior of other individuals in the organization and the interaction between the organization and its environment. Examples of skills required in an administrative position are influencing, motivating, communicating, delegating, networking, negotiating, consensus building, conflict management, and other interpersonal and human management skills.

In addition to leadership qualities, an administrator must possess technical and analytical skills. These skill areas are aimed at organizational planning and evaluation, promoting efficiency in the allocation of resources, and reducing variability and promoting quality in the production of services. Examples include systems assessment and analysis, the application and use of information technology, implementing quality assurance systems, budgeting, financial analysis and management, community/consumer needs assessment and technical planning, risk assessment and management, pro-

Table 2.1. Clinical and Administrative Approaches to Practice in Interdisciplinary Organizations*

Clinical	Administrative
Single-case-oriented	Population- and organization-oriented
Focused on direct care of patient/client/family	Focused on issues in environment surrounding case
Expertise in technical fields affecting case	Expertise in general processes and management Recommends optimal care within limited resources
One-on-one communication emphasized	Whole-group communication emphasized
Work is done by self	Work is delegated to others

* taken from Kazuk (1987).

gram evaluation, and environmental scanning and policy analysis. Such skills are sometimes seen as the "science" of administration.

Although these domains have been discussed discretely, it is simplistic to think that these skills are employed independently of one another. For example, an administrator needs to be very aware of the impact that technical decisions have upon clinical and administrative staff. The implementation of an information system is more than just identifying and implementing needed technology. The administrator must understand the information needs and concerns of staff, and encourage their involvement in the development and decision-making process to ensure cooperation and participation once the system is in place. All aspects of these areas of practice must come together in the administration process. The technical/analytical skills are critical to designing and managing the organizational processes (management of human, financial, and information resources). The leadership skills and the attention to the values and cultural of the organization are equally important, as well as meeting the expectations of clients and other external groups.

Educational and Training Requirements

A person who becomes an administrator may do so from a variety of career paths. Depending on their background, administrators will have obtained different knowledge and skills: for example, either a clinical or administrative preparation. An individual may study in a clinical discipline such as social work and then accept a position in an agency for individuals with developmental disabilities and their families. Opportunities for advancement may lie in accepting more organizational and supervisory experience in the particular setting, such as becoming Director of Social Work Services. The person may then further expand his opportunities by accepting a promotion into an Assistant Director or Director position which extends beyond his education and training.

In another instance, a person may be trained in some general administrative function such as accounting, budgeting, or human resource management. This person may accept a position developing and managing budgets in an organization serving individuals with developmental disabilities and their families. Her opportunity for advancement may be the same as that of the social worker cited in the previous example. In order to advance, she may seek the position of Director of Accounting and Budgeting if the organization is large enough to support such a Department, and then seek the position of Assistant Director or Director.

Yet a third scenario is an individual with administrative training who is specifically recruited for the position of Assistant Director or Director. Alternatively, a person with clinical training and practical experience may be recruited directly into the position of Assistant Director or Director because of previous experience in a similar role. In these instances, clinically-trained persons may elect to return for a graduate degree or special training in administration to supplement their experience and reinforce their administrative role.

These contrasting scenarios raise an interesting issue about preparation for administrative positions, which becomes an important and potentially political topic when an administrator is recruited. What emphasis should the recruitment process place on administrative training and experience versus clinical background and skills? The question is also raised about the type of training necessary prior to assuming an administrative position, as well as continuing training requirements following employment.

The individual who desires administrative training has several options. These include undergraduate and graduate programs in health, business, or public administration. Such programs offer training in the leadership, technical and analytical skills of administration and management. In all

three instances, the master's degree is generally viewed as the terminal degree for professional practice as an administrator or planner/analyst, although many programs also offer doctoral-level training for those interested primarily in research and teaching. Graduate programs in public health, generally aimed at practicing health professionals who want to improve their research and analytical skills, may also include a concentration in administration. They may offer both master's and doctoral-level preparation in public health.

In many universities, there is a trend toward interdisciplinary training in administration which includes business, health, and public administration. For example, a graduate program in health administration may be organizationally located within the Health Sciences but actually be a joint venture between related schools such as business and public affairs. Another approach is to combine clinical and administrative training by offering dual degrees. Examples might include dual master's degrees in nursing and business, or social work and health administration.

Health administration training prepares students for careers in areas related to health and social sciences. Graduates of these programs often secure positions as planners, administrators, and analysts in hospitals, physician group practices, integrated health networks, community/public health clinics, and agencies such as home health and rehabilitation. They may also work in related areas such as insurance, consulting, government, professional organizations, or with policy making bodies such as legislatures. Business schools emphasize the generic practice of administration and management, and their graduates enter a wide range of industries, including health and social services. These positions may include administration in settings similar to those in which health administration graduates are found. Public administration training programs prepare their graduates to assume positions in the public sector, which may include health care. Examples are governmental agencies responsible for health-related issues, policy-making bodies such as legislatures, and community-based clinics.

Different disciplines and curricula emphasize different knowledge and skills in administration, although leadership preparation is essential in both clinical and administrative training programs. Clinically trained individuals will have a strong understanding of the care process and be effective in advocacy for the individual client. They will be well prepared to understand the professional values and culture of clinicians in the organization. In addition, many of the skills necessary to a caring, nurturing provider of services are transferable to understanding staff behavior and management. Individuals who are trained in administration are prepared to undertake the technical/analytical tasks of administration. In addition, they are trained to view the organization as a whole, and understand the necessity of considering the impact of organizational decisions on other clients and staff, instead of solely focusing on an individual client. This perspective is sometimes called *systems advocacy*, since the organization is conceptualized as an entity. This perspective is very important when dealing with the external environment including funding agencies and policy makers.

Licensure, Certification, and Continuing Education

Due to the diversity of roles and academic backgrounds of administrators, licensure is generally not required, with one notable exception: virtually all states have a requirement for licensure for administrators of nursing homes. For this particular license, preparation and requirements vary on a state-by-state basis.

Continuing professional education is an important consideration for administrators in organizations serving persons with developmental disabilities. Continuing professional education needs to be flexible enough to address those areas in which administrators have not been trained, while offering advanced preparation in the areas of their backgrounds or disciplines. Since clinicians and administrators may assume joint decision making responsibilities, training is often interdisciplinary in nature and includes personnel in both of these roles.

Continuing education is available through programs sponsored by universities, professional organizations, and other profit and non-profit entities. The nature of the training may vary greatly depending on the background and training of the target audience. For an administrator who has come to this type of position through a clinical route, one option is further graduate training. This can be pursued through any of the three graduate programs which have been described (health, business, or public administration). A growing number of programs are offering concentrated courses in certified executive training. "Distance learning" options which lead to master's degrees in administration have also become increasingly attractive to individuals who are mid-career and cannot return to school on a full-time basis.

There are a variety of professional organizations for administrators in health and social services, many of which provide certification and/or continuing education. Examples include the American College of Health Executives (ACHE), American Association of Medical Administrators (AAMA), American College of Nursing Home Administrators (ACNHA), Association of Mental

Health Administrators (AMHA), and American College of Physician Executives (ACPE). In addition, professional organizations for clinicians may contain subgroups for administrators. An example is the National Association of Social Workers (NASW), which includes a subgroup of Social Work Administrators, and the Administrative Division of the American Association on Mental Retardation (AAMR). These organizations may provide continuing education and/or credentialling services in administration for their members.

Administrators who work in organizations serving persons with developmental disabilities may elect to seek membership in any of the organizations cited. However, only three specifically reference developmental disabilities or mental retardation in their membership experience. These organizations are the American College of Health Administrators (ACHE), the Association of Mental Health Administrators (AMHA), and the Administration Division of the American Association on Mental Retardation (AAMR).

The American College of Health Executives (ACHE) is the largest of the organizations citing administration in mental retardation and developmental disabilities in their mission statement. ACHE has become a national leader in providing continuing education and certification for administrators, many of whom are employed in settings which serve individuals with developmental disabilities. Examples include acute and long-term health care settings, as well as specialty care organizations such as mental health and mental retardation facilities. ACHE offers Fellowship, Diplomate, and Associate status based on professional experience and the ability to meet continuing education and certification requirements. Individuals who are able to successfully complete the ACHE Board of Governor's Examination in Healthcare Management are allowed to use Certified Health Executive (CHE) after their names.

Most professional organizations have various levels of membership and use continuing education and certification as two criteria for advancement. An analysis by the authors of twelve professional organizations which cite the advancement of professional administration as a significant part of their mission indicate that over half (58%) offered two or more organizational levels of membership. Fifty-eight percent offered a status of "Accredited" or "Certified." Forty-two percent required an examination for membership and the majority (75%) of those who had more than one level required an examination to progress to a higher level. Continuing education is a requirement by 42% of organizations for continued certification.

Contributions to Interdisciplinary Practice

Administrative practice is focused upon the organization as an entity, the total population to be served, and the available resources. The administrator is responsible for the effective management of agency resources, which often involves weighing conflicting demands and priorities. As a member of the interdisciplinary team, the administrator is able to assist the other members in understanding how team practice and use of resources ultimately affects all clients served by the organization. The administrator can also assist the team in evaluating the services that are being provided, understanding the environment in which they are practicing, and recognizing and acting upon new opportunities and trends which may impact team functioning. An effective administrator contributes greatly to maintaining an open and productive organizational climate, which supports interdisciplinary team functioning and assures a high-quality and meaningful experience for clients and families.

A major role of the administrator is developing and overseeing the administrative systems which support interdisciplinary team functioning. These include the financial and clinical data systems, which provide information for evaluation of current activities and future planning. An administrator must also provide leadership in the human resources systems that define the roles and activities of clinical and administrative staff and set standards for compensation. Other administrative processes that are important to effective team functioning include materials procurement and management, risk management and quality assurance, and records management and maintaining confidentiality.

Although the technical skills of administration are the most concrete and visible, the leadership skills are the ones that contribute the most toward effective team functioning. The administrator must work with a wide range of people, including staff within the organization and external groups who are affected by the organization. The major constituency groups include (a) clinical and administrative staff within the organization, (b) external groups such as referral organizations, governmental bodies, advocates, and other interested citizens, and (c) consumers and their families.

Each of these three constituency groups may share in the vision of the organization and support the mission and goals, but each may view these goals from a different perspective. Clinical staff want to work in an environment that provides adequate and appropriate resources, and offers autonomy and flexibility in clinical decision making. External groups are primarily concerned with access and cost-effectiveness in the delivery of those services. Consumers and their

families want a responsive, caring environment, and well-coordinated, high-quality services. Each of these perspectives must be taken into account by the administrator in making decisions about the service organization.

Regardless of the level of authority held by the administrator, he or she plays a major role in drawing upon the perspectives of all constituents, particularly when confronted by difficult decisions such as resource allocation and quality-of-care issues. The administrator ultimately plays many roles in communicating and integrating various concerns and perspectives. At times, the administrator is the "expert" in designing an effective organizational structure that clearly designates roles and responsibilities for clinical and administrative personnel, or in assuring that staff have the appropriate resources necessary to carry out their roles. In other situations, he or she is a facilitator and assumes the responsibility for bringing clinical experts, consumers and families together to address important program issues. In another situation, the administrator is the broker of information, responsible for assuring funding agencies and other interested community members that the organization is serving the community well. All of these roles and activities ultimately impact the ability of interdisciplinary teams to carry out their work on behalf of clients.

A well-trained administrator will have good team organization and management skills. Complex professional organizations, such as those which serve individuals with developmental disabilities, will continue to rely heavily upon team approaches to the delivery of services. The administrator serves as a facilitator of the team process, helps interdisciplinary teams to work together effectively, manages conflict, assesses team function, and considers innovative new services and program approaches. Administrative practice may extend beyond service to the interdisciplinary team and include a variety of teams created within the organization. Many organizations use team approaches to accomplish goals that integrate related organizational and clinical functions, such as efficient delivery of quality care by assessment of cost related to clinical outcomes.

Total Quality Management (TQM) is one application of administration in team functioning aimed at integrating clinical and administrative practices. TQM is being adopted in many health and human service organizations because this approach promotes worker involvement in the identification and maintenance of quality production of services, creates and sustains the values of consumer orientation, assures that all services offer added value, and utilizes scientific measures for managing the service delivery process (Widfeldt & Widfeldt, 1992). The underlying values of TQM are promoting quality services, consumer empowerment, emphasizing the importance of well-trained staff, and utilizing scientific methods for assuring the highest quality services even with limited resources. The basic values of the TQM approach are quite consistent with the mission of organizations serving individuals with disabilities and their families.

The implementation of TQM requires an administrative perspective, although its success is dependent upon adoption by all staff. It must be oriented towards the needs of the organization, emphasize communication throughout the organization, promote the empowerment of clinical and administrative staff by delegating work appropriately, and utilize effective management processes. The success of TQM is ultimately measured by the satisfaction and benefit received by each individual consumer. TQM reflects the manner in which clinical and administrative processes come together to accomplish a common goal, and serves to demonstrate the importance of the administrative role in that effort. In many respects, this is an enhancement of the traditional interdisciplinary team process, that moves beyond the consideration of the services being delivered, and attends to the processes which assure the best service delivery.

A brief example may help to illustrate the administrator's contribution to effective team function utilizing TQM methods. Managing client records is a very important activity in any organization serving persons with developmental disabilities. Often this function is a source of contention between clinical and administrative staff. Poorly managed records may result in inappropriate and/or inadequate care. Records management becomes even more difficult when information must flow from one organization to another, as in cases of a referral to another program. Thus the problem is of concern to the client and family, to the clinical and administrative staff, and possibly to external groups such as advocates and/or other professional organizations.

The principles of TQM require that identifying and resolving problems with records management start by determining the most desirable client outcomes. Addressing this issue requires full commitment on the part of the administrative and clinical leadership in the organization, and the involvement of any staff member whose job responsibilities are related to records management. The administrator may take the responsibility for forming the team, implementing and guiding the process. In addition to clinical and administrative staff, the team might be expanded to community members who represent referral organizations, and even consumers/advocates who must live with the results of the records management system. The team would identify "benchmarks" or measures of excellence in records management. Next, they would begin to identify the process by which client records are currently handled. Once the process is well described, the team will identify desired changes and improvements aimed at meeting their "benchmark" criteria, and develop a plan for monitoring progress and continued quality through ongoing information collection and evaluation.

Although this example is a simple one, it illustrates the potential role of the administrator in facilitating effective teamwork to assist with identifying problems and solutions between clinical and administrative staff. To begin the process, the administrator plays a key role in selecting the right members for the team process. Then he or she must be sure that information is made available to the team to adequately describe the records management process, and subsequently to address resources that may be needed to implement changes and monitor the outcome. Moreover, the administrator plays a vital role in bringing about the necessary changes throughout the organization in order to implement improvements in the process. This may require formal changes in procedures, role definitions and functions, or informal encouragement to certain staff members to adopt new methods of work. Further, the administrator may need to communicate the work being undertaken by the team to other organizations and/or community groups so they have an opportunity for input and can, if needed, participate in successful implementation.

This type of administrative function is often carried out through a team process. The outcome is to promote effective service delivery across an organization, especially when organizations face difficult decisions and conflict. An effective administrator can hold consumer benefit paramount in the decision-making process, ensure the involvement of all concerned parties, minimize conflict, and promote trust and effective communications across an organization. Ultimately clinical and administrative staff will feel valued and consumers will be better served. Interdisciplinary teams can appropriately expand their activities to incorporate problem-solving strategies, ultimately improving their function and better serving the client.

Assessment and Intervention

Since administrators do not have a clinical role to fulfill as part of their responsibilities, assessment and intervention will be addressed together in this chapter.

The administrator is trained to view the organization within the context of the community in which it operates and the population within that community as a whole. Thus administrative assessment, rather than focusing on the individual client, will focus on the community: who resides in the community and how they may be served by the programs offered by the organization, how effectively the organization functions, and how well programs and services target community needs. In addition, community assessments often promote important support from multiple-constituency groups.

Community and organizational assessment is the basis for planning and implementing programmatic improvements and assuring continuous evaluation and reassessment. These efforts will provide important information and support to the function of interdisciplinary teams. Such assessments can be very formal in nature and utilize structured methodology and analysis, or be less formal and utilize informal networks, key informants, and other such approaches. Table 2 summarizes the information which is gathered as part of an evaluation and assessment for both an organizational and community perspective.

Both organizational and community assessments must be undertaken with the cooperation and participation of clinical and administrative staff. Community assessments must also include the cooperation and participation of community leaders. The assessment process lends itself quite well to a team approach. The administrator can serve as the leader in designing, organizing, and implementing the assessment. Ongoing assessments, whether formal or informal, will bring together clinical, administrative, and community perspectives in assuring that organizational goals are aligned with community expectations. Further, information gained from assessments forms the basis for ongoing quality improvement.

Table 2.2. Organizational and Community Assessments

Organizational assessments offer an opportunity to review:

- the organization's mission and goals.
- the authority and/ or legislation under which the organization operates and how that integrates with mission and goals.
- the allocation of resources towards the accomplishment of organizational goals.
- the indicators of quality service and the mechanims for assessing quality.
- the effectiveness with which internal systems (e.g., information management systems, client data system) assist in managing organizational resources.
- the effectiveness of clinical functions and service delivery.
- staff and consumer satisfaction.
- relationships between the organization and external groups.

Community assessments provide information which describes:

- the population to be served and their needs.
- social and demographic characteristics of the community.
- how well community needs are addressed by the programs and services offered.
- other provider organizations in the community.
- social, economic, and political trends within the community which may affect the organization.
- potential changes in demand, needs for services.
- the degree to which the organization is known in the community.
- the degree of satisfaction or dissatisfaction felt towards the organization by key constituency groups.
- potential sources of community support for the organization.

Case Example: Problem and History

Early one afternoon the telephone rang in the administrator's office. It was the Director of Clinical Services for the Citywide Developmental Center, and he was agitated. A group from the city's Association for Retarded Citizens (ARC) had just left his office. They had been there to complain about the "poor service" at the Center. Many parents had been referred there for evaluation and services for their children with special needs. They were impressed with the array of people available to them during the evaluation and the quality of their expertise, but they also voiced some strong concerns.

Their main issue was the way the Center staff interacted with parents. One complaint was that appointments were scheduled at the convenience of the staff. If the initial appointment was missed, the parent had to begin the application process from the beginning. Above all, parents received very mixed messages from the staff about their importance and their role. On one hand, parents were involved in all of the evaluation appointments and sat in on the interdisciplinary team meeting when findings and recommendations were discussed. They were asked for their input and about their opinions. However, they felt that the staff talked in a private language to each other and that the parent was not really part of the group. If parents asked questions, they usually received explanations which they perceived as condescending. These explanations made them feel inadequate and reinforced their belief that they were not actually a part of this closely knit work-group. From the parents' perspective, the entire experience was demeaning.

The administrator readily agreed to bring this issue to Monday's management team meeting in the Center. The team consisted of the administrator (who held a master's degree in health administration), the director of clinical service (a psychologist), and the program directors (two social workers, a nurse practitioner and an educator). The administrator asked the staff to organize preliminary data in preparation for the upcoming meeting.

At the meeting the administrator reported that during the past six months the Center had conducted 54 interdisciplinary meetings with parents to discuss findings and recommendations. These data suggested that in most cases (44%), only one parent attended the interdisciplinary meetings. Most of the time, the mother was the parent in attendance. In 33% of the cases, both parents came to the meeting sessions, but 20% of the time, neither parent was there.

Data were also presented about the charges and billing for the sessions. Families paid out-of-pocket for these sessions almost half of the time (45%). Insurance picked up about a fourth of the costs (23%). Outstanding amounts accounted for 37% in the billing process.

After these data were presented to the Center staff, a lively discussion followed. Several staff members were surprised, mystified, and bewildered by the parents' complaint. Two members of the group had been on the staff when the Center started inviting parents to attend these conferences. To them, the inclusion of parents seemed like a giant step forward. They questioned whether the decision to include parents had backfired.

Everyone concurred that they truly wanted to integrate parents into the team. It was decided that the best solution would be to employ a parent as a full-time consultant to help bridge this gap and make services responsive to parents. At this particular Center, social workers, psychologists, and educators all had been especially involved in working with parents, and they all offered to help. In the end, everyone agreed that it would be best for the administrator to take the lead in setting up this new position.

Recommendations for Problem Resolution

The administrator knew that she would have to deal with two major issues to establish the new position in the agency. These were (a) creating the position and defining the role, and (b) assuring a meaningful role and acceptance by the other team members. She decided to link the two issues. By engaging the members of the management team in the elements of getting the position established (e.g., developing the job description, thinking about the compensation level, methods of financing the position, organizational location, and recruitment strategies), both issues would be addressed.

A parent-consultant organizing group was established with the Administrator as the chair. The group was given the name of COG by one of the members, which is an acronym for Consultant's Organizing Group. It contained a representative sample of disciplines on the clinical teams, since typically staff in these positions had the greatest level of interaction with parents. Members included a social worker, psychologist, educator, and nurse. A pediatrician was invited but unable to join due to time constraints.

Meeting 1. The initial meeting was designed to develop a consensus regarding the purpose of the position and initiate discussion of the job description. The administrator focused discussion on the question "What do we want this position to accomplish at this Center?" The group skirted the issue and the administrator had to keep the focus on the question. Such phrases were heard as "empowering parents," "integrating them into the team," "parents as case

managers," and "parents as advocates." They started talking about the parent-consultant as a "bridge" between the Center and parents, who could "translate" the explanations that were given in the conferences, and who could help parents use the Center's services more appropriately and effectively. One group member finally ventured the observation that the staff must need some help if they had been so insensitive that the parent group had to call the problem to their attention.

COG members finally agreed to a statement. The position would have three purposes: (a) to sensitize staff to the parents' dilemmas and feelings, and improve communications between these groups; (b) to monitor and provide accurate feedback regarding parents' satisfaction with their experiences at the Center; (c) to act as an ombudsman for parents when problems surfaced. At the next meeting, the job description would be discussed. The administrator was asked to develop a "discussion draft" to speed and facilitate the discussion.

Meeting 2. The draft description provided by the administrator incorporated the information from the last meeting. It also included statements describing typical activities, required skills and competencies, supervision/reporting relationships, and minimum qualifications. Interestingly, the group agreed rather quickly on each topic until it came to "supervision/reporting relationships." Each person attempted to establish his or her own credentials as the best qualifications to supervise this new position. The educator and nurse gradually withdrew from the contest, leaving both the social worker and psychologist unwilling to concede. The administrator suggested that they discuss what other elements should enter into the decision, assuming that both were professionally qualified and competent to supervise the position. The group quickly iterated such factors as (a) ability to support the ombudsman activities, (b) ability to help formulate methods for tracking, evaluating, and reporting parental response to their experience, (c) sophistication in understanding the dynamics of the team conference, (d) current supervisory workload of the social worker and the psychologist.

After this clarifying activity, the group concluded that "discipline" was not as important as role and function for the parent who served in the new consultant role. Issues involving supervision were tabled at this point and would be discussed with the community services director. When it came to minimum qualifications and compensation, the group felt that being a parent and possessing the necessary skills was more important than specific training or discipline. They suggested that compensation be commensurate with a candidate's experience and with the pay of other members of the interdisciplinary team, reasoning that if the parent were the lowest-paid member of the team, he or she would again feel an outsider.

Meeting 3. This was a short meeting. The members of COG felt unable to address the issues of funding as they were unfamiliar with the options. This issue was referred to the personnel committee of the board of directors for resolution.

Meeting 4. The Administrator reported that she was having trouble getting the position approved by the personnel committee—due largely to difficulty in establishing the compensation level, since no other duty statement in the classification system was comparable. COG members considered finding a local group, such as the parent association, who would hire the parent-consultant and then have the person work at the Center under a contractual arrangement. Ultimately COG found this alternative unacceptable, since it created too much "separateness." Their recommendation was that an entire new classification be created

for this position that would ensure adequate compensation. Their recommendation was accepted, and the group decided to review the position in six months. Recruiting was implemented through local newspaper advertisements and announcements in the offices of local parent groups and service organizations. The members of COG agreed to serve on a pre-screening committee. However, they asked that a parent who would not be a candidate for the position also serve on this committee. Approximately six months after the original decision by the management committee, the parent-consultant was hired.

Implementing Change

Initially, the relationship between the parent-consultant and the Center staff was extremely positive. She was articulate, witty, and sensitive, and team members accepted her as a colleague. The perception of Center personnel was that a consumer would be a very worthwhile addition to the group.

Over time, however, members of the team began to feel uncomfortable as she confronted them with their failure to engage parents in considerations for changes in plans. Team members felt that this intimate engagement of parents was impractical, time-consuming, and inconsequential to either the Center or the parent. Moreover, parents themselves were starting to become more challenging of team decisions, and pressures were again starting to mount. All these issues arose within one month, out of the required six-month appraisal period of the position. The management committee recommended that the COG be reactivated to consider these issues, and that the parent-consultant be included in this process.

To address these pressing concerns, COG met twice more. The parent-consultant was quite assertive (some said defensive) during these sessions. She gave a report on her activities during the first six months in the new position. The parent consultant had attended about 70% of the evaluation team conferences and had interviewed an additional 50 parents. In conjunction with one of the psychologists, she had also designed a parent-satisfaction survey form.

In addition to sharing her accomplishments, she also shared her observations about the team process. She said staff members were inclined to relate to persons with developmental disabilities and their parents as subjects instead of people. However, she concluded that this role differentiation was currently inevitable. She saw a definite improvement in team understanding of parents' opinions. She also stated that it was inevitable that parents will not feel like members of the team, nor should the staff expect them to. After all, the staff worked closely together on a daily basis, while the parents only interacted with them periodically around the special needs of their child.

After more discussion, the COG concluded that the stress of this new venture was to be expected. They strongly recommended that the position be continued for another six months to give time for working relationships to stabilize and outcome data to be collected. Each team was asked to set aside 30 minutes to discuss the role of the parent-consultant and what had happened during the first six months. The administrator and director of clinical services were asked to be present during these meetings. At the end of the year the parent consultant was clearly accepted as a member of the team. One outcome was the perception of other parents and the team that their present interaction was more realistic and effective. This impression was backed by survey results which showed a very high level of satisfaction by parents. Interestingly, other positive outcomes were observed since the parent-consultant had joined the Center. The frequency of both parents in a family attending a case conference had increased from 33% to 50%. The collection of fees for service had also increased from 45% to 60%.

References

Bennis, W.G., & Nanus, B. (1985). *The strategies for taking charge*. New York: Harper and Row.

Covey, S.R. (1990). *The seven habits of highly effective people*. New York: Simon and Schuster.

Drucker, P.F. (1985). *The changing world of the executive*. New York: Times Books.

Fiedler, F.E. (1971). *Leadership*. New York: General Learning Press.

Kazuk, E. (1987). *Introduction to administration*. Baltimore, MD: Dome Learning Systems.

Maslow, A. (1971). *The further reaches of human nature*. New York: Viking.

Peters, T., & Waterman, R. (1987). *In search of excellence: lessons from America's best run companies*. New York: Harper and Row.

Quinn, R.E., Faerman, S.R., & McGrath, M.R. (1990). *Becoming a master manager*. New York: Wiley & Sons

Ross, A. (1992). *Cornerstones of leadership*. Ann Arbor, MI: Health Administration Press.

Toffler, A. (1980). *The third wave*. New York: Bantam Books.

Widtfeldt, A.K., & Widtfeldt, J. (1992). Total quality management in American industry. *American Association of Occupational Health Nursing Journal*, 40(7), 311-318.

3

Audiology

Sandra K. Keener, M.A., CCC-A

Hearing loss affects a large portion of the population in the United States, with estimates of over 21 million Americans with a hearing impairment. It is also estimated that 1 in every 1,000 infants born has profound deafness, with more frequent occurrences of lesser degree of hearing losses (American Speech-Language-Hearing Association, 1993a). Further, a significant number of children are affected by hearing losses that occur in early childhood. Despite these statistics, audiology has only recently become recognized as an essential health-care profession.

The term *audiology* is generally defined as the study of hearing (Davis, 1970). Clinical audiology initially developed as an outcome of World War II, when rehabilitative services were needed for veterans affected with hearing impairment as a result of intense noise exposure. Presently, audiologists are professionals involved in many areas of specialization such as pediatric, rehabilitative, medical, and industrial audiology. Audiologists may perform a variety of duties including administration, teaching, research, supervision of clinical trainees, and clinical service provision. Employment settings may also vary, including universities, hospitals, specialty clinics, rehabilitation facilities, schools, government health agencies,

and private practices. As a clinical discipline, audiology can be broadly described as a health-care profession concerned with the prevention, identification, diagnosis, and rehabilitation of individuals at risk for and with hearing impairment (Bess & Humes, 1990).

The goal of prevention programs in audiology is conservation of normal function of the auditory system. These programs exist in different practice settings and include services for clients in various age groups. For example, programs may include developing and implementing services to facilitate hearing conservation in neonatal intensive care units, which often exhibit noise levels considered hazardous to fragile newborns. Programs may also be part of a worksite; occupational hearing conservation programs are essential for employees at risk for hearing loss as a result of exposure to industrial noise sustained during employment.

Appropriate identification programs are essential for accomplishing early diagnosis and intervention services for persons with impaired hearing. Screening programs are provided to identify individuals with or at risk for hearing impairment. Such programs may take place in newborn nurseries, neonatal intensive care units, preschools, traditional educational settings, government agencies, private corporations, industry, and various other sites.

Despite legislation requiring the provision of audiological services and screening programs to optimize early identification and intervention, the average age of initial identification of congenital or early-onset hearing loss is 2½ to 3 years of age. At this age, unfortunately, the most important period for communication development has passed. The ideal goal for identification and treatment of congenital hearing impairment is 6 months of age. The National Institutes of Health (NIH) (1993) recommends that universal screening be implemented for all infants within the first 3 months of life. NIH estimates that current screening programs only identify about 50% of hearing-impaired newborns, even though these programs are based on high-risk criteria. An additional recommendation of NIH includes comprehensive intervention and management programs as integral parts of a universal screening program.

An accurate and early diagnosis of hearing impairment is essential to minimize the serious and global impact a hearing impairment may have on communication, academic, vocational, and social functions. While medical technology has extended the life expectancy of geriatric populations, who account for a large proportion of persons with hearing impairment, these advances have also had significant impact on the prognosis for survival of premature infants and children with cancer and other chronic illnesses. Patients in all of these categories are at risk for hearing loss, as a result of their condition and also as an outcome of their treatment. To address the need for effective and objective assessment tools, computer and electronic technology has increased to meet the demands of a growing at-risk population. Objective diagnostic assessment of auditory function is now possible immediately after birth.

The rehabilitative services provided by an audiologist are as essential as an early and accurate diagnosis of hearing impairment. Rehabilitation includes the selection, fitting, and dispensing of amplification, assistive listening, and alerting devices. In addition, rehabilitative audiology services include extensive training on the use and care of amplification systems as well as techniques for teaching individuals and/or their families how to use their residual hearing ability to maximize performance. The area of rehabilitation is dynamic due to technological advances in amplification systems for persons with hearing impairments. The overall goal of these systems is to improve the quality of amplified sound, thereby enhancing speech comprehension.

Educational and Training Requirements

Educational and training requirements have increased to meet the demands of increasing technology and to produce professionals appropriately trained to provide exemplary service and treatment to a diverse and expanding population. The American Speech-Language-Hearing Association (ASHA) is the scientific and professional organization for speech-language pathologists and audiologists. ASHA determines standards for certification, grants certification and membership, conducts accreditation for university graduate programs, and develops and defines the scope of practice, preferred practice patterns, position statements, practice guidelines, and ethical standards for practice (American Speech-Language-Hearing Association, 1992). In order to qualify for certification through ASHA, audiologists must complete a graduate degree, obtain a minimum of 375 supervised

clinical contact hours, pass a national examination, and complete a professional
clinical practicum supervised by a certified
audiologist.

The foundation of graduate study in audiology is the completion of a well-rounded
undergraduate curriculum. The *Membership
and Certification Handbook for Standards in
Certificates of Clinical Competence in Speech-
Language Pathology and Audiology* (American
Speech-Language-Hearing Association,
1992) outlines the requirements for education and certification. Baccalaureate level
preparation includes coursework in mathematics, physics, biological sciences, human
development, and psychology. Effective
January 1, 1994, an audiologist must possess a master's degree from an accredited
educational program. Certain educational
requirements must be fulfilled for certification in audiology. Applicants for certification must have completed 75 semester
credit hours, including at least 27 credits
in basic sciences and at least 36 credits in
professional coursework. Basic science
coursework includes biological/physical
sciences and mathematics. At least 15 credit
hours must be in basic human communication processes. Professional coursework
includes a curriculum covering prevention,
evaluation, and treatment of speech, language and hearing disorders. Thirty of the
36 hours must be graduate level coursework,
and at least 21 must be in audiology. Professional coursework should include content regarding normal function, disorders,
instrumentation, assessment, rehabilitation,
and conservation across the life span. At
least 6 credit hours of professional
coursework must be in speech-language pathology dealing with disorders unassociated
with hearing impairment.

The clinical practicum experience required for certification is as important as
the didactic preparation. Prior to beginning
clinical practicum, 25 clock hours of supervised clinical observation of children
and/or adults with communication disorders and/or hearing loss must be completed.
Clinical practicum requirements are currently set at completion of 350 hours of
supervised clinical contact. Minimum hours
must be completed in the following areas:
evaluation of hearing in adults and children, selection and use of amplification in
adults and children, and rehabilitation
therapy. In addition, 35 hours must be completed in speech-language screening and
treatment.

In addition to the successful completion
of a graduate program and supervised clinical practicum, a passing score on a national
examination in audiology must be obtained.
The National Examinations in Speech-Language Pathology and Audiology (NESPA)
are comprehensive in nature. The exam is
offered three times per year and must be
passed within two years of initially taking
the examination.

A final requirement for eligibility for certification is the completion of a supervised
professional experience, the Clinical Fellowship. This component of training is essential, since academic and practicum requirements for the master's degree do not completely prepare a clinician to provide services independently. The Clinical Fellowship consists of at least 36 weeks of full-
time professional experience (or the part-
time equivalent) and is designed to promote
the practitioner's transition from supervised
graduate clinician to independent professional.

Licensure, Certification and Continuing Education

As of March 1994, 41 states required
licensure to practice audiology and one state
requires registration (American Speech-Language-Hearing Association, 1994). Requirements for licensure are generally the same

as previous requirements which mandated 275 clinical contact hours for certification. However, some states specify that more current ASHA requirements be met, with consideration given to years of professional practice. Fees for application, license, and renewal vary by state, as do renewal requirements, reciprocity with other states, and exemptions.

Continuing education requirements for licensure also vary. Only 22 of the 41 states which require licensure for the practice of audiology have guidelines for continuing education. States mandating continuing education for license renewal range from requirements of 10 hours of continuing education credit annually to 50 hours every three years (American Speech-Language-Hearing Association, 1993b).

In addition to requirements for audiology licensure, the majority of states also require an audiologist to obtain a separate license to dispense hearing aids. State requirements for hearing aid dispensers are a high school diploma and a passing score on a state examination. However, a hearing aid license does not allow the holder to diagnose hearing impairment or to be called an audiologist. Fifteen states requiring licensure in audiology accept a license as sufficient to dispense hearing aids. Audiologists are currently lobbying to have that standard adopted in the remaining states.

Certification requirements were described in the previous section regarding education and professional preparation requirements. Upon completion of all the requirements for certification, application is made to the American Speech-Language-Hearing Association for the Certificate of Clinical Competence in Audiology (CCC-A). Certification is granted only following successful completion of a graduate degree in audiology, clinical practicum requirements, passing score on the national examination, and completion of the Clinical Fellowship. Certification allows the audiologist to provide independent clinical services as well as to provide supervision to subsequent applicants. Audiologists who practice in public school systems are required to have additional coursework and certification in some states.

Certification is maintained via annual payment of dues. There are currently no continuing education requirements for certification, however, audiologists practice under a Code of Ethics written and governed by the professional association. Despite the current lack of continuing education requirements for certification, ASHA does sponsor and encourage continuing education opportunities.

Contributions to Interdisciplinary Practice

Recent figures suggest that the prevalence of hearing impairment in children from birth to 18 years of age is as high as 5% (American Speech-Language-Hearing Association, 1993a). Approximately 30% of children who are profoundly deaf have additional health impairments (Fritsch & Sommer, 1991). Many children with hearing loss have additional sensory impairments, neurological problems, and developmental delays in several areas. Cherow, Diggs, and Williams (1982) estimate that 25–33% of persons with hearing impairment have an additional handicapping condition. These authors also report that the incidence of hearing loss in children receiving special education services is higher than children who are not special education students.

These estimates suggest that many individuals with developmental disabilities benefit from auditory services. The role of the audiologist in providing services to the population with developmental disabilities is to provide identification, assessment, evaluation, and treatment. The audiologist also works to enhance hearing capacity by training families, providing consultation with other professionals or agencies, and serving as an advocate when required.

Because development of communication is heavily dependent on auditory input, early identification and intervention of hearing impairment is essential to reduce the significant negative impact hearing loss may have on speech and language development. The type and degree of hearing loss and the age of onset have significant effects on communication, regardless of other factors. Auditory deprivation interferes with the development of sound production, grammar, speech perception, and language learning. These deficits may have a subsequent impact on cognitive and social development, overall academic achievement, vocational choices, and family relations.

The audiologist has a prominent role in determining the nature and treatment of hearing problems for people with developmental disabilities. Audiologists have comprehensive knowledge of normal auditory function, hearing impairment, associated difficulties, and appropriate intervention. If an auditory impairment is present, the audiologist can determine the severity of the hearing loss and location of the lesion within the auditory system, estimate the extent of developmental delay that may be caused by the hearing loss, determine the habilitation or rehabilitation needs, and make recommendations for medical follow-up.

As a member of the interdisciplinary team, the audiologist benefits from and contributes to the effective treatment of people with developmental disabilities. Through a comprehensive team approach, the audiologist is provided information regarding global development and medical issues which can assist in decisions regarding appropriate assessment, treatment, and intervention recommendations. Other team members rely on the audiologist's accurate assessment of hearing status to make their diagnoses. For example, a psychologist requires information regarding auditory status before making a diagnosis such as attention deficit disorder or mental retardation. A hearing loss must also be eliminated as a cause of the discrepancy between a performance and a verbal IQ score. A speech-language pathologist needs an accurate assessment of auditory function to make recommendations regarding a speech or language delay. Before assuming that all of a motor delay is the result of inadequate function, the physical and occupational therapists must be assured that their instructions were actually heard by the individual.

The audiologist also plays an essential role in educating other members in the social network of the person with a hearing impairment. Parents, other family members, and service professionals require information about risk factors for congenital and acquired hearing loss, behavioral signs of hearing impairment, and the need for comprehensive assessment. In addition, the audiologist may provide consultative services to classroom teachers or vocational instructors.

Assessment of Individuals and their Families

Not all audiologists or audiology clinics are prepared to accurately assess a person with a developmental delay. Reliable assessment often requires more than one audiologist, expensive and often highly technical equipment, and expertise in developmental disabilities. Referrals are often made to audiologists and clinics specializing in the assessment of persons who have developmental delays.

Mass screening programs are rarely successful in ruling out hearing impairment in persons with developmental disabilities. Depending on the severity of the disability and cooperation of the client, assessment methods and procedures will vary. In many instances, assessment must be performed in a timely manner because families cannot return for multiple visits. Procedures can quickly be performed to rule out hearing losses of sufficient magnitude to cause developmental delays or interfere with progress in programming. The test procedures and response tasks which are administered must be appropriate to the client's cognitive and physical ability. The best strategy is to obtain limited data by presenting tasks the client can complete rather than getting limited information because of unreasonable demands. Regardless of the procedure used to measure hearing sensitivity, audiological assessment begins with a detailed case history. An accurate case summary includes not only medical records but also reports from individuals knowledgeable about the client, who can give additional information regarding developmental history, behavior, likes/dislikes, and general observations that prompted the assessment. Concern regarding a person's auditory responsiveness is sufficient information to prompt an immediate referral and is often the initial indicator that a problem exists.

The assessment process and instruments vary depending upon the functional and cognitive level of the client. For infants and children functioning at less than 5-6 months, two instruments, the Auditory Brainstem Response (ABR) and Otoacoustic Emissions (OAE), are currently considered to be the most reliable and objective indicators of auditory sensitivity. Previously, the Behavioral Observation Audiometry (BOA) was more widely used. In administration of the BOA, noise makers are generally used to elicit a behavioral response such as a

startle. However, this procedure is not widely considered an accurate or reliable measure of hearing sensitivity (Thompson and Folsom, 1981). BOA generally fails to identify those infants with less than severe-to-profound hearing loss.

The Auditory Brainstem Response (ABR) is an electrophysiologic response to a rapid auditory stimulus, for example, a click sound. The procedure is performed when the person is asleep and therefore is highly sensitive to hearing loss. Sedation is often required to achieve this state, especially in older infants and children. Limitations of the ABR are that the equipment to perform the procedure is generally expensive, it reflects hearing ability in the high frequency region, it cannot determine type of hearing loss, and it does not measure understanding of sound at the level of the cortex.

The Otoacoustic Emissions (OAE) is an assessment of inner ear function at the level of the outer hair cells and provides information regarding hearing status. This procedure is also most successful with a sleeping or sedated individual. The presence of OAE response suggests normal hearing or minimal hearing loss. The absence of a response generally indicates at least a mild loss but cannot pinpoint the degree or type. Since the OAE procedure can estimate hearing ability from low to high frequencies, it provides more complete information regarding the range of hearing than the ABR.

For clients who function between 6 months to 2 years of age, soundfield audiometry is performed. A variety of stimuli may be used including speech and frequency specific stimuli. Visual Reinforcement Audiometry (VRA) uses operant conditioning and reinforcement of a response via a visual stimulus. If the client is a child, these tests are usually performed with the client seated on the parent's lap. The procedures may require one examiner to present the test signals and another to be in the room with the client to maintain attention and judge responses. One limitation of soundfield audiometric techniques is that the procedure lacks ear-specific information unless earphones are used and a visual response is reliably trained. Statements can only be made regarding the status of one ear, and unilateral hearing losses cannot be ruled out. However, sufficient information is obtained to enable the audiologist to make statements regarding the likelihood of a hearing impairment of sufficient degree to interfere with communication development.

For clients who function at the 2-year-old cognitive level or above, the most complete audiometric information can be obtained under earphones with some type of conditioned response to sound stimuli. The particular tests are selected depending upon the specific referral questions. A comprehensive audiometric assessment includes measurement of speech reception threshold, pure tone hearing sensitivity, word recognition, and middle ear function.

Assessment typically begins with measurements using speech stimuli, where a *speech awareness threshold* or *speech reception threshold* is obtained. This threshold is the lowest level at which a client indicates a speech signal is heard. The client indicates hearing the signal by performing a task (such as dropping an object on command) or pointing to a picture. If speech and language delays limit the ability to repeat a spoken word or identify a picture, procedures may be adapted to match the client's developmental level. This threshold alone provides limited information regarding overall hearing ability.

The next step in the assessment process is to determine hearing sensitivity to frequency specific stimuli. The goal is to obtain thresholds which are the softest sounds that can be heard at each pitch, using earphones half of the time. If a hearing loss is present, testing is repeated using a bone oscillator to determine the site of lesion.

Hearing losses fall into four categories, depending upon which part of the ear is affected. Those which involve the outer and middle ear are referred to as *conductive* hearing losses. Those that involve the inner ear and auditory nerve are referred to as *sensorineural* hearing losses. Additionally, multiple parts of the ear can be affected, resulting in a *mixed* hearing loss. Hearing impairments may also exist in which the site of lesion is considered *central*: the outer, middle, and inner ear are intact, and the difficulty is with the VIII cranial nerve (auditory nerve), brainstem or cortex.

When a client has sufficient speech and language skills, word recognition testing is performed. The client may repeat a single syllable word or point to a picture representing the spoken word. The words are presented at a normal conversational loudness level or at a sufficient level to be easily audible in cases of hearing loss. Word recognition ability is often reduced in sensorineural hearing loss, since speech is heard in distorted forms with this type of loss.

Another test included in a comprehensive hearing evaluation is tympanometry which is the most common test of middle ear function. Middle ear pathology is common in children and individuals with developmental disabilities in general. If the audiologist determines that the test result is abnormal, a medical referral would be recommended, as middle ear problems are generally treatable.

Methods of Service to Persons with Developmental Disabilities

Because assessment of hearing impairment in persons with developmental delays is often difficult and time-consuming, intervention may be initiated based on limited information. Treatment has two main components: amplification and programming. While some aspects of the treatment process may vary according to the age of the client, there are some standard steps involved in the process.

The first step in treatment of a hearing loss is referral to an otolaryngologist (ear, nose, and throat physician). This procedure is performed to determine if medical or surgical intervention is required to improve the hearing loss, or if treatment is needed for the health of the patient. In cases when medical treatment could not improve all of the hearing loss, amplification or instrument selection is pursued.

If amplification is warranted, several factors must be included in hearing aid selection. These factors are based on the type and degree of hearing loss, physical aspects, and behavioral considerations. There are different types (behind the ear, body worn, in the ear) and power ranges (mild gain, moderate gain) in hearing aids. Regardless of the severity of hearing loss or the type of hearing aid selected, the overall goal of fitting a hearing aid is the same: to make speech loud enough to be understood by the client.

The type and degree of hearing impairment is a significant factor in the selection of amplification. For many persons who have developmental disabilities, exact audiometric information is difficult to obtain, which requires that a hearing aid be flexible in its power range. Complete information is often not obtained until years following the initial diagnosis of hearing impairment, and clearly it is not feasible to wait to fit the aid until such information is obtained.

A second consideration in selection involves the physical attributes of the client. Hearing aids range in type and size to accommodate various characteristics of the client. Modifications may also be made in a hearing aid to allow flexibility in fitting individual needs.

A third consideration in the selection of appropriate amplification is based on the behavior of a client. For example, some children with significant behavior disorders will not tolerate the placement of a hearing aid. There are some approaches that can be used to make removal of a hearing aid by the user difficult; nevertheless, most physically able and determined children can remove their hearing aids at will. This issue may be addressed in a behavior modification program, if one is in place. If not, the audiologist will assist the parent in devising a system to decrease the possibility that the hearing aid would be lost if removed. The audiologist must also be alerted to the possibility that refusal to wear the hearing aid, or behavior problems during use, may be indicative of a problem that deserves further assessment, such as an incorrect power range supplied by the instrument.

Once a hearing aid is selected, the device is fitted specifically to the client. An evaluation of the client's hearing with the amplification in place is also performed to ensure an appropriate amount of power is being provided at the needed pitches. The type of evaluation performed will vary depending on the client. Evaluation of hearing aid performance is an ongoing process, since immediate changes are often not seen, particularly in more severely hearing impaired persons who have little or no sound experience. Benefit from amplification is sometimes difficult to measure until a year or more following initial fitting; however, behavior observations often provide helpful insight. As more is learned about the hearing impairment, adjustments may be easily made to a carefully-selected flexible instrument.

Part of the treatment process includes an orientation for individuals who have significant relationships with the client. These sessions may include parents, other family members, and service providers such as teachers. The session is essential because a hearing aid must be functioning properly to improve hearing ability. For example, parents frequently come to the audiologist thinking a hearing aid is broken when the battery is merely dead or the earmold plugged with wax. The information received in a hearing aid orientation is extensive, technical, and often occurs at an emotional time for the family. The audiologist must be sensitive to those issues, and schedule multiple sessions with the client and family, if necessary.

After identification and decision-making concerning amplification are completed, the second component in treatment is initiated. This step involves referral to an aural habilitation/rehabilitation program to help clients develop or improve communication abilities. Appropriate programming depends on factors such as age of the client, age of onset of hearing loss, other delays, and family issues. Although audiologists have significant input regarding programmatic considerations, other disciplines are essential in assisting the audiologist to plan an appropriate program. For example, children with poor vision or blindness will not have the opportunity to supplement auditory signals with visual cues, which is one type of educational approach. Other handicapping conditions may inhibit communication development despite amplification.

There are no straightforward guidelines to follow when selecting the appropriate program. Many considerations must be taken into account when choosing a program, particularly for children with other delays unrelated to their hearing impairment. Intervention may include some form of manual communication, fingerspelling and sign language, in addition to spoken language. This approach is referred to as *total communication* and combines the use of hearing with visual presentation of language. In another educational approach, known as *auditory-oral*, emphasis is placed entirely on the auditory system to develop speech and language. A third approach relies solely on manual communication. The decision regarding the "best" approach is surrounded with controversy. Whatever the choice, hearing-impaired clients for whom amplification has been chosen should be encouraged to make maximum use of their residual hearing capacity.

Case Example

Referral

Eric is a 2-year-9-month-old male referred for an interdisciplinary team evaluation by his pediatrician due to concerns regarding his overall physical and developmental status. Specifically, his parents expressed concern regarding Eric's hearing, communication, and motor skills. Eric was diagnosed with *Hemophilus influenza* meningitis at 18 months of age, before which time he was described as developing normally. Due to the family's concern regarding Eric's hearing status and the history of meningitis, the audiologist was chosen as evaluation coordinator for this case.

Review of medical records and a family interview were completed in order to obtain complete case history information. This information was compiled and presented by the evaluation coordinator. A pre-assessment staff meeting was conducted with members of the interdisciplinary team to provide input as necessary.

History

Eric lives at home with his parents and is an only child. His mother is a homemaker and his father is currently unemployed. The client is covered by state medical insurance which is paying for the assessment. Eric's parents are both currently seeking employment out of the home.

Eric was the product of a full-term, uncomplicated pregnancy and vaginal delivery. He was discharged as a healthy newborn after a 24-hour hospital stay. Neonatal health history was unremarkable. Eric was followed regularly through well-baby visits and his immunizations are up to date.

Medical history was significant for chronic otitis media and upper respiratory infections which had been successfully treated with antibiotics. At age 18 months, Eric was seen in the emergency room due to high fever for more than 24 hours, ataxia, and irritability. He was subsequently diagnosed with *H. influenza* (bacterial) meningitis and was hospitalized for 8 days during which time he was treated with ampicillin. In addition to complete medical treatment, a hearing assessment was completed prior to discharge due to the diagnosis of meningitis and ampicillin treatment, both of which are considered high-risk factors for hearing loss. An Auditory Brainstem Response (ABR) was obtained, resulting in 30 dB HL thresholds in both ears, indicating mild hearing loss in at least the high frequencies in both ears. Follow-up in 4 weeks was recommended, as hearing levels following meningitis may fluctuate. However, further assessment was not performed due to reports that Eric seemed to respond normally to voices. There were no concerns regarding his hearing until more recently, when expected advances in his speech and language skills were not observed.

Developmental milestones were reportedly achieved at age-appropriate levels prior to Eric's illness. Currently, communication skills are reported as delayed. At age 33 months, he is reported to have less than a 100-word vocabulary. He communicates primarily through pointing and gestures and his speech is difficult to understand. Motor development is described as normal with the exception of reports of clumsiness; however, that is felt to have improved since his illness.

Behaviorally, Eric's parents describe him as having a limited attention span. He is easily frustrated and difficult to discipline. They question whether this behavior is typical of a child in the "terrible twos" stage. In order to address referral and parental concerns, the following disciplines were asked to evaluate Eric over a three-day assessment period: developmental medicine, audiology, speech-language pathology, occupational therapy, physical therapy, and psychology.

Findings

Eric was found to be a generally healthy boy. His physical growth was within normal limits. Neurological examination was normal, with no evidence of the seizures which are often a sequela of meningitis.

Conditioned Play Audiometry was performed under earphones. A speech awareness threshold was obtained at 25 dB HL, which is considered in the borderline normal-to-slight range of hearing loss. Responses to tones were in the borderline normal-to-slight hearing loss range in the low frequencies and beginning at 2000 Hz sloped sharply to a moderately severe to severe sensorineural hearing loss bilaterally. Responses were considered reliable. Eric's responses to speech were reflective of his better hearing ability for low-frequency sounds. Word recognition abilities were not formally assessed due to apparent communication delays; however, informal observation revealed some difficulty in word recognition abilities that were not felt to be due to unfamiliar vocabulary. Tympanograms, obtained to evaluate eardrum mobility, were normal in both ears. Acoustic reflex thresholds were consistent with the above hearing loss.

Communication abilities were assessed by a formal battery of tests including vocabulary comprehension, expressive language abilities, observation of structured play, and informal observation. The speech and language assessment revealed significant speech and language impairment characterized by reduced language comprehension and limited expressive language abilities. Multiple articulation errors were noted. Eric was not stimulable for many of the sounds in error such as *f, s, z, th,* and *v.* These errors were not felt to be developmental in nature, since they coincided with the frequencies for which he had significant hearing impairment, making these sounds inaudible.

Psychological assessment revealed low average performance on nonverbal measures of intelligence. Verbal IQ scores were significantly lower and were commensurate with the findings of speech-language pathology. A limited attention span was noted, but Eric could be easily redirected with verbal prompts paired with gestures. He was noted to become frustrated when the complexity of tasks exceeded his abilities or when verbal items were presented. The psychologist noted that the findings should be interpreted with caution if a hearing loss was present, as even the "nonverbal" performance items required verbal instruction.

Motor assessment revealed age-appropriate fine motor skills. Gross motor skills were also within a broad range of normal. However, qualitative concerns regarding balance and unsteady gait were noted.

Treatment Recommendations

The above findings were discussed in a post-assessment staff meeting with input from all disciplines involved. Based on the information provided by the interdisciplinary assessment and input from the family, the following recommendations were made.

Referral to an ear, nose, and throat physician was made. The ENT will medically evaluate hearing loss, address vestibular concerns, and provide medical clearance for hearing aids. Eric's primary care physician will provide the proper referrals for evaluations and procedures required.

Following a complete medical assessment of Eric's hearing loss and medical clearance for two hearing aids, he will return to the audiologist for hearing aid selection. Because Eric is covered by a state medical card, the hearing aids will be purchased through Medicaid upon submission of appropriate paperwork. Eric will be fitted with loaner hearing aids pending approval and funding for his personal hearing aids.

Audiological follow-up will be ongoing for Eric for hearing aid services and continued assessment. Hearing loss associated with meningitis can often be progressive and fluctuating in nature for as long as 18 months following diagnosis. In this case, the audiological findings in the high frequencies were significantly poorer than the ABR results in the hospital, suggesting some progression in hearing loss. Hearing aids will be chosen that provide a good amount of flexibility in case Eric's hearing changes in the next few months. Prognosis for oral speech development and improvement in communication abilities was judged as good due to the degree of hearing loss, previously normal hearing, and motivation of the family.

Referral was made to a center-based program for hearing-impaired children that has three normal-hearing children in attendance in addition to four children with hearing impairments. The program emphasizes a total communication approach which was judged to be appropriate for Eric. He will attend this program in the mornings, four days per week. The program is transdisciplinary in nature and is staffed by a hearing-impaired teacher, an audiologist, a speech-language pathologist, an occupational therapist, and a social worker. A home visit will take place for one hour one time per week to assist the family.

Transitions from the preschool setting to kindergarten must be carefully planned. Consultation between the preschool and elementary school setting are essential. Follow-up cognitive assessment is recommended in six months, at which time an assessment normed for hearing-impaired children will be given.

References

American Speech-Language-Hearing Association (1992). *Membership and certification handbook for standards in the certificates of clinical competence in speech-language pathology and audiology.* Rockville, MD: Author.

American Speech-Language-Hearing Association (1993a). Guidelines for audiology services in the schools. *ASHA*, 35(10), 24-32.

American Speech-Language-Hearing Association (1993b). Implementation procedures for the standards for the certificates of clinical competence. *ASHA, 35,* 76-83.

American Speech-Language-Hearing Association (1994). Report to the members. *ASHA, 36*(3), 10-14.

Bess, F. & Humes, L., (1990). *Audiology: The fundamentals.* Baltimore, MD: Williams & Wilkins.

Cherow, E., Diggs, C., & Williams, P., (1982). Demographics and description of the problem. In E. Holzhauer, K. Hoff, & E. Cherow (Eds.), *Hearing impaired developmentally disabled children and adolescents: An interdisciplinary look at a special population* (pp. 11-122). Rockville, MD: American Speech-Language-Hearing Association.

Davis, H. (1970). Audiology. In H. Davis & S. R. Silverman (Eds.), *Hearing and deafness*, 3rd ed. (pp. 3-6). New York: Holt, Rinehart and Winston.

Fritsch, M., & Sommer, A. (1991). Demographic overview. In M. Fritsch & A. Sommer (Eds.), *Handbook of congenital and early onset hearing loss* (pp. 1-2). New York: Igakushoin Medical Publishers, Inc.

National Institutes of Health (1993). *Consensus Statement.* Washington, DC.

Thompson, G. & Folsom, R. (1981). Hearing assessment of at-risk infants. *Clinical Pediatrics, 20,* 257-261.

4

Behavior Analysis

Rolando G. Figueroa, Ph.D., Bruce E. Davis, Ph.D.,

& Kathryn H. Smith, Ph.D.

From the perspective of the behavior analyst, analysis of an individual's behavior involves determining the environmentally-based antecedents and consequences which influence particular target behaviors. Michael (1985) suggests that Skinner's 1938 book, *The Behavior of Organisms: An Experimental Analysis*, was the first overt affirmation of the association between behavior and such environmental analysis. Morris (1992) indicates that Skinner's 1931 article, "The Concept of Reflex in the Description of Behavior," actually first presented the argument that the purpose of behavior analysis was "prediction and control." Morris added that an essential element of prediction and control was also "description." But it wasn't until 40 years later, in the 1970's, that the term "behavior analysis" gained widespread use. This is a matter of nomenclature rather than discipline evolution, as most who called themselves "behaviorists" before the 1970s and "behavior analysts" afterwards did not change their practice or philosophy (Morris, Todd, Midgley, Schneider, & Johnson, 1990).

The basic difference between general psychology and behavior analysis is the nature of experimental design within each discipline (Baron, 1990; cf. Sidman, 1960). Psychology has tended to use methods of statistical inference to determine "significant" differences between groups; BA utilizes single-subject designs to ascertain treatment effects.

Morris (1992) describes the evolution of BA over the last half century as having resulted in three predominant and enduring branches:

1. the *experimental* analysis of behavior, basic research that is typically confined to the laboratory;
2. *applied* behavior analysis, addressing clinical and community applications (which can also be considered "experimental"); and
3. the *conceptual* analysis of behavior, dealing more with the theoretical and philosophical venues of the discipline.

Baer, Wolf, and Risley (1968) indicated that *applied behavior analysis* must be *applied*, *behavioral*, and *analytic* (what Morris, 1992, referred to as "conceptual"). Morris (1992) laments that "As robust as these three branches may be, however, they are not mainstream psychology; worse yet, behavior analysis is sorely misunderstood and mischaracterized" (p. 3). Baer et al. (1968) also suggested that applied behavior analysis is technological, conceptually systematic, effective, and generalizable. These dimensions have withstood the test of time (Baer, Wolf, & Risley, 1987) and merit brief discussion in order to better grasp the nature of BA.

Applied. As Baer et al. (1968) point out, in behavior analysis, the target behavior(s) generally selected for "analysis" are those which society deems either necessary for, or interfering with, effective functioning. Behaviors of most concern in the field of developmental disabilities are those which significantly impede one's ability to function independently, e.g., self-injurious behavior, aggression, or stereotypy (abnormal repetition of an action or abnormal maintenance of a single position or posture).

Behavioral. The focus of the behavior analyst generally continues to be observable behavior, i.e., what an individual actually *does* (Baer et al., 1968). Focusing on observable behaviors allows more precise measurement, providing the sensitivity to detect even subtle changes in behavior. Frequency and/or duration data may be collected that permit us to make inferences about the effect of antecedents and/or consequences on behavior, as well as to evaluate the efficacy of interventions. Systematic self-reports of the patient's thoughts, private behavior, or affective states are also increasingly amenable to investigation using behavior analysis.

Analytic. Analysis of a behavior requires identification of the environmental contingencies (again, antecedents and consequences) associated with a particular behavior. The analysis is complete if the information gathered permits the behavior analyst to "exercise control" over a behavior, to "turn the behavior on and off, or up and down, at will" (Baer et al., 1968, p. 94). Morris (1991) indicates that analysis within applied BA means demonstration and discovery. Analysis will demonstrate the effectiveness of general behavior principles as well as discovering the functions and/or

causes of behavior. The focus of the analysis are those natural relationships which occur in society that maintain the behaviors of interest.

Technological. The technological aspect of applied BA is directly associated with the analytic dimension; it requires clear definition and description of all aspects of a particular treatment (e.g., "stimuli, contingency, [and] schedule"; Baer et al., 1968, p. 95). If a procedure is technologically sound, a trained reader should be able to replicate it and accomplish the same results. Morris (1991) is more explicit about technology and concludes that its import lies in the process of discovery. "To demonstrate change in problem behavior by applying a technology is not necessarily to discover the contingencies responsible for the problem in the first place" (p. 414). It is important that the behavior analyst not only demonstrate change in a particular behavior, but also discover the original functions of that behavior. In developmental disabilities, such a *functional analysis* of behavior is one of the most essential elements of effective BA and will be addressed later in the chapter.

Conceptual, Effective, Generalizable. Baer et al. (1968) further posit that applied BA should be conceptually related to the fundamental principles of "behaviorism" (i.e., reinforcement, punishment, conditioning, etc.). Also, in order to be effective, the changes in behavior produced through this technique have to be substantial enough to produce clinically practical results, not just statistically significant differences. These changes should be constant across time and generalizable across settings.

Within the last 40 to 50 years, changes in research and services in the field of developmental disabilities have been due predominantly to the application of classical and operant conditioning procedures previously confined to laboratory settings (Johnston, 1991; Matson & Coe, 1992). Such approaches to the treatment of individuals with a developmental disability have proven to be particularly useful in treating so-called mental health problems as well (cf. Matson, 1990). BA continues to have a considerable role in the treatment of persons with a developmental disability, not only because the methodology of BA lends itself so well to this population, but also due to lack of interest from other disciplines (Johnston, 1991).

Education and Training

Psychologists often conduct the functions of BA in applied settings. However, having a psychology degree does not necessarily prepare an individual for the practice of BA. Shook (1993) points out that state licensure in psychology does not require competence in BA (at times even disallowing internships with a focus on BA), and suggests that the broad credential offered by the American Board of Behavioral Psychology (1989) recognize BA as a specialty. This is particularly appropriate since BA has been described as a "discipline unto itself" (Morris, Todd, Midgley, Schneider & Johnson, 1990). The reality, however, is that although variously referred to a "science," "discipline," or "field," BA has no cogent educational guidelines. Johnston (1991) notes that the field as a whole has not confronted the need for establishing minimum or recommended curriculum standards in academic settings.

There are only 19 colleges or universities listed in the *Directory of Graduate Training Programs in Behavior Analysis* that list programs containing the term "behavior analysis," and 21 traineeships with this emphasis (Association of Behavior Analysis: International [ABA], 1992). This is not to say that these institutions are the only ones providing training, or even specialization, in BA. Nonetheless, the *Directory of Gradu-ate Training Programs in Behavior Analysis* only lists three programs in the United States that offer a graduate degree in "Behavioral Analysis;" only one offers a Ph.D. (ABA, 1992). This paucity of programs testifies to the need for a nationally recognized core curriculum. The Association for Behavior Analysis has been investigating this issue for several years now, as has Division 25 (The Experimental Analysis of Behavior) of the American Psychological Association.

BA, then, is not yet deemed an independent *profession* in most of the United States. In recent years, students have been able to receive training with an emphasis on behavioral analysis from departments of psychology, rehabilitation, and special education; most programs are found within departments of psychology. There are some, however, who would argue that persons of varied backgrounds can function just as well as BAs (Kunkel, 1987; Tharp & Wetzel, 1969).

There is no publication addressing training in BA at the undergraduate level, but attempts were made over 20 years ago to bring a sense of formalization to the training needs at this level as well. Keeley, Shemberg, and Ferber (1973) described a very successful program at Bowling Green University training bachelor level students of psychology as behavior analysts. The training was conducted at two levels: formal education in behavioral precepts, and use of this technology to write intervention programs and consult with persons who would implement them.

Certification

Florida (since 1979) and Oklahoma (as of 1993) are the only states that currently offer certification in BA (Starin, Hemingway, & Hartsfield, 1993). At least four other states—Alabama, California, Georgia, and Texas—are currently pursuing certification

of some sort. To take the certification examination in Florida, one must only furnish proof either of college credits from
course work in behavioral analysis, or of
having taken a workshop preparing for the
certification test. Also, there are no requirements for continuing education to maintain certification. It is important to note,
however, that Florida is light years ahead
of most, if not all, of the country in meeting the challenge of establishing exemplary
guidelines and meaningful standards.
Florida is currently well underway in revis-
ing the certification process and has two
proposals under review. One alternative
would only grant certification to individuals who have a minimum of a master's degree with a major emphasis on BA; they
would receive the title "Certified Behavior
Analyst." The other option would add another level of certification below the Certified Behavior Analyst. These individuals
would have an undergraduate degree and
some specialized training in behavior analysis and would be referred to as "Certified
Behavior Specialists" (Starin et al., 1993).

Contributions to Interdisciplinary Practice

Behavior analysts have a unique orientation
toward understanding the consumer's behavior. This orientation puts us in the position of advocating for meeting particular
needs expressed by the consumer's behavior. The BA serves as the primary consultant for the interdisciplinary team (IDT) with
respect to the consumer's maladaptive
behavior(s). The IDT meeting provides an
appropriate venue for interviewing team
members to complete the assessment begun
at the direct care level. The BA then summarizes this assessment of the behavior(s)
and leads the team in identifying areas for

intervention. Not only is this a fertile environment for information gathering, but the
team can immediately use the information
to assist in designing interventions. The IDT
often looks to the behavior analyst to provide suggestions for intervention in maladaptive behaviors and guidance in determining appropriate replacement behaviors.
Just as critical to the IDT is the assistance
the BA brings in recommending procedures
for the acquisition of *appropriate* behaviors.

The BA relies on all members of the IDT
to assist at every level of assessment and intervention. Particularly important are the
staff who function at the direct care level.
It is these individuals who spend the most
time with consumers and therefore know
them most intimately. It is often only the
direct-care worker who enlightens us about
the nuances of behaviors that elude even
the most experienced professional.

An integral partner, when available, in
conducting the behavioral analysis is the
psychologist (see the chapter on Psychology
in this volume). Unfortunately, fiscal realities often prohibit such associations. In most
settings, psychologists are only called on a
consultant basis to review the most intractable cases. Should a psychologist be in the
same setting, however, he or she can provide
additional insights from a perspective similar to the behavior analyst's. It is imperative, though, that the psychologist also have
a background in BA and training in developmental disabilities. More often than not,
such an individual is not readily available.

As BA more and more reveals the communicative functions of behaviors, particularly in persons with more significant intellectual disabilities (Carr & Durand, 1985),
the speech-language pathologist serves as an
essential adjunct to service delivery. A thorough communication assessment must be
conducted, not only to determine strengths
and weaknesses, but also to suggest what mode
of communication training may be most ef-

fective (e.g., augmentative/alternative communication systems, sign language, articulation training, etc.). This often serves as the focus of training in developing replacement behaviors for the maladaptive behaviors.

Bailey and Pyles (1987) stress the importance of addressing physiological variables when assessing a particular behavior. For instance, a significant increase in aggression in the spring and fall that remits when given antihistamines and corticosteroid nasal sprays clearly suggests a medical etiology for the problem of aggression (a reaction to subjective discomfort?).

Special education teachers provide critical feedback to the BA about the behavior(s) of concern and are integral players in the development of the Individual Program Plan. They are particularly important because so much of the support plan relies on the acquisition of replacement behaviors. We frequently have to rely on the expertise of special education teachers to develop plans to teach functional skills. In the case above, one would teach the student to utilize augmentative communication to indicate pain/discomfort. And, to promote independence, an effort would be made to teach the student to self-administer the medications.

The social worker is our link to reality; a liaison with and between community and familial resources. As one of the main goals of BA is generalizability of results, the social worker provides a vital link to the family in setting up visitations and training sessions. Involvement with the community may consist of setting up training sessions similar to those presented to the family, as well as mobilizing available community resources. This establishes a three-dimensional support delivery system that greatly enhances the probability of generalizing positive treatment results across settings and maintaining them over time.

Assessment

As expressed earlier, BAs have as their primary goal the assessment of overt behavior and its environmentally based causes and consequences. Consultation and intervention efforts stem directly from evaluation of behavior, and appropriate and effective interventions result from thorough, accurate, data-based assessments.

Behavioral analysis attempts to isolate the details of individual behavioral events by attending to what occurs in the environment before, during, and after the target behavior. In effect, we attempt to take a series of snapshots, then put them together into a moving picture of a person's behavior. Just like the photographer, the BA continues to take snapshots across time from several different angle, continually seeking a more complete account of what occurs in behavioral events for the person. Once he or she takes enough snapshots, the BA tries to develop a theme for the photographs and puts them in a sensible order so that others understand them.

The ABC Model

Many behavior analysts use the ABC model to structure accounts of behavioral events. The ABC model involves assessing the *Antecedents*, *Behaviors*, and *Consequences* of the behavioral event. These refer respectively to what events occur before the behavior, a definition/description of the behavior, and what events follow the behavior.

Antecedent Conditions. Axelrod (1987) refers to the process of assessing antecedent conditions as *structural analysis*. In structural analysis, the BA looks for the situations in which the target behavior is most likely to occur. At this stage, the BA typically has two questions: What are the typical conditions when the person participates in activities of daily living? What are the typical conditions when the person avoids participation in those activities?

Stimulus control describes conditions that demonstrate a reliable relationship between particular behaviors. *Stimulus* refers to a particular condition or situation that stimulates the occurrence of behavior. For instance, asking someone to brush his teeth may stimulate a behavior. Control occurs when a stimulus *predicts* the occurrence of a particular behavior. Thus, if a person generally brushes his teeth when asked, asking him to brush his teeth has stimulus control over toothbrushing. If the person generally hits or slaps a person requesting him to brush his teeth, asking him to brush his teeth has stimulus control over hitting or slapping. The behavior analyst seeks to determine the conditions that have stimulus control over the behavior in question.

Behavior. To a large extent, BAs respond to social desirability when identifying behaviors for assessment; i.e., to what extent does this behavior violate societal norms? The type of target behavior often has implications in determining what type of intervention is chosen. For example, while analysis may reveal that an aggressive or self-injurious behavior gains attention, to completely ignore such a behavior may present a risk to safety. For this reason, behavior analysts attempt to provide the team with a specific definition of the behavior and its consequences and will use the information gained through assessments to help the IDT design appropriate interventions.

BAs also attend to the frequency, intensity, and duration of the behavior. *Frequency* is the number of times the behavior occurs in a specified time period. *Intensity* describes the energy the person exerts on the behavior, or the behavior's effect on the environment. *Duration* represents a different measure of intensity and simply describes how long the behavior occurs. These pieces of information help the team determine the social significance of the behavior and the need for intervention.

Consequent Conditions. The BA asks the question, "What occurs after (or as a consequence of) the behavior?" When interpreting the effect of a particular behavior, one must take into consideration the desirability of the consequences for both the consumers and those around them. For instance, a verbal reprimand punishes an approval-seeking behavior, but may positively reinforce an attention-seeking behavior.

Consequences may take at least five basic forms: *Positive reinforcement* refers to the presentation of consequences following a target behavior's occurrence, which results in an *increase* in the target behavior's future frequency, intensity, or duration. Positive reinforcement is colloquially known as "reward." *Negative reinforcement* involves the removal of some stimulus following the occurrence of the target behavior, which also leads to a future *increase* in the target behavior's strength, i.e., frequency, intensity or duration. Negative reinforcement, colloquially known as "relief," is one of the most frequently misunderstood terms in psychology–by professional and lay persons alike (Iwata, 1987). *Positive punishment* occurs when the behavior is followed by presenting stimuli, such consequences resulting in a future *decrease* in the frequency, intensity, or duration of the target behavior. *Negative punishment* occurs when stimuli are removed, contingent upon the occurrence of the target behavior, with the result that the future likelihood of the target behavior is decreased. This is colloquially known as a "fine." The removal of reinforcing consequences that maintain a target behavior leads to a decrease in the future probability of that behavior, through a process called *operant extinction*.

Iwata et al. (1982) have identified some typical functions for the self-injurious behaviors of persons with developmental disabilities. Negative intrinsic reinforcement occurs when the self-injurious behavior removes physical pain or discomfort. Positive intrinsic reinforcement occurs when the self-injury results in the production of the body's natural pain killer, endorphin. Positive extrinsic reinforcement occurs when the self-injury results in attention from others, or in a tangible reward. Negative extrinsic reinforcement occurs when the behavior results in escape from a difficult task.

Functional Analysis. This method is currently the backbone of BA in the field of developmental disabilities and has been used to describe the assessment of the consequences of a particular behavior (Iwata et al., 1982). O'Neil, Horner, Albin, Storey, & Sprague (1990) define functional analysis as an information-gathering process (assessment) with three objectives:

1. an operational definition of the behavior(s) in question
2. prediction of the circumstances when and where the behavior will and *will not* occur
3. subsequently determining the function the behavior serves for the consumer

Lennox and Miltenberger (1989) differ in their account of functional analysis by distinguishing it from *functional assessment.* They describe functional assessment as the *identification* of antecedents and consequences that maintain a behavior; *functional analysis* alludes to the *manipulation* of the variables putatively regulating the behavior. Such hypothesis testing permits us to make inferences about the causes of certain behaviors with more certainty.

Methods of Assessment

Interview. Most BAs make extensive use of interview information. Typical infor-

mants work closely with the client/consumer displaying the target behavior. The BA gains the most accurate information by interviewing two or more informants from multiple disciplinary perspectives. The BA may complete the interviews with a group or with individuals.

Observation. In this method, a person working with the behavior records the time, location, situation, and consequences for episodes they have observed. Observation sometime takes place by setting up particular antecedent and consequent conditions in a controlled environment in analog situations (cf. Iwata et al., 1982). Trained observers then record the frequency, intensity, and/or duration of the behavior under different conditions.

Rating Scales. There are a multitude of rating scales available to assess behavior, but few specifically developed for use in the field of developmental disabilities. Durand and Crimmins (1988) devised the *Motivation Assessment Scale* to classify the functions of problem behaviors. The scale attempts to classify the motivation for behaviors into four functions: tangibly reinforcing, attention-seeking, demand-escaping, and self-stimulatory. Rourke, Dorsey, Geren, and Kimball (1991) provide evidence, however, that the MAS may not be applicable to types of behavior other than self-injury.

Behavioral Analysis Service Delivery

Indirect Services

Most of the BA's responsibilities fall under the category of indirect services. As shown above, he or she completes most assessments based on the observations of others. The BA also implements most recommendations through direct care staff.

Behavior Support Planning. The BA

typically fashions the IDT's feedback into a *behavior support plan* or *behavior management plan*. Most facilities require behavior support plans to have strategies geared toward increasing appropriate alternative (replacement) behaviors, preventing maladaptive behaviors, and intervening in maladaptive behaviors. In institutional settings, behavior support plans must undergo review to ensure that they include technically sound strategies that observe the rights of the individual they intend to support; behavior management and human rights committees may serve these functions. The BA acts as the team's representative on these committees to provide a rationale for their approach and respond to questions. The BA also revises the plans to meet the recommendations of the review committees. In some states, as many as 80–93% of community programs require some sort of approval of a behavior support plan as well, prior to its implementation (Jacobson & Ackerman, 1989). Other states do not have a formal approval procedure for individual behavioral support plans, but may be required to have a Quality Assurance/Client's Rights committee review the policies related to behavior management and techniques of physical restraint.

Medication Monitoring. The BA provides key data to assess the effectiveness of behavior-modifying medications. He or she helps the team define diagnostic criteria for psychiatric disorders in terms of easily observable behaviors. The BA then reports on various dimensions of those behaviors before and after changes in the medications. The ethical use of behavior-altering medications requires that we use a data-based approach to determine the minimum dosage that produces optimal desired behavioral effects. In many settings, interdisciplinary teams call on the behavior analyst to devise medication reduction plans. (A more appropriate term would be "medication management plans," as titration to the most effective dose could easily mean an increase as well as a decrease.) These plans provide objective criteria for the team to utilize when considering a change in medication status. Writing these plans requires that the behavior analyst translate the IDT's goals with respect to a certain behavior into a functional procedural guide.

Training direct care staff. As primary authors of behavioral support plans, BAs provide training to direct-contact personnel on behavior support plans. Generally, they are responsible for at least "training the trainer." In other words, they provide training to a person in a leadership position, who then provides training to the direct contact persons. Time constraints on the behavior analyst frequently make it difficult to provide effective training to all staff who have direct contact with the consumer. Video technology provides one alternative to direct training; we may see an increased reliance on this method in the future.

In settings where violent behavior occurs, the BA is often required to develop expertise in the physical management of aggression. Many clients require the use of blocking or brief physical restraint techniques during the course of their daily life routine. The behavior analyst aids the team by providing initial training to incoming personnel on aggression management techniques.

Direct Services

While most of the BA's activities center around indirect services, he or she occasionally provides some direct services to clients.

Therapy. Many clients with developmental disabilities can benefit from structured talk therapies. It is important to note, however, that BAs may not be not trained in psychotherapy (just as most psychologists are not trained in behavior analysis). However, the BA can often provide skill acquisition "therapies" such as social skills training (McClennen, Hoekstra & Bryan, 1980), assertiveness training, or relaxation training. The BA may also provide training for a person learning to implement a behavioral skill in a particular situation (i.e., learning to make his bed in the morning). Supportive verbal therapy may also fall under the purview of a behavior analyst's competence. Again, time constraints limit the BA's ability to consistently provide these services in a direct fashion. Instead, he or she often provides these services by training others to implement these procedures and supervising them to assure quality control.

Modeling. As part of training, the BA frequently works directly with a client to demonstrate the techniques outlined in behavior support plans. The BA may perform this function to train staff on redirection techniques or reinforcement strategies. Given the role of aggression management expert, BAs may often demonstrate techniques for de-escalating potentially violent situations by physically intervening when violence actually occurs. The BA is the interdisciplinary team member who is often called upon to manage the most physically difficult situations.

Case Example

One of the most frequent reasons for admission to intermediate care facilities for the mentally retarded (ICF/MR) is severe aggressive behavior. This case report describes the treatment of an eleven-year-old boy who has been hospitalized since the age of nine in an ICF/MR serving school-aged consumers because he escaped from his home, entered a nearby school playground, and attacked a young child (previously reported in Figueroa, Thyer, & Thyer, 1992).

He had a significant history of aggression prior to this incident.

At the time of the intervention, the student was functioning in the severe range of mental retardation; he was additionally diagnosed with cerebral palsy, manifesting in partial left hemiparesis. He attained a mental age equivalent of 3-10 on the Slosson Intelligence Test, a mental age of approximately 1-8 on the Bayley Scales of Infant Development, and an Adaptive Behavior Composite on the Vineland Adaptive Behavior Scale of 2-4. The Stanford-Binet, Form L-M, was attempted, but a basal could not be established. (Note: neither the Slosson Intelligence Test–Revised nor the Fourth Edition of the Stanford-Binet were available at the time the student's psychological assessment was conducted.)

While at the ICF/MR, numerous interventions had been attempted with minimal success. For instance, he had been taught to say, "Move," if anyone got too close. This helped some, but he often aggressed nonetheless. Other interventions that had been attempted included redirection, differential reinforcement of other behavior (DRO), a time-out room, and physical restraint. The severity of his behavior required that he be kept away from peers for their safety. The aggression took the form of biting, scratching, pulling hair, tearing others' clothes, spitting, hitting, and kicking. These behaviors occurred at an extremely high frequency and had resulted in countless and costly injuries to workers and peers. As a consequence, the student was essentially isolated from his peers at virtually all times. He would eat at a table by himself. In the classroom, a makeshift partition was constructed out of bookshelves and a desk to keep him segregated, and recreational outings were seldom attempted.

Further analysis of his behavior led to the hypothesis that the aggression was a negatively reinforced operant response. For reasons that we could not determine, the student found the close proximity of others extremely aversive. The poor motor skills associated with the cerebral palsy prohibited quick active avoidance of others who approached him. Thus, to him, the aggression was functional in that it resulted in staff-assisted escape from anxiety-laden situations; i.e., aggression was negatively reinforced by removal from uncomfortable situations. Requiring him to stay in the situation to prevent the escape response would often result in physical confrontations that could last for hours, terminating only when the student was too physically exhausted to continue. Concern was noted that these interactions, in turn, may have been paradoxically turning into *positively* reinforcing confrontations where he could have staff on a one-to-one basis.

That aggression can be negatively reinforcing has been previously reported in the literature (cf. Carr, Newsome, & Binkoff, 1980) and certainly seemed to be occurring in this case. The dilemma was how to deal with the fact that attempting to prevent the escape response was not effective, resulting in numerous staff injuries, and that these very efforts seemed to be prolonging the episodes. So we returned to the basics of behavioral analysis for an answer.

If aggression was an operant, then removing the consequences presumed to be reinforcing should result in a decrease of that behavior. In practice, this would mean that individuals would need to invade and persist in his perceived personal space. They should refuse to move despite the student's efforts to elicit an escape response by means of requests or attacks. We surmised, based on the principle of extinction, that if the student could be maintained in very close proximity to several persons at the same time, and find that the violent behavior no longer produced reinforcing consequences, the frequency of the behaviors would decrease sig-

nificantly. As well, we felt that it was important that the student come to associate the putatively reinforcing presence of staff with behaviors other than aggression. Previous accounts in the literature have addressed the concurrent use of extinction and DRO procedures (Deitz, 1985), which may produce a quicker decrease than extinction alone. This seemed like a prudent choice.

Typically, IDT's convene in an effort to integrate respective discipline assessments to produce an individual program plan. The individual program plan is usually implemented by direct care staff or by single (or at most dual) disciplines; i.e., programs devised by interdisciplinary teams are almost exclusively implemented in a *trans*disciplinary manner. Our IDT was activated in a way not normally associated with interdisciplinary practice: members of *all* disciplines and *all* levels of staff (from the Unit Director to the newest direct care worker) were recruited and participated in implementation of an intensive three-day intervention.

The intervention consisted of 7 consecutive hours on 3 consecutive days of extinction and DRO. Figueroa et al. (1992) described the procedure as follows:

> Immediately following breakfast on the first day, Anthony [a pseudonym] was escorted to the treatment room, stocked with toys and games, and staffed with at least three members of the facility's professional and direct care employees. The employees were rotated on and off duty (on an hourly basis), always keeping at least three other persons in close proximity to Anthony. The staff engaged Anthony in conversation, games, and in toy play. One professional staff member provided DRO using nonfattening edibles and social reinforcement (on a variable schedule averaging approximately 30 seconds). Staff employed protective equipment as they desired. Ag-

gressive behavior was ignored, blocked or redirected, but in any case did not result in the withdrawal of the staff (or physical restraint). Close proximity to Anthony was continuously maintained by the staff for 7 hours each day, except when he left the treatment room to go to the bathroom. During mealtimes, Anthony was taken to the cafeteria and ate his lunch with several staff remaining close to him. To further promote generalization and maintenance of this program, Anthony's father joined the staff during several of these sessions. Each 7-hour session was videotaped through the observation mirror by a member of the psychology staff. (p. 138)

Data revealed that aggression decreased within each day and across days (see Figure 4-1). Subjectively, the intensity of the aggression decreased significantly as well.

After the 3-day intervention, direct care staff continued to collect data on a continuous basis (delineated in Figure 4-2) on the frequency of aggressive behavior. As might be expected, there was an increase in the frequency of aggression when Anthony first returned to his normal schedule. It is natural that once he returned to the natural environment, expecting previous contingencies to be in place, he would escalate—i.e., have an extinction burst. It follows that if contingencies previously maintaining the behavior in the natural environment were no longer present, we would see a decline in the frequency of aggression. Figure 4-2 clearly reveals this trend despite great variability on a day-to-day basis. The decrease in the natural environment is attributable not only to Anthony's desensitization to the presence of staff, but largely to *staff's* desensitization to Anthony. This was a logical, but unanticipated, result of the sessions.

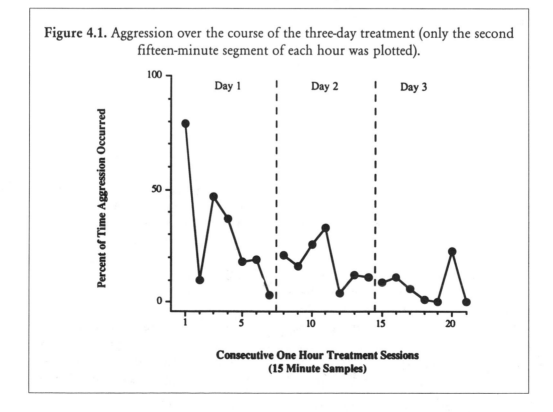

Figure 4.1. Aggression over the course of the three-day treatment (only the second fifteen-minute segment of each hour was plotted).

Consecutive One Hour Treatment Sessions (15 Minute Samples)

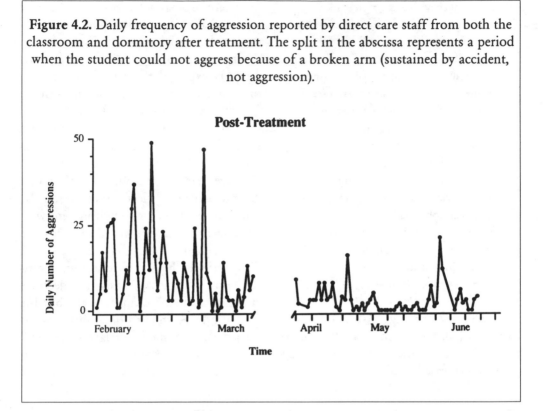

Figure 4.2. Daily frequency of aggression reported by direct care staff from both the classroom and dormitory after treatment. The split in the abscissa represents a period when the student could not aggress because of a broken arm (sustained by accident, not aggression).

Part of Anthony's problem was the staff's reluctance to get close to him for fear of an attack. Staff's distancing from Anthony had been negatively reinforced by avoidance of attacks and injury. The treatment sessions forced *everyone* to be in close proximity; over the course of the 3 days both Anthony and staff became accustomed to each other's physical closeness. This effect carried over to the naturalistic environment and explains why after a couple of weeks the frequency of aggression dropped precipitously. The decreasing slope might perhaps have been steeper had we continued the same intensity of staffing into the natural environment.

Summary

Behavior analysis provides the framework to observe an individual's behavior and to investigate possible relationship of environmentally-based antecedents and consequences which may establish and maintain that behavior. Clinically speaking, BA may be defined as applying behavioral principles toward increasing desirable behaviors and/or decreasing maladaptive ones. In the area of developmental disabilities, attention should be turned to not only behaviors which interfere (maladaptive), but more importantly, to those which promote (adaptive) that person's ability to function in society as independently as possible. Techniques should be based on sound behavioral principles, be replicable across individuals, and result in changes in behavior that are durable over time and generalizable to other settings.

References

American Board of Behavioral Psychology (1989). *Procedures and regulations for the creation of the diplomates in behavior therapy*. New York: Author.

Association for Behavior Analysis: International (1992). *Directory of Graduate Training in Behavior Analysis*. Kalamazoo, MI: Author.

Axelrod, S. (1987). Functional and structural analyses of behavior: Approaches leading to reduced use of punishment procedures? *Research in Developmental Disabilities, 8*, 165-178.

Baer, D.M., Wolf, M.M., & Risley, J.R. (1968). Some current dimensions of applied behavioral analysis. *Journal of Applied Behavioral Analysis, 1*, 91-97.

Baer, D.M., Wolf, M.M., & Risley, J.R. (1987). Some still current dimensions of applied behavioral analysis. *Journal of Applied Behavioral Analysis, 20*, 313, 327.

Bailey, J.S., & Pyles, D.A.M. (1987). Behavioral diagnostics. In E. Cipani (Ed.), *The treatment of severe behavior disorders: Behavior analysis approaches* (pp. 85-107). Washington, DC: American Association on Mental Retardation.

Baron, A. (1990). Experimental designs. *The Behavior Analyst, 13*, 167-171.

Carr, E.G., & Durand, V.M. (1985). Reducing behavior problems through functional communication training. *Journal of Applied Behavior Analysis, 18*, 111-126.

Carr, E.G., Newsome, C.D., & Binkoff, J.A. (1980). Escape as a factor in the aggressive behavior of two retarded children. *Journal of Applied Behavior Analysis, 13*, 101-117.

Deitz, S.M. (1985). Differential reinforcement of other behavior. In A.S. Bellack & M. Hersen (Eds.). *Dictionary of behavior therapy techniques* (pp. 110-112). New York: Pergamon Press.

Durand, V.M., & Crimmins, D.B. (1988). Identifying the variables maintaining self-injurious behavior. *Journal of Autism and Developmental Disorders, 18* , 99-117.

Figueroa, R.G., Thyer, B.A., & Thyer, K.B. (1992). Flooding and DRO in the treatment of aggression in a child with severe mental retardation. *Journal of Behavior Therapy and Experimental Psychiatry, 23*, 133-140.

Iwata, B.A. (1987). Negative reinforcement in applied behavior analysis: An emerging technology. *Journal of Applied Behavioral Analysis, 20*, 361-378.

Iwata, B.A., Dorsey, M.F., Slifer, K.J., Bauman, K.E., & Richman, G.S. (1982). Toward a functional analysis of self-injury. *Analysis and Intervention in Developmental Disabilities, 2*, 3-20.

Jacobson, J.W., & Ackerman L.J. (1989). *Use of behavior management procedures in group homes: Positive and negative approaches* (Report No. 89-1). A Report from the Best Practices Research Project. New York: Planning Unit, New York State Office of Mental Retardation and Developmental Disabilities.

Johnston, J.M. (1991). What can behavior analysis learn from the aversives controversy? *The Behavior Analyst, 14*, 187-196.

Keeley, S.M., Shemberg, K.M., & Ferber, H. (1973). The training and use of undergraduates as behavior analysts in the consultative process. *Professional Psychology, 4*, 59-63.

Kunkel, J.H. (1987). The future of JABA: A comment. *Journal of Applied Behavioral Analysis, 20*, 329-333.

Lennox, D.B., & Miltenberger, R.G. (1989). Conducting a functional assessment of problem behavior in applied settings. *Journal of the Association for Persons with Severe Handicaps, 14*, 304-311.

Matson, J.L. (1990). *Handbook of behavior modi-*

fication with the mentally retarded (2nd ed.). New York: Pergamon Press.

Matson, J.L., & Coe, D.C. (1992). Applied behavior analysis: Its impact on the treatment of mentally retarded emotionally disturbed people. *Research in Developmental Disabilities, 13*, 171-189.

McClennen, S.E., Hoekstra, R.O., & Bryan, J.E. (1980). *Social skills for severely retarded adults: An inventory and training program.* Champaign, IL: Research Press.

Michael, J.L. (1985). Behavior analysis: A radical perspective. In B.L. Hammonds (Ed.), *The masters lecture series: Vol. 4. Psychology and learning* (pp. 99-121). Washington, DC: American Psychological Association.

Morris, E.K. (1991). Deconstructing "Technological to a Fault." *Journal of Applied Behavior Analysis, 24*, 411-416.

Morris, E.K. (1992). ABA presidential address: The aim, progress, and evolution of behavior analysis. *The Behavior Analyst, 15*, 3-29.

Morris, E.K., Todd, J.K., Midgley, B.D., Schneider, S.M., & Johnson, L.M. (1990). The history of behavior analysis: Some historiography and a bibliography, *The Behavior Analyst, 13*, 131-158.

O'Neil, R.O., Horner, R.H., Albin, R.W., Storey, K., & Sprague, J.R. (1990). *Functional analysis of problem behavior.* Sycamore, IL: Sycamore Publishing Company.

Rourke, D.A., Dorsey, M.F., Geren, M.A., & Kimball, J.W. (1991, May). *The motivation assessment scale: A failure to extend to aggression.* Paper presented at the meeting of the Association of Behavior Analysis: International, Atlanta, GA.

Shook, G.L. (1993). The professional credential in behavior analysis. *The Behavior Analyst, 16*, 87-101.

Sidman, M. (1960). *Tactics of Scientific Research: Evaluating experimental data in psychology.* New York: Basic Books.

Skinner, B.F. (1938). *The behavior of organisms.* Englewood Cliffs, NJ: Prentice-Hall.

Starin, S., Hemingway, M., & Hartsfield, F. (1993). Credentialing behavior analysts and the Florida behavior analysis certification program. *The Behavior Analyst, 16*, 153-166.

Tharp, R.G., & Wetzel, R.J. (1969). *Behavior modification in the natural environment.* New York: Academic Press.

5

Pediatric Dentistry

Edward S. Sterling, D.D.S., & Paul S. Casamassimo, D.D.S., M.S.

Dentistry has no specialist equivalent to the special educator or developmental pediatrician. In fact, within dentistry, only pediatric dentistry's definition specifically mentions persons who are developmentally disabled. Pediatric dentistry is defined as "the practice and teaching of and research in comprehensive preventive and therapeutic oral health care of children from birth through adolescence. It shall be construed to include care for special patients beyond the age of adolescence who demonstrate mental, physical and/or emotional problems" (American Academy of Pediatric Dentistry, 1992-1993). Pediatric dentistry, unlike any other recognized specialty in dentistry, does not limit the range of services provided but, rather, limits *for whom* the services will be provided.

The pediatric dentist is the dental professional most likely to recognize and utilize the skills and knowledge obtainable in an interdisciplinary setting. Virtually every discipline represented in interdisciplinary teams (IDTs) has a body of knowledge and range of skills which can be adopted by the pediatric dentist and adapted to fit the needs of the pediatric dentist in the delivery of dental services.

Dentistry, however, has often been overlooked in the interdisciplinary setting; it is often considered adjunctive at best. Even the federal agencies which support such programs often view dentistry as not basic to the needs of these programs. Yet in an unpublished study conducted at a University Affiliated Program (UAP), the two most common unmet needs of a random sample of children referred to the program were dental and visual.

Oral health is certainly recognized as a part of overall general health and self-esteem. It can affect nutritional status. It can affect learning, job placement, speech production, social acceptance and general appearance. In doing so, dentistry touches and crosses other discipline boundaries and shares many of the same concerns.

An often-cited statistic claims that 65% of children eventually diagnosed as mentally retarded are not detected until school age. If one considers this "unidentified" preschool age child and asks, "Who are the professionals with whom this child may have contact?", the professionals with whom this child is most likely to have contact are physicians and dentists. If one takes this another step and analyzes the time these professionals spend in direct contact with the child and the frequency with which they see the child, the answers may surprise some. The average dental appointment is 30–45 minutes in length, and almost all of that time is in direct contact with the dentist. Additionally, because dentistry has such a strong preventive orientation, the child is seen at regular intervals, usually not exceeding six months. If properly trained and attuned, pediatric dentists could become a major referral resource for various early detection and intervention programs. Added to this is the recommendation that a child's first dental appointment should occur not later than one year of age (American Academy of Pediatric Dentistry, 1992-1993).

Dentistry has not necessarily recognized the major role it could play in early identification. Many dentists, including pediatric dentists, have often taken a rather narrow role and view (Burtner, Jones, McNeal & Low, 1990). Since the vast majority of dentists are in private practice in isolated offices, they do not have the opportunity for regular interaction with professionals from other disciplines. It is unlikely that the primary setting for private practice will change significantly.

A colleague once described "interdisciplinary" as a way of seeing the world. He stated that a person could be "interdisciplinary" even alone in a closet. The training necessary to learn to see the world this way requires interaction with other professionals, but once the skills have been obtained, the ability to see and think in an interdisciplinary fashion has been established. One can view toothbrushing as an oral health or dental task, but from the slightly different perspective of the movements and actions involved, it can readily be seen to fall within the domain of the occupational therapist.

Just as the genesis of University Affiliated Programs was based on the notion that developmental disabilities were not the responsibility of any one discipline or profession but crossed many boundaries, pedi-

atric dentistry can integrate elements from many different disciplines. This will be discussed and described in more detail later in the chapter.

Educational and Training Requirements

Dentists traditionally begin dental school after four years of college, although some opt to forego a bachelor's degree and start dental training after only three years. Most dental school training lasts four years. For a brief period in the 1970s and 1980s, dental schools tried a three-year curriculum spurred by federal funds aimed to address a national shortage of dentists. Today, all dental schools but one have a four-year curriculum and a few have moved to five years.

The dental curriculum resembles that of medical school for the first year or two, then diverges into clinical areas specific to dentistry. Predoctoral students (the preferred term to describe dental students) treat patients in dental school clinics under the direct tutelage of faculty or in off-site clinics under similar supervision. This latter half of the dental school curriculum exposes students to the various specialties of dentistry, gives them experience in hospitals, and provides training in related areas, including interdisciplinary team functioning in some schools. The operational concept of dental and medical training is to provide basic science training early and build on it with clinical experiences that, ideally, integrate the science into clinical care. Most would agree that today, with the explosion of knowledge and technology, four years is the minimum needed to train a dentist. In fact, accreditation standards only validate the provision of minimal competencies of dental graduates to render care.

All dentists graduate from dental school

with either a D.M.D. (Doctor of Medical Dentistry) or a D.D.S. (Doctor of Dental Surgery) and the differences between the two degrees are philosophical rather than real. Unlike the D.O. and M.D. degrees, which can be differentiated by training and curricular differences, the D.M.D. and D.D.S. training programs cannot. Both meet accreditation standards of the Commission on Dental Accreditation, the national accrediting body; both are recognized by all states in licensure; and practitioners are indistinguishable by their degree in clinical practice.

Unlike medicine, dental education attempts to prepare its graduates for licensure and practice immediately after dental school. No postdoctoral residency or internship is required for dentists to be licensed. Within the last two decades, however, the number of one-year residencies has increased dramatically, mainly due to interest and the realization by graduates that the four-year curriculum is too short to prepare dentists for the complexities of the clinical practice of dentistry. Most of these residencies are hospital-based; some are based in schools of dentistry. Participation is competitive and voluntary, but the additional year gives the graduate dentist the opportunity to refine skills, learn more complex procedures, gain speed in provision of care, and work with more challenging patients such as those who have handicaps or chronic illnesses. A residency-trained dentist will be more likely to have treated a larger number of more complex patients than one who has completed only four years of dental school. Our health care system has also directed care of the older patient with disabilities to residencies of this type because of their school affiliation, access to resources and support services and willingness to treat these people.

Dentistry recognizes eight specialties and provides accredited training programs for all of them.

1. *Endodontics* concerns treatment of the dental pulp; endodontists primarily provide root canals and related procedures.
2. *Oral pathology,* the dental equivalent of pathology in medicine, concerns histological diagnosis of oral disease; oral pathologists may examine patients and obtain biopsy specimens but render no other care.
3. *Oral and maxillofacial surgery* is the surgical specialty of dentistry that performs tooth extraction, jaw surgery, tumor removal, implants and more complex surgical procedures of the head and neck; surgeons perform implants and may also have M.D. degrees.
4. *Orthodontics* is the specialty concerned with braces for patients of all ages.
5. *Pediatric dentistry,* the only age-related specialty, cares for children—and also the disabled of all ages; many patients with disabilities see pediatric dentists because they are the dental providers most able to meet their needs.
6. *Periodontics* treats the gums and bone supporting teeth rather than the teeth themselves; most periodontal therapy is surgical in nature and provided to adults.
7. *Prosthodontics* concerns the artificial replacement of teeth with bridges and dentures.
8. *Public health dentistry* is concerned with the dental health of populations and is the only specialty not related to an age or a procedure; public health dentists may provide clinical dental services in some settings, but usually do not provide direct dental services.

All specialty programs must be accredited by the Commission on Dental Accreditation. Most programs are two or three years in length; a few are four years (e.g., oral and maxillofacial surgery). The focus of specialty training is development of proficiency in that area; training may occur in a school of dentistry or a hospital.

Another dental professional who may be involved with interdisciplinary function is the dental hygienist. *Dental hygiene* is the profession concerned with prevention of dental disease and removal of calculus and stain from teeth (Hofer, 1988). Dental hygienists can also perform certain procedures that dentists can, such as dental sealants. These procedures are specified by law and vary from state to state.

Licensure, Certification, and Continuing Education

Every state maintains a board of dentistry, which may be called the Board of Dental Examiners or State Dental Board and may fall into various places in the regulatory scheme of the state's administrative or executive branch. This body, which today usually includes dentists, consumers and dental hygienists, is responsible for oversight of public safety and licensure of dental professionals in that state.

Dental licensure remains a somewhat antiquated system, varying from state to state in requirements. All states require dental licensure for practice. Dentists must pass a series of examinations in addition to having graduated from an accredited school of dentistry. In a few states, graduates of foreign dental schools are given the opportunity to demonstrate skills and knowledge and can take a licensing examination along with graduates of accredited U.S. schools.

Each state has its own licensing process. As a general rule, a graduating dentist must present evidence of passing both parts of the National Board Examination, pass an additional clinical examination that in-

volves several examples of the dentist's skills, and provide information to support his or her ethical and moral character. States have moved to additional measures (again, quite variably) such as requiring immunity against certain diseases, mandating malpractice coverage, requiring continuing education for relicensure, and demonstrating proof of knowledge of that state's particular laws related to delivery of dental care.

The national dental licensing mosaic also includes variations that permit simpler licensing of teaching dentists who must limit their practice to the university teaching program; entry of foreign-trained dentists; licensing by reciprocity for established licensed dentists who wish to enter the state; and specialty-license of dentists in the specialties listed previously.

Board certification exists for all recognized specialties in dentistry, but unlike medicine, achievement of what is termed "diplomate" status, or board certification, has no tangible benefit beyond the gratification of the recipient. Hospital privileges, marketing advantage, and academic advancement don't seem affected by board status in dentistry. Pragmatically, achievement of board status has little effect on care; other factors such as extent of training exert far greater influence.

Many states have moved to require continuing education for relicensure, but the application of the concept of lifelong learning in dentistry sees many variations, and enforcement is equally unpredictable even when mandated by law. Problems with continuing education for dentists include the quality of education, the evaluation of learning, the relationship of education to patient need, and regulation of adequate hours to maintain quality. Interestingly, continuing education in the care of persons with disabilities is rare and, even when offered, often under-utilized by practitioners.

Contributions to Interdisciplinary Practice

Dentistry touches many facets of a person's day-to-day life and also crosses many disciplinary lines in the conduct of an oral evaluation or provision of services. Some of the contributions are immediately visible; others are more subtle.

Oral health is an integral part of general health. A physical survey would be incomplete without an adequate oral examination. The dental health professional's knowledge of the oral structures supplements a physical evaluation, just as the occupational therapist's precise assessment of fine motor coordination and the psychologist's evaluation of the intellectual capabilities help describe the person's skills and abilities. Lack of oral health certainly affects general health and well-being. One need only think of the pain of a toothache to recognize the broad impact poor oral health can have. When in pain, it is unlikely someone will perform to optimal level, whether in school or at work. The ability to concentrate and stay on task is certainly impacted.

Often, families with a child who has a developmental disability overlook dentistry. Given the trauma of a diagnosis, or the focus on various developmental therapies to enhance and improve the child's ability to function, it is easy to see how dental health can be overlooked. This is why professionals from other disciplines need to be aware of the basics of oral health and recommend regular dental services to these families.

Many diseases and syndromes have oral manifestations which are pathognomonic to a diagnosis (Sterling, 1992). For the person who does not clearly manifest particular clinical signs, an evaluation by a dental professional can help confirm or rule out a diagnosis under consideration.

The pediatric dentist performing an oral evaluation examines the oral and facial structures, noting form as well as function. The structures need not only to be intact but to function as a unit. The structures may be of normal shape and form, but if the neuromusculature is damaged, normal function will probably not occur.

It is not uncommon for children who are developmentally delayed to be on prolonged soft food diets. These soft, adhesive foods can lead to early, extensive dental decay which in turn can affect the child's ability and desire to eat foods which require more chewing. Often, once the teeth are restored to good health, improvement in eating habits is noted.

The child who is tube fed exclusively receives little to no oral stimulation. This can lead to severe breakdown of the supporting dental tissues. An oral hygiene program for this child not only helps promote good dental hygiene, but can also produce stimulation to the oral structures so that when oral feeding is re-instituted, the child has not lost all oral motor responses.

Teeth play a minor role in speech sound production. The classic lisp of a child who is missing primary front teeth and awaiting the eruption of the permanent teeth is transitory, assuming the misarticulation was not present previously. More commonly, misarticulations are due not to the teeth or their position, but rather to either immature neuromusculature or insult which affects the sequencing necessary for concise sound production; i.e., reflective of a central insult rather than a peripheral difference in shape or alignment.

The soft palate, however, plays an important role in speech sound production. An inactive or short palate can cause speech sound production similar to that heard in a person with a cleft palate. A submucous cleft usually has little clinical significance, and speech sounds can be produced clearly.

The teeth provide an indelible record of

development. Primary or baby teeth begin to form in approximately the fourth month of pregnancy. Secondary or permanent teeth develop from around birth through adolescence. Defects in form or shape of the primary teeth can reflect insults during the prenatal period. Generally, the permanent teeth begin formation around the time of birth, so variations in form or shape of the permanent teeth are reflective of post-natal development, if not genetic in origin. Observed defects can help piece together *when* insults may have occurred but usually are not specific enough to describe *what* insult(s) may have occurred.

To provide a thorough evaluation, the dental health professional must have the cooperation of the child. To accomplish this, the dental health professional must assess both the child's expressive and receptive language or communication skills. Once the method(s) of communication have been determined, the levels of understanding can be assessed. Does the child respond similarly to other children of the same chronological age? At what level of language development is the child operating? Based on these judgments, requests can be made of the child.

Similarly, how the child responds to new settings and separation can be assessed. Dental services are very demanding; the range in which the child can maneuver is very limited. Physical activity must be controlled; the child's thoughts can wander but the child cannot wander physically. The child with autism who deflects or rejects physical contact presents a unique challenge. The provision of dental services, by its very nature, invades life space and can be threatening to some people.

An understanding of the family's values is an important element of service provision. The dental health professional needs to be aware of the family's wishes and develop treatment options with those in mind.

Generally, these issues are broached during initial contact while reviewing the health history. Skills in interviewing are basic to accomplishing this. The elements of empathy, concern, warmth, and openness must be transmitted effectively and sincerely for a strong professional relationship to be established.

Dental health status can certainly impact on self-esteem. Whether it is severe breakdown of tooth structure from decay, bad breath from periodontal disease, or significant malalignment of teeth, oral problems can cause a person to be withdrawn, shy or avoided by others. Our society places a high premium on appearance. For many years, aesthetics was not as recognized in the field of developmental disabilities. A higher value was placed on skill development while the "packaging" was overlooked. This has changed with the help of the families and persons with disabilities. Their requests and demands for such services have caused providers to be more aware and responsive.

Dental Assessment

Dental evaluation of persons with disabilities involves procedures identical to those used in the population in general. Few if any disabilities create oral problems not seen elsewhere in the patient population. What may occur in the disabled population is a specific pattern of disease, such as malocclusion (orthodontic problems), or an exacerbation of relatively common diseases like dental caries (cavities) and periodontal disease (gum disease). Some disabilities may have an associated dental problem that is characteristic of and frequently coincident with that disability.

Dental evaluation involves a medical model of chief complaint, past health history, physical and oral examination, diagnosis, and treatment plan. A history taken by a dental professional has several parts.

The first is a general health history: since dental care may involve stress on the patient, administration of medication, surgery of hard and soft tissue and care of a prosthesis, a general health history is required in as much detail as for any other health care procedure. Most histories involve a review of systems with emphasis on those areas which may have an impact on delivery of dental care, such as bleeding.

The dental aspect of the history would address tooth development, fluoride exposure, trauma, previous dental care experiences, personal hygiene practices, dental concerns and problems specific to that patient. For children, a dental history may involve more detailed questioning about pre- and early post-natal experiences related to feeding, fluoride ingestion, dental development, and behavior in the dental setting or other settings where separation occurs.

For persons with disabilities, history taking should look more in-depth at issues related to the specific disability as they relate to the oral cavity and the delivery of care. A paradigm for this has been suggested, using a problem orientation that looks at potential obstacles to delivery of care and dental health (Entwistle & Casamassimo, 1981). The following examples illustrate the types of historical data that might be uncovered which would have a direct impact on the outcome of the dental care intervention. This format is itself interdisciplinary, in that it looks at issues beyond dentistry that play a role in dental health; intervention may require cooperation of dental and non-dental professionals.

1. *Accessibility*: Can the person get to the dentist? Is the person ambulatory? Is the office accessible? Is dental care available in the community?
2. *Psychosocial*: Does the person fear dental care? Is dental health a priority for the family? Is behavior an issue to be considered?
3. *Financial*: Can the person afford care? What are the competing costs of care and therapy?
4. *Communication*: Can the person understand and respond to the dental professional? Should medication be used to bypass the need to communicate? Can aids assist in normalized communication?
5. *Mobility and Stability*: Can the person sit still for care in a normalized setting?
6. *Medical*: Are there overlying medical problems that will affect care delivery? Are there medical problems that will affect long-term oral health?
7. *Continuity of Care*: Are resources available to maintain health? Are other disciplines attuned to dental needs and are dental professionals attuned to other needs?

This problem-oriented format is not universally applied, nor is it applied without fragmentation. However, dental professionals who care for persons with disabilities will routinely use some variant of this historical paradigm to facilitate care.

A dental examination involves visual, tactile and radiographic evaluation of the structures of the entire head and neck. For the person who is disabled, it would also involve a general appraisal of ambulation, mobility, manual dexterity, and oral motor function. The process of examination is general to specific, with absence of disease and approximation of norms as baselines. The patient is usually examined in a dental chair and with adequate lighting. Larger extra-oral and intra-oral structures are palpated manually, while teeth are examined using a dental probe, with a dental mirror to improve visibility. For older patients, a specialized probe with millimeter graduations is used to measure the depth of the gingival sulcus around teeth. The depth is an indirect indicator of disease and a direct indicator of damage from disease.

The objective of the examination is to identify abnormalities such as dental caries, periodontal disease and malocclusion as well as neoplasia and other soft tissue pathosis. The results of dental examinations are charted on records, which vary somewhat but include abnormal findings from the examination of the soft tissues, the teeth and functional relationships such as the occlusion (bite).

Radiographic examination is integral to dentistry and varies slightly from radiography in medicine. The preponderance of dental disease prompts "routine" documentation of patients in certain circumstances. In other words, patients who present certain clinical characteristics (not necessarily disease), such as tightly aligned teeth, would receive radiographic examination based on the probability of occult disease, usually dental caries. Most dental radiographs, however, are exposed based on selection criteria that are disease-related. The person who is disabled may experience difficulty complying with the positioning or stability requirements for radiography and treatment may be done without radiographs, relying solely on clinical findings. Sedation or general anesthesia to obtain radiographs for dental diagnostic purposes is deemed too costly and rarely done. In other instances, other techniques or positioning may be employed to obtain the necessary radiographic views.

Dentists may employ a variety of additional diagnostic techniques and procedures when circumstances deem them appropriate. Teeth suspected to be non-vital or abscessed may be tested with electrical or temperature probes to determine their responsiveness in a process called pulp testing. Orthodontic care requires a variety of "records" to be made, including plaster models of the teeth, which are obtained from molds; cephalometric radiographs, which provide standardized, measurable ra-

diographic representations of the teeth and jaws that can be placed against norms for diagnostic purposes; and measurements of the dental arches or rows of upper and lower teeth to determine if enough space is available for the teeth within each jaw.

Diagnostic information is analyzed to create a treatment plan specific to that patient. Today, in dentistry, no standards exist as to appropriateness of treatment and what constitutes a realistic treatment plan within the general population. Historically, dental treatment of the person with a disability was problematic: goals for oral health were not the basis for care, and treatment was relegated to management of acute situations. If a general operational standard or goal exists today, it is to aim for optimal health in a functional framework. This would be the goal for anyone and everyone and implies significant input by the patient/consumer in the establishment of this goal.

Consideration of the needs of the person with a disability can alter what would be considered the "ideal" treatment plan when compared to a non-disabled person with the identical dental disease pattern and dental treatment needs. A realistic treatment plan for a person who is disabled should take the person's needs into account and establish outcomes acceptable to that patient or caretaker. It is similar to the preparation of an Individualized Educational Plan (IEP), with important consideration given to the strengths and needs of the individual, long- and short-term outcomes, and areas of individual and shared responsibility. The best dental treatment plan is one that maximizes the potential for good oral health by realistically addressing needs and resources. Ultimately, like any individually developed plan, the patient and primary care giver(s) need to agree to the plan and participate in the development of it.

Dental Intervention

The specific techniques used to treat the dental needs of persons with developmental disabilities are no different from those applied to the population in general. What may differ are the techniques used to obtain patient cooperation and stability. These techniques can be divided into the following areas:

1. *Behavioral modification techniques.* These are commonly used with children or persons with disabilities to obtain cooperation in a variety of settings. Positive reinforcement, negative reinforcement, extinction and distraction may be used to obtain desired behavior. Non-invasive and invasive procedures can often be provided using these non-threatening and short-acting approaches (Pinkham, 1994). Modeling and desensitization techniques may also be employed (Gordon, Terdal & Sterling, 1974). Complicating the application of behavioral techniques, however, are the dentist's lack of skill, the time limitations involved in dental delivery, and the lack of sufficient frequency to reinforce behaviors by applying the techniques.

2. *Non-pharmacologic aids.* These restraining and positioning techniques are to be used in concert with established policies. Restraint by device or by personnel is used mainly to obtain diagnostic information with the expectation of no additional treatment, or of escalation to more effective methods of control if treatment is required. Devices include a papoose board, restraining straps, or body wraps (Weddell, McKown, Sanders & Jones, 1994). Positioning devices might include pillows or other chair adaptations and use of adjustable wheelchairs as the dental chair. Mouth props may also be used to permit safe and extended oral procedures (Posnick & Posnick, 1975).

3. *Pharmacologic techniques.* Two main approaches for pharmacologic management are sedation and general anesthesia. Sedation is usually done in a dental office with the patient seated in the dental chair (Melamed, 1985). A variety of routes are used including intravenous, oral, and intramuscular. Sedation is subdivided into two levels, *conscious* and *deep*, according to the guidelines of the American Academy of Pediatric Dentistry (1992-1993). For conscious sedation, protective reflexes must be intact and the patient must be arousable. Deep sedation begins to approach general anesthesia. Today, policies directing providers in appropriate monitoring exist and should be followed (DuBose, 1991). The person with a disability may present additional risks for sedation, and monitoring of vital signs, even for conscious sedation, is the standard of care. Here, also, licensing requirements in various states may limit who can provide sedation.

   General anesthesia is often the procedure of choice for care of certain persons due to their medical risk, inability to cooperate for care, lack of suitability for sedation, and/or extent of treatment required. Dental procedures under general anesthesia are considered an operation and usually performed with the same rigors as any operation; hospital operating rooms are usually used. For patients who are good anesthesia risks, the procedure of dental rehabilitation under general anesthesia is a same-day event with no overnight stay required. The intent of treatment under general anesthesia is to allow treatment to "catch up" to the needs of the patient. Once this has been accomplished, it is unlikely the patient will require a second treatment under general anesthesia. Aggressive preventive programming and regular dental follow-up should allow future treatment to be completed in the office setting.

Case Example

Since each interdisciplinary team has its own unique personality and method of reaching its goals and objectives, the following example is provided to illustrate how one team operates.

After some preliminary information is obtained from the referring party, usually by telephone, contact is made with the family/primary caregiver. Again, some preliminary information is sought to determine the nature of the family's concerns, whether these are in agreement with the concerns of the referring party, and additionally, whether other community resources are more appropriate for the family. If another agency or team is better suited to address the questions, a referral is made at that point. If the referral is appropriate to the interdisciplinary team, a detailed questionnaire is sent to the family/primary caregiver. The document contains questions which pertain to: the family constellation; other professionals familiar with the child; programming in which the child is enrolled; family health; history of the pregnancy and delivery; early infant, child and adolescent development; child health and habits; current and past medication history; vision and hearing status; dietary and eating habits; physical skills; independent functioning skills; leisure-time activities; family life; agreement among family members as to the nature and significance of the problems; discipline and treatment programs; the child's strengths and major concerns. Approximately half the questions are open-ended, permitting the person filling out the questionnaire to expound on the subject. A family picture or a picture of the child is also requested.

Additionally, adaptive behavior measures may be requested of the family and teacher to provide an overview of the child and how the child interacts with his or her environment at home as well as at school; these are reviewed by the psychologist. In addition to the questionnaire, consent forms to request information are included. These consent forms enable the team to obtain information from agencies or professionals with whom the child and family have had significant contact.

As this information is being obtained, a case coordinator is assigned. The case coordinator is usually selected on a rotational basis unless there has been an individual request by the family or a professional. The role of the case coordinator is to act as liaison among the family, the interdisciplinary team, and the community agencies/professionals. Additionally, the case coordinator is the "team leader" for the interdisciplinary team. The team leader might also serve as an advocate for the family.

The team leader sifts through the acquired documents to obtain a clear and concise picture of the child's history, and will contact the family to further clarify issues or questions. In fact, the team leader may also make a home visit and/or school visit to see the child in his or her own environment. While this is occurring, other members of the team also review the information which has been obtained.

After all the pertinent materials have been gathered, the team meets to review the questions, issues, strengths and weaknesses as gleaned from the materials. Based on this exchange with the additional input of the team leader, a list of questions and/or concerns is developed. From this list of questions, team members are selected to be part of the interdisciplinary assessment team. Outside professionals are often requested to participate as well. The intent is to create a team specific to the needs of the family, as determined by the referring party, the family themselves and the interdisciplinary team. As much as possible, community professionals, agency representatives or school personnel are invited to participate in the evaluation and/or subsequent family informing conference. Community participation is encouraged, but schedules do not always permit it to occur.

Depending on the number of team members participating in the evaluation, the evaluation may be completed in one day or require part of a second day. Following the professional assessments, the team will meet to exchange information, findings and concerns. The team leader will chair this meeting and help focus the discussions. By the end of this meeting, the questions initially raised will have been addressed, plans of action discussed, and contingencies examined. At this time, a decision will be made among the interdisciplinary team members to determine which members of the team should be part of the "informing conference." The intent is to not overwhelm or intimidate the family, which can happen when a family walks into a room full of professionals. The team leader, by virtue of the increased contact with the family, is relied upon to make the final decision as to the size and composition of the informing team. If, for example, school placement or support services were a major issue, the special educator or someone familiar with the support services in the particular community would be part of the informing team.

The informing conference is held with the family. The child may or may not be present, depending on age or ability to participate. Any persons the family selects to participate, and community persons who have ongoing significant contact with the

child and family, are invited also. During this informing conference, the team leader will conduct the meeting and guide the discussion. After introducing everyone present at the conference, the team leader will review the intent(s) of the evaluation, reason(s) for referral, and a brief overview of the evaluation team. The team leader is the primary liaison among the family, interdisciplinary team and community professionals present.

The focus is on the questions raised and then those disciplines which have an impact or input into those issues. For example, a concern may have been raised in regard to the child's eating habits. In response to this, the nutritionist may review the findings of the dietary history; the pediatric dentist may address the oral structures, their health and functional relationships; the occupational therapist may address the ability of the child to manipulate the utensils and/or foods and oral motor skills. This concern may now very well be addressed by only one professional who has been provided findings and analysis from the others; i.e., who can summarize the other professionals' findings and provide guidance on how to improve the child's eating habits.

The team leader has the additional responsibilities to be cognizant of professional jargon, request clarification on behalf of the family, and actively support the family's participation. The aim is to have an exchange—a dialogue between the family and the interdisciplinary team where questions can be asked, the family is not overwhelmed, and concrete constructive recommendations are made with the assistance of the family and the community representatives. At this time, follow-up evaluations are determined as well. In some instances these may occur in one year or at the end of a school year, or be left unscheduled and open for the family to establish. Also, if there is to be individual professional follow-up or service, these contacts are established at this time.

In addition to the meeting with the team, the family receives a brief written list of the recommendations made by the interdisciplinary team. This is meant to be a concise listing of the prescriptive recommendations, written devoid of professional jargon. Usually, the team leader will develop this as one handwritten page and give it to the family at the conclusion of the conference. A copy is kept in the child's file for future reference.

After the conference, clinical staff will collect the various discipline reports and send copies to the various professionals and/or agencies designated by the parents or primary caregivers. A copy of each discipline's report is available to the family, as well, upon request. The team leader continues as the link and advocate for the family as long as necessary. This period is determined by mutual agreement of the family and the agency.

The process described takes about two to three months to complete. Most often, the delays occur in waiting for reports from outside agencies and professionals. Occasionally, if the situation appears urgent, the process will go on as described, but will not wait for all the supporting agency and professional reports to be received. In this case the process is often completed within one to two months.

To further illustrate how the interdisciplinary process relates to direct services, a specific example follows. Since the focus of this chapter is pediatric dentistry, the other recommendations or therapies will not be included.

Jack was thirteen years, two months old when first seen for an evaluation. The previous year, he developed Reye's syndrome as a sequela to the flu he contracted (Zamula, 1990). He had spasticity in all four limbs, great difficulty speaking, and less than 50% intelligible speech. His receptive speech and language were age-appropriate.

Because of poor oral motor control, feeding was difficult and prolonged. He had been out of school for the year, and home tutoring had only recently been initiated. He had spent most of the previous year in and out of hospitals and physical rehabilitation facilities. With the aid of a walker, Jack was able to walk short distances. Subsequent to orthopedic surgery, he was able to use a typewriter with difficulty. He could not feed, dress or toilet himself. He had no food or drug allergies and was otherwise healthy. He was on a daily regimen of muscle relaxants, to help alleviate the spasticity, and a stool softener. Jack resided with his father and his father's housemate; his three younger siblings resided with his mother. Jack's father and the father's housemate were the primary care givers. During the day, when they were working, Jack was attended by an in-home worker. Since Jack was not able to respond to emergencies or use the telephone, constant supervision was required.

At the time of his evaluation, he was being followed on a regular basis for therapy by a physical therapist, an occupational therapist and a speech therapist. He was receiving regular medical care from the family physician.

Reye's syndrome occurs most frequently in children under fifteen years of age (Gauthier, Guay, Lacroix & Lortie, 1989). The course can be mild and self-limiting, or it can progress rapidly, leading to death within hours of onset (American Society of Dentistry for Children, 1989). Death is usually the result of swelling of the brain. Recovery can be complete. Reye's syndrome is usually associated with a viral illness. The child seems to be recovering when suddenly the following clinical symptoms appear: fever, nausea, vomiting (usually quite severe), lethargy (listlessness), stupor or coma followed by seizures, internal irritability, aggressiveness, confusion, and irrational behavior.

Liver biopsy demonstrates fat accumulations, and high levels of liver enzymes and ammonia are found in blood samples. Other more reasonable explanations for the liver or brain abnormalities (e.g., toxic substance ingestion or viral hepatitis) are excluded from diagnosis (Partin, 1975).

Jack had been in a coma for eight days and spent more than 125 days in the hospital during the previous year. His was one of the most severe examples of Reye's syndrome seen in the area.

Specific recommendations were made regarding Jack's therapies, and plans for returning to school were outlined. One of the services he needed was dental care. He had not been seen by a dentist for approximately two years.

Oral examination revealed a very responsive, handsome young man who was in the early stages of a completed permanent dentition; i.e., all the permanent teeth with the exception of the third molars (wisdom teeth) had erupted. His dental development was consistent with his chronological age. The interdigitation of his teeth (occlusion) was normal, with the exception of an open bite secondary to a tongue thrust: Jack tended to carry his tongue forward in his mouth, which caused the teeth to separate. When he closed his teeth together, only the molars occluded but the rest of the teeth were progressively apart.

Volitional tongue control was fair at best. He could control tongue movement with much effort and thought. Tongue control was better to the left than the right.

Oral hygiene was only fair, the result of so much time spent in hospitals and rehabilitation centers where the focus was on other issues. The gingival (gum) tissues were mildly inflamed from lack of oral stimulation. He had one cavity which required restoration. Time was spent with Jack's father to assess oral hygiene practices. Specific recommendations were made regarding methods to improve oral hygiene and return the gingival tissues to an optimal state of health. The techniques for accomplishing this were demonstrated to both Jack's father and the housemate, since they shared the responsibility for Jack's day to day care.

The necessary dental treatment was completed and Jack was placed on a regular six month regimen for recall. In a very short period of time, with some guidance from dental health professionals, Jack's oral hygiene had improved significantly and the gingival tissues were healthy.

Prior to his check-up visit, a call was received from the speech therapist. She requested the pediatric dentist attend a staffing with the occupational therapist and physical therapist regarding some new findings. At this meeting the discussion focused on Jack's speech. It had been discovered serendipitously that when he held a tongue blade in his mouth, his speech improved significantly. Following this meeting, Jack was seen by the pediatric dentist and speech therapist together in the dentist's office. When Jack held a tongue blade between his teeth on one side, the clarity of his speech improved dramatically. The problem was the unacceptable appearance of Jack going to classes or socializing with a tongue blade sticking out of the side of his mouth. With the tongue blade in place, salivation also increased and led to drooling—the tongue blade acting as a wick.

After some discussion with the speech therapist and Jack, impressions and models were made of Jack's teeth. From these models, a mouthguard type of appliance was made for Jack's lower teeth and then cut so that it only fit on one side of his mouth (Netsell, 1985). Some clasps were added to the appliance to assure retention in the mouth. After some trial and error, the appliance was completed. Jack tolerated the appliance well; it was secure so that it would not be swallowed or aspirated. Jack, after some training, could insert and remove the appliance himself. This was important, since the appliance aided speech but interfered with chewing and eating. Because it fit only one side, it created an eccentric bite and, in fact, with the appliance in place, the teeth on the non-prosthesis side could not meet fully. The appliance required some refinement and modification over time, but Jack, his family and the professionals involved could all hear the significant improvement in sound production and clarity. Jack was understood now even by people unfamiliar with his speech.

When last seen for a dental check-up, Jack was preparing to graduate from high school and was looking forward to going to college. His physical status and motor control had not changed significantly in the past five years, but he was ambulatory with the support of his walker and certainly able to express himself and be understood by others.

As professionals, we are trained in our individual disciplines to a high level of competence. We seek continuously to update and upgrade our skills to keep pace with advancements in our professional field. It is the belief of the authors that the professional trained in an interdisciplinary setting not only is highly competent in the primary discipline, but also has acquired many skills from the other professionals and disciplines which are represented in a University Affiliated Program and other interdisciplinary settings. This professional is able to see more things and observe more domains than the traditionally trained professional. Whether alone in an office, involved in an interdisciplinary milieu or working in a community agency, the interdisciplinary professional is more ready and better trained to see the "whole person" and respond in a client/consumer/patient centered, community based fashion.

References

American Academy of Pediatric Dentistry (1992-1993). *Reference Manual, 1992-1993*. Chicago, IL: Author.

American Society of Dentistry for Children Newsletter (1989). Reye's syndrome. *American Society of Dentistry for Children Newsletter*, *9*, 3.

Burtner, A.P., Jones, J.S., McNeal, D.R., & Low, D.W. (1990). A survey of the availability of dental services to developmentally disabled persons residing in the community. *Special Care in Dentistry*, *10*, 182-184.

DuBose, R.A. (1991). Pediatric equipment & monitoring. In C. Bell, C. W. Hughes and T. H. Oh (Eds.) *The pediatric anesthesia handbook* (pp. 81-96). St. Louis, MO: Mosby Year Book.

Entwistle, B.A., & Casamassimo, P.S. (1981). Assessing dental health problems of children with developmental disabilities. *Developmental and Behavioral Pediatrics*, *2*, 115-121.

Gauthier, M., Guay, J., Lacroix, J., & Lortie, A. (1989). Reye's syndrome: A reappraisal of diagnosis in 49 presumptive cases. *Journal of Dentistry for Children*, *143*, 1181-1185.

Gordon, D.A., Terdal, L., & Sterling, E.S. (1974). The use of modeling and desensitization in the treatment of a phobic child patient. *Journal of Dentistry for Children*, *40*, 102-105.

Hofer, D.J. (1988). Role of the dental hygienist in the private office setting. In J. P. O'Donnell (Ed.) *Dental management for developmentally disabled persons in the community* (pp. 153-159). Boston, MA: Department of Public Health, Division of Dental Health.

Melamed, S.F. (1985). *Sedation: A Guide to Patient Management*. St. Louis, MO: C.V. Mosby.

Netsell, R. (1985). Construction and use of a bite-block for the evaluation and treatment of speech disorders. *Journal of Speech and Hearing Disorders, 50,* 103-106.

Partin, J.C. (1975). Reye's syndrome, diagnosis and treatment. *Gastroenterology, 69,* 511-518.

Pinkham, J.R. (1994). Patient management. In J. R. Pinkham (Ed.). *Pediatric dentistry, infancy through adolescence* (pp. 339-353). Philadelphia, PA: W.B. Saunders Company.

Posnick, W.R. and Posnick, I.H. (1976). Dental care in the private practice. In A. J. Novak (Ed.) *Dentistry for the handicapped patient* (pp. 193-211). St. Louis, MO: C.V. Mosby.

Sterling, E.S. (1992). Oral and dental considerations in Down syndrome. In I. T. Lott & E. E. McCoy (Eds.) *Down syndrome: Advances in medical care* (pp. 125-147). New York: Wiley-Liss.

Weddell, J.A., McKown, C.G., Sanders, B.J., & Jones, J.E. (1994). Dental problems of the disabled child. In R. E. McDonald & D. R. Avery (Eds.) *Dentistry for the child and adolescent* (pp. 592-653). St. Louis, MO: C. V. Mosby.

Zamula, E. (1990). Reye's syndrome: The decline of a disease. *FDA Consumer,* November, 21-23.

6

Information/Instructional Technology

Kathy L. Mayfield-Smith, M.A., M.B.A., & Brian C. Smith, Ed.D.

There have been enormous developments in technology over the last few decades. With this change, several fields dedicated to the application of technology for persons with disabilities have evolved and expanded. Almost all recent disability-related federal legislation has fueled this evolution by either mandating or encouraging the development and implementation of technological applications to foster the development, education, independence and inclusion of persons with disabilities.

Two technology-related disciplines, information/instructional technology and assistive technology, offer valuable contributions to interdisciplinary practice that are crucial to the full inclusion of persons with disabilities in all aspects of society. What may appear to be overlap is primarily due to the fact that these disciplines often use the same technology and tools, such as microcomputers. In most other aspects, however, each has a distinct identity based on the applications and contributions to human services and persons with disabilities. Assistive technology focuses on the use of technology to support individuals in daily living, for example, providing individuals with devices such as microcomputers, augmentative communication devices, and mobility aids; and the implementation of environmental adaptations. By contrast, information/instructional technology concentrates on the application of technology for information management, information dissemination, instruction, and education (i.e., microcomputers, interactive videodiscs, CD-ROM, etc.).

Although it could be argued that information technology and instructional technology are two unique and separate fields, the terms are often used synonymously in the literature. For the purposes of this chapter, the authors combine them to provide an overall perspective in relation to interdisciplinary practice. Hopefully, the presentation of the two as a combined discipline also will increase the understanding of the importance of technology to persons with disabilities, their families, and the professionals who work with them.

The first section will briefly define both information and instructional technology, but the remainder of the chapter will treat them as one discipline.

Information technology is a broad term that focuses on the application of computer-based technology to the management, manipulation, and dissemination of information. The goal of information technology, specifically in relation to developmental disabilities, is to enhance the efficiency and effectiveness of access and utilization of information to enhance the lives of persons with disabilities and their families. It is the technology of organizing, managing, acquiring, using, and disseminating information that is most applicable to the interdisciplinary practice of developmental disabilities.

As a discipline, *instructional technology* focuses on the application of technology to educational environments to enhance the learning experience. This may be accomplished by structuring an individual student's learning environment, consulting with individual or groups of teachers, or more broad-based training of professionals. The Association for Educational Communications and Technology (1977) defines instructional technology as a "systematic process of problem-solving using people, procedures, devices, and organizations [and applying] scientific principles in the design, implementation and evaluation of solutions" (p. 3).

Information/instructional technologists are employed in a variety of settings serving persons with disabilities. These settings include: public schools, direct service programs, higher education institutions, University Affiliated Programs, clinical education programs, government agencies, and private sector businesses. The role of the information/instructional technologist varies from setting to setting and includes: identifying and managing media and related technologies; designing, developing, producing and evaluating educational and administrative programs; assessing learner needs; assessing family information needs; providing programs to enhance learning; training other professionals in instructional design and other technological applications; and conducting research.

Although formerly information/instructional technology simply assisted in the utilization of media and other instructional devices, the field has evolved to emphasize the roles of needs assessment, design, development, production, and evaluation of educational, service and administrative programs (Ely, 1992). It is in these more current roles that technologists provide major contributions to interdisciplinary practice for persons with developmental disabilities. Unfortunately, in some settings the role of the instructional technologist continues to be limited somewhat by the perceptions of other professionals, who see instructional technologists only as resources for instructional materials (Lewis & Rossett, 1981a), and more related to hardware and software than to the broader applications for teaching and learning (Ely, 1992). In a study of special educators' perceptions of instructional technologists, Lewis and Rossett (1981b) conclude that "special educators are overlooking a valuable team member by misunderstanding the contemporary functions of the educational technologist" (p. 44). These continuing misperceptions recently led the Association for Educational Communications and Technology to begin to develop a new definition of educational technology.

The contribution of information/instructional technology to persons with disabilities has continued to develop as a result of the increased access to computers and other instructional technologies within the schools, the increased affordability of these technologies, and the increased home use of computers. Even with this movement, the use of technology within the education and direct service systems is lagging. This situation is partially due to the role changes for teachers and service personnel that result from the incorporation of technology. Former Secretary of Education Terrel H. Bell suggests that the incorporation of innovative technological practices into the school curriculum could occupy one-third of a student's day, freeing the teacher to give children more individualized attention

(Bell & Elmquist, 1991). In 1992, the National Education Association adopted a resolution supporting the application of instructional technology opportunities in the classroom to develop skills, further research, and expand knowledge in our society. The role of instructional technologists is to help teachers and other service personnel develop the competencies to incorporate instructional technologies in a student's educational curriculum or in the program plan for an individual with disabilities.

Education, Training, and Certification Requirements

The education, training, and certification requirements of information/instructional technologists vary depending on the level of service and employment setting. Education and training in instructional technology is provided under several program headings, including instructional technology, educational technology, educational communications, and media technology. Each year, the ERIC Clearinghouse on Information Resources and the Association for Educational Communications and Technology publish the *Educational Media And Technology Yearbook*, which lists degrees offered at the bachelor's, master's and doctoral levels in Instructional Technology (Ely & Minor, 1992). Some schools also offer a six-year specialist/certificate program in instructional technology and related media. These specialist/certificate programs vary significantly from institution to institution and are offered as degree and non-degree programs. These programs are designed to provide additional certification for school media specialists, to provide a higher level of study in instructional design and application of technology, or to lead to a doctoral level program of study.

Information/instructional technology programs of study are usually offered through departments of Education, Library Science, or Information Sciences. Curriculum requirements include courses in computer science, computer-based instruction, media production, education, instructional design, evaluation and administration. The continual evolution of technology challenges higher education to look to the future in preparing professionals in the field of information/instructional technology. More future-oriented doctoral programs, especially in instructional technology, are emphasizing instructional design and development, interactive technologies, and technology integration in order to prepare professionals to bridge communication and information technologies (Caffarella, 1992).

Licensure, Certification, and Continuing Education

As evolving fields, information and instructional technology are struggling to define their roles and responsibilities and to establish standards, requirements, and certification criteria. States generally have minimal certification requirements for persons practicing in the public schools. These requirements generally include a bachelor's degree and the completion of annual continuing education requirements. Individuals whose roles encompass the design, development, application and evaluation of enhanced learning systems will have earned a masters' or specialists' practitioner-level degree, or a doctorate degree emphasizing research and evaluation. Standards of practice are being developed by professional associations such as the Association for Educational Communications and Technology (AECT), the American Association of School Librarians (AASL), the Forum for Information Networking in Disabilities

(FIND), and the Alliance of Information and Referral Systems (AIRS).

Contributions to Interdisciplinary Practice

With the implosion of information in the 21st century and the explosion of technology, all disciplines will be forced to incorporate and often rely on technology to enable them to serve persons with disabilities. The field of information/instructional technology is by nature interdisciplinary in approach. It builds on the constructs of various disciplines, especially cognitive psychology and education, and applies these constructs to improve performance outcomes within educational, instructional, service and training contexts, regardless of the specific discipline or setting within which they are applied (Caffarella, 1992).

The information/instructional technologist has knowledge and resources that are significant in interdisciplinary practice for people with developmental disabilities. On all levels, technology will be the key that unlocks the door for many persons with disabilities to achieve full participation and inclusion in society. Information and instructional technologists have a variety of responsibilities in the interdisciplinary team, including (a) direct service to individuals with disabilities and their families, (b) training of other information/instructional technologists at the preservice and inservice levels, (c) training of other disciplines on the incorporation of technology into practice, (d) research and evaluation of technological application, (e) consultation with other disciplines, and (f) consultation with the organization and community in areas of policy development.

The major goal of technology-related fields is to increase the efficiency and effectiveness of people and service delivery systems. Families of children with disabilities have multiple needs and must frequently deal with many service systems. A major obstacle is obtaining complete and coordinated information about the needs of their child and the services available to the child and family (Bailey & Simeonsson, 1988; Harris & Associates, 1986; Mayfield-Smith, Toon, Morse, & Yajnik 1990). Through an interdisciplinary approach, information technology has addressed this need by developing information and referral programs. These programs blend the technology of information management with telecommunications so that human service professionals can coordinate access to information for families of children with disabilities (Jones & Chandler, 1990; Mayfield-Smith, Yajnik, & Wiles, 1990; Sharp, Siff, & Reichle, 1990).

A practice dilemma faced by human service providers is the need to reduce paperwork and increase professional time available for direct services. Information technology offers many possible solutions that enable professionals to focus on service by reducing the time spent performing bureaucratic functions. Specific applications have shown how to enhance the delivery of service coordination in early intervention (Winborne & Vowels, 1992), social services (Bakken & Boss, 1989), and services to children with disabilities and medically fragile conditions (Coble & Massey, 1992; Corrigan, 1989; U'Deen & Hamlin, 1992; Vafeas, 1989). Another application is the automation of the Individualized Family Service Plan (Kaplan & Kregness, 1990). The Coordinating Center for Home and Community Care, Inc. (CCHCC) has used information technology in the service coordination organization to increase efficiency in service delivery, to monitor cost comparisons between residential and in-home care options, and to help evaluate and improve their team approach to service delivery.

In addition to its organizational uses, technology is beneficial in the actual interventions for people with disabilities. In an educational system, students with a developmental disability often have difficulty generalizing skills across different contexts. The two ideas central to formal learning in a discipline are *exercise* and *appropriate use* of developed faculties, which are now subsumed under the term *transfer of learning*. Transfer of learning studies have demonstrated that learning is exceptionally complex, and the application or generalization of content from a specific field to other problem areas is complex (Cormier & Hagman, 1987; Milton, 1972). Unfortunately, the traditional approaches to learning, such as small-group activities, discussions, and instructor/learner meetings, are often ineffective (Cormier & Hagman, 1987; Milton, 1971). Each of these is related only peripherally to learning, and collectively their popularity has aided in obscuring the central learning issues.

Traditional teaching strategies, as well as the capacity of the public schools and many treatment facilities, are limited by shortfalls in staff and money. It is almost impossible for teachers to provide the amount of individualized instruction needed by many children, especially those with disabilities. Microcomputers are one example of technology that is especially well suited to the special needs of learners with disabilities; they offer many enhancements to the learning experience. The benefits of technology to educators include the use in either individual or group instruction, provision of immediate feedback and reinforcement to learners, collection and analysis of learner performance data, flexibility in terms of level of instruction and type of learner-computer interactions available, self-paced instruction, and errorless practice (Behrmann, 1984).

Types of Technology

Some misunderstandings of the technologically related disciplines stem from the misperception that technology is only machines. In fact, technology is the application of scientific tenets to solve practical problems; the machines are merely the medium through which the principles are applied. Ely (1992) describes technology as a "process that deals with problem solving. It is not machines; it is not software. It is a systematic blend of people, materials, methods, and machines to solve problems" (p. 27). A brief description of major and emerging technologies—the hardware, the software and the methods—is essential to a complete understanding of the fields of information and instructional technology and how they are incorporated into interdisciplinary practice for persons with developmental disabilities.

Microcomputers. Microcomputers (or personal computers) are at the heart of the expansion of these fields. They provide a significant capacity for data storage and manipulation, audio and graphical presentation and interactive applications. Many technological developments are extensions of microcomputer technology.

Computer assisted instruction (CAI). CAI refers to the direct interactive instruction when a learner is using a computer (Cawley and Murdock, 1987). Based on the theory of programmed instruction, it presents material in logical, sequential steps. Learners are able to proceed at their own pace, to master one unit of study before advancing, to receive immediate feedback, and to repeat material if necessary. Intelligent Computer Assisted Instruction (ICAI) incorporates artificial intelligence that significantly enhances the system's capabilities, especially in the area of learner diagnostics.

Artificial intelligence/expert systems. An *expert system* is a type of computer program that is designed to engage the user in a dialogue that simulates a conversation one might have with an expert consultant. The computer is programmed to ask questions of the user to detail the problem or situation (Barr & Feigenbaum, 1981). Through a question and answer process, the program branches, giving the user options at each step while maintaining the needed structure for the process. Many educational leaders believe that expert systems hold great potential for improving services to children with disabilities (Bruyere, 1984; Hofmeister, 1984; Vandergoot, 1984). One example of expert systems applied to the interdisciplinary process is the *Mandate Consultant* that was designed to help special educators and others through the process of referral, and organization of assessment and placement teams (Parry, 1986).

Interactive multimedia. Interactive multimedia has been defined as "the integration of text, audio, graphics, still image and moving pictures into a single, computer-controlled, multimedia product" (McCarthy 1989, p. 26). Current multimedia productions rely on optical storage methods such as laser videodisc and CD-ROM technologies.

Interactive video (IV). Interactive video instructional systems allows the incorporation of visual imagery into the instruction program, through a new integration of computer and video technologies. This combination provides some of the most promising instructional devices of recent times (Cawley & Murdock, 1987; Hofmeister & Thorkildsen, 1981). Interactive video enables the presentation of selected video segments followed by appropriate questions via the computer. It blends the best features of videotape (i.e., motion, color, and graphics) with the best features of computer-assisted instruction (i.e., immediate feedback for correct or incorrect responses, frequent repetition of materials if needed, and appro-

priate record keeping). Where visual, temporal, sequential stimuli are presented at a rapid rate (such as in fingerspelling and speechreading), a great deal of practice is required to become skilled. Interactive video is a perfect format for providing this necessary practice time (Pollard, 1985). The increasing application of this type of technology is based on the potential to rapidly provide students with an array of concrete visual representation of concepts and relationships (Carnine, 1991; Gersten & Kelly, 1992; Hofmeister, Engelmann, & Carnine, 1989).

Laser videodisc. This optical storage medium is primarily used to store audio and video. Videodiscs provide excellent video still frames and rapid access to audio and video material contained on the videodisc (Thorkildsen, 1992). The pages of a book, motion sequences complete with sound, still pictures such as slides and photographs, and graphic animations can be stored on a single disc. Interactive videodisc technology has been successfully applied to teach a variety of skills to persons with developmental disabilities. Examples include beginning reading skills (Thorkildsen & Friedman, 1986), basic math skills including fractions (Gersten & Kelly, 1992; Woodward & Gersten, 1992), social skills (Thorkildsen, Fodor-Davis & Morgan, 1989) and daily living skills such as grocery shopping (Wissick & Kinzie, 1989). They also offer advantages for teachers in that they are easy to use, can be operated from a distance and can facilitate group as well as individual instruction (Woodward & Gersten, 1992).

Compact disc read only memory (CD-ROM). CD-ROM is the most widely used optical storage system and is ideal for distributing large amounts of prerecorded data (Rizzo, 1989). Because it can store large amounts of text, audio and graphics, a great potential exists for use in information management, information dissemination, and training in all areas of interdisciplinary practice. One current example is HyperAbledata (Vanderheiden, 1991), a database cataloging information about assistive devices for person with disabilities. This technology blends the advantages of easily disseminated service directories and catalogs with the quick search, easy update, and space-saving features of a computerized database. The use of a compact disc requires a CD-ROM player interfaced with a personal computer.

Telecommunications. The field of telecommunications is the link connecting education and disability-related services to the world. Telecommunications is a broad term that describes electronic point-to-point connections between individuals and groups using telephone lines, lines dedicated to transmission of data, and cable and satellite transmission (Ely, 1992). Applications encompassed by telecommunications include some electronic mail (e-mail) networks, computer conferences, and one or two-way audio and video conferences. The more interactive forms are charting the future directions of this technological medium. E-mail networks have opened doors for widescale dissemination of information, professional consultation and collaboration, and networking for persons with disabilities. Several organizations have developed 'pen pal' e-mail networks, such as "Kids.Talk" through the National Learning Disabilities Network, that enable children with learning disabilities to share experiences with each other via modems and personal computers.

Distance education. Building on the telecommunications technology, distance education refers to any medium that electronically transports instruction immediately to a learner who is distant from where the instruction is being provided. Usually, the delivery methods are similar to traditional instructional techniques: live instructor, videotape, overheads, slides, videodisc, pro-

grammed learning segments, and sequential learning segments. The differences are the methods of transporting the audio and video to the learner, and what happens at the reception site. The transport methods include: cable (both national and local), satellite, teleconferencing, interactive television, fiber optic, and microwave transmission. Two current applications of this technology to interdisciplinary practice for persons with developmental disabilities include: (1) a parent and early-intervention-provider training model that uses distance education technology to reach families and providers in rural communities (Lopez-De Fede, 1994); and (2) an expert consultation model (West, 1993) using distance technology to provide individualized consultation to special education teachers of children with severe behavioral disorders.

Assessment

The purposes of assessment vary from a focus on diagnosis in some disciplines to determination of program eligibility in others. The instructional technology assessment focuses on identification of aspects of learning that can be translated into specific intervention efforts. The purpose of the assessment provided by the instructional technologist is to identify both the needs of the learner and the appropriate strategies for intervention using available technologies.

Most often, the instructional technologist will not be part of the initial interdisciplinary team, but will be included after preliminary information is gathered and specific problems have been identified. Frequently, an assessment is conducted through an interdisciplinary approach that involves consultation, with observation conducted by other interdisciplinary team members. When possible, the instructional technologist directly assesses the child's ability to use specific technological interventions.

Evaluation data. Referral records provide information regarding the nature of the problem prompting the request for evaluation including teacher, provider, or parental observations. This information usually provides a gauge of the person's actual performance and current difficulties and sometime includes specific examples of performance. Results from other discipline evaluations are reviewed for a variety of factors that would impact not only the types of instructional technology interventions that might be used, but whether instructional technology interventions may be appropriate at all.

Medical evaluations provide specific diagnostic indicators, including type of disability and etiology. Additional health related or physical factors that may affect the learning process, such as vision and hearing screening, will be included. Evaluations also address pharmacological interventions that may affect the individual's attention and energy level.

Psychological evaluations provide information about cognitive abilities, giving indications of a child's general ability or potential to learn, as opposed to actual performance. The psychologist also factors in behavioral and emotional characteristics of a child as well as functional and adaptive behavior measures to provide an estimate of expected levels of performance. Given that adaptive behavior ratings are crucial in determining a diagnosis of mental retardation, specific deficiencies in this area are important to note when examining educational objectives, especially in planning for transition from school to adult life.

Special education evaluations are designed to facilitate remediation. They provide very useful information regarding the development of prerequisite skills necessary for learning, the level of basic information needed to comprehend the tasks, and specific strengths and weaknesses of a student's current performance (Hannafin, 1986). Specific deficiencies in basic skills or academic areas are pinpointed for which technological applications can be used.

Speech and language evaluations provide information regarding language development, including the ability to understand language (receptive language skills) and communicate to others (expressive language skills). Because speech and language development depend on a variety of cognitive, physical, social and developmental skills, understanding the cause of speech and language difficulties significantly affects intervention methods. Speech and language development also have tremendous impact on a person's development and performance in school and life.

Physical and occupational therapy evaluations provide detailed assessments of the individual's physical abilities, both gross and fine motor skills. For individuals with physical limitations, this information is essential in determining appropriate technological interventions and strategies. Occupational therapy evaluations also may suggest difficulties related to perceptual-motor and sensorimotor development especially in children with learning disabilities.

Observation. A major part of any assessment process is the observation of the person. This process often begins before formal assessment, usually before the child or adult is aware he or she is being observed and it continues throughout the assessment and intervention. Ideally, although this is not always possible, observation occurs in different settings and a variety of activities, e.g., in the classroom or service setting, in structured and unstructured activities, during leisure time, at home, and during formal assessment. Observation provides valuable information about: (a) student-teacher interaction, (b) interaction with peers, (c) behavior when left alone, (d) general information about overall abilities, (e) obvious factors that might affect the person's use of technological applications, and (f) specific factors to be examined during formal assessment.

Observation of the classroom setting and knowledge of the school concerning technology integration are extremely important in assessing the use of instructional technology interventions with a student with disabilities. Successful intervention using technology is significantly related to the teacher's willingness and ability to help the student and to incorporate the technology into the overall curriculum. To be useful to the student, assessment and interventions must be practical, in terms of the realities of the particular school setting. Consequently, the actual interventions and level of consultation provided by the instructional technologist may vary depending on the teacher's skills, the availability of technological applications, and the school's policies on technology integration.

Evaluation of instructional resources. Before recommending instructional technology solutions for a learner with disabilities, it is essential to determine the individual's abilities to use the technology of choice and decide if adaptations in technology or presentation of material are needed. This is best accomplished by demonstrating the equipment and application to the learner and observing the learner's attempt to use the computer or other equipment. For students who may require specific adaptations to the computer, this direct assessment would best be done in collaboration with an assistive technology specialist so that structural and instructional adaptations can be noted simultaneously.

Intervention

The instructional technologist provides interventions directly to persons with developmental disabilities, as well as assisting other service providers to most effectively incorporate the benefits of technology into their own practice. Two overarching types of interventions will be discussed in this section: direct practice and consultation. Although this section addresses work with children and adolescents in the school system, principles can be applied to work with adults in vocational settings.

Direct intervention. Once the specific needs of the child have been identified, the instructional technologist, in cooperation with other disciplines, develops specific objectives targeted to meet the child's needs. The instructional technologist specifically examines the application of the wide range of available technological solutions that could be used with the child, then develops specific objectives to address these issues.

In cases where the assessment has suggested motivation to be a key factor, care is taken to select or develop an instructional program that is challenging yet provides opportunity for necessary feedback, reinforcement, and success. Many computer-based educational programs are similar to video games or can be developed with "real life" experiences to enhance the child's understanding of the applicability of the instructional lesson to real events. The utilization of videodisc technology opens many avenues to incorporate the realism of motion pictures into the instructional sequence.

When the child's disability involves severe physical limitations, the instructional technologist works closely with an assistive technology professional to ensure that the computer is appropriately adapted. Adaptation usually involves a modified keyboard, key guard, voice synthesizer, or other modification to enable the child to use the technology freely. The adaptations are especially necessary in cases where the child has upper body restrictions or severe visual limitations.

Some children need to use a computer as both an instructional tool and an assistive device. This is the situation for many children with severe learning disabilities or cerebral palsy. For these children, the instructional technologist works with the assistive technology professional and the family to determine if the student needs a computer at home to facilitate homework or practice exercises. If so, training other family members also may be necessary.

Technology can help children develop language, master developmental and academic material, and improve social skills. For example, children with severe hearing impairments must develop receptive and expressive language skills, but often in an alternate form of communication. Pollard (1985) describes many advantages of interactive video for teaching fingerspelling and sign language to children who have severe hearing impairments. Across the special education curriculum, many technological applications have been developed, and are currently being used, to address basic skills of language development, sight reading and math concepts.

Enhancement of social skills and adaptive behaviors is often identified as a need in children with disabilities. The literature shows that children with disabilities often do not learn appropriate social behaviors through observation and must be taught these skills in a systematic way (Cartledge & Milburn, 1986; Gresham, 1982; Kaufman, 1989). Using videodisc training programs, Thorkildsen et al. (1989) demonstrated effective teaching of social skills to children with mild disabilities that resulted in increased cooperative interaction skills, improved positive social behaviors, and improved teacher satisfaction in regular education settings.

As children with disabilities approach adulthood, planning for transition from school to adult life becomes an integral part of the Individualized Education Plan (Individuals with Disabilities Education Act, 1992). Collaboration between the special educator, vocational rehabilitation counselor, instructional technologist, parent, and student is necessary to develop specific objectives to prepare the student to move successfully into the next stage of life. To learn life skills effectively, the student needs to be placed in settings which are often difficult to arrange, given the logistical and fiscal limits of the school setting. Interactive videodisc technology, however, enables simulation of real life situations so that appropriate behaviors and skills can be modeled in the setting in which they would normally occur. One example includes training of grocery shopping skills that can be done with a videodisc simulation (Wissick & Kinzie, 1989).

Technology can play a major role for students whose attendance at school is difficult or impossible. Children with disabilities and associated health conditions may experience frequent absences. The break in academic stimulation and the exclusion from the school environment are detrimental to the student's learning process. Even with homebound instruction, the student who is out for extended periods of time is excluded from routine academic and social interaction. Although not appropriate for all students, schools must begin to examine the use of interactive telecommunications via cable television media as a more inclusive alternative for educating children with disabilities and chronic health conditions.

Consultation. The consultant role is a very important one for instructional technologists, especially with the special educator. This role may involve teaching the educator to use specific equipment or applications to teach a particular student. A collaboration between the instructional technologist and teacher may also be necessary to develop or adapt the learning program to meet the needs of a specific child.

There is a need for instructional technologists to assist educators on the mechanics of using technology, and also to increase the likelihood that it will be used for the full range of benefits. Computers are used routinely in special education classes, but almost exclusively for drill and practice exercises (Becker & Sterling, 1987), or to improve motivation, self-confidence and self-discipline. Additionally, little evidence exists that teachers have successfully integrated computer-assisted instruction into their traditional curriculum (Woodward & Gersten, 1992). Even with the ease of use of videodisc technology for teachers, adequate integration into the teaching repertoire is greatly enhanced by a facilitator or coach helping the teacher when first using a videodisc application (Gersten & Kelly, 1992; Woodward & Gersten, 1992). The use of videodisc technology, especially for group instruction, shifts the teacher's role from that of primary presenter of information to one of clarifying, motivating and monitoring progress (Woodward & Gersten, 1992). The instructional technologist's role of helping teachers adjust to this shift becomes essential to successful technology integration.

Telecommunications is another emerging type of technology that has been useful for people with disabilities. A major difficulty encountered in serving many individuals with disabilities results from geographic distance. Technical assistance to teachers and other providers is severely limited by time and cost associated with travel, which even further limits the number and scope of services available to persons with disabilities and their families. The use of new technologies such as telecommunications greatly increases the ability of all professionals to provide service and technical assistance, especially to persons with disabilities and professionals in rural areas.

Rule and Stowitschek (1991) have demonstrated the effectiveness of telecommunications in providing inservice support to teachers who were working to effect changes in the social skills and behavior of students with disabilities. Using audioteleconferencing and interactive television, experts were able to provide extensive consultation from a central location to teachers at four separate sites, 120 to 300 miles away. With combined technologies, rural preschool special educators were able to access expertise that would have otherwise been unavailable.

Case Example

To illustrate the information/instructional technologist's role in the interdisciplinary process, a case involving a child who has cerebral palsy will be presented. Cerebral palsy is defined as a nonprogressive disorder of posture and movement (Behrman, Kliegman, Nelson, & Vaughn, 1992). It is often associated with a spectrum of disabilities including visual, hearing, speech, cognitive, and behavioral difficulties and epilepsy. This type of disability is relatively common, appearing in approximately 2 of every 1,000 live births (Behrman et al., 1992). Spastic quadriplegia is the most severe form of cerebral palsy, characterized by marked motor impairments of all extremities and a high association with mental retardation and seizures.

Referral

Denise is a 17-year-old African-American female who has spastic quadriplegia with mild mental retardation. She was referred for evaluation based on her mother's request that the team begin planning for "life after school." Her mother is a single working parent with a younger child at home and is concerned that Denise needs to be prepared for some type of employment or other activity upon leaving the public school system in four years.

History

The medical history indicates that Denise's cerebral palsy was initially diagnosed at 18 months of age. She currently exhibits marked motor impairment in all extremities and has used a wheelchair since early childhood. She appears to have cognitive delays, but the extent is not certain due to the severity of her motor and speech limitations. Her vision and hearing are not affected, nor does she have any type of seizure activity.

Denise has been in special education classes since beginning school at age 5. Although her expressive speech is significantly impaired by her motor limitations, she speaks well enough to be understood by her family, teachers and others. Her receptive language skills are better developed than her expressive skills. Although she shows frequent frustration with her limitations, she has never exhibited severe behavior problems.

The core members of the interdisciplinary team were the psychologist, special educator, physical therapist, occupational therapist, instructional technologist, and parent. The team was lead by Denise's service coordinator from the state's Department of Disabilities and Special Needs. The team was charged with developing a comprehensive individualized transition plan to facilitate Denise's vocational development and prepare her to move into adult life. As part of her educational program, Denise had been using computers on a limited basis for the past two years. Her mother was especially interested in examining the potential for technological applications to expand Denise's learning opportunities and to make her fully integrated into her own educational and transition plan.

Assessment

After initial evaluations by the core team members were completed, the team met to discuss the results and to begin developing the plan for transition. The psychological evaluation results showed an IQ of 69. The educational evaluation provided a baseline measure of current academic performance. Although Denise had made some progress in the last two years, she was performing only at a pre-readiness level in reading and math areas.

The instructional technology assessment showed several areas in which the computer could be incorporated into the curriculum to better structure the presentation of material and systematically monitor Denise's performance, especially the types of errors made. This monitoring would enable her teacher to focus on the "difficult-to-master" areas when needed. Although the computer had been used for the past two years, the utilization had been more for drill and practice than for systematic instruction and analysis of errors. Computer literacy had not been addressed at all. Additionally, full utilization of the computer was significantly impaired by Denise's motor limitations, and it was evident that equipment modification was necessary.

As the team discussed what approach would be best, supportive team members were called in to provide additional assessments targeted at developing realistic transition goals. To identify the specific adaptations necessary for adequate computer utilization, the assistive technology specialist from the local Assistive Technology Project was called. The rehabilitation counselor from the Department of Vocational Rehabilitation also provided a complete vocational assessment to determine her employment potential.

After completing the interdisciplinary assessments, the team followed a more transdisciplinary model to develop the transition plan. As opposed to developing individual discipline objectives, the team members, including Denise's mother, developed a comprehensive transition plan. Although individual discipline members maintained responsibility for implementing specific objectives, many objectives crossed over into the responsibilities of other professionals. Given the importance of the home and activities outside the educational or service setting, the family was responsible for implementing many of the objectives.

Recommendations

The assessment process from the various disciplines and input from Denise and her family emphasized four objectives for interventions. These were: (a) fully integrating technology to support educational and vocational development, including both instructional technology and assistive technology at school and at home, (b) improving academic skills to a level that supported vocational goals, (c) developing vocational skills that would enable employment upon leaving high school, and (d) coordinating the necessary family support to facilitate transition to the next stage of life. Implementing these objectives required expertise from each of the individual disciplines as well as well-coordinated efforts among the professionals. Coordination was particularly important in addressing the goal of technology integration because of the involvement of an assistive technologist, physical therapist, occupational therapist, instructional technologist, special educator, and parent.

It was determined that Denise would

need a computer both at school and at home. Since the school already had a computer, the first priority involved the assistive technologist, who had appropriate modifications made (especially to the keyboard) to enable Denise to use it with more flexibility. The home computer would take more effort, since resources had to be coordinated to obtain the computer. The physical therapist addressed seating and positioning issues to facilitate comfortable computer use for Denise, and the occupational therapist began therapy on fine motor activities to help her use the modified keyboard. The occupational therapist also worked closely with the special educator and parent so that fine motor development could be reinforced both in classroom and home activities.

The instructional technologist implemented a structured academic program using interactive videodisc applications that targeted reading readiness skills, specifically sight word vocabulary and writing skills. This program presented material in units with graduated degrees of difficulty. The computer monitored Denise's responses and errors so that subsequent interventions could be structured by her teacher. When Denise made continuous errors on the same tasks, the teacher was signalled to provide immediate assistance. Since this was the first time the teacher had used this technology, the instructional technologist provided training to both the teacher and Denise, and provided consultation with the teacher during the first few weeks to ensure appropriate use of the equipment. This support also helped the teacher adjust her teaching strategies to maximize appropriate use of the technology while increasing her interaction with Denise as a motivator and clarifier of more difficult material.

Through coordinated efforts of the Assistive Technology Project, the Department of Vocational Rehabilitation, the school, and the family, an adapted computer for the home was obtained in about four months. Although the interactive videodisc could not be used at home, other appropriate software was purchased and the instructional technologist worked with the family to ensure adequate training and understanding of the hardware and software.

Summary

The value of technology in the lives of persons with developmental disabilities increases with every new development. Although it will not be appropriate for every individual, it will provide opportunities for increased and full inclusion and participation in society that otherwise would not be available. The potential applications of information/instructional technology for individuals with disabilities and for improving access to services and training for professionals make this discipline an integral part of the interdisciplinary practice for persons with developmental disabilities and their families.

References

Association for Educational Communications and Technology (1977). *The definition of educational technology.* Washington, DC: Author.

Bailey, D. B., & Simeonsson, R. J. (1988). Assessing needs of families with handicapped infants. *Journal of Special Education, 22,* 117-127.

Bakken, G., & Boss, B. (1989). Case management with laptop computers. In K. Mayfield-Smith & D. L. Wiles (Eds.), *Proceedings of the Fourth Annual National Symposium on Information Technology* (pp. 187-200). Columbia, SC: University Printing Department.

Barr, A., & Feigenbaum, E. A. (Eds.). (1981). *The handbook of artificial intelligence.* Los Altos, CA: William Kaufman.

Becker, H., & Sterling, C. (1987). Equity in school computer use: National data and neglected considerations. *Journal of Educational Computing Research, 3,* 289-311.

Behrmann, M. M. (Ed.). (1984). *Handbook of microcomputers in special education.* San Diego, CA: College-Hill Press.

Behrman, R. E., Kliegman, R. M., Nelson, W. E, & Vaughn, V. C., III (1992) *Nelson textbook of pediatrics* (14th ed.). Philadelphia: W. B. Saunders Company.

Bell, T. H., & Elmquist, D. L. (1991). *How to shape up our nation's schools: Three critical steps.* Salt Lake City, UT: Terrel Bell and Associates.

Bruyere, S. M. (1984). Impact of high technology on the rehabilitation professional: Changing roles and skills. *Technology and Rehabilitation of Disabled Persons in the Information Age: A Report of the Eighth Mary E. Switzer Memorial Seminar* (pp. 49-57). Washington. DC: National Rehabilitation Association.

Caffarella, E. P., (1992). Current developments in educational technology programs: The Ph.D. program in educational technology at the University of Northern Colorado. In D. P. Ely & B. B. Minor (Eds.), *Educational Media and Technology Yearbook* (Vol. 18, pp. 52-63). Englewood, CO: Libraries Unlimited, Inc.

Carnine, D. (1991). Curricular interventions for teaching higher order thinking to all students: Introduction to the special series. *Journal of Learning Disabilities, 23,* 261-269.

Cartledge, G., & Milburn, J. F. (Eds.). (1986). *Teaching social skills to children: Innovative approaches* (2nd ed.). New York: Pergamon Press.

Cawley, J. F., & Murdock, J. Y. (1987). Technology and student with handicaps. *Contemporary Educational Psychology, 12,* 200-211.

Coble, D. H., & Massey, S. (1992). Automation of targeted care management. In D. Lesser (Ed.), *Proceedings of the Seventh Annual Na-*

tional Symposium on Information Technology (pp. 125-139). Columbia, SC: University Printing Department.

Cormier, S.M. and Hagman, J.D. (1987). *The transfer of learning: Contemporary research and applications.* San Diego: Academic Press.

Corrigan, A. (1989). Automated case management systems. In K. Mayfield-Smith & D. L. Wiles (Eds.), *Proceedings of the Fourth Annual National Symposium on Information Technology* (pp. 157-170). Columbia, SC: University Printing Department.

Ely, D. P. (1992). Trends in education technology 1991. In D. P. Ely & B. B. Minor (Eds.), *Educational media and technology yearbook* (Vol. 18, pp. 1-30). Englewood, CO: Libraries Unlimited.

Ely, D. P., & Minor, B. B. (Eds.). (1992). *Educational media and technology yearbook* (Vol. 18). Englewood, CO: Libraries Unlimited, Inc.

Gersten, R., & Kelly, B. (1992). Coaching secondary special education teachers in implementation of an innovative videodisc mathematics curriculum. *Remedial and Special Education, 13*(4), 40-51.

Gresham, F. M. (1982). Misguided mainstreaming: The case for social skills training with handicapped children. *Exceptional Children, 48*, 422-433.

Hannafin, J. J. (1986). Special education assessment. In D. L. Wodrich & J. E. Joy (Eds.). *Multidisciplinary assessment of children with learning disabilities and mental retardation* (pp. 77-108). Baltimore, MD: Paul H. Brookes.

Harris, L., & Associates, Inc. (1986). *Disabled Americans' self perceptions: Bringing disabled Americans into the mainstream* (Study No. 854009). New York: International Center for the Disabled.

Hofmeister, A. M. (1984). *CLASS.LD: An expert system for classifying learning-disabilities* [computer program]. Logan, UT: Utah State University.

Hofmeister, A. M., Engelmann, S., & Carnine, D. (1989). Developing and validating science education videodiscs. *Journal of Research in*

Science Teaching, 26, 665-667.

Hofmeister, A. M., & Thorkildsen, R. J. (1981), Videodisc technology and the preparation of special education teachers. *Teach Education & Special Education, 4*(3), 34-39.

Individuals with Disabilities Act Amendments of 1991, PL 102-119. (October 7, 1991). 20 U.S.C. 1400.

Jones, G. H., & Chandler, B. R. (1990). Automating information and referral systems: Establishing an effective partnership between system user and system developer. In K. Mayfield-Smith (Ed.), *Proceedings of the Fifth Annual National Symposium on Information Technology* (pp. 128-140). Columbia, SC: University Printing Department.

Kaplan, A., & Kregness, S. (1990). An automated IFSP for the case management monitoring and tracking process. In K. Mayfield-Smith (Ed.), *Proceedings of the Fifth Annual National Symposium on Information Technology* (pp. 208-214). Columbia, SC: University Printing Department.

Kaufman, J. (1989). *Characteristics of children's behavior disorders* (4th ed.). Columbus, OH: Merrill Publishing.

Lewis, R. B., & Rossett, A. (1981a). Educational technology as perceived by special educators. *Journal of Special Education Technology, 3*(2), 43-49.

Lewis, R. B., & Rossett, A. (1981b). Educational technology in special education. *Teacher Education and Special Education, 4*(3), 44-48.

Lopez-De Fede, A. (1994). Personal communication. Center for Developmental Disabilities, University of South Carolina, Columbia, SC.

Mayfield-Smith, K., Toon, T. L., Morse, T., & Yajnik, G. G. (1990). *Nationwide information and referral for persons with developmental disabilities: A feasibility study.* Columbia, SC: Center for Developmental Disabilities.

Mayfield-Smith, K. L., Yajnik, G. G., & Wiles, D. L. (1990). Information and referral for people with special needs: Implications for the Central Directory of Public Law 99-457.

Infants and Young Children, 2(3), 69-78.

McCarthy, R. (1989). Multimedia: What the excitement's all about. *Electronic Learning*, 8(3), 26-31.

Milton, O. (1972). *Alternatives to the traditional.* San Francisco: Jossey-Bass.

Milton, O. (1971). Learning transfer. *Teaching-Learning Issues. 15*, 1-11.

Parry, J. D. (1986). Mandate consultant: An expert system for reviewing implementation of regulatory procedures for handicapped. Logan, UT: Utah State University.

Pollard, G. (1985). The nuts and bolts of interactive video: How it works and how to get started. *American Annuals of the Deaf, 130*, 386-390.

Rizzo, J. (1989, November). Letting in the light. *MacUser*, 132-155.

Rule, S., & Stowitschek, J.J. (1991). Use of telecommunications for inservice support of students with disabilities. *Journal of Special Education Technology*, 11(2), 57-63.

Sharp, M., Siff, E., & Reichle, N. (1990). The family support network: An experiment in integrating community parent programs. In K. Mayfield-Smith (Ed.), *Proceedings of the Fifth Annual National Symposium on Information Technology* (pp. 52-66). Columbia, SC: University Printing Department.

Thorkildsen, R. (1992). Using laser videodiscs and DVI to develop visual databases. In D. Lesser (Ed.), *Proceedings of the Seventh Annual National Symposium on Information Technology* (pp. 247-260). Columbia, SC: University Printing Department.

Thorkildsen R. J., & Friedman S. G. (1986, Spring). Interactive videodisc: Instructional design of a beginning reading program. *Learning Disability Quarterly*, 9(2), 111-117.

Thorkildsen, R., Fodor-Davis, J., & Morgan, D. (1989). Evaluation of a videodisc-based social skills training program. *Journal of Special Education Technology*, X(2), 86-98.

U'Deen, J. V., & Hamlin, E. (1992). Integrating information and referral with client tracking systems. In D. Lesser (Ed.), *Proceedings of the Seventh Annual National Symposium on Information Technology* (pp. 205-217). Columbia, SC: University Printing Department.

Vafeas, J. G. (1989). Goal oriented case management systems: A personal computer based model. In K. Mayfield-Smith & D. L. Wiles (Eds.), *Proceedings of the Fourth Annual National Symposium on Information Technology* (pp. 236-250). Columbia, SC: University Printing Department.

Vandergoot, D. (1984). The potential of technology for rehabilitation. *Technology and Rehabilitation of Disabled Persons in the Information Age: A Report of the Eighth Mary E. Switzer Memorial Seminar* (pp. 92-93). Washington, DC: National Rehabilitation Association.

Vanderheiden, G. (1991). *HyperAbledata* [machine-readable data file]. Madison, WI: Trace Research & Development Center.

West, R. (1993). Personal communication. Center for Persons with Disabilities, Utah State University, Logan, UT.

Winborne, D., & Vowels, E. (1992). Tracking system for at-risk and disabled infants: A model for service coordination. In D. Lesser (Ed.), *Proceedings of the Seventh Annual National Symposium on Information Technology* (pp. 221-225). Columbia, SC: University Printing Department.

Wissick, C. A., & Kinzie, M. B. (1989). The developmental and design of a videodisc simulation for training grocery shopping skills to students with moderate or severe handicaps. In R. Fox (Ed.), *Proceedings from the Eleventh Annual Society for Applied Learning Technology Conference on Interactive Videodisc in Education and Training* (pp. 28-31). Warrenton, VA: Society of Applied Learning Technology.

Woodward, J., & Gersten, R. (1992). Innovative technology for secondary learning disabled students: A multi-faceted study of implementation. *Exceptional Children, 58*, 407-421.

7

Neurology, Child Neurology, and Developmental Pediatrics

Patricia L. Hartlage, M.D., & Graham Pereira, M.D.

I. Neurology

Neurology is a medical specialty which deals with disorders of the central and peripheral nervous system. The child neurologist specializes in the disorders that affect infants and children. It is the task of the neurologist to apply knowledge of neuroanatomy, neurophysiology, and neurochemistry to solving clinical problems. For example when the problem is a child's recurring loss of consciousness, the neurologist first tries to identify whether or not there is disease of the nervous system, since heart problems or behavioral disorders could have similar presentations. If it appears that the problem is a neurological one, the neurologist makes an effort to identify where within the nervous system the disorder is occurring, what is the probable nature or cause, and finally how best this problem can be managed.

Which individuals with developmental disabilities should be referred to a neurologist or child neurologist? An individual who exhibits a precipitous or progressive decline in motor, sensory, or cognitive behavior would be very appropriately referred to a neurologist, as would an individual with episodic interruptions of normal functioning, especially when seizures are suspected. We believe that every mentally retarded individual should have a comprehensive medical examination as soon as the problem is recognized, because for an important minority, medical, nutritional, or surgical treatment may be available. Recognition of the hereditary forms of mental retardation, and identification of environmental factors which might be modified, may lower the recurrence risk for subsequent siblings. The more severe the physical or cognitive disability, the more likely it is that a specific cause will be found.

Cost-effective use of medical specialists is best done through the individual's primary-care physician, who knows what various specialists have and do not have to offer and may know individuals with expertise in dealing with a particular problem or in dealing in an especially effective manner with developmentally disabled clients.

Education and Training Requirements

After a year of general medical training beyond the medical degree of M.D. or D.O., the neurologist spends three years in residency training. The child neurologist spends two years of post-doctoral training, one of which must be in Pediatrics, before entering a three-year residency training program in Neurology, one year of which is exclusively devoted to the neurological problems of infants and children. Many physicians, especially those interested in academic careers, will spend an additional year or two of fellowship which is usually a combination of research and practice in a restricted interest area such as epilepsy, muscle disease, cerebral vascular disease or behavioral neurology.

While the general neurologist spends at least three months in child neurology, the amount of experience in dealing with developmentally disabled adults varies from program to program. Rotations in psychiatry and neurosurgery as well as neuroscience research are encouraged. In contrast, over half the patient contacts of the child neurologist, in training or in practice, are the result of some developmental disability. The trainee works with a variety of medical and surgical specialists each day, as well as with occupational and physical therapists, speech pathologists, social workers, nurses, and nurse practitioners, neuropsychologists, child life specialists, and a variety of skilled neurodiagnostic technicians—all of these individuals contributing to the training of the child neurologist. Less predictable is the exposure to educational professionals, nutritionists, pediatric dentists, audiologists, and vocational specialists.

Licensure, Certification, and Continuing Education

All physicians are licensed by the state in which they practice, and continuing education is mandated to maintain this licence. The American Board of Neurology and Psychiatry awards board certification in Neurology and for over twenty years has also awarded certification in Neurology with Special Competence in Child Neurology, following the successful passing of a two-part examination, the first a written examination and the second an oral examination which includes patient examinations.

Contributions to Interdisciplinary Practice

Within the care network of a developmentally disabled individual, the physician interacts with a variety of other professionals serving the same client. Typically this communication is a written one, verifying that certain ancillary services are needed and providing annual health care statements and recommendations. For some individuals with limited support systems in the professional or social community, the physician may also play an advocacy role. Some of us are privileged to work with interdisciplinary teams which provide comprehensive care to an individual patient and provide a unique learning experience for our trainees. As the cost of health care increases and as health care for the developmentally disabled becomes increasingly dependent on the individual's own health insurance, the expense of such an approach limits its use. Neurologists and child neurologists frequently serve as consultants to schools, mental health and mental retardation facilities, the social security administration, vocational rehabilitation, and statewide programs for handicapped children.

Assessment

An increasingly complex array of neurodiagnostic tests has been developed to help better understand problems in the nervous system, including imaging studies like ultrasound, computerized tomography, and magnetic resonance imaging to look at brain structure, and more dynamic imaging studies, like positron emission tomography and single photon emission computerized tomography, which yield information about localized metabolic function in the brain. Electrophysiological studies include the electroencephalogram (EEG) or brain wave test, electromyogram (EMG) which records the electrical pattern of muscles, and a variety of other studies involving stimulation which measure the capacity of various nerve pathways to carry information to and from the nervous system and various organs of function. Examples are peripheral nerve conduction studies, electroretinograms, visual evoked potentials, auditory evoked potentials, and somatosensory evoked potentials.

Invasive studies (e.g., sampling blood or spinal fluid, or the surgical removal of a small piece of tissue for microscopic study) are employed in certain situations. In the evaluation of an individual with medically intractable focal seizures as a potential candidate for surgical treatment, video EEG's and comprehensive neuropsychological assessments are first performed. Cerebral angiography, the injection of dye into the major arteries feeding the brain, is also performed, and a short-acting barbiturate drug is injected into each carotid artery to briefly impair the function of one half of the brain. During this time, motor, sensory, and memory functions are measured. In the evaluation of a pre-schooler with moderate mental retardation of unknown etiology, a urine metabolic screen, thyroid function test, lead level, chromosome analysis, and fragile-x screening would commonly be chosen. The neurologist must make appropriate choices as to which, if any, of the neurodiagnostic tests would contribute information that could be translated into a specific management approach for the individual patient.

Of course, the single most important diagnostic tool the neurologist employs is the medical history, which includes a family history and a developmental history as well as a detailed survey of health problems, especially the specific concerns which brought this child and his family to the office. This next most important diagnostic tool is the examination of the patient. In some cases, there is no need to proceed beyond this point to have an excellent understanding of what is going on and what action is called for.

Intervention

The neurologist may serve as a diagnostician. Having a medical diagnosis is often a necessary prerequisite to gaining specific services for an individual. At times the neurologist is called upon to confirm a diagnosis, especially when the prognosis is ominous. The child neurologist often functions as an educator for the patient, the family, the primary physician, and persons from other disciplines offering care. We make good use of our nurse clinicians, other patients, families with similar problems, and information available through a variety of voluntary health agencies in our educational program. For certain individuals, the neurologist becomes the manager for some part of the medical treatment—for example, if seizures are difficult to control, or in monitoring and preparing for the relentless series of more severe symptoms that accompanies progressive or degenerative neurological disease.

Case Example

Eddie was referred to the cerebral palsy evaluation team at age three and a half. His parents asked if something could be done surgically to help him walk. Born 6 weeks prematurely, he had developed sepsis at 24 hours of life and was treated with intravenous antibiotics for 10 days. He had had a hernia repaired at 3 months of age and a cranioplasty at 5 months for premature closure of a cranial suture.

At one year his parents became concerned because he was not sitting or crawling; his legs were stiff and his trunk floppy. He was examined then by a child neurologist, who diagnosed moderately severe spastic diplegia and mild left hemiplegia and referred him to a physical therapist.

His general health and language development were good. He attended a church nursery 4 days a week and spent the other day with his grandparents, who usually provided transportation to his therapy sessions. His therapist reported progress in many areas, good range of motion but increasing dynamic spasticity both in sitting and standing. During a lengthy day of evaluation, a nurse clinician took Eddie, his therapists, and his family to appointments with three physicians, two therapists, and a social worker. They shared their opinions and recommendations with each other and then the family at a team conference.

The social worker commented on the strong family support and expressed concerns about the limited health insurance coverage, especially in the case of outpatient therapy, and about some statements the father had made about Eddie walking. The other team members had also picked up on Dad's fixation on Eddie walking independently. As a body builder, he felt that if you work hard enough at something it would get done. The nurse mentioned this family had no ongoing association with other families with handicapped children.

The physical therapist noted generally good range of motion and good strength in the trunk and upper body. He had videotaped his evaluation, including Eddie's rapid but usually bunny-hopping-style crawl and his ability to stand and take a few steps in a scissoring-sideways fashion with maximal assistance and wearing ankle-foot orthoses. He felt Eddie's sitting balance was good despite tight hamstrings, but the occupational therapist remarked that falling off the potty chair was impeding his completing toilet training.

The occupational therapist described Eddie as dependent in every area of activities of daily living and felt some of this was due to the parents and grandparents doing so much for him. She proposed additional occupational therapy for the next six months.

The orthopedic surgeon described multiple tight muscle groups in the lower extremities, even at rest, and bilateral hip flexion contractures. Because of marked increase in spasticity in action, he favored a selective dorsal rhizotomy to reduce tone. If this was not done, he felt Eddie would need multiple tendon lengthening within the next two years.

The child neurologist described the absence of any persistent primitive reflexes as a favorable sign for ambulation. The pattern of weakness seemed compatible with periventricular leukomalacia secondary to complications of prematurity, but the CT scan done at the time of the child's skull surgery would be reviewed to exclude any brain anomalies, since dorsal rhizotomy results had been better in the former group. A standard recorded examination for cerebral palsy was submitted as a preoperative baseline.

The neurosurgeon felt Eddie would be an excellent candidate for selective dorsal rhizotomy and pointed out the commitment that would be necessary to more intensive physical therapy pre- and postoperatively. The goals would be improved upper body use and for Eddie to be ambulatory with the aid of a walker, perhaps using a wheelchair at times, and to avoid the need for tendon lengthening which might slightly reduce his strength. Eddie's family thought the following summer would be a good time for this procedure.

The neurosurgeon would meet again with the parents to review the risks and benefits of the procedure which all of the team had agreed seemed best for Eddie as well as alternative surgical and non-surgical treatments. During the surgery, a neurologist would be stimulating the exposed sensory nerve roots and recording the responses of the leg muscles to help direct the surgical approach.

The nurse gave Eddie's family information about the therapeutic recreation programs available through the local United

Cerebral Palsy chapter. The social worker agreed to assist Eddie's family in working out a payment plan to cover the additional physical and occupational therapy.

Postscript: Two years postoperatively, Eddie has successfully completed regular kindergarten at the public school. He required no special assistance and his teacher is confident of his readiness for first grade. Mild stiffness and weakness are still apparent in the legs and left arm. His gait with Lofstrand crutches is functional but not fluent. He enjoys displaying his ability to perform chin-ups. He still sees his physical therapist weekly and has been discharged by the specialists to the care of his pediatrician.

II. Developmental Pediatrics

Developmental Pediatrics is a subspecialty of Pediatrics which deals mostly with cognitive competence and the physical and mental disabilities that limit children from enjoying normal lives. The developmental pediatrician studies normal neonatal, infant, and child development in order to identify deviations from normal which indicate problems. He or she evaluates and treats children with delays in gross motor, fine motor, cognitive, language, and behavior areas, and provides care for children with chronic handicapping conditions such as cerebral palsy, meningomyelocele, muscular dystrophy, mental retardation, chromosomal abnormalities, and congenital anomalies. The developmental pediatrician also serves as an advocate for such children and provides active participation and

leadership in their multidisciplinary care by coordinating their care based on their specific needs.

Educational and Training Requirements

After four years of medical school, three years are spent in pediatric residency. During these years, training is received in the evaluation and treatment of all disease processes affecting infants and children. The emphasis, however, is on acute illnesses, with limited time spent on chronic handicapping conditions like mental retardation, learning disabilities, muscular dystrophies, spina bifida, etc. Following residency, a two-year fellowship in developmental pediatrics provides specific knowledge and understanding of the basic principles and milestones of child development, dysmorphology, pediatric neurology, child psychiatry, behavior management, and the medical implications of chronic conditions.

Licensure, Certification, and Continuing Education

Developmental pediatricians are licensed as physicians with training in pediatrics. Pediatric Boards are encouraged but not mandatory. There is as yet no board certification in developmental pediatrics because of differences in the areas of emphasis in the different training programs around the country. Some centers specialize in neonatal behavior, others in learning disabilities, and yet others in chronic physically handicapping conditions, making it very difficult to devise a test that would examine knowledge in all these areas in a fair way.

Contributions to Interdisciplinary Practice

One major contribution of the developmental pediatrician is as a diagnostician. Although some conditions have subtle signs and symptoms, making early diagnosis difficult, the developmental pediatrician strives for early diagnosis, which is prerequisite for eligibility for infant stimulation programs that enhance the chances of a child achieving his full potential. The pediatrician also coordinates all the services required by his patients, since he knows what conditions are associated with the particular disease process and what complications may arise from a given condition. Cerebral palsy, for example, may be associated with mental retardation, epilepsy, visual handicaps, hear-

ing impairments, dysarthria, scoliosis, and joint contractures. Thus, longitudinal care might include physical therapy, occupational therapy, neurology, special education, ophthalmology, and orthopedics. This requires coordination and the knowledge that these needs and services exist. There are also many psychosocial problems in families who have children with chronic handicapping conditions; therefore, psychology and social work play key roles in the long-term management of follow-up of these patients.

Assessment

As with any medical evaluation, the medical history and the medical examination provide most of the initial information required to draw up a differential diagnosis. Is the problem inherited or congenital? Is it a chromosomal abnormality? Is the problem secondary to central nervous system damage or malformation? Is it a peripheral nervous system problem? A muscular problem? A metabolic disorder? Was the child exposed to environmental or gestational toxins? Or is it due to a psychosocial problem? Most of these questions can be answered with a thorough history and physical examination.

Once the diagnosis is established, the child undergoes a full battery of developmental tests to determine the severity of the delay and the specific areas in which delays have occurred. Infants and very young children are best assessed by the Bailey Scale of Infant Development, which uses a deviation score method to calculate the standardized mental and/or motor indices rather than the ratio method. Although the long-term predictive value of the Bailey mental scale is poor in the general population, repeated testing up to age six enables one to predict with some certainty the children who will develop mental retardation. Neuro-developmental examination in later years can be accomplished adequately with the Pediatric Early Elementary Examination for Children. Mostly used on children in first, second, and third grades, this exam looks at various areas, including neurological indicators, temporal sequential organization, visual spacial orientation, auditory language function, fine motor function, gross motor function, and memory. This test complements the various psychometric tests that will be given by a psychologist, such as the Wechsler Intelligence Scale, the Peabody Picture Vocabulary Test, the Peabody Individual Achievement Test, and the Woodcock Johnson. Appropriate assessments involve administration of tests that will clarify the symptomatology and the etiology of the developmental delay and/or of the learning problem.

Intervention

Developmental pediatricians first and foremost provide primary care for children with disabilities. Children with special needs have a myriad of medical problems which vary with the different etiologies. A child with PKU (phenylketonuria) requires special diets and nutritional supplements throughout life. A child with a meningomyelocele (spina bifida) has problems with hydrocephalus, requiring VP shunts which may become infected or obstructed, has problems with neurogenic bladder or recurring urinary tract infections, has orthopedic problems with hip dislocations and flaccid paralysis requiring adaptive devices, has learning disabilities requiring special education, or may develop epilepsy requiring anticonvulsant medication. A child with Trisomy 21 (Down Syndrome) may have heart failure from a congenital heart defect, may have seizures, hyper- or hypothyroidism requiring medication, etc. Thorough knowledge of the underlying disease processes will determine the required therapies in children with special disabilities, and many different treatments have to be individualized.

Case Example

A six-month-old male is referred for evaluation because of weakness and gross motor delay. As mentioned earlier, the first step in evaluating any child with a medical problem is a thorough history and physical. The history includes gestational/prenatal history. Were there any complications during pregnancy, e.g., fever, bleeding, infections, alcohol or drug abuse, exposure to any kind of medication? Were the fetal movements *in utero* normal? Were there any complications during the labor and delivery? Did the fetus have any heart decelerations? Was there any meconium aspiration? Did the infant have an oxygen requirement at birth? Did the neonate have any seizures? Did he have any feeding difficulties? Did he have hyperbilirubinemia? Were there any central nervous system infections? Was the neonate small or large for gestational age? Did he have a small or big head?

The family history is important. A family tree is constructed to look for any history of muscular problems, congenital disorders, or metabolic disorders. Developmental history is taken. Was the child floppy from birth? Have his motor milestones been normal? Did he have any feeding problems? Did he have any increased or decreased tone? Does he focus and follow? Does he reach and grasp? Did he develop a social smile between the first and second month of life?

Past medical history includes questions about head trauma, possible child abuse or neglect, any problems after immunizations, any heart disease, any recurrent infections, chronic diarrhea, weight loss, seizures, central nervous system infections, recurring respiratory difficulties. Much information is to be gained from a thorough history.

Physical examination includes a look at linear growth. This is easily evaluated by closely monitoring the head circumference, the weight, and the length in standardized curves. Is the child small or large for his age? Is the head circumference above the 95th percentile or below the 5th percentile?

Observation of the child's general appearance and behavior for a few moments will give valuable information. Does he have an unusual facies? Does he have ear abnormalities? Does he have any extremity abnormalities or dysmorphic signs that would point to a certain syndrome? Does he have weak or involuntary movements of the eye or face muscle pointing to a cranial nerve involvement? Does he have facial paralysis with tent shaped mouth that would point to a congenital myotonic dystrophy? Dissymmetry of movement and posture needs to be evaluated and can be done by observation. The state of alertness, lack of response to visual and auditory stimuli, or inability to suck and swallow point toward central nervous system damage. Marked generalized weakness with hypotonia, particularly if the legs are more affected than the arms, in a child with bright and unaffected facial movements points towards a spinal muscular atrophy.

An increase in the tone, persisting primitive reflexes, and increase in deep tendon reflexes can all point towards cerebral palsy. Normal infants, when picked up from the supine position, will flex their hips and knees. Spastic infants, on the other hand, will tend to extend their hips and knees and come to a standing position. When held in vertical suspension, hypertonic infants have excessive extensor tone of the head with hyperextension of the neck, head and trunk. If scissoring of the lower extremities upon vertical suspension occurs after six months of age, an increase in tone of the hip ad-

ductors is present.

Deep tendon reflexes are difficult to obtain in neonates and young infants due to the normal flexor attitude of the extremities. The deep tendon reflexes are also affected if the child is tense or crying. The position of the child is important when assessing reflexes because if the head is not midline, the asymmetric tonic neck reflex may alter the response. A knee jerk elicited by tapping over an area at some distance from the patellar tendon (e.g., by percussing over the shins) can be considered confirmation of an exaggerated response. Several beats of clonus can be normally seen in neonates and in infants up to six to nine months of age. Persistent clonus, on the other hand, is abnormal at any point in time. These would be suggestive of central nervous system or upper motor neuron damage.

Certain primitive reflexes offer assistance in making a diagnosis of cerebral palsy. The asymmetric tonic neck reflex, which appears between two weeks and two months of age and disappears between four and six months of age, is elicited by turning the infant's head to one side and holding it there for thirty seconds. The infant will then assume a fencing posture with the arm in front extended and arm in back flexed. If the child cannot get out of this position, even when crying, this is considered an obligatory response and is always abnormal. This has been associated with the development of cerebral palsy. Also, if the reflex is present after six months of age, this is considered abnormal. The Moro reflex, or startle reflex, would be abnormal if present beyond six months of age. The crossed extensor reflex, which normally disappears by four months of age, is elicited with the baby in the supine position. When a stimulus is applied to the sole of one extremity with the knee extended, the contralateral foot normally responds by flexor withdrawal and rapidly moving to extension, abduction and then adduction. Finding this response after four months of age, whether on one side or both, suggests a possible presence of cerebral palsy.

If on examination the child showed hypotonia and weakness with associated signs of either respiratory problems sucking and swallowing difficulties, facial weakness, ophthalmoplegia, multiple contractures and arthrogryposis, dysmorphic features, and fasciculation of the tongue, a congenital myopathy should be considered. The classic Duchenne's muscular dystrophy patient usually does not show clinical symptoms until after the child starts walking. Hypotonia may be noted early in life, and careful observation may show evidence of weakness in this preclinical phase; there is usually a delay in motor development as well.

Further evaluation of a patient with this clinical presentation might include amino acid screens, electromyography, muscle biopsy, MRI or CAT scan of the head, nerve conduction velocities, chromosomal analysis if indicated by the presence of dysmorphic features on the child, a complete blood count and blood chemistry profile, urinalysis, and a CPK muscle enzyme test.

All of these would be done as an initial workup, and with the information gained from the history and physical and the different tests, one should be able to come up with a definite or probable diagnosis. The child would then be started on an early infant stimulation program with specific therapies in the area of physical therapy and occupational therapy. Any other medical therapies indicated would be instituted at the time.

8

Nursing

Ann W. Cox, Ph.D., R.N.

As a relatively young profession, nursing has evolved from the care of the sick by untrained individuals to a profession characterized by several entry-level educational programs and many advanced graduate-level specialties. The American Nurses' Association's *Nursing: A Social Policy Statement* (1980) defines nursing as follows:

> The practice of nursing means the performance for compensation of professional services requiring substantial specialized knowledge of the biological, physical, behavioral, psychological, and sociological sciences and nursing theory as the basis for assessment, diagnosis, planning, intervention, and evaluation in the promotion and maintenance of health; the casefinding and management of illness, injury, or infirmity; the restoration of optimum function; or the achievement of a dignified death. Nursing practice includes but is not limited to administration, teaching, counseling, supervision, delegation, and evaluation of practice and execution of medical regimen (p. 2).

Further, the American Nurses' Association (1980) identifies the "phenomena of concern" to nurses as "human responses to ac-

tual or potential health problems" (p. 9). Human responses are viewed as (a) reactions of individuals and groups to actual problems (health-restoring responses) and (b) concerns of individuals and groups about potential problems (health-supporting responses). Interventions that have a health-restoring function ameliorate or attenuate the impact of illness upon the client and family. Health-supporting responses provided by nursing professionals are structured to monitor potential problems and include educational and skill training programs with at risk populations and communities. These types of interventions exemplify the diversity within the profession of nursing.

Historically, the focus of nursing has been individual, family, or community needs relevant to health and welfare. These needs have ranged broadly from environmental health in a community to energy conservation in an individual. Generalizing across specialties and practice settings, the broad concern of nursing has consistently been humans' optimal functioning in their environment. To achieve this professional mission, nursing practice takes place in a wide variety of settings, including hospitals, community-based health clinics, primary care centers, schools, day care centers, residential services, industry, and the client's or family's home.

The specific phenomena nursing addresses are potential or actual functional problems (Carpenito, 1987). Potential problems can result from health-related practices and may predictably contribute to future disability of an individual, family, or community. For example, smoking is a practice with considerable adverse consequences on the health of the individual. The nursing profession has been involved in strategies to help individuals overcome an addiction to tobacco, as well as waging campaigns to prevent people from beginning to use tobacco products. Nurses intervene in an array of other health-related practices such as excessive alcohol consumption during pregnancy, exposure of infants and young children to the dangers of an environment high in lead, or resistance to fastening seat belt restraints during automobile use. Each of these examples impacts the development or acquisition of developmental disabilities.

Actual problems occur in association with illness or with social, occupational, or maturational changes. In clients with developmental disabilities and their families, actual problems frequently encountered include lack of information regarding management of a condition, ineffective coping on the part of the individual or family, alterations in parenting, disturbance in self-concept, alterations in patterns of functioning, and impaired mobility. The functional perspective of nursing views the individual within the context of the family and community. This theoretical viewpoint is well suited to work effectively with individuals with developmental disabilities in community-based and acute care settings.

Nurses seek to understand phenomena in the domain of health-related behavior at the level of human organism–environment interaction. Clinical problems are viewed as expressions of the person and environ-ment interactional model. In order to intervene effectively at this interface, nursing practice requires both "art" and "science" components. Theories, concepts, principles, and methods of treatment compose the "science" of nursing. "Art" is the way knowledge is used, especially in human interactions, and reflects attitudes, beliefs, and values. Concerned with a broad range of human functional responses to life situations, nursing has traditionally taken a holistic view of clients and their situations (Jackson & Lubkin, 1990).

Educational and Training Requirements

Entry into professional nursing practice can occur through various educational routes (diploma, associate, and baccalaureate degrees). In this chapter, the term professional nurse refers to the registered nurse (RN). Other designations, such as licensed practical nurse, vocational nurse, or nursing assistant or aide, are not considered members of the profession and will not be discussed.

Nursing education includes coursework in the biological, behavioral, and social sciences. Basic courses include biology, anatomy and physiology, pharmacology, pathophysiology, nutrition, growth and development, systems theory, and interpersonal relationships. Nursing curricula include content and application courses in practice with adults and children and emphasize health promotion and health restoration. In addition, nurses prepared at the baccalaureate level (BSN) receive education in community health, including principles of interdisciplinary, interagency service coordination, and nursing research.

In addition to their basic preparation, many nurses choose to further their education in preparation for advanced practice roles. Typically, this occurs through further academic preparation at the master's or doctoral degree levels. Advanced practice nurses are prepared to engage in research, develop and test theory, and synthesize and utilize a broad range of knowledge, theories, and skills in clinical practice (American Nurses' Association, 1990).

As generalists or advanced practice specialists, nurses are involved in all levels of health care and with all ages of individuals with developmental disabilities. Health services can be categorized into three levels of care: (a) *primary care*, with a focus on health maintenance and preventive care; (b) *secondary care*, which encompasses long term care needs of persons with chronic conditions and disabilities and may include hospitalization; and (c) *tertiary care*, which frequently requires the sophisticated technology of specialized units. Nurses who are advanced practice specialists hold additional expertise in different types of practice: (a) settings, such as community health; (b) age groups, such as geriatrics and child health; and (c) health problems, such as maternal, medical-surgical, or psychiatric-mental health specialties.

Licensure, Certification, and Continuing Education

In order to become a registered nurse (RN), professional nurses must pass an examination following completion of their nursing education program. Since states develop their own acceptable criteria for licensing, each applicant is licensed in the state in which he or she passes the examination. A nurse must be registered in the state in which he or she practices. A system of reciprocity has been developed among many states in order to facilitate the registration process when nurses relocate. Each state regulates the profession through the development and implementation of a Nurse Practice Act. This act describes the scope of nursing practice and the standards for

licensure in a particular state. In addition to the basic registered nurse licensure, many states have developed continuing education requirements for nurses. These requirements vary greatly among states and are part of the periodic review of nurses for renewal of licensure.

Nurses with advanced degrees and specialty experience may sit for a national certification examination in their area of specialty. The development of these certification exams is based upon a set of standards developed by specialists in a given area. For example, the nursing divisions of the American Association of University Affiliated Programs and the American Association on Mental Deficiency developed standards for the Clinical Nursing Specialist in Developmental Disabilities/Handicapping Conditions (American Association of University Affiliated Programs, 1987). Once the standards are accepted, the national certifying organization develops a certification examination which is made available to nurses fulfilling criteria acceptable for advance practice specialties. Standards and certification examinations have been developed for a number of advanced practice specialties. Recently, standards have been developed for nurses practicing in the field of early intervention (Early Intervention Consensus Committee, 1993).

Contributions to Interdisciplinary Practice

In the field of developmental disabilities, nurses practice within a variety of team models including multidisciplinary, interdisciplinary, and transdisciplinary. The interdisciplinary team model recognizes that efforts of human service professionals are more successful when they work together with professionals from other disciplines.

Thus, there is an interdependence inherent in effective interdisciplinary teams. Further, team members acknowledge that the result of the team's activity is synergistic, providing more benefit to the client and family than each could accomplish individually or separately (American Congress of Rehabilitation Medicine, 1992).

The domain of nursing practice is not static; instead, it tends to increase as the needs and capacities of society change. Collegial, collaborative practice with other health-care professions further extends the boundaries of nursing practice. Diller (1990) observed that interdisciplinary rehabilitation teams often involve members who engage in problem solving beyond the confines of their particular discipline. Nurses, physicians, social workers, and others have to collaborate if clients are to receive coordinated care. Understanding others' professional viewpoints as well as one's own is the first step toward collaborative practice.

For service to people with developmental disabilities, the profession of nursing intersects with and complements other professional roles in health care. Nursing professionals seek to diagnose and treat the response to the disability. The concerns of nursing are varied and address numerous health and psychosocial problems, including limitations of a client's self-care ability; impaired ability to function in any fundamental area such as sleeping, breathing, eating, or maintaining circulation; pain, anxiety, fear, loneliness, grief, or other physical or emotional problems related to health, illness, or treatment; impaired social or intellectual processes; impaired ability to make decisions and choices; alteration of self-image as required by the change in health; dysfunctional perception of health or health-care activities; extra demands posed by such normal life processes as birth, growth, or death; and difficulty in interpersonal relationships (Fraley, 1992; George, 1985).

The *nursing process* is the underlying scheme that provides order and direction to nursing care and is the essence of professional nursing practice. The nursing process can be defined as a deliberate intellectual activity whereby the practice of nursing is approached in an orderly, systematic manner (Fraley, 1992). As a tool or methodology, the nursing process also provides a means for evaluating the quality of nursing care given by nurses and assures accountability and responsibility to the client/patient. This process includes data collection (assessment), diagnosis, planning, treatment (intervention), and evaluation.

The process of nursing is supported by standards that provide specific guidelines for practice. Standards mandate the systematic, continuous collection of client health data which must be compiled into a form that is both accessible and communicable. From these data is derived a nursing diagnosis which provides the basis for construction of a plan for nursing care. The treatment phase involves nursing actions which are selected and performed with the client's participation. The selected interventions provide for the promotion, maintenance, or restoration of health and serve to maximize the health care abilities of the client. The progress toward goals is mutually determined by the client and the nurse, resulting in reassessment, reordering of priorities, establishment of new goals, and revision of the plan for care.

Assessment

A holistic view during the assessment phase ensures that the biological, psychological, social, and spiritual spheres of the individual are considered in nursing treatment. All nursing assessment guidelines need to include the following basic categories of information: biographical data, a health history including family and social history, and subjective and objective data about the current health status, including reasons for contact with the health care professional, and a medical diagnosis if the client/patient has a medical problem. Additional and supplemental information may need to be included such as past strategies to cope with a particular health problem, or religious and cultural beliefs about health status and services.

The health history is a vital component of the assessment. This is the client's story of past and present events which may affect current and future health status. The current health status of the client is ascertained through these subjective data (from client interviews) and objective data (from past health records, examinations, and observations). For example, a client's description of pain in relation to malpositioning is considered subjective data, whereas vital signs, physical assessment data, or observation of a pressure sore are examples of objective measurements of physiological data.

Systematic, continuous, and comprehensive assessment includes assessment of the following parameters:

1. health perception and health management practices
2. nutritional needs and metabolic functioning
3. factors that affect activity, exercise and self help such as neuromuscular, cardiovascular, respiratory and developmental functioning
4. cognitive/perceptual functioning
5. roles, relationships and social supports
6. coping and stress responses including family strengths and resources
7. self-perception/self-concept
8. sleep/rest patterns and needs
9. problems/concerns with sexuality/reproductive functioning
10. family values, beliefs, concerns and priorities within their cultural context

Within each of these parameters, nurses may engage in more specific screening and assessment to determine the extent and nature of a potential or actual health problem. Some examples of more specific parameters include the interactive relationship between an infant and his/her caregiver, the functional assessment of an adult client with mobility limitation, a family assessment that focuses on identifying means of natural supports available to an individual with developmental disability, a 24-hour dietary intake record to determine the need for referral to a dietitian, or developmental screening for the purpose of early identification and referral.

Intervention

Nurses possess physical, behavioral, and psychosocial skills that enable them to address many needs of individuals with developmental disabilities and their families across the life span. Because practice is built on this broad base of knowledge and skills, the nurse is an essential and valuable member of the interdisciplinary team. The interventions in nursing include dependent functions such as initiating and monitoring treatment protocols and techniques which are prescribed by others, most notably physicians; independent functions derived from nursing diagnostic statements; and interdependent functions derived through collaborative problem solving among interdisciplinary team members. Due to this broad orientation, several functional roles in service provision will be addressed, including care coordinator, practitioner, educator, counselor, advocate, and consultant.

Service coordinator. Nurses provide an array of direct services and interventions for individuals with developmental disabilities. Often referred to by others as "the generalist on the team" (Rothberg, 1992), nurses frequently serve in the role of service coordinator, also termed *case manager* or *care coordinator*. The functions of a nurse as service coordinator vary with the setting, the individual and family, and the type of services required (American Nurses' Association, 1988).

Because the needs of individuals with developmental disabilities are quite often complex and involve many specialist team members, direct service is frequently organized and provided within a transdisciplinary model of delivery. With this model, usually only one member of the team actually delivers the interventions, with the support and consultation of others. This service delivery model is common in early intervention in the community and in public school systems (Sobsey & Cox, 1991).

The person who will function in the service coordinator role is typically the one having the background discipline whose services most closely match the needs of the person with the disability. The selection of a service coordinator is a decision that is jointly made by the other team members, the client, and the client's family. The nurse on the team is viewed as a likely service coordinator and primary service provider because of his or her diverse health education background; knowledge and skills in many aspects of prevention, health maintenance, and health promotion; and holistic family-centered approach.

For children and adolescents with developmental disabilities, the nurse often fills a coordinator role for services provided within the school system. If a school nurse is available, he or she is particularly useful to coordinate the health services required by the child during the school day. This is accomplished through regular communication with the parents, child, teacher, and physician. Health service planning in the school can include anything from addressing primary health care needs, to medica-

tion monitoring and administration and performance of specialized health related treatments (American Nurses' Association, 1988).

Practitioner. Children and adults with developmental disabilities continue to have health needs, either related to their disability, related to other health concerns, or preventive in nature. As a practitioner, the nurse may be in contact with the individual during an initial crisis in an acute-care or rehabilitation setting (Hanlon & Sharley, 1989). The nurse provides direct care to the client until skills necessary for self-care have been developed, and assesses and monitors responses of the individual to treatment and planning services offered by the team. Further, health care can be provided in the home and community following discharge. Understanding that individuals' health problems also affect their families, the nurse plays an important role in helping families cope and deal with their own needs and concerns.

Educator. In order for the individual and family to make informed decisions, accurate and current information must be provided about the disability, its prognosis and treatment, available services, and the probable outcome of participation in these services (Bobb & Lubkin, 1990). As educator, the nurse furnishes the individual and family with information related to the disability and its treatment and management. Further, nurses are instrumental in preventing disabilities through participation in individual, group, or community education and screening programs (Godfrey, 1991).

Counselor. The counseling function of nursing is to help individuals describe, analyze, and respond to their current situation. Miles (1986) views counseling as an ongoing process of helping people solve and effectively cope with their concerns. The chronic nature of disability requires continuous adjustment and readjustment, acceptance and rejection, and adaptation throughout life. For example, parents are encouraged to express the common feelings of denial, anger, guilt, and sorrow associated with the birth of a child with a disability. Likewise, the nurse encourages the person with quadriplegia to express feelings of anger, frustration, and helplessness related to his or her chronic, lifelong condition.

Not all individuals with disability or their families will need extensive counseling. However, if the requirements for counseling are beyond the nurse's level of knowledge and skill, referral is made to an appropriate mental health professional.

Advocate. As an advocate, the nurse uses influence effectively to further the individual's and family's well-being. The nurse becomes a coach, teacher, liaison, and friend to help resolve existing problems (Jackson and Lubkin, 1990). For example, the nurse functions as an advocate in helping to obtain appropriate early intervention services for a child born with Down syndrome. In an advocacy role, the nurse also initiates or supports community and legislative activities that promote the rights of persons with disabilities or provide for their unique needs.

Consultant. In assuming a consultant role, the nurse functions as a resource person. Consultation services may be provided to various persons involved in developmental disability services including individuals and families, nursing staff, interdisciplinary team members, health care professionals, community agencies, and any other person or group providing services (American Nurses' Association, 1988). As a consultant, the nurse should possess and demonstrate advanced levels of expertise acquired through clinical practice and advanced education.

Case Example

Myelomeningocele, or spina bifida, is a neural tube defect that occurs during early fetal development. The defect is visible at birth, and surgery to close the lesion is performed within 24 to 48 hours after birth. Varying degrees of nerve involvement occur as a result of the defect, which typically occurs in the lumbar or lumbosacral of the spinal column. Nerve damage often leads to varying degrees of paresis or paralysis of the lower extremities and can cause neurogenic bladder dysfunction. Musculoskeletal problems can affect later locomotion. Hydrocephalus is an problem associated with spina bifida, occurring in approximately 90% of infants (Anderson, 1989).

Health History

Tony, a seven pound infant, firstborn of Mr. and Mrs. A. Stanley, was born at 36 weeks of gestation with myelomeningocele. The anomaly occurred in the lumbosacral area of the spinal column, giving rise to symptoms such as flaccid paralysis of the lower extremities and varying degrees of sensory deficit. Initial care included the surgical closure of the lesion within 48 hours of birth and the placement of a shunt to deal with developing hydrocephalus. The multidisciplinary assessment and approach to care during hospitalization involved the specialties of neurology, neurosurgery, pediatrics, urology, orthopedics, social work, physical therapy, and nursing. The collaborative efforts of these specialists were directed toward five major problems associated with this defect—the surgical closure of the myelomeningocele, placement of a shunt to correct the hydrocephalus, assessment and planning regarding urinary tract dysfunction, locomotion, and rehabilitation and education of both the child and family.

The social worker and nurse were asked to assess the family's ability to manage Tony's care upon discharge. With some initial instruction, Tony was able to go home—following a three-week hospital stay—seemingly stable, growing and eating well, and without infection. An appointment was given to Tony's parents for a follow-up visit with the neurosurgeon in two weeks, and a referral was made to the local early intervention interagency coordinating council service coordinator.

Mr. and Mrs. Stanley, Tony's parents, brought Tony to the clinic for the follow-up appointment with the neurosurgeon. Medically, Tony was healing well and stable. Yet Mrs. Stanley seemed despondent, asking few questions and becoming teary when the doctor asked how things were going. Mr. Stanley did all of the talking, indicating that Tony was a happy, quiet baby. He was particularly pleased that Tony had gained almost three pounds since discharge from the hospital.

The clinic nurse, who also had noticed Mrs. Stanley's emotional state, inquired whether someone from early intervention services had been in touch with the family. Mr. Stanley indicated that a service coordinator had contacted the family, but that they were waiting until the neurosurgeon gave them a "good report" on Tony's medical condition. Understanding that families find initial contact somewhat difficult, the nurse asked if the Stanleys would like her to inform the service coordinator that Tony was stable and could begin services. A brief discussion about early intervention options was followed by a question-and-answer session regarding Tony's future needs. Emphasis was placed on the preventive aspect of his physical care, including prevention of skin breakdown associated with urinary and bowel incontinence and positioning techniques, and his socialization needs early in childhood, including normalized childhood experiences.

Throughout the sessions with the service providers, each parent appeared to have a different response to the condition of their child. Mr. Stanley was eager to discuss the future care needs of his son. Mrs. Stanley, on the other hand, seldom smiled or asked questions. Both, however, agreed that early intervention home services would be useful.

Assessment

Two weeks following the clinic visit, the service coordinator from the local interagency council visited Mrs. Stanley. The visit was primarily an initial contact to determine what the family saw as their needs and resources. A nurse from the intervention program accompanied the service coordinator because Mrs. Stanley had expressed concern regarding some puffiness of the healing incision on Tony's back. A physical assessment performed by the nurse indicated that Tony was in good health. The puffiness around the surgical incision had lessened and no signs of infection were evident. However, Mrs. Stanley indicated that Tony had no primary physician.

During the visit, Mrs. Stanley expressed considerable concern regarding Tony's future abilities and the belief that her eating habits and smoking had caused the defect. She was hopeful that therapy would help Tony walk so that he could play with other children. An appointment was made for an interdisciplinary assessment to address the family's concerns. Mrs. Stanley agreed that the assessment would involve the disciplines of physical therapy, social work, pediatrics, and nursing.

Assessment data indicated that Tony, now 10 weeks old, was a fussy infant with initial delays in gross motor development. He was a robust baby who apparently had gained significant weight since birth.

Clearly, lower motor functioning was minimal, and the physical therapist felt that some positioning and exercise techniques were indicated to facilitate later locomotion.

Family assessment data indicated that Mrs. Stanley felt isolated and alone. Living in a rural area of the county, she had few friends and felt she had very little in common with the friends she had. She expressed recurring guilt regarding Tony's condition. Mr. Stanley, who was not in attendance for the assessment, worked long hours and traveled frequently. Although supportive, he was seldom available to assist with Tony's care and appointments.

Several areas of health concern were expressed by Mrs. Stanley, including being unsure whether Tony's shunt was working properly, concerns about recurrent rashes in the diaper area, when to begin immunizations, his feeding schedule, and his fussiness. Mrs. Stanley indicated that Tony's fussiness seemed only to be relieved by feeding. Tony currently took seven, six ounce bottles of formula a day and his current weight was 11 pounds, 4 ounces. However, he slept through the night and usually took two 3-hour naps during the day. It was apparent that, as her first child, Mrs. Stanley was unsure of the typical care needs of infants and tended to attribute all concerns to the medical condition.

Treatment Recommendations

The following list of concerns were identified by the team, which included Mrs. Stanley:

1. Mrs. Stanley wants to find a pediatrician who understands Tony's needs.
2. She needs information regarding what to expect from Tony, the baby, as opposed to what to expect because he has myelomeningocele.
3. She wants to get out by herself and find some friends who understand her situation.
4. She wants Tony's fussiness to decrease.
5. She wants to understand more about Tony's medical condition and what she can do to help him learn to move.
6. She wants information about how to deal with his frequent diaper rashes.

An Individualized Family Services Plan (IFSP) was developed based on these concerns, and initial prioritization was made. Mrs. Stanley preferred beginning with Tony's daily care schedule, feeling that it would be helpful to have a health professional available "in case something happened with Tony's shunt." It was the team's decision to have the early intervention nurse serve as the service coordinator and primary infant-service provider for the first six months, believing that Mrs. Stanley needed the support of a health professional who could serve also to implement the IFSP. A transdisciplinary team model was chosen for direct services with the physical therapist, social worker, and pediatrician serving as consultants to the nurse.

As Tony grew, Mrs. Stanley became more confident in her parenting abilities, including managing the medical regimen. Another parent of a child with myelomeningocele contacted the family and provided support, enabling Mrs. Stanley to express her feelings of guilt and frustration and to locate a physician familiar with the needs of children with myelomeningocele. Tony's weight gain stabilized, an appropriate feeding schedule was instituted, and Tony's fussiness decreased. Diaper rashes continued to be a concern, but Mrs. Stanley developed confidence in her ability to keep them under control. Tony "scooted around" with the help of a rolling board designed by the physical therapist and built by Mr. Stanley.

At Tony's one-year reassessment, the team decided to gradually transition from the nurse as primary service provider to the physical therapist. The psychological assessment indicated that Tony performed at age level in cognition, language acquisition, fine motor skills, and psychosocial development. His gross motor abilities were significantly delayed. Tony's needs included more integrated mobility activities, specialized positioning techniques, and possibly bracing. The early childhood special educator, occupational therapist, nurse, social worker, and pediatrician served as consultants to the physical therapist.

Since Tony has experienced recurrent urinary tract infections, intermittent catheterization was suggested. If this became a necessity, the physical therapist and nurse would jointly make visits to the home until Mrs. Stanley was comfortable with performing this treatment.

The strong friendships which developed between the Stanleys and a parent support group provided essential ongoing supports for the family, including periodic respite, socialization, information about the future, and occasional playmates for Tony. Mrs. Stanley considered being a parent partner for families of infants born with myelomeningocele.

The Stanleys are now looking to the future in terms of planning their family. They continue to have many questions regarding the reoccurrence of myelomeningocele. Their pediatrician has been able to address many of their initial questions, but has referred the family to a geneticist for further counseling.

Summary

The profession of nursing has been actively engaged in interdisciplinary teaming for many years. As one of the required disciplines when the Maternal-Child Health Bureau began funding training programs in interdisciplinary teamwork in developmental disabilities during the late 1960's, nursing embraces the need for a collaborative approach with colleagues and families to address the needs of persons with developmental disabilities. Nursing's unique contribution to the team effort is that of assessing, diagnosing, and intervening in the human responses of individuals and families to altered functioning. Together with colleagues in many disciplines, nurses bring a holistic perspective to the often complex issues challenging families and individuals with developmental disabilities.

References

American Association of University Affiliated Programs (1987). *Standards for the clinical nurse specialist in developmental disabilities/handicapping conditions.* Silver Spring, MD: Author.

American Congress of Rehabilitation Medicine (1992). *Guide to interdisciplinary practice in rehabilitation settings.* Skokie, IL: Author.

American Nurses' Association (1990). *Standards of clinical nursing practice.* Washington, DC: Author.

American Nurses' Association (1988). *Nursing care management.* Kansas City, KS: Author.

American Nurses' Association (1980) *Nursing: A social policy statement.* Washington, DC: Author.

Anderson, S.M. (1989). Secondary neurologic disability in myelomeningocele. *Infants and Young Children, 1*(4), 9-21.

Bobb, A., & Lubkin, I. (1990). Teaching. In I. M. Lubkin (Ed.), *Chronic illness: Impact and interventions* (2nd ed., pp. 279-299). Boston, MA: Jones and Bartlett.

Carpenito, L. J. (1987). *Nursing diagnosis: Application to clinical practice* (2nd ed.). Philadelphia: J. B. Lippincott.

Diller, L. (1990). Fostering training in interdisciplinary teamwork, fostering research in a society in transition. *Archives of Physical Medicine and Rehabilitation, 71*, 275-278.

Early Intervention Consensus Committee (1993). *National standards of nursing practice for early intervention services.* Lexington, KY: Author.

Fraley. A. M. (1992). *Nursing and the disabled.* Boston, MA: Jones and Bartlett.

George, J. B. (Ed.) (1985). *Nursing theories.* Englewood Cliffs, NJ: Prentice-Hall.

Godfrey, A. C. (1991). Providing health services to facilitate benefit from early intervention: A model. *Infants and Young Children, 4*, 47-55.

Hanlon, D., & Sharley, E. (1989). Professional practice of rehabilitation nursing. In S. Dittmar (Ed.), *Rehabilitation nursing: Process and application* (pp. 73-79). St. Louis, MO: C.V. Mosby.

Jackson, E., and Lubkin, I. (1990). Advocacy. In I. M. Lubkin (Ed.), *Chronic illness: Impact and interventions* (2nd ed., pp. 300-316). Boston, MA: Jones and Bartlett.

Miles, M.S. (1986). Counseling strategies. In S.H. Johnson (ed.). *High-risk parenting: Nursing assessment and strategies for the family at risk.* (2nd ed., pp. 343-360). Philadelphia, PA: J.B. Lippincott.

Rothberg, J. S. (1992). Knowledge of discipline roles and functions of teamwork members. In American Congress of Rehabilitation Medicine, *Guide to interdisciplinary practice in rehabilitation settings* (pp 44-71). Skokie, IL: Author.

Sobsey, D., & Cox, A. (1991). Integrating health care and educational programs. In F. Orelove & D. Sobsey (Eds.), *Educating children with multiple disabilities: A transdisciplinary approach* (pp 155-185). Baltimore, MD: Paul H. Brookes.

9

Nutrition

Lois Ann Wodarski, Ph.D., R.D.

The science of nutrition involves the study of nutrients in foods and of the body's handling of them. Qualified nutrition experts—that is, those who are trained to deliver nutrition counsel and care—are registered dietitians (RD). The registered dietitian has completed a program of study that entails the development and application of knowledge of food, nutrition, biochemistry, physiology, management, and behavioral and social sciences to promote health, prevent disease, and speed recovery from illness. Registered dietitians have earned an undergraduate degree from a college or university by completing a dietetics training program that has been approved or accredited by the American Dietetic Association (ADA). The Canadian counterpart is the Canadian Dietetic Association, or CDA.

The ADA (or CDA) is recognized as the accrediting agency for dietetics programs. Through accreditation and approval, the ADA assures the public that these programs of dietetic study meet high standards of quality (American Dietetic Association, 1988). The approved or accredited program requires approximately 60 semester hours devoted to the study of nutrition and food science, 900 hours of preprofessional practice (clinical internship or the equivalent), and passing a national examination designed to assess knowlege and performance competencies deemed critical by the ADA. Continuing education activities are required to maintain up-to-date knowledge. The certification process encourages high standards of performance in order to protect the health, safety, and welfare of the public.

Most registered dietitians maintain membership in the American Dietetic Association, which is the nation's largest professional organization for dietitians, dietetic technicians and nutritionists. The purpose of the Association is to provide direction and leadership for quality dietetic practice, education, and research and to promote the optimal health and nutritional status of the population. The underlying philosophy of membership is "to embrace all dietetic professionals who may contribute to the goals of the Association" (American Dietetic Association, 1988).

Dietitians are employed in a variety of settings, many of which serve those individuals with developmental disabilities. For example, dietitians' roles pertinent to care of those with disabilities include provision of client care, coordination of care as members of nutrition support teams, management of food-service systems, and research in intermediate and long-term care facilities, hospitals, public health departments and home health agencies.

The University Affiliated Programs (UAPs) have included the discipline of nutrition in their training programs from the outset, and the federal government recognizes the discipline as possessing the knowledge and skills to assess and develop care and intervention plans for preschool and school-age children with disabilities. PL 99-457 lists nutritionists among the health professionals with expertise in assessment and development of family service plans (Smith, 1993).

Many states require the possession of a state license to practice as further evidence of competency to practice in the area of nutrition and dietetics, or to use a title which implies such competency. Licensure of dietitians and nutritionists was first initiated in 1974. Since that time, 29 states have enacted some form of regulation. Nineteen states have a licensure law, nine have certification laws, and one has registration (American Dietetic Association, 1993). Licensure is state-regulated, with each state having its own requirements backed up by licensure bills. By definition, licensing statutes include an explicitly defined scope of practice. In states that require licensure, practice in the profession is illegal without possessing a license from the state. Statutory certification limits the use of particular titles, such as "nutritionist" or "dietitian," to those who have met certain requirements. Certification requirements, however, do not prohibit the practice of the occupation. Registration is the least restrictive form of state regulation in that it protects the use of the title but not the practice of the profession (American Dietetic Association, 1993).

Contributions to Interdisciplinary Practice

Optimal nutrition is essential for the health and well-being of every person. The profession of dietetics recognizes nutrition as the interaction between food and the living organism that is influenced by myriad psychological, social, economic, and technogical factors (American Dietetic Association, 1983). It is critical that the influencing factors be considered in planning for nutrition care. The nutritional status of an individual depends on the ingestion of food and, once ingested, the availability of the nutrients contained in the food to meet the body's need for energy, growth and maintenance. Variables infrequently encountered in normal nutrition affect food intake and nutrient availability, and thus affect the nutritional status, of individuals with developmental disabilities (Ekvall, 1993). When nutrition care does not include attention to all factors, voids in treatment occur, and the individual is at high risk of nutritional deficiency (Wodarski, 1985).

Food intake may be impaired by physical handicaps. Down syndrome, for example, is often characterized by poor tongue and lip control and impaired fine and gross motor control (Springer, 1982). Cerebral palsy and brain damage may result in lack of mouth, head and trunk control. Lack of sitting balance; the inability to bend one's hips, to stretch one's arms to grasp and maintain a grasp and bring one's hands to one's mouth; and the lack of eye-hand coordination further hamper the eating process (Finnie, 1970).

Behavior disorders such as autism, minimal brain dysfunction, and hyperactivity may result in inadequate food intake and subsequent malnutrition. Low attention spans and disruptive behaviors make mealtimes a challenge. Congenital metabolic aberrations such as phenylketonuria (PKU) require diet modification to increase or decrease intake of critical nutrients.

Drug-induced abnormalities, likewise, may affect the use of nutrients once they have been ingested. Medication may be the cause of anorexia, nausea, and diarrhea, all of which have negative effects on nutrient ingestion and utilization. Constipation is a common side effect of anticonvulsant drugs and tranquilizers (American Dietetic Association, 1981). The problem is frequently compounded by lack of mobility and decreased opportunity for exercise. Medications commonly used in treatment can lead furthermore to problems with teeth and gums (American Dietetic Association, 1981). Dental caries, gingivitis, and bacterial infections can cause gastrointestinal infections and consequent malnutrition. Bruxism, or teeth grinding, is characteristic of children with brain damage. The grinding wears down the cusps and bumps of the teeth and results in poor mastication and subsequent malabsorption of nutrients (Palmer & Ekvall, 1978).

Emotional distress of the parent or caretaker may have adverse effects on diet availability and acceptance. Frustrations experienced in feeding a person with oral-motor or behavioral difficulties may result in the caretaker's giving up before sufficient food has been eaten. Children who are fed foods inappropriate to their level of development may gag or spit them out. Caretakers frequently mistake those behaviors for signals of lack of hunger and stop feeding the children. Caretakers may also use food as a reward to compensate for other pleasures in life that are frequently denied to individuals with handicaps. Parents or caretakers may need to recognize when they use food inappropriately to reward or punish and should be taught alternate means for controlling behavior or expressing love and concern.

Finally, high medical expenses may place severe strain on a family budget and thereby restrict the availability of food. The problem may be compounded in many instances when the parent or caretaker is required to provide 24-hour care for the handicapped individual and therefore is unable to maintain employment.

The multitude of factors that influence the nutritional status of people with disabilities requires an approach to care that incorporates information and assistance from several disciplines. This approach entails the interaction of several professions in the diagnosis, treatment planning, program implementation, and evaluation phases of service (Smith, 1993). A model for viewing the interactions of selected disciplines in achieving optimal nutritional health for clients with developmental disabilities has been described elsewhere (Wodarski, 1985).

In an ideal situation, the physician and nurse conduct physical examinations and relay pertinent clinical and laboratory findings, along with a diagnosis, to other members of the interdisciplinary team. Psychologists provide information on developmental level, fine and gross motor skills, and emotional or personality factors that influence eating behavior. The social worker gathers information dealing with socioeconomic status, family interaction patterns, and other information pertinent to implementation of team recommendations and the mobilization of community resources and social services to support care. Occupational and physical therapists evaluate sensory-motor development, prescribe adaptive feeding equipment and make recommendations regarding food consistency and texture. Dentists evaluate oral health and provide information on the functional capabilities of the oral structures as they affect feeding. If drug therapy is prescribed, the pharmacist is called upon to provide information on diet-drug interactions that is essential to modify the diet to alleviate problems associated with drug prescriptions. The dietitian completes the nutrition evaluation and fills the diet prescription based on medical, psychological, and sociological information. He or she may also work in conjunction with the speech therapist in attempts to remediate speech and language problems frequently associated with feeding difficulties. Finally, recreation therapists and health educators may be called upon to develop exercise programs to enhance diet therapy and improve neuromuscular functioning (see Wodarski, Bundschuh & Forbus, 1988).

Nutritional Assessment

The following interdisciplinary treatment protocol is suggested based on current knowledge in the treatment of developmental disabilities that includes results of three recent research studies of the nutritional status of developmentally disabled children and adolescents who received comprehensive nutritional care in an interdisciplinary setting (Nicholson, 1989; Pesce, Wodarski & Wang, 1989; Wodarski, McMillian & Doshi, 1993).

Referral and Record Review

The physician's written referral, including diagnosis and pertinent physical examination and laboratory findings, is reviewed by the dietitian. When possible, parents or caretakers are requested to supply a three-day food and activity diary and a typical snack or meal to be fed to the client during the evaluation period.

Dietary History

Ideally, an intake interview is conducted with a parent or other caretaker. During the interview the dietitian obtains a diet history with the following components:

1. methods of feeding (e.g. breast, bottle, gavage, spoon, cup)
2. gavage, bottle and breast weaning
3. type, order, and age of introduction and present intake of solid foods
4. foods that cause difficulty in terms of aspiration or gagging
5. current and past special diet orders, including texture modifications
6. use of nutritional supplements, vitamin/mineral supplements
7. food intolerances/allergies
8. current and past medications and noted side effects
9. pica (inappropriate food consumption)
10. appetite, regularity of meals
11. fluid preferences and intake pattern
12. fad, cultural, or religious diet preferences
13. nutritional knowledge and attitude of caretaker regarding meal planning and diet of client
14. use of food as reinforcer/pacifier
15. where and with whom food is consumed
16. participation in school/child care breakfast and/or lunch programs, or other meal programs

The three-day food/activity diary is used as a basis for discussion and/or confirmation of much of the above.

Medical History

The physician's medical record serves as the basis for discussion and clarification with the caretaker of client and family history and physical data. The following items are considered:

1. chronic/metabolic disorders
2. records of any substance abuse
3. incidence of vomiting, nausea, diarrhea

or constipation

4. acute or recurring illnesses and/or infections
5. obvious manifestation of nutritional deficiencies
6. physical activity
7. dental screening
8. socioeconomic data including home environment, adequacy of resources, educational status of primary caretaker, social/economic habits, parenting skills, support system for caretaker, and influential sources of information.

Anthropometric Assessment

Anthropometric measurements are obtained by the dietitian, or by the occupational and/or physical therapists. Height and weight are usually the most necessary indications of proper development (Kalisz & Ekvall, 1984) and must be determined for each client. Midarm muscle circumference and triceps skinfold are used in addition when muscle wasting or overabundance of fat tissue are suspected.

Techniques recommended for use with the general population can be used with adaptations as needed for clients with disabilities. To measure length, measuring boards are preferable to platform scales with movable measuring rods which tend to give inaccurate results. Weight is determined by beam-balance scales. Infants and non-ambulatory children are weighed on pediatric scales with pans; older, ambulatory clients are weighed on standard platform-type scales. Height and weight are plotted on the growth charts from the National Center for Health Statistics to determine percentile rankings.

Feeding Assessment

Following anthropometric measurement and dietary interview, the parent or care-taker, client, dietitian, and other interdisciplinary team members in settings where this is possible, engage in feeding assessment. The client is observed by the team as he or she is fed in a "typical" manner by the caretaker or, if independent in feeding, as he or she self-feeds. As the client eats the meal or snack, team members observe techniques and discuss any feeding problems of particular interest to the caretaker. It is important that the caretaker participating in the assessment be the person usually responsible for feeding the client. Other family members are encouraged to participate in addition.

The dietitian and/or the occupational and speech therapists consider the following in their assessments of the client's oral-motor mechanisms and feeding skills:

1. Neurological dysfunction or mechanical obstructions reflected in inefficient sucking and swallowing, bite reflex, strong or hypoactive gag reflex, tongue thrust, protrusion reflex, poor lip control, impaired chewing, malocclusion and high arched palate, and lack of head and trunk control.
2. Dysphagia caused by gross congenital anatomical defects of the tongue, palate, mandible, pharynx, larynx, esophagus, and thorax; neuromuscular causes such as delayed maturation, cerebral palsy, muscular dystrophy, various syndromes, and bacterial and viral infection; and acute infective conditions such as stomatitis.
3. Particular problems associated with feeding difficulties, such as delayed introduction of solid foods, delays in self-feeding, mealtime tantrums or disruptive behavior, coercive or manipulative interactive patterns between client and caretaker, and inappropriate uses of rewards/punishment for eating/mealtime.

Clinical Assessment

During clinical assessment the client's hair, skin, eyes, nails, face and skin are evaluated for clinical signs of malnutrition. Skeleton and musculature and general appearance are noted. Examination of the lips, teeth, gums and tongue are likewise important.

Nutritional Intervention

The multifactorial nature of nutritional problems associated with developmental disabilities requires a well organized, interdisciplinary effort. According to the interdisciplinary approach, a team composed of professional and support staff, the client, and the family is involved in an integrated approach to service. The team members share their knowledge and expertise in developing an individual program plan to meet identified needs in the most cost-effective and efficacious manner possible (Wodarski, 1991).

Following the client's assessment, the team discusses general impressions and sets initial treatment goals that are defined according to the specification of major problems. For example, one problem frequently encountered is growth retardation. Each discipline is responsible for setting objectives aimed at the remediation of the problem. In this case, the dietitian would look at the incorporation of appropriate supplements following the analysis of current nutrient intake. The speech and occupational therapist would work on feeding problems that hamper intake. The physician and pharmacist would be consulted for possible drug/ nutrient interaction, medication timing to reduce possible anorectic effects, and so forth (Wodarski, 1991).

Dietary intervention must consider data from the anthropometric, laboratory, food intake and feeding evaluations.

Anthropometric

Mental retardation, regardless of cause, is frequently associated with delays in physical growth and variances in body composition (Kalisz & Ekvall, 1984). With few exceptions, norms to evaluate the status of youth with developmental disabilities have yet to be established. Thus, following the individual's growth patterns may provide a more realistic interpretation of development than will comparison with standards. A smooth curve with a positive slope will indicate optimal growth, whereas an erratic curve and/or a negative slope alerts the therapist to the need for further evaluation to determine the etiology of the growth failure (Culley, Goyal, Jolly & Mertz, 1965). Correlation between height and weight percentiles is used to determine the degree of over- or under-weight. When either is suspected, it is desirable to use body fat, lean body mass, and muscle mass measures for confirmation of problems. Again, due to lack of standards for this population, baseline values serve as the control by which changes will be measured.

Determination of energy and nutrient needs requires the critical analysis of anthropometric, dietary, and physical activity data (Kalisz & Ekvall, 1984). The child's "height-age," as opposed to chronological age, is used to figure the Recommended Dietary Allowances (RDAs) when growth retardation is evident (American Society of Parenteral and Enteral Nutrition, 1983). To determine height-age, the child's height is located on the growth chart at the 50th percentile and the age corresponding to this point is noted. The height-age is used then as the basis for calculation of energy and nutrient needs. For example, a thirteen year-old child with a developmental disability may measure only 132 cm tall. According to the height-age calculation, his RDAs are more realistically determined to be those in the category of the 7-10 year old child.

Adjustments for calories are then made up or down in the usual manner based on physical activity data. It is important to note that with growth failure (stunting), energy intake generally must be higher for recovery. In these cases, it has been suggested that energy requirements be assessed according to kilogram of ideal weight. Ideal weight is calculated according to mean parental stature rather than the client's present height.

Low muscle mass and increased fat percentage may be an indication of the need for increased physical activity. Diet therapy should incorporate exercise within the parameters of the client's physical condition. Consultation with the physician, physical therapist, and when appropriate, school health education and recreation staff are called for in developing and implementing this facet of the intervention plan.

Food Intake Data

Data from the caretaker's three-day food/activity diary are analyzed in the normal manner, by hand calculation using food composition tables or by any of a number of available nutrient analysis computer software programs. Deficiencies or excesses are noted and intervention is based on the general recommendations for treatment of the over- or under-weight child, adolescent or adult.

Counseling for the caretaker includes an explanation of the nutritional needs for the client's growth and development with regard to "Daily Food Guide" concepts and/or RDA. If food or formula supplements are prescribed, the caretaker is instructed in the choice and use of the various options. In some cases clients require the services of social workers who are consulted for assistance in locating funds or mobilizing resources when these are needed to insure provision of an adequate food intake.

Feeding Skills

Poor feeding skills place the client with disabilities at increased nutritional risk due to inadequate energy and nutrient intake. Results of the study by Pesce et al. (1989) revealed that mean energy intake was the highest in children and adolescents with adequate feeding skills (93% of the RDA), as contrasted with nonfeeders and feeders requiring behavior modification whose intakes averaged 91% and 81% of the RDA, respectively. It should be noted that in this study intakes of all groups are high, due most likely to the comprehensive care these institutionalized clients received.

Assessments by the occupational and physical therapists and the speech therapist serve as the basis for counseling the caretakers. Food consistency (texture) is prescribed according to the client's stage of oral-motor development. Clients requiring no modifications in diet other than texture should be provided regular table foods which may be puréed, ground or chopped. Exceptions include nuts, seeds, coconut and hard or stringy vegetables and fruits. Doughy or pasty items such as pizza and rice are also difficult to modify in texture. Dry foods are made more palatable by the addition of broth, milk, gravy or fruit or vegetable juice. Swallowing and cup drinking are often facilitated by thickened liquids. Baby cereals, puréed fruit or commercial thickeners are useful in adjusting fluid consistencies. General feeding goals include the gradual introduction of foods of firmer texture to encourage chewing, the incorporation of a variety of finger foods to encourage finger feeding, and self-feeding with a spoon using items that will stay on the spoon such as mashed potatoes and puddings.

The social and psychological aspects of food are also considered in the intervention. Unless corrected early, feeding difficulties may quickly turn into difficult-to-remediate behavioral problems. Knowledge of what to expect in terms of self-sufficiency in feeding, messiness, and acceptance of foods according to the client's developmental level is imperative. Caretakers should be cautioned against the improper use of food reinforcers, withholding of food as punishment, or overcompensation through the use of food.

In the study by Pesce et al. (1989), suboptimal intakes of children with behavioral problems reflected the need for early identification and remediation of these problems. Severe behavioral problems in the client or emotional problems of caretakers that influence feeding require input from psychology or behavior analysis staff or—based on the client's resources—other appropriate community services. At the same time, it may be necessary to incorporate smaller, more frequent feedings high in nutrients to insure adequate intake of clients whose behaviors interfere with eating (Pipes, 1985). Spacing of meals to coincide with medication regimen may relieve some difficulties, e.g., anorexia or drowsiness, which aggravate the feeding situation.

Proper body positioning to facilitate feeding and feeding equipment adaptations are major components of treatment. Caretakers are trained in how to achieve proper body alignment to improve posture and muscle tone necessary to optimal food intake. Likewise, equipment is modified or arrangements are made to purchase what is needed. Again, social services staff may be consulted to facilitate the acquisition of essential items.

Dental caries, gingivitis and bacterial infections can cause problems with food intake and nutrient utilization. Pesce et al. (1989) found that subjects with dental problems had significantly lower food intakes than those without problems. Dental problems may require changes in food consistency or the limitation or exclusion of some foods.

Caretakers might also need help in locating a dentist who specializes in the care of clients with developmental difficulties. The UAP or the community's mental health organizations have access to information on available resources.

Laboratory Data

Information regarding clients' serum nutrient values frequently is absent or difficult to obtain. At the very least, hemoglobin and hematocrit values must be available. Ideally, serum ferritin will be determined as a measure of iron stores. Serum ferritin is the first to decrease during the early development of iron deficiency (Caliendo, 1981). Thus, while hemoglobin and hematocrit may be within normal range, iron stores may be inadequate. This proved to be the case in the subjects of Pesce et al. (1989), indicating the need to include serum ferritin measurement in the routine screening of clients whose food intake data and/or clinical examination show evidence of iron deficiency.

Serum albumin levels within normal range indicate that visceral protein stores are adequate. Somatic protein stores, however, may be low in this population (Pesce et al, 1989). Serum creatinine and midarm muscle circumference measurements are necessary to determine somatic protein stores or striated muscle mass. With underweight or evidence of muscle wasting, these tests are called for.

A disturbance in bone metabolism resulting in osteomalacia has been demonstrated in individuals receiving anticonvulsants, especially dilantin and phenobarbital (Caliendo, Booth & Moser, 1989; Latner, 1975; Pipes, 1985; Tolman, Jubiz & Sannella, 1975). It has been hypothesized that these drugs cause an increased metabolic requirement for vitamin D because they induce hepatic microsomal enzymes that interfere with the metabolism of vitamin D to its 25-hydroxymetabolite. The induction of liver enzymes by anticonvulsants shortens the biological half-life and leads to decreased levels of vitamin D despite adequate intake. This alteration in vitamin D metabolism subsequently leads to increased alkaline phosphatase levels (Latner, 1975; Pipes, 1985; Richens & Rowe, 1974). One might assume, then, that the measurement of alkaline phosphatase is necessary to screen for possible osteomalacia. However, elevated alkaline phosphatase levels may also be an indication of the increased rate of bone formation in growing children (Latner, 1975). Screening therefore becomes a complicated matter requiring a combination and sequencing of steps. In the study by Nicholson (1989), institutionalized children and adolescents with developmental disabilities were screened for possible osteomalacia by systematically looking at serum calcium, phosphorus, and alkaline phosphatase. Subjects with hypocalcemia and hypophosphatemia and high alkaline phosphatase levels were further evaluated by radiographs to detect bone demineralization. Following this protocol resulted in the detection of bone demineralization in only 2 out of the 35 residents of an Intermediate Care Facility where comprehensive interdisciplinary nutrition services are routine.

Folic acid deficiencies likewise have been noted in individuals on anticonvulsant therapy (Cimino, Epel & Cooperman, 1985; Garabedian-Ruffalo & Ruffalo, 1986). It is encouraging to note that in the study by Pesce et al. (1989), subjects on anticonvulsant regimens but having adequate nutrient intakes did not have serum folate levels significantly different from subjects not on anticonvulsants.

Hypercholesterolemia has been observed in children and adolescents with developmental disabilities (Wodarski et al., 1993). In clients treated with anticonvulsants which are known to induce choleresis, the changes have been associated with increased plasma cholesterol levels (Luoma & Sotaniemi, 1985). The mechanism is probably related to hepatic enzyme induction causing proliferation of hepatic endoplasmic reticulum and increasing protein and lipid synthesis. This involves an increase in hepatic phospholipid and protein concentration and hypertrophy of liver cells. Phenobarbital-induced choleresis has also been noted to increase the formation and pool size of bile acids, secondary to a change in Na+K+ATPase activity, which in turn may increase the abdominal absorption of cholesterol by facilitating micelle formation (Okuda & Sorrentino, 1988). This also results in an increase in total plasma cholesterol.

Serum cholesterol is influenced also by thyroxine (Fichsel & Knopfle, 1978). Medications which depress the function of the thyroid, for example Tegretol and Depakote, in turn increase levels of blood cholesterol. The total serum cholesterol level increase, however, is due to the increased HDL fraction, and high HDL decreases the risk for cardiovascular disease (Gordon & Castell, 1977). In the study by Wodarski et al. (1993), children and adolescents with developmental disabilities were observed to have elevated serum cholesterol, but these elevations did not necessarily increase their risk for coronary heart disease. The authors recommended that all children and adolescents with special health care needs be screened for abnormal serum lipid levels as well as for other known risk factors. It was further recommended that, based on the results of that screening, individualized treatment interventions should be planned and implemented according to results of the lipoprotein analysis and other pertinent aspects of the dietary and medical history.

It is evident that close monitoring of serum nutrient values is necessary to detect nutrient deficiencies or excesses in this population. Clients on medications, especially anticonvulsants, should be followed for vitamin D and calcium status. Clients with familial histories of hypercholesterolemia should be screened early and appropriate dietary management instituted when indicated. Those on anticonvulsants should have, in addition, a lipid profile to determine degree of cardiovascular risk. Decisions regarding obtaining pertinent laboratory test data will be made by the physician in collaboration with the caretaker(s). Other team members, however, contribute information useful in making the decisions (Wodarski, 1991).

Follow-Up

Follow-up and evaluation are scheduled according to the objectives of the treatment plan. Many clients with developmental disabilities receive ongoing occupational or physical therapy services. Thus, subsequent visits to follow up on diet therapy should be scheduled to coincide with these regular visits. Follow-up visits consider growth changes, laboratory values, dietary intake and reinforcement of positive changes and progress.

Case Example

Prader-Willi syndrome provides an example of a problem in which interdisciplinary treatment is indicated for its resolution. Prader-Willi syndrome (PWS), described originally in 1956 by Andrea Prader, Alexia Labhart, and Heinrich Willi, is a complex multi-system disorder that is gaining increased recognition. This disorder is manifested by marked obesity, mental deficiency, hypotonia, hypogonadism, and shortness of stature (Bray, Dahms, Swerdloff, Fiser, At-

kinson & Carrell, 1983). Behavior problems such as temper tantrums and non-compliance are common in children with PWS. These aberrations often evolve into serious personality problems by late adolescence (Otto, Sulzbacher & Worthington-Roberts, 1982).

Due to the diversity of symptoms, the treatment of PWS must incorporate knowledge and skills from a variety of areas. From a strictly disciplinary perspective, treatment would require at a minimum the services of a physician, a nutritionist, a psychologist or behavior specialist, and a physical educator. Other supportive services are enlisted to provide additional knowledge or skills necessary for formulating a full spectrum treatment plan (Wodarski et al., 1988).

Implementation of the Interdisciplinary Model

The following case example illustrates the implementation of the interdisciplinary model. The example incorporates theory-based treatment and the interdisciplinary approach to problem solution. The subject was a fifteen-year-old Caucasian female referred to an Intermediate Care Facility for the Mentally Retarded (ICFMR). She exhibited all of the characteristics considered essential for Prader-Willi syndrome diagnosis. At the individual program plan meeting, the client's interdisciplinary team, led by a QMRP (Qualified Mental Retardation Professional), documented level of functioning, needs, goals, and objectives. The physician's diagnosis included mild mental retardation, morbid obesity, compulsive eating, small hands and feet, aggressive behavior, unsocialized behavior, and hyperkinesis. The obesity/hyperphagia and behavior anomalies were addressd by the team from a problem-solving perspective. Two major goals developed for the client were: (1) to exhibit more compliant, cooperative behaviors as indicated through data recorded for the behavior management plan; and (2) to decrease weight through a calorie-controlled diet and an increase in physical activity.

The core members of the interdisciplinary team—i.e., those working most directly with the individual—were the physician, dietitian, psychologist, physical educator, and social worker. These professionals, utilizing the skills and perspectives provided by their training and experience, guided the development of an individual program plan to be carried out by themselves and other members of the team. Information was pooled and reviewed by the team. Team members then implemented the program facets for which they were assigned responsibility. Periodic meetings provided the opportunity to review the client's needs and the appropriateness of the program in light of the progress. The principles which guided the development of the diet and exercise regimens, behavior modification programming, and family support components represented the state of the art, according to the practice literature (see Wodarski et al., 1988).

Several other disciplines provided supportive services. Education staff contributed programming to increase self-help and socialization skills. Teachers worked with the dietitian to develop lesson plans that incorporated mathematical concepts to teach the differences between high and low calorie foods and portion sizes, and language concepts to teach recipe interpretation. Nutrition concepts were reinforced in art education classes where the client made collages of pictures of high- and low-calorie foods and various forms of physical activity. Likewise, the client worked with various media to produce pictures or models of healthy foods or meals. In music therapy, staff engaged the client in physical activities set to music and taught food concepts through song and other music accompaniment. The activity therapist emphasized group as well as individual activities. The client was taken into the community as much as possible to train in appropriate socialization skills. These activities underscored the need to improve communication and community integration.

In addition to providing direct and support services, the aforementioned discipline staff functioned frequently in a transdisciplinary capacity. In this approach to service, professionals maintained their credentialed accountability but shared specialized skills with, and released their intervention roles to, facilitators who implemented the intervention. In the case example, the transdisciplinary approach is exemplified by the assumption of duties from the psychologist by the classroom teacher and physical educator, who carried out the behavior management program in the classroom and gymnasium and on recreational outings. Likewise, dormitory staff enhanced the programming specified by the occupational and physical therapists through engaging the client in appropriate activities during nontreatment hours. The family served as perhaps the ultimate example of the transdisciplinary process, as they were responsible for virtually all elements of programming in the home and community environments.

According to data collected, the client made considerable progress following her admission to the ICFMR. Non-compliant behavior decreased from a 50% weekly average to a 2% weekly average in three months. Furthermore, the client's weight decreased from 175.5 pounds upon admission to 161.5 pounds after six months of treatment intervention.

In the foregoing example, the obesity/hyperphagia and behavior anomalies were addressed from a problem-solving perspective. Goals (i.e., match energy intake to energy output and increase compliance) were determined jointly by the client's interdisciplinary case management team. The expertise of each team member was drawn upon in the development and implementation of a comprehensive treatment program. Coordination of all aspects of the program was achieved through regularly scheduled team meetings and through informal channels of communication which exist ideally in interdisciplinary settings.

Interdisciplinary treatment, however, does not require an institutional or clinical setting to function. Communication among disciplines is the vital component. Professionals are responsible for the identification of therapeutic needs and for seeking out staff/persons capable of providing services to meet those needs. Interdisciplinary cooperation involves the coordination of these services in an efficacious and cost effective manner.

In many instances professional services must be solicited from a variety of sources including individual practitioners, private and state operated agencies, and community clinics. The interdisciplinary process in these cases must still provide for the pooling, review and evaluation of individual practitioners' reports. A comprehensive evaluation would identify the client's needs and establish goals and objectives for meeting them. When possible, face-to-face meetings of core team members is desirable, but telephone conferences and written correspondence may suffice.

Interdisciplinary case management provides many advantages to the practitioner as well as to the client. A major benefit is the opportunity for ongoing education and role expansion of team members. Face-to-face contact with representatives of other disciplines on a problem-solving team provides the opportunity to learn what the disciplines may contribute. Thus each team member increases awareness of services and methodologies and of the interdisciplinary

process (Accreditation Council for Facilities for the Mentally Retarded, 1977). Dietitians, along with other specialists, have much to gain from the process.

Summary

Poor nutritional status is not necessarily concomitant with developmental disabilities. Results of the Pesce et al. study (1989) of the nutritional status of children and adolescents with developmental disabilities suggest that clients who received comprehensive interdisciplinary nutritional services were, in general, adequately nourished and had nutrient intakes that met the RDA. Furthermore, there is evidence that improvements in growth, in terms of height and weight, occur where comprehensive nutritional intervention is provided in an interdisciplinary setting (Nicholson, 1989). Thus, it appears that nutritional problems may be eliminated or ameliorated when anomalies common to developmental disabilities are recognized and remediated by an interdisciplinary team that includes the disciplines of medicine, dietetics, psychology, occupational therapy and other support services. In the study by Pesce et al. (1989), clients received comprehensive nutrition-related services. Moreover, there was consistent application within this group of interdisciplinary case management in diagnosis, treatment planning, implementation of plans, and evaluation. According to the interdisciplinary approach to case management, factors which place a resident at risk for nutritional deficiencies are identified by an interdisciplinary team, and appropriate interventions are planned to prevent and/or ameliorate problems. A variety of professionl services are coordinated in a problem-oriented approach to case management.

References

Accreditation Council for Facilities for the Mentally Retarded (1977). *Standards for Residential Facilities for the Mentally Retarded*. Chicago, IL: Joint Commission on Accreditation of Hospitals.

American Dietetic Association (1981). Infant and child nutrition: Concerns regarding the developmentally disabled. A statement by the American Dietetic Association. *Journal of the American Dietetic Association, 78*, 443-448.

American Dietetic Association (1983). Conceptual framework for the profession of dietetics. *ADA Courier, 22*(1), 5.

American Dietetic Association (1988). *The American Dietetic Association*. Chicago, IL: Author.

American Dietetic Association (1993). Licensure of dietitians and nutritionists. *Journal of the American Dietetic Association, 93*, 272.

American Society for Parenteral and Enteral Nutrition (1983). *Nutritional assessment of the handicapped child*. Rockville, MD: Author.

Bray, G.A., Dahms, W.T., Swerdloff, R.S., Fiser, R.H., Atkinson, R.L., & Carrell, R.E. (1983). The Prader-Willi syndrome: A study of 40 patients and a review of the literature. *Medicine, 62*, 59-80.

Caliendo, M.A., Booth, G., & Moser, P. (1981). Iron intakes and serum ferritin levels in developmentally delayed children. *Journal of the American Dietetic Association, 81*, 401-406.

Cimino, J., Epel, R., & Cooperman, J.M. (1985). Effect of diet on vitamin deficiencies in retarded individuals receiving drugs. *Drug-Nutrient Interactions, 3*, 201-204.

Culley, W.J., Goyal, J., Jolly, D.H., & Mertz, E.T. (1965). Caloric intake of children with Down's syndrome. *Journal of Pediatrics, 66*, 772-775.

Ekvall, S.W. (1993). Introduction to chronic diseases and developmental disorders. In S. W. Ekvall (Ed.). *Pediatric nutrition in chronic diseases and developmental disorders* (pp. 4-5). New York: Oxford University Press.

Fichsel, H., & Knopfel, G. (1978). Effects of anticonvulsant drugs on thyroid hormones in epileptic children. *Epilepsia, 19*, 323-336.

Finnie, N.R. (1970). *Handling the young cerebral palsied child at home*. New York: Dutton.

Garabedian-Ruffalo, S.M., & Ruffalo, R.L. (1986). Drug and nutrient interactions. *American Family Physician, 33*, 165-174.

Gordon, R.A., & Castell, W.P. (1977). High density lipoprotein as a protective factor against coronary heart disease. *American Journal of Medicine, 62*, 707-714.

Kalisz, K., & Ekvall, S. (1984). A nutritional interview for clients with developmental disorders. *Mental Retardation, 22*, 279-288.

Latner, A. (1975). *Clinical biochemistry*. Philadelphia, PA: W.B. Saunders.

Luoma, P.V., & Sotaniemi, E.A. (1985). Serum low-density lipoprotein and high-density lipoprotein cholesterol and liver size in subjects on drugs inducing hepatic macrosomal enzymes. *European Journal of Clinical Pharmacology, 28*, 615-618.

Nicholson, K. (1989). *Skeletal growth in mentally retarded children*. Unpublished master's thesis. Athens, GA: University of Georgia.

Okuda, J., & Sorrentino, D. (1988). Bile acid secretion and pool size during phenobarbital induced hypercholeresis. *Proceedings of the Society for Experimental Biology and Medicine, 197*, 202-208.

Otto, P.L., Sulzbacher, S.I., & Worthington-Roberts, B.S. (1982). Sucrose-induced behavior changes of persons with Prader-Willi syndrome. *American Journal of Mental Deficiency, 86*, 335-341.

Palmer, S., & Ekvall, S. (1978). *Pediatric nutrition in developmental disorders.* Springfield, IL: Charles C Thomas.

Pesce, K.A., Wodarski, L.A. & Wang, M. (1989) Nutritional status of institutionalized children and adolescents with developmental disabilities. *Research in Developmental Disabilities, 10*, 33-52.

Pipes, P.L. (1985). *Nutrition in infancy and childhood* (3rd ed.). St. Louis, MO: Times Mirror/Mosby.

Richens, A & Rowe, D.J. (1974). Disturbances of calcium metabolism by anticonvulsant drugs. *British Medical Journal, 4*, 73-76.

Smith, M.A.H. (1993). Nutritional assessment for persons with developmental disabilities. *Topics in Clinical Nutrition, 8*(4), 7-49.

Springer, N.S. (1982). *Nutrition casebook on developmental disabilities.* Syracuse, NY: Syracuse University Press.

Tolman, K.B., Jubiz, W., & Sannella, J.J. (1975). Osteomalacia associated with anticonvulsant therapy in mentally retarded children. *Pediatrics, 56*, 45-51.

Wodarski, L.A. (1985). Nutrition intervention in developmental disabilities: An interdisciplinary approach. *Journal of the American Dietetic Association, 85*, 218-221.

Wodarski, L.A. (1991). An interdisciplinary nutrition assessment and intervention protocol for children with disabilities. *Journal of the American Dietetic Association, 90*, 1563-1570.

Wodarski, L.A., Bundschuh, E., & Forbus, W.R. (1988). Interdisciplinary case management: A model for intervention. *Journal of the American Dietetic Association, 88*, 332-335.

Wodarski, L.A., McMillian, C., & Doshi, N. (1993). Hypercholesterolemia in developmental disabilities. *Topics in Clinical Nutrition, 8*(4), 66-74.

10

Occupational Therapy

Rita R. Hohlstein, M.S., O.T.R., & Rae E. Sprague, M.S., O.T.R.

The fundamental concern of occupational therapists is the development and maintenance of an individual's capacity to perform the tasks and roles that are essential to productive living, self-determination, and mastery of the environment.

> Occupational therapy is a profession which incorporates both art and science to help direct an individual's participation in selected tasks to restore, reinforce, and enhance performance; facilitate learning of those skills and functions essential for adaption and productivity; diminish or correct pathology; and promote and maintain health (American Occupational Therapy Association, 1991a, p. 1076).

The term "occupation" does not relate specifically to employment. Instead, this term has a much broader meaning and relates to an individual's goal-directed use of time, energy, interest, and attention.

Occupational therapy shares interests and skills with many other professions. The feature which distinguishes it from related fields is a focus on functional activity. Occupational therapists work to support people of all ages, with many different disabilities, to accomplish the activities which are meaningful to them. In order to structure appropriate interventions, the occupational therapist must have a holistic understanding of the individual person, including personal desires, values, and cultural factors.

Occupational therapists serve a diverse constituency and work to provide supports and services to people with a wide range of disabilities across the entire life span. For example, infants and young children are served by occupational therapists at neonatal intensive care units, high risk follow-up clinics, diagnostic and treatment clinics, and home- or center-based early intervention programs. Children and adolescents receive services or supports in schools, hospitals, specialty diagnostic and treatment clinics or programs, and community health care clinics or programs. Adults and aging persons may receive supports or services from occupational therapists at specialty clinics, hospitals, residential facilities, nursing homes, or their place of employment.

Most occupational therapists provide services and supports as a member of an interdisciplinary or multidisciplinary team. However, some OTs are private practitioners and work independently on specific problems with their clients. Regardless of the settings, the services and supports provided by OTs focus on one of three approaches:

1. improving the functional ability of a person,
2. providing adaptive equipment or assistive technology,
3. adapting or modifying the environment to enhance personal functioning.

The first approach, improving personal ability, focuses on assisting the individual in completing functional activities. Supports or services to assist a person to accomplish tasks include physical improvements such as increasing strength, range of motion, coordination, dexterity, fine or gross motor skills, and perceptual-motor skills. Improving personal ability also includes interventions that are aimed at increasing interpersonal skills, such as interpersonal interactive skills and communication.

Occupational therapists also provide adaptive equipment or assistive technology supports and services. These interventions require that the OT be able to analyze the factors which are impeding function and to identify the most logical and effective way to provide assistance. Assistive technology ranges from low technology, which is simple and frequently inexpensive, to high technology, which is complex and usually quite costly. Although there is a temptation to identify the most advanced technology available, people are often more successful using the most basic and simple technology. For example, a person who requires augmentative communication and needs to speak before groups of people will probably want and need to use a voice synthesizer. When communicating on a more personal level, a communication board may be faster and more effective. The most advanced equipment is not necessarily the best solution for every person or situation.

Interventions are also structured to improve personal abilities by adapting the physical or human environment. Physical modifications may include rearranging a closet in the home or locker at school so a person can dress independently. Modifications in the human environment can also improve functioning ability. An example of this type of intervention is to work with a parent to facilitate a son's or daughter's self-care skills instead of having the parent perform the tasks.

Education and Training Requirements

The official accrediting agency for entry-level educational programs is the American Occupational Therapy Association (AOTA). This organization works in collaboration with the Committee on Allied Health Education and Accreditation of the American Medical Association. For accreditation to educate entry-level occupational therapists, a college or university must document an ability to provide appropriate didactic and clinical instruction (American Occupational Therapy Association, 1991b).

The curriculum for an OT degree includes a liberal arts base, specialized course content, and a practical component. Specific requirements for the content of occupational therapy educational programs include biological, behavioral, and health sciences; occupational therapy theory and practice; management of occupational therapy services; research; professional ethics; and fieldwork education. Fieldwork is a crucial component of an occupational therapist's education and must include opportunities for professional role modeling and for carrying out professional responsibilities under supervision. All occupational therapy programs have a beginning and advanced level for their fieldwork components.

There are three ways to acquire the credentials for entry-level practice in occupational therapy. The majority of therapists prepare to enter the field by completing baccalaureate degree programs. However, people who already have a baccalaureate degree in another field may choose to complete a certificate program to fulfill the academic requirements. Others choose to complete a professional or entry-level master's program.

In addition to the baccalaureate (entry) level, there are two other levels in occupational therapy. It is possible to fulfill the requirements to become an occupational therapy assistant (OTA) through associate degree programs or through certificate programs. These programs have more emphasis on intervention than on evaluation, and the educational programs place a heavy emphasis on clinical fieldwork.

Master's degree programs and doctoral degree programs in occupational therapy are also available. Because these are not required to enter the profession or to practice, the AOTA is not involved in the accreditation process. These programs are accredited or approved by the university or college offering them.

Licensure, Certification and Continuing Education

The profession of occupational therapy is regulated by jurisdiction, meaning states, districts (District of Columbia), or commonwealths (Puerto Rico). These regulations define and regulate entry-level competency for professional practice. Most jurisdictions utilize licensure to regulate practice; however, some use certification, title control, or registration for regulation purposes. Licensure prohibits unlicensed individuals from practicing occupational therapy, whereas the other forms of regula-

tion do not prevent individuals from providing services under different titles. Most jurisdictions mandate continuing education to maintain licensure or certification, but the amount and documentation of the continuing education required varies.

Occupational therapists can also receive national certification through the American Occupational Therapy Certification Board (AOTCB). This is voluntary, not a legal requirement for practice unless so designated by jurisdiction. The purpose of the AOTCB is to protect the interest and welfare of the general public by establishing high standards for certification, developing valid and reliable certification examinations, and investigating and taking disciplinary actions against individuals who are either unethical, impaired, or incompetent. Many jurisdictions use the AOTCB certification examination as one of the criteria for regulation.

Additionally, occupational therapists who work in developmental disabilities can qualify for optional specialty certifications. The AOTA has developed and administers a Specialty Certification in Pediatrics. Some of the additional certifications that occupational therapists earn include those in Sensory Integration (SI), Neurodevelopmental Therapy (NDT), and mental retardation (Qualified Mental Retardation Professional, QMRP).

Contributions to Interdisciplinary Practice

The contributions of occupational therapy to interdisciplinary practice for persons with developmental disabilities involve supporting people in the functional activities which are needed and desired to lead satisfying and productive lives. Occupational therapists have traditionally worked in collaboration with families and other professionals to understand the needs and wants of people with developmental disabilities and to design appropriate intervention plans. These include activities of daily living, self-care skills, and adaptive skills or behaviors. In all instances, the abilities are those needed to perform the basic or fundamental tasks in which people engage for self-care, work, and leisure pursuits. These abilities are necessary for people to fulfill their roles in life in a way that is self-satisfying.

All individuals have several roles which change with age and life transitions. Examples of roles include the following: student, worker/volunteer, recreator/player, personal maintainer, supervisor, caregiver, employer, citizen/neighbor, family member, friend/companion, consumer. Associated with each role are underlying activities, skills, and components. For example, the student role is based on a need or desire to learn and to engage in relevant student activities. The skills needed to be a student include: being able to get to and from school and maneuvering around the school buildings and campus; participation in classes; studying in school or at home; using the tools of school, which may include writing utensils, computers, books, and notebooks; and using special equipment for science, art, or music. To develop these skills, one needs certain cognitive, sensory, neuromuscular, psychological, and social abilities.

Role integration occurs when an individual functions comfortably in all of his or her life roles and achieves a balance between those roles. In the beginning phases of work with an OT, a person with a developmental disability must determine the roles he or she wishes to fulfill. The task of an occupational therapist is to work with the person with developmental disabilities and with other members of the interdisciplinary team to determine which activities, skills, and components can be influenced in order to support the individual in his or her chosen roles. If an individual is intrinsically unable to perform the needed activities to fulfill these roles, the occupational therapist may help to determine what assistive technology, environmental modifications, or human supports can be provided.

The contributions of occupational therapists to research are often marked by a collaborative and interdisciplinary nature. The basic research of occupational therapists ranges from using animal models to study the effects of prenatal factors, such as stress and alcohol exposure, on fetal development and infant behavior (Schneider, 1992) to the systematic study of the human as an occupational being who is engaged in culturally and personally meaningful activities (Clark, PArham, Carlson, Frank, Jackson, Pierce, Wolfe, & Zemke, 1991). The clinical or applied research done by occupational therapists is equally broad. For example, some therapists work with other team members to investigate the ability of individuals with specific disabilities to accomplish tasks such as safe driving (Galski, Bruno, & Ehle, 1992). Others examine the effects of specific interventions on persons with specific disabilities (Reisman, 1993).

Assessment

Occupational therapists employ a variety of assessment methods and instruments. Although the philosophy of occupational therapy has always been client-centered and holistic, the realities of current health care may force therapists, and other members of interdisciplinary teams, to mainly address specific problems of disease or disability. To construct an integrated picture of an individual's functioning, both qualitative and quantitative measures are used.

Within an interdisciplinary assessment team, the role of an occupational therapist may vary greatly from setting to setting. Because different disciplines have overlapping areas of expertise, each ID team decides which discipline should assess specific areas. For example, depending on the setting and expertise of the team members, a feeding evaluation may be done by an occupational therapist, a speech and language clinician, a nutritionist, a nurse, or any combination of these professionals. Occupational therapists use a wide variety of screening instruments and standardized and non-standardized instruments in their assessment of individuals with developmental disabilities.

In a traditional approach to assessment, a therapist asks specific questions, elicits specific behaviors or responses, makes detailed observations and records findings, scores and computes results, and then makes interpretations.

Some of the formal screening instruments used by occupational therapists include the Denver Developmental Screening Test (Frankenburg & Dodds, 1990), the Miller Assessment for Preschoolers (Miller, 1988), the Hawaii Early Learning Profile (HELP) (Furuno, O'Reilly, Hosaka, Inatsuka, Allman & Zeisloft, 1979), the Milani-Comparetti and Gidoni Motor Development Screening Test (Milani-Comparetti & Gidoni, 1977), and the Quick Neurological Screening Test (Mutti, Sterling & Spalding, 1978). Many therapists have developed informal clinical screening tests to help identify individuals who require comprehensive assessments.

The formal assessments used by occupational therapists serve multiple purposes. Some may examine specific components that underlie function, while others may evaluate adaptive behavior or overall development. Some of the instruments used to evaluate specific areas of function include the Bruininks-Oseretsky Test of Motor Proficiency (Bruininks, 1978), the child and adult versions of the Motor-Free Visual Perception Test (Colarusso & Hammill, 1972), the Peabody Developmental Motor Scales (Folio & Fewell, 1983), the Sensory Integration and Praxis Tests (Ayres, 1989), the Adult Skills Evaluation Survey (Lowe, 1990), and the Vocational Adaptation Rating Scales (Malgady & Barcher, 1980). Examples of the instruments used to assess development include the Minnesota Child Development Inventory (MCDI) (Ireton & Thwing, 1974), the Bayley Scales of Infant Development, second edition (Bayley, 1993), the Developmental Profile II (Alpern, Boll, & Sheafer, 1980), Lindner's Transdisciplinary Play-Based Assessment (Lindner, 1990), and the Vineland Adaptive Behavior Scales (Sparrow, Dalla & Cicchetti, 1984).

Computer technology has also been used in functional assessment processes. A computerized functional assessment tool, OT FACT (Smith, 1993), provides an innovative way to look at the overall functioning of individuals. OT FACT represents a significant contribution to the interdisciplinary understanding of people with developmental disabilities and provides new ways to think about function. This tool utilizes a hierarchial model to examine:

a) role integration,
b) activities involved in the performance of those roles,
c) the skills needed to complete the activities, and
d) the underlying components of the skills.

While OT FACT does not change any evaluation procedures, the program organizes data collection to give a clear and comprehensive understanding of a person's functional abilities.

Computerized assessment procedures such as OT FACT have expanded the ways that functional performance data can be collected and used. This computerized interdisciplinary assessment, directed by occupational therapists, provides multiple informant perceptions of performance and environmentally sensitive evaluations.

Another approach to assessment is through an ethnographic assessment process. This type of assessment requires that therapists examine a person's experience—relative to a specific disease, disability, or injury—in the context of that person's culture. Ethnographic assessment enables occupational therapists to be more sensitive to a client's perceptions and priorities (Spencer, Krefting, & Mattingly, 1993). Occupational therapists who use an ethnographic assessment process focus either on a specific role and associated tasks, or on the total role set of an individual. Assessments are done with a person in the various environments in which she or he functions. As part of this process, the therapist must describe how specific routines or tasks are usually accomplished, how routines are completed, the other individuals who are involved, and the value of the tasks performed. The OT must also analyze the individual's performance and make recommendations for changes.

Interventions

Occupational therapy interventions focus on different aspects of functional difficulties. Intervention may include working to improve the intrinsic skills and abilities of an individual, adaptation to the physical environment, or modifications in the human environment or support system. Specific intervention approaches in each of these three domains will be discussed.

The contributions of the occupational therapist to intrinsic skill development encompasses multiple theoretical bases. Intervention approaches can be categorized as physical or neurobiological; sensory-motor or sensory-integrative; adaptive or self-care; and behavioral. Most neurobiological treatment implemented by therapists is based

on the work of Margaret Rood (1956) or Karl and Berta Bobath (Bobath & Bobath, 1972). Rood was concerned with the effects of sensory inputs and motor responses on the autonomic resting base of individuals. From the beginning of her work, Rood stressed the importance of linking all therapeutic input to functional activity. Therapists using Rood's approach might use gentle rocking, neutral warmth, or inversion to calm a person or to get her or him to function more on the parasympathetic side of the autonomic nervous system. The therapist might also use stretches or resistance exercises to facilitate stability around the proximal joints while a child is playing with a toy.

The Bobaths based much of their treatment on the tenet that normal movement both depends upon, and results in, the generation of normal sensory feedback (Fisher, Murray & Bundy, 1991). They advocated the use of physical handling to give appropriate input to individuals with motor dysfunction. They initially relied heavily upon reflex inhibiting patterns but evolved to focus on eliciting automatic, goal-directed movement patterns. Their therapeutic approach also emphasized posture and the quality of movement. Treatment could include facilitating weight shifting and trunk rotation while a child is engaged in play activities. The ultimate goal is for the therapist to be able to withdraw physical support and have the client be able to move appropriately and spontaneously.

Sensory integrative treatment uses controlled sensory stimulation in the context of meaningful, self-directed activities to elicit adaptive behaviors (Ayers, 1972). The emphasis of sensory integration treatment is on the integration of vestibular-proprioceptive and tactile sensory input, not just on specific motor responses. This is done in order to improve motor planning and higher-level functioning. Examples of activities that may be used in sensory integration include swinging on bolsters suspended from the ceiling, maneuvering through a simple to complex sensorimotor maze, or applying tactile stimulation with a rough cloth or surgical scrub brush.

The adaptive behavior treatment approach is used to teach the skills needed for self-care, work, or play. To facilitate task success, activities are analyzed and broken down into small segments or component parts. Chaining is the process of sequentially teaching the steps or components for skills development. This type of approach is essential in many occupational therapy programs to increase intrinsic abilities to accomplish tasks. Behavioral theory forms the basis for some of the techniques that therapists employ to support people with developmental disabilities. Natural reinforcers such as smiles, positive comments, and food are often used to increase or maintain desirable behaviors. Ignoring negative behaviors while focusing attention on desirable behaviors is also used.

The contributions of occupational therapists related to adaptations of the physical environment fall under the category of assistive technology. According to the Technology-Related Assistance for Individuals with Disabilities Act of 1988 (Public Law 100-407), assistive technology devices are defined as "any item, piece of equipment, or product system, whether acquired commercially off the shelf, modified, or customized, that is used to increase, maintain, or improve functional capabilities of individuals with disabilities." Occupational therapists frequently work with rehabilitation engineers, physical therapists, physicians, educators, and speech and language clinicians to evaluate an individual's need for and ability to use technologically advanced equipment. This can range from basic or low technology to complex or high technology. Examples of adaptive equip-

ment (low technology) that occupational therapists may recommend include built-up handles for eating utensils, plates or bowls with raised edges to ease scooping of food; special writing tools; keyboard guards; velcro closures for shoes, pants and shirts; and adapted bathing or toileting equipment. Technologically advanced equipment that may be considered for people with developmental disabilities includes equipment for seating and positioning; powered mobility; computer access (alternative keyboards, special software, graphical user interfaces); reading devices; page turners; and switch-activated toys.

The application of technology is not an end in itself but must be considered part of an ongoing therapeutic process. Technology and the new tools it offers can be used to simplify work and to extend human performance. However, in order to be helpful, technology must be properly installed and maintained, and the person using it must be supported and monitored across time.

An occupational therapist may work with an interdisciplinary team to recommend modifications in the human environment, or in the way that assistance is provided, to enable the individual with developmental disabilities to accomplish necessary or desired tasks. For example, an individual with severe physical limitations may be able to dress herself, but this process may take so much energy and time that it interferes with the other activities that she wants to do. Therefore, she may decide that an attendant should do the majority of the dressing on school or work days, but on other days the person will do her own dressing with only minimal assistance.

Another way that the environment is being changed to support people concerns individuals with challenging behaviors. In the past, when an individual with developmental disabilities presented challenging behaviors (previously called disruptive or negative behaviors), a behavior modification program would have been developed to attempt to change the person. Occupational therapists are now working as part of interdisciplinary teams to redefine the issues and the way that behaviors are viewed. Utilizing the work of Lovett (1985), Perske and Perske (1988), Mount, Beeman and Ducharme (1988), and O'Brien (1990), professionals and family members working to support people with challenging behaviors now look at the environmental and the human precursors to these behaviors in order to construct safe, supportive environments and to facilitate positive relationships (White, 1992).

Case Example

History

Jamie is a 13-year-old boy with a diagnosis of autism. During a recent telephone interview, his mother was asked to describe how and when she first knew Jamie had problems, his strengths and areas of difficulty, and the contributions of occupational therapy to his interdisciplinary treatment. The information obtained from this interview, combined with data from the medical records, was used to construct this case study.

Jamie's mother said that he was a difficult, irritable baby who needed to be held and rocked much of the time. He never rested easily and was 4 years old before he slept through the night. As a young infant, all of Jamie's interactions were intense, and he closely watched everything and everybody. Initial contacts with physicians left his parents feeling frustrated because their main concerns were not addressed nor were they given specific advice or help. When Jamie was not walking at 18 months, the family was referred to an orthopedist. X-rays were taken, and his parents were told that Jamie's bones structure was unremarkable. He began walking at 19 months.

In describing Jamie's current status, his mother said that he has a great personality, that he truly likes people, but that he has not always known how to relate to others. She also said that he has a great memory, especially for baseball trivia and world politics. These topics have provided him a link to the outside world. Jamie is also strongly motivated to cope with the difficulties he encounters and to learn new things. He never gives up on tasks and works much harder than his classmates to be successful. Although he has a great visual memory, his fine motor skills and coordination are poor, which made elementary school difficult for him. With additional instruction, reading has become one of his strengths; however, math continues to be a challenge.

During Jamie's childhood years, his mother kept looking for resources to support the family. She was referred to the Wisconsin University Affiliated Program (UAP) when he was six. The UAP interdisciplinary assessment team was composed of professionals from developmental pediatrics, clinical genetics, occupational therapy, speech and language, special education, and child psychiatry. Jamie was diagnosed with autism, attention deficit hyperactivity disorder (ADHD), hypotonia with hyperextensible joints, and developmental delays. Significant phonological errors and underdeveloped motor skills were noted. His motor skills were influenced by difficulties with motor planning, poor proximal stability and visual motor integration, and difficulties with modulation of sensory information.

Treatment Recommendations

The family and the professionals from the UAP assessment team developed a plan to support Jamie's full inclusion in their home community. Most of Jamie's educational intervention was to be implemented by personnel at his neighborhood school; however, the parents requested that this be supplemented by direct treatment, consultation, and support by UAP and community staff. A UAP speech and language clinician was to provide therapy with an emphasis on improving his pronunciation of sounds and his communication. A child psychiatrist was to provide consultation and support to the parents regarding pharmacological issues, the management of anxiety and challenging behaviors, and the development of interpersonal skills. A reading specialist in the community was to work with Jamie on developing reading skills. A UAP occupational therapist was to provide treatment for Jamie's sensorimotor delays and dysfunction. The OT would also provide treatment to Jamie and consultation and support to his parents and school personnel related to the functional capabilities Jamie needed to develop for his home and school activities. Jamie also needed a full-time educational aide to help with his social interactions, to help alleviate his anxiety, and to help him function in the school environment. His parents would continue to function as the service coordinators for Jamie and their family, calling upon professionals for support and consultation as needed.

Because of Jamie's complex clinical picture, the interdisciplinary team working with him needed to incorporate components of developmental, behavioral, neurobiological, and sensory integrative approaches into his intervention plan. The UAP occupational therapist focused on the immediate concerns and challenges identified by Jamie, his parents, and school personnel, and on the formal and clinical assessment findings as the basis for treatment. She developed incremental components for each sensory integration activity or func-

tional skill Jamie needed to learn. By breaking down all activities into small steps, Jamie's anxiety level would be minimized and some degree of success could be guaranteed. She established a relationship of trust with both Jamie and his parents so that the family could work on treatment activities but also enjoy their accomplishments and each other. This component was especially important to the family because they had experienced many frustrating periods and had missed chances to celebrate the achievements taking place in their family.

As a member of the treatment team, the initial focus of the UAP occupational therapist was to help Jamie move better. Activities were planned to develop better stability and control of his neck, trunk, hips, and shoulders; to increase his endurance for activity; to improve his awareness of where his head, trunk, and extremities were in space; and to improve his ability to plan and carry out movements in the proper sequence. The interventive approach was accomplished through combined neurobiological and sensory integration strategies, including experiences on swinging equipment; balancing on uneven and moving surfaces; and walking, jumping, and changing positions on a trampoline to provide input to vestibular and proprioceptive receptors in the inner ear, muscles, and joints. Weights were used to increase proprioceptive input, facilitate proximal stability, and increase endurance. Eye-hand coordination demands were incorporated into wholebody activities by asking Jamie to throw a ball at a target while balancing on a moving surface or to knock down bowling pins. Many of the gross motor activities involved challenging balance skills, which included complex planning and sequencing of movements on Jamie's part.

Sensory-integrative treatment has been advanced as an approach to improve praxis or motor planning (Fisher et al., 1991). The ABA design used to evaluate this treatment was based on work described by Ottenbacher (1986). To measure the effects, Jamie was asked to trace around a maze. The amount of time Jamie needed to complete the maze while staying within the lines was recorded in seconds. In order to determine the effect of sensory integration treatment on his ability to do a paper and pencil motor planning task, data were collected at ten different times prior to beginning treatment, during the implementation, and after treatment had been withdrawn. The amount of time that it took Jamie to complete the maze with the required level of accuracy decreased during the treatment phase and leveled off when treatment was withdrawn (see Figure 10-1). The mean time for completing the maze was 133 seconds at baseline, 101 seconds during treatment, and 98 seconds at post-treatment. It was determined that the sensory integration treatment was effective, because his performance time was significantly longer at baseline than at the post treatment measure.

Other goals that were established by Jamie, his family, and school personnel addressed his functional abilities. Some of the activities that needed to be enhanced were writing, cutting, zipping, tying shoes, coloring, ball playing, swallowing pills, bike riding, regulating the water temperature in the bathroom, and drying his hands. Although the shoe-tying was one of the first requests, Jamie did not accomplish this task until right before he entered sixth grade. He and the OT worked on this goal intermittently over the years, but at times it became too frustrating and anxiety-producing. At this point, the shoe-tying goal was suspended and they decided to continue to use shoes with velcro closing until later.

Another functional goal which presented challenges for Jamie was swallowing pills. Jamie's inability to take pills presented significant problems, since many medications are unavailable in liquid form and are difficult to break down and conceal in food. Because he was afraid of choking, Jamie became extremely anxious about swallowing pills. The UAP occupational therapist assisted Jamie to break up this difficult task into successive steps. He was first taught how to move and control the position of objects in his mouth, then how to spit objects from his mouth, before the actual swallowing of pills was attempted.

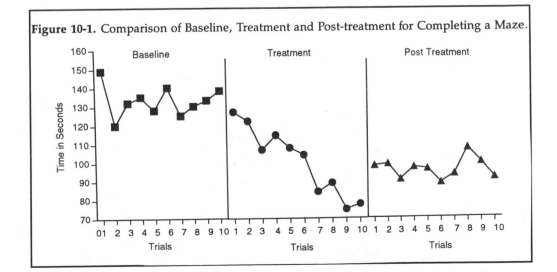

Figure 10-1. Comparison of Baseline, Treatment and Post-treatment for Completing a Maze.

The treatment plan included high-level skill acquisition to facilitate Jamie's educational program. Long before Jamie was expected to use computers in school, the UAP occupational therapist began teaching him keyboarding. The goal was to have these skills ready and available when he needed them.

Social interaction goals were included in all parts of the treatment process and were reinforced by all members of the interdisciplinary team. All of the professionals and his family members consulted and worked with each other to support Jamie in broadening the topics of his conversations, expanding his interactions with other people, establishing trust in new people, and discussing alternative ways to handle his social situations with peers. Collaboration between service providers was an inherent part of this process. For example, both the school and UAP therapists foreshadowed all art and sewing activities before they were presented in class. This enabled Jamie to learn the new activities ahead of time and to participate with his class on each activity.

Part of the intervention plan included an ongoing assessment process to evaluate progress. OT FACT was used shortly after Jamie had started sixth grade to compare perceptions about his performance, to reinventory the level and type of support needed, and to identify ongoing or new areas for intervention. Table 10-1 presents the results of a comparison of Jamie's, his mother's, and the UAP occupational therapist's perceptions of his intrinsic functional performance using OT FACT Levels I and II. The findings at this point in the treatment process resulted in clarification of some skills that could benefit from additional work. For example, the occupational therapist did not realize that Jamie does not identify a need to blow his nose, does not grasp his nose with a handkerchief, or wipe adequately. She also learned that Jamie did not go to the neighborhood grocery store, did not prepare any snacks for himself when he came home after school, and did not independently use any public transportation. A discussion between the OT, Jamie, and his family led to changes in the occupational therapy intervention plan to include work in Jamie's home and at the neighborhood store.

Perceptions were also compared on a

Table 1

Perceptions of Functional Performance, OT FACT Levels I & II				
Category	**Definition**	**Respondent**		
		Jamie	Mother	OTR
I. Role Integration	Functions appropriately in all life roles and balances roles in unified life activity. Does not demonstrate overemphasis or skill in some roles to the deficit of others.	100%	75%	58%
II. Activities of Performance	Personal Care and occupational role related activities	97%	88%	86%

breakdown of education-specific activities and skills (see Table 10-2). Jamie's education aide sees herself as contributing much more to his performance than do either Jamie or his mother. Although Jamie is capable of navigating the school building independently, the sensory overload which occurs when large numbers of students are in the halls makes him anxious. Frequently he waits for the aide to accompany him to different rooms.

Other examples indicate diverging perceptions on Jamie's abilities within the educational context. The trend in the data suggests that Jamie has the highest perception regarding his function in school. His

Table 2

Perceptions of Functional Performance — Education-Specific

Category	Definition	Jamie	Mother	Aide
a. Indicates Need	Demonstrates cognitive awareness of need/desire for further education	50%	100%	100%
b. Studentship Acquisition Activities	Accepts the student role; applies to educational programs, registers, plans a course of study	n/a	n/a	n/a
c. Studentship Maintenance Activities	Attends educational activities regularly and on time; studies; performs homework; gets along with peers and instructors; physically negotiates campus	100%	92%	47%
d. Mobility	Negotiates educational	100%	100%	50%
e. Participate	Attends activities on time, regularly	100%	100%	100%
f. Stores materials	Manages personal space and storage (lockers)	100%	0%	50%
g. Records information	Takes notes/records important information	100%	50%	0%
h. Studies	Organizes studies, completes assignments (in class, homework)	100%	100%	33%
i. Tools, supplies	Manages tools, supplies and equipment necessary for learning activities	100%	100%	50%
j. Non-classroom	Participates in activities across settings in school (cafeteria, hallway, playground)	100%	100%	50%

mother has varying perceptions, her lowest perception being of Jamie's ability to record information at school (take notes) and store material (manage his locker). The educational aid has the lowest overall perception of his performance. Her highest rating of Jamie was in participation, such as attending classes punctually and regularly. A comparison of the overall perceptions of Jamie, his mother, and his educational aide are presented in Figure 10-2.

The use of OT FACT clarified where the differences of opinion existed and provided a format for discussing the differing perceptions. It also identified those areas where additional work needed to be done to support Jamie's full inclusion in his school and community. Finally, it provided information related to the effectiveness of the assistive technology and human supports now being incorporated into Jamie's school and home environments.

Currently, Jamie is doing well, as indicated by his mother's positive statement earlier in the case example. Her impression reflects the success of Jamie's interdiscipli-

nary intervention program. This would not be the situation without the ongoing and open interaction of the parents and all involved professionals. Jamie's parents have done a superb job of requesting the supports and services that they have felt were needed. With support from the UAP and the school staff, Jamie has expanded his capabilities, and the family has been able to continue to meet Jamie's needs. The UAP occupational therapist continues to collaborate with the interdisciplinary team and Jamie's family to support his full inclusion in his community.

References

Alpern, G., Boll, T., & Shearer, M. (1980). *Developmental profile II*. Los Angeles, CA: Western Psychological Services.

American Occupational Therapy Association (1991). Position paper: Occupational therapy and assistive technology. *American Journal of Occupational Therapy, 45*, 1076.

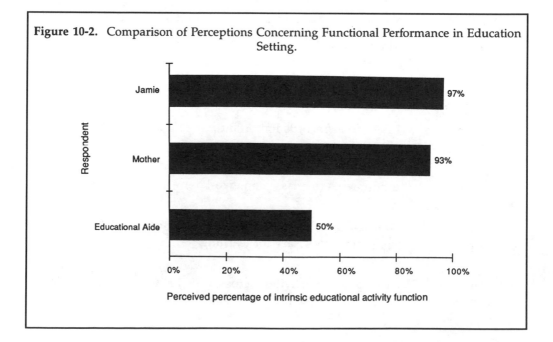

Figure 10-2. Comparison of Perceptions Concerning Functional Performance in Education Setting.

American Occupational Therapy Association (1991). *Essentials and guidelines for an accredited educational program for the occupational therapist*. Rockville, MD: Accreditation Division, American Occupational Therapy Association.

Ayres, A.J. (1989). *Sensory integration and praxis tests*. Los Angeles, CA: Western Psychological Services.

Ayres, A.J. (1972). *Sensory integration and learning disorders*. Los Angeles, CA: Western Psychological Services.

Bayley, N. (1993). *Bayley scales of infant development* (2nd ed). San Antonio, TX: Psychological Corporation.

Bobath, K., & Bobath, B. (1972). Cerebral palsy. In P.H. Pearson (Ed.), *Physical therapy services in the developmental disabilities* (pp. 31-186). Springfield, IL: Charles C. Thomas.

Bruininks, R.H. (1978). *Bruininks-Oseretsky test of motor proficiency*. Circle Pines, MN: American Guidance Service.

Clark, F., Parham, D., Carlson, M.E., Frank, G., Jackson, J., Pierce, D., Wolfe, R.J., & Zemke, R. (1991). Occupational science: Academic innovation in the service of occupational therapy's future. *American Journal of Occupational Therapy*, 45, 300-310.

Colarusso, R.P., & Hammill, D.D. (1972). *Motor-free visual perception test*. Novato, CA: Academic Therapy Publications.

Conrad, C. (1992). *Scholars explore role of master's degrees in American education*. (School of Education Newsletter, Vol. 21, No. 1). Madison, WI: University of Wisconsin.

Fisher, A., Murray, E., & Bundy, A. (1991). *Sensory integration: Theory and practice*. Philadelphia, PA: F.A. Davis Company.

Folio, M.R., & Fewell, R.R. (1983). *Peabody developmental motor scales*. Allen, TX: DLM Teaching Resources.

Frankenburg, W.K., & Dodds, J.B. (1990). *Denver II*. Denver, CO: Denver Developmental Materials.

Furuno, S., O'Reilly, K.A., Hosaka, C.M., Inatsuka, T.T., Allman, T.L., & Zeisloft, B.

(1979). *Hawaii early learning profile*. Palo Alto, CA: VORT Corporation.

Galski, T., Bruno, R.L., & Ehle, H.T. (1992). Driving after cerebral damage: A model with implications for evaluation. *American Journal of Occupational Therapy*, 46, 324-332.

Ireton, H.R., & Thwing, E.J. (1974). *Minnesota child development inventory*. Minneapolis, MN: Behavior Science Systems, Inc.

Linder, T.W. (1990). *Transdisciplinary play-based assessment*. Baltimore, MD: Paul H. Brookes.

Lovett, H. (1985). *Cognitive counseling for persons with special needs: Adapting behavioral approaches to the social context*. New York: Praeger Publishers.

Lowe, H.E. (1990) *Adult skills evaluation survey for persons with mental retardation (ASES): A manual for vocational assessment*. Pasadena, CA: New Opportunity Workshops, Inc.

Malgady, R.G., & Barcher, P.R. (1980). *Vocational adaptation rating scales*. Los Angeles, CA: Western Psychological Services.

Milani-Comparetti, A., & Gidoni, E.A. (1977). *Milani-Comparetti motor development screening test*. Omaha, NE: Meyers Children's Rehabilitation Institute, University of Nebraska Medical Center.

Miller, L.J. (1988). *Miller assessment for preschoolers*. San Antonio, TX: Psychological Corporation.

Mount, B., Beeman, P., & Ducharme, G. (1988). *What are we learning about circles of support?* Manchester, CT: Communitas, Inc.

Mutti, M., Sterling, H.M., & Spalding, N.V. (1978). *Quick neurological screening test*. Novato, CA: Academic Therapy Publications.

O'Brien, J. (1990). *What's worth working for: Leadership strategies to improve the quality of services for people with severe disabilities*. Lithonia, GA: Responsive Systems Associates.

Ottenbacher, K.J. (1986). *Evaluating clinical change: Strategies for occupational and physical therapists*. Baltimore, MD: Williams & Wilkins.

Perske, R., & Perske, M. (1988). *Friendship*. Nashville, TN: Abingdon Press.

Reisman, J. (1993) Using a sensory integrative approach to treat self-injurious behavior in an adult with profound mental retardation. *American Journal of Occupational Therapy, 47*, 403-411.

Rood, M.S. (1956). Neurophysiological mechanisms utilized in the treatment of neuromusculary dysfunction. *American Journal of Occupational Therapy, 4*, 220-225.

Schneider, M.L. (1992). The effect of mild stress during pregnancy on birthweight and neuromotor maturation in rhesus monkey infants. *Infant Behavior and Development, 15*, 389-403.

Smith, R.O. (1993). Computer-assisted functional assessment and documentation. *American Journal of Occupational Therapy, 47*, 988-982

Sparrow, S.S., Dalla, D.A., & Cicchetti, D.V. (1984). *Vineland adaptive behavior scales.* Circle Pines, MN: American Guidance Services.

Spencer, J., Krefting, L., & Mattingly, C. (1993). Incorporation of ethnographic methods in occupational therapy assessment. *American Journal of Occupational Therapy, 47*, 4, 303-309.

Technology-Related Assistance for Individuals with Disabilities Act (1988). Public Law 100-47, Sec. 3.

White, P. (1992). Community support to people with developmental disabilities and challenging behaviors. Paper presented at the Challenging Behaviors Conference sponsored by the University of Wisconsin, Madison, WI.

11

Pediatric Medicine

I. Leslie Rubin, M.D.

In order to understand the role of the pediatrician (or any other physician for that matter) in the interdisciplinary team (IDT), it is helpful to look at some of the history of the role of the medical profession in serving children and adults with developmental disabilities. It should also be noted that the role of the medical professional in providing services for individuals with mental retardation and related developmental disabilities parallels and reflects society's attitudes, social philosophies and expectations. This is particularly evident in the United States over the last century.

Clinical Diagnosis and Terminology

The 19th century and the early part of the 20th century employed a set of terms which described the intellectual, cognitive or social functioning of individuals. These terms were considered scientific classifications of ability and their application was quite serious. They were to be found all major texts on neurology, psychiatry, or general medicine. The terms included: *feeble-minded*, for those individuals with the mildest degree of cognitive limitation, through the terms

moron, idiot, and *imbecile.* As may be appreciated, this collection of terms in no way reflected any specific frame of reference or any root understanding. Although these words were in wide use across all strata of society, the formal labeling was the domain of the physician.

Mental Retardation

As the science of intelligence testing evolved, it became clear that there could be a more formal interpretation—or gradation of the measurement—of function of individuals with intellectual, cognitive, and social limitations. This appreciation then led to the development of the concept of "mental retardation" and its classification of degrees by achievement on formal test items. This provided a tool for scientific investigation and further understanding of the nature of and expectations around this new terminology and classification.

It is of further interest to note that the view of mental retardation as a discrete and separate entity that could be viewed in isolation lent itself readily to scientific exploration. This concept has now come under scrutiny, however, because it does not adequately explain the associated complexities and implications. It has yielded to a broader understanding and conceptualization that includes all levels of functioning and adaptation.

Furthermore, the term *mental retardation* is by no means universally embraced. Indeed, in European countries the terms *intellectual disability*, *learning disability*, and *mental handicap* are used to describe similar conditions. A task force of the American Association on Mental Retardation looked at reconsideration of the term *mental retardation*; it toyed with the notion of changing the term but chose to retain it for the time being. This decision allows for conceptual continuity—although the issues are by no means clear. The challenge is to understand and conceptualize the expression of central nervous system impairment on cognitive functioning and social ability.

Neurological Basis

If we acknowledge that the physical and physiological basis for our cognitive, social, and emotional well-being is coordinated in the central nervous system—the brain and its complex sensory and integrative components—then its dysfunction will result in alterations or modifications of the individual's manifest activities. By the introduction of the term *central nervous system dysfunction*, we begin to conceptualize the notion of mental retardation, cognitive impairment, intellectual disability, and so forth as being a consequence of some alteration in brain function. The alteration in brain function creates difficulties in dealing with information from the environment and interpreting this into meaningful function towards survival. In this particular

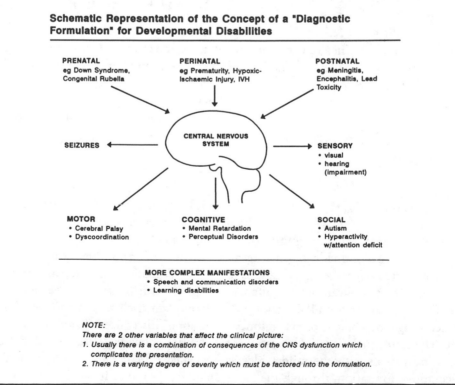

Figure 11-1. Construct of CNS Dysfunction, Recognizing Etiology (Pre-, Peri-, or Postnatal) and Types of Disorders (Motor, Cognitive, or Social).

Schematic Representation of the Concept of a "Diagnostic Formulation" for Developmental Disabilities

PRENATAL
eg Down Syndrome, Congenital Rubella

PERINATAL
eg Prematurity, Hypoxic-Ischaemic Injury, IVH

POSTNATAL
eg Meningitis, Encephalitis, Lead Toxicity

SEIZURES

CENTRAL NERVOUS SYSTEM

SENSORY
• visual
• hearing (impairment)

MOTOR
• Cerebral Palsy
• Dyscoordination

COGNITIVE
• Mental Retardation
• Perceptual Disorders

SOCIAL
• Autism
• Hyperactivity w/attention deficit

MORE COMPLEX MANIFESTATIONS
• Speech and communication disorders
• Learning disabilities

NOTE:
There are 2 other variables that affect the clinical picture:
1. Usually there is a combination of consequences of the CNS dysfunction which complicates the presentation.
2. There is a varying degree of severity which must be factored into the formulation.

notion, the term *mental retardation* becomes merely one aspect of a functional spectrum of human attributes.

Cerebral Palsy

At this point it might be interesting to consider the history of the term *cerebral palsy* and the role of the medical profession in the definition of this clinical diagnostic entity. In the early 19th century, a physician by the name of William John Little underwent surgery to correct a congenital anomaly of his foot. This surgery, which has come to be known as *heel cord lengthening*, enabled Dr. Little to walk better. Little, being a thoughtful and compassionate person, determined to learn the procedure and performed it on many people. Being an astute clinician, he then discovered that although some individuals seemed to benefit as he did, for others the benefit was less than optimal and their difficulties returned.

After careful deliberation, he came upon the unifying concept that for those children on whom he had performed the procedure whose difficulties later recurred, there had been the experience of a difficult birth. After analyzing a series of his patients, he presented his findings to the Royal College of Obstetricians. He reported that difficulties during birth can have a serious damaging effect on the brain, which then can translate into functional problems in the intellectual, social and motor areas.

Since Dr. Little's major intervention was surgical, and related to muscles and joints, his findings became a significant area of interest for orthopedic surgeons. For many years the clinical condition of cerebral palsy remained the domain of orthopedists, physical therapists and neurologists.

Once again, it is important to note the unifying concept that we are dealing with a neurologically based disorder of the brain (or central nervous system) that then mani-

fests in disorders of movement and posture which have come to be known by the term *cerebral palsy*.

Cerebral palsy has not always been the prevailing diagnostic term. Indeed, it was originally known as *Little's disease*, named after William John Little. Subsequently, in the French neurological literature, it came to be differentiated from other palsies or weaknesses by the term *palsy cerebral*, which distinguished it from the peripheral nerve palsies, e.g., of polio. Thus, *palsy cerebral* became, in English, *cerebral palsy*.

Other Manifestations of CNS Dysfunction

It should be noted here that other functional alterations as a result of central nervous system involvement could include:

1. behavior, e.g. hyperactivity, depression, autism
2. sensory limitations, blindness or deafness
3. neurological disorders, such as seizure disorders and movement disorders
4. secondary consequences, such as muscle contractures and orthopedic complications
5. medical complications, particularly if the degree of involvement is severe

Paradigms of Treatment

Metabolic

The next phase of our history begins in Switzerland, where, at the top of the mountains, a group of people were identified who had similar features that constituted the diagnostic syndrome of "Cretinism with goiter." Scientific exploration gave rise to the astute observation that the single significant element lacking in the diets of this group was iodine. The water in the higher elevations in Switzerland lacked the essential iodine, and as a result, thyroid function was impaired. Thyroid function assures optimal growth and development of the body as well as the brain. The people who were thus affected had significant cognitive and functional limitations. Introduction of supplemental iodine into the diet helped to restore normal thyroid function and thus improve metabolism of the whole body, particularly the brain, thereby allowing the people to once again participate more actively in society.

The diagnosis of Cretinism was applied to individuals whose physical features and functional abilities were altered by the absence of adequate iodine and hence of appropriate amounts of thyroid hormone. This was the beginning of the appreciation of the fact that alterations in diet can affect not only well-being and overall nutritional status, but growth and cognitive function as well. It was also the beginning of the recognition that growth and cognitive status could be recovered by the introduction of the missing agent. The challenge that arose out of this was to discover what other conditions might have such simple and reversible explanations. The notion of reversibility of developmental disabilities, in particular, began to feature prominently.

Along similar lines, the discovery of PKU in the 1920's, and the subsequent improvement in outcome by dietary elimination of phenylalanine, set off an explosion of interest in the biochemistry of mental retardation. The conditions that were then discovered included the amino acidopathies (e.g., PKU), the mucopolysaccharoidoses (e.g., Hunter and Hurler syndromes), and the lipidoses (e.g., Tay-Sachs disease). The exploration of underlying biochemical disorders produced more than a few notable and highly significant successes: in understanding many conditions, in developing screening programs for newborns, particularly with PKU, and in reversing a number of conditions which would inevitably have resulted in cognitive impairment.

Screening and Prevention

The examples described above spurred the development of two vital elements in the array of professional activities in the field of developmental disabilities: screening and prevention. The two concepts are intimately linked in that each implies the other's existence. Once a mechanism of any illness or disorder is identified, there is an exploration as to how the particular disorder arises, then a search for ways in which the condition can be treated, cured, reversed, ameliorated, or just prevented.

One of the classic success stories of such an approach was a result of the outbreak of rubella in the mid-1960s and the consequent epidemic of congenital rubella, with its profound effect on the body's organs—particularly the heart, hearing and vision—and on the central nervous system, affecting cognition, socialization, communication, learning, and even motor performance. After the mechanism and the offending organism were identified, an immunization against rubella was developed. The screening for susceptibility, and immunization as a preventive measure, of young women of childbearing age rapidly followed. Now all infants are routinely immunized, and congenital rubella and its consequences have been virtually eliminated.

This cohort of children born in the mid-60's, who had congenital rubella and its central nervous system consequences, swelled the special education systems of public (and private) schools. These children challenged professionals to become creative in responding to their multiple and complex needs and the needs of their families.

This example illustrates the need for professionals from a variety of disciplines to collaborate at many different levels to identify disorders, understand their mechanisms, and develop expertise to work together in different ways at different times to help individuals with developmental disabilities and their families throughout their lifetime of changing needs.

Currently there are many different screening tests at many different levels that operate from a prenatal period in the recognition of increased risks with certain genetic conditions that occur in families or among specific population groups. The high rate of Tay-Sachs disease among people of Jewish lineage has resulted in the availability of pre-conception screening of both parents for the conditions. Screening also takes place during pregnancy, looking for the possibility of chromosomal disorders, particularly Trisomy 21 (Down syndrome), and also non-chromosomal conditions such as myelodysplasia. In the immediate newborn period, there is screening for PKU, hypothyroidism, and other metabolic conditions. During infancy, screening for neurological features that might predict neurodevelopmental disorders occurs, particularly if the infant had been at high risk (e.g., maternal illness or substance abuse, prematurity or intracranial hemorrhage) If the presence of a developmental disorder is established, continued screening for health-related medical issues is vital.

Other Medical Interventions

There are of course a number of categories of medical intervention where, although 'mental retardation' was not specifically reversed or prevented, function was significantly improved, such as with the use of medications to treat and control seizures, surgical interventions to prevent or correct deformities, or physical therapy to enhance function.

Educational Interventions

The other area that was approached and developed within the medical establishment dealt not so much with the reversal of biochemical or organic conditions as with the enhancement of function through overcoming particular disabilities. The classic example of this was the story of the wild boy of Avernon. A physician found a boy in the forest living alone and surviving off natural resources. He brought this boy into his home and attempted to educate him in the more traditional social manners. He was only partially successful and viewed his attempt as a failure; however, others viewed it as a success. The lesson learned was that changes could be made, and that perhaps for each individual the right kind of education and the right changes could produce a desired effect.

This concept was adopted again in the mountains of Switzerland by a physician who opened a school for children with mental retardation and claimed success with this method. As a result, he traveled around the world touting the methods of his success. The notion of special schools then took off, and in the United States large schools began to spring up around the country.

Patterns of Practice

Evolution of the Medical Model in Institutions

Although the early phase in the development of institutions appeared to have merit, it soon became evident that the knowledge base for this "special education" was limited. The educational services for the children rapidly deteriorated, leaving only the traditional medical model of care. Very soon these schools became institutions, and these institutions then degenerated into the human warehouses that have been so abhorrent to society.

It is interesting to note that the physicians who had been part of the initiation of the process of education and the superintendents of these schools continued to hold control in the management of these institutions and ran them on the same model as hospitals. It was this situation that gave the term *medical model* its negative connotation. The term refers to the way in which individuals with mental retardation were being dealt with and served by the medical and nursing profession within these institutional settings.

Traditional Medical Practice

The traditional pattern of physicians' practice is based on a rather simple formula (see Figure 11-2). The formula is that a problem of a health-related nature is brought to the attention of the physician. The physician will ask questions, perform a physical examination, and perhaps get some tests. The physician will then collate the information, come up with a diagnosis, and prescribe a treatment—e.g., medication or surgery. The

desired outcome is to correct the problem or to make it go away.

This is a familiar pattern. It generally works well with acute problems, but it falls short in dealing with chronic disorders and particularly with permanent conditions that cannot be readily reversed. In other words, the model cannot be readily used to understand or address the complex issues related to an individual with mental retardation or other developmental disabilities.

Interdisciplinary Practice

In the late 1960s, when University Affiliated Programs (UAPs) were first established, the model for an interdisciplinary approach was developed. This model spoke of *evaluation* rather than *diagnosis*, and of *making recommendations* rather than *prescribing treatment*.

The framework was similar to the earlier model except that, instead of consulting only with a physician, an individual with mental retardation would come to an interdisciplinary team. The interdisciplinary

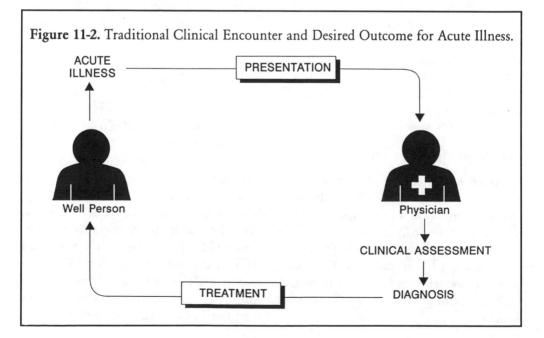

Figure 11-2. Traditional Clinical Encounter and Desired Outcome for Acute Illness.

team would perform an evaluation and, through that evaluation, offer a composite set of recommendations to enhance function (see Figure 11-3).

With this change in concept, from the unidisciplinary diagnosis–treatment model to the interdisciplinary evaluation–conceptualization–recommendations model, the physician became part of the team rather than operating in isolation. This paradigm shift, from independent diagnostician to participant in an interdisciplinary process, required significant re-examination of a physician's identity. This examination brought into focus the meaningful role that the physician could play, by participating with colleagues from other professional disciplines, in improving the understanding of a particular individual who is being evaluated.

The idea of working intimately with a variety of disciplines was not foreign to physicians. However, the notion of sharing center stage and relinquishing omniscience was. It became clear to physicians that the observations and interpretations of the physical therapist for assessing motor function,

the nutritionist for eating and optimal growth, the audiologist for hearing, the ophthalmologist for vision, the speech pathologist for speech, the psychologist for intellectual function, the special educator for learning styles, the psychiatrist for behavioral issues, the social worker for social issues, etc., contributed perspectives, information, and observations towards greater understanding of the individual being served than the physician alone could bring.

Over time the role—and value—of a physician as part of an interdisciplinary team became clear. This role can be spelled out as follows:

Diagnostic Understanding. With knowledge of genetics and neurology, the physician is able to come to a diagnostic understanding of the individual being evaluated. This allows for conceptualization of the reasons for the disability; the nature of the disability; possible medical treatments which may help to reverse, alleviate or prevent further disability; and some appreciation of the natural history of any particular condition that might be applied to the individual being evaluated. This forms the structural

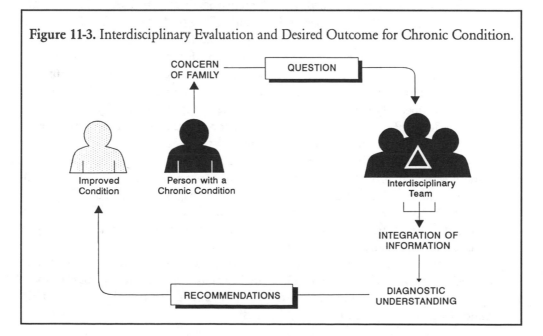

Figure 11-3. Interdisciplinary Evaluation and Desired Outcome for Chronic Condition.

diagnostic understanding which will help determine practical and other benefits.

Health-Related Issues. Through an understanding of the many facets and complexities of health, a physician can offer an understanding of the relationship between a particular health-related condition and other aspects of ability and function. This is true for acute as well as chronic health care issues.

Coordination of Specialty Health Care Needs. People with developmental disabilities are likely to have additional needs of a functional or health-related nature that require attention. Because of the central nervous system involvement, there may be additional complications: neurological factors, sensory involvement (e.g., hearing and vision), psychiatric and psychological issues, as well as other medical complications (e.g. nutritional, gastrointestinal, respiratory, cardiovascular, renal, and certainly orthopedic). Thus it can be appreciated that a physician plays a significant role in determining the need for, and the value of, a specialty consultation, and interpreting the results of such an evaluation. In addition, a physician may be required to coordinate and interpret multiple specialty services and help to integrate the care for the individual, the family and other providers.

Education and Training. Not only is the physician required to provide health care, coordinate specialty care, and have a working knowledge of the genetics, neurology, and other health-related aspects of people with developmental disabilities; there is also an obligation to provide training and education around these issues to all involved people. This is not meant to be informative only, but to help guide decisions, plan programs, and orient daily living towards physical, emotional, and social well-being.

Improving the Knowledge Base. The physician has a responsibility to add to existing knowledge and play a part in improving the understanding of the health and well-being of people with developmental disabilities. This knowledge should be applied to enhance health, function, and quality of life for individuals with developmental disabilities, their families, and their communities.

Advocacy. The physician also has a responsibility and an obligation to participate in the development of policy and the formulation of practices at a broader social level that will improve the lives of people with developmental disabilities.

Adaptation to Working in an Interdisciplinary Team

It is within the context of the IDT that the physician may have the greatest difficulty. This difficulty may not be specific to physicians on the interdisciplinary team, but may well be a common phenomenon among disciplinary professionals on an interdisciplinary team. Be that as it may, I will address the question of the identity of physicians on an interdisciplinary team.

Conceptually, the domain of clinical practice is determined by a professional identity. This professional disciplinary identity is what distinguishes an individual in a specific profession from those in another disciplinary category. Indeed, training in a particular discipline focuses on cultivating a strong disciplinary identity at a cultural, linguistic, social, and philosophical level. Medical training in specific disciplines is broad and deep, marked by attention not only to intercurrent ills of a relatively minor and manageable nature, but also to life-threatening conditions in a desperate and critical situation. In training, hours may be long and demands may be great if not excessive (This description is meant not to make excuses for physicians, but as an attempt to explain some cultural characteristics).

In order for physicians to subscribe to and embrace the interdisciplinary concept, and to participate in an actively committed fashion within an interdisciplinary team, a process of re-education or acculturation is required. This involves the dismantling of the previously established, traditional professional identity and the restructuring and redefining of professional identity. During the process of re-education and redefinition, there will inevitably be a point in which the identity of the professional will be at its most vulnerable. A point will be reached where one's professional identity will be brought into question and may even take the form of an "identity crisis."

It should be appreciated by the non-physician that at times, physicians in the interdisciplinary process may feel redundant to some extent and may feel that their discipline-specific clinical offerings may not be of significance or relevance. At other times, they may feel that their offerings are of supreme significance or relevance, to the exclusion of all others. Why this rather polarized view exists is not clear, but the fact that it does should be given some consideration. Whereas each of the other disciplines has a specific focus in the developmental intervention, the physician's role is somewhat broad, ill-defined, and relative, and may not be unique to the area of development specifically.

There are two elements operating under this set of circumstances :

1. The physician must appreciate the nature of the discipline-specific contributions that can be offered generically in an interdisciplinary team.
2. The degree of involvement, and hence participation, of the physician will vary depending on the nature of the individual's condition.

In addition, improvements in the knowl-edge and understanding of clinical conditions that affect individuals with developmental disabilities are being appreciated and taught within residency training programs, and even within medical schools. The first has been a direct consequence of four major phenomena:

1. The rejection of the discipline-dominated "medical model" for the more enlightened interdisciplinary and dynamic developmental model.
2. The process and social philosophy of deinstitutionalization and noninstitutionalization, towards inclusion into the mainstream of clinical practice, of individuals who would have been previously confined to the Siberias of modern civilization.
3. Public Law 94-142, which holds that all children are entitled to a free and appropriate education, and that there should be a commitment on the part of the community to provide these services to the child regardless of the nature of the disability.
4. The appreciation within pediatric and medical training programs that the physician cannot operate in isolation, particularly in treating children or adults with chronic disorders, but must collaborate with professionals from all domains in the psychosocial, biomedical, and educational/vocational spheres, and in the neurodevelopmental formulation. These phenomena have promoted civil rights tenets of respect and dignity of all, regardless of disability, towards full inclusion for *all* members of society.

A pediatrician's contribution to the interdisciplinary team process can include the following practical and conceptual elements:

1. A sense of history, including: the family history, from a genetic point of view; the pregnancy, from the point of view of finding possible etiological factors; the birth, from the point of view of determining biological influences; and the health and developmental history, which provides patterns of insight into biomedical and neurodevelopmental well-being.

2. Monitoring the development of an infant—the pediatrician is the professional who is most likely to encounter the child within the first few years of life (i.e., before school)—so as to appropriately manage and coordinate developmental problems in children.

3. A sense of the physical strengths or weaknesses related to neurodevelopmental or biomedical factors that influence health in general or function in particular.

4. The awareness of medications or therapies that can improve or adversely affect functioning and how these may be used or abused.

5. Investigations of biochemistry, hematology, toxicology, neurophysiology, radiology, and all the other special investigations that help shed light on causes and identify treatable problems.

6. The appreciation of where consultants from other medical disciplines and specialty medical knowledge can be drawn upon to assist in evaluating health-related issues or neurodevelopmental function.

7. Ensuring and providing health care for individuals with developmental disabilities, that they may achieve optimal functioning potential and enjoy the benefits that family, the community, and society offer.

8. Advocacy on behalf of all children and their families for whom developmental disability is a major issue, and helping to change policy.

Shifting Paradigms

While we saw a shift in pattern of practice from the traditional to the interdisciplinary model beginning a quarter of a century ago, we are now seeing a further shift towards a more inclusive model. In this model, the traditional "patient" (or parent or other family member) has become a *consumer* and is actively engaged in the clinical process. This participation of the consumer in the team has been viewed as foreign to the traditional interdisciplinary team process, just as the interdisciplinary team was viewed when the concept was first introduced to the traditional solo clinical practice. What may not be appreciated by the detractors is that *all models exist to serve a single purpose*: responding to the problem, question, or need of the consumer. It is only the way in which it is done and the philosophy underlying the specific practice that differ. In the first model, the patient is the sufferer; the physician is the omniscient practitioner providing "help" or a cure where and when possible. In the second model, the client obtains an interdisciplinary evaluation which acknowledges the complexity of the situation, and once a diagnostic formulation has been articulated, a set of recommendations are made. The client then must try to use the recommendations to negotiate the variety of educational, social, and/or vocational systems. In the third model, the consumer is included in the process as an active participant, and his or her needs are addressed in an active fashion (see Figure 11-4).

In all the models, the professionals are there for the consumer, yet they differ in how they specifically respond to the issues in relation to the consumer. Only in the third model is the contribution of the consumer/parent actively sought and incorporated into the process. This does not mean that the other models do not acknowledge or respect their patients or clients, but that

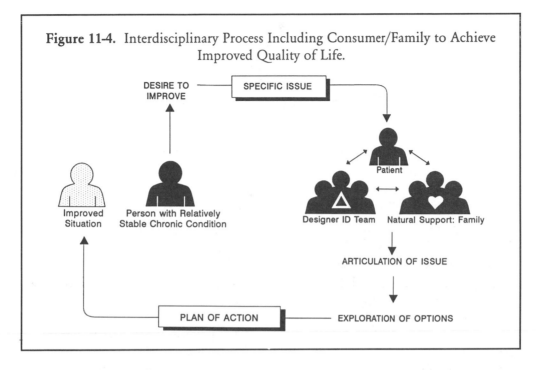

Figure 11-4. Interdisciplinary Process Including Consumer/Family to Achieve Improved Quality of Life.

the third process actually includes the consumer.

To put it simply, pediatricians (as well as other physicians and health professionals) have a depth of knowledge in their specific field of practice, and a breadth of experience in dealing with many individuals. In that context, they become aware of the issues, feelings, treatments, and other resources available. The consumer (also parent, guardian, other family member, friend, etc.) has the best perspective and sense of the individual and his or her characteristic strengths, needs, and resources. Together, they will develop a shared understanding of the conditions that exist, the resources available, and the best ways of accessing these to ultimately benefit both the consumer, in the sense of helping to satisfy needs, and the professional(s), in providing new knowledge, experience, and insights for the development of self and understanding of others in the future.

References

Kanner, L.A. (1964). *History of the care and study of the mentally retarded*. Springfield, IL: Charles C. Thomas.

Levine, M.L., Carey, R., & Crocker, A.C. (1993). *Developmental-behavioral pediatrics*. Philadelphia, PA: W.B. Saunders.

Rubin, I.L., & Crocker, A.C. (1989). *Developmental disabilities: Delivery of medical care for children and adults*. Philadelphia, PA: Lea & Febiger.

12

Physical Therapy

Susan L. White, M.S., P.T., & Ellen A. Kaplan, M.S., P.T.

The major goal of physical therapy is to enhance human movement and function through the use of therapeutic techniques that prevent disability, provide alternate methods for compromised skills, and improve ability. Thus, physical therapy contributes, in an active and positive fashion, to improved competence for individuals with developmental disabilities. The scope of physical therapy includes acute care, rehabilitation, orthopedics, neurology, cardiopulmonology, pediatrics, geriatrics, sports medicine, and industrial medicine.

Physical therapy in the United States originated as a profession during World War I, when the U.S. army trained "Reconstruction Aides" to work with injured soldiers. During World War II, the profession received further recognition. In the civilian population, trained health professionals were also needed to work with people weakened by infantile paralysis (poliomyelitis) during recurring epidemics. The procedures developed to treat and retrain these patient populations evolved into the body of knowledge and techniques presently known as physical therapy (Pinkston, 1989).

In 1921, the American Physical Therapy Association (APTA) was established. The following definition of physical therapy was adopted in 1986 by the APTA House of Delegates:

(a) treatment by physical means; (b) the profession which is concerned with health promotion; with prevention of physical disabilities; and with rehabilitation of a person disabled by pain, disease, or injury; and which is involved with treating through the use of physical therapeutic measures as opposed to medicines, surgery, or radiation (Pinkston, 1989, p. 13).

Educational and Training Requirements

A physical therapist must be a graduate of a physical therapy program accredited by the Commission on Accreditation in Physical Therapy Education of the American Physical Therapy Association (APTA). Prerequisite skills are attained through extensive classroom, laboratory and clinical education. Several types of academic programs leading to professional competence in physical therapy are available. Entry-level baccalaureate programs combine elements of a strong liberal arts program integrated with a specialized curriculum emphasizing medical sciences and therapeutic modalities. The required medical science courses include human anatomy, physiology, neuroanatomy, and pathology. Therapeutic topics include kinesiology, specific physical therapy modalities (e.g., use of heat, cold, electric, and hydrotherapies), therapeutic techniques and exercise, and adaptive and assistive equipment (prosthetics, orthotics, ambulation equipment, mobility aids, and postural control devices).

Entry-level graduate programs are available for students who have obtained their undergraduate degree in another field. These programs, leading to a master's level degree, offer similar curricula, clinical education experiences, and research methodology. Programs providing an entry-level doctoral degree (DPT) are now available.

Physical therapists often enhance their basic education with postgraduate certificate courses within a specific area of interest (e.g., neurodevelopmental treatment, myofacial release, joint mobilization, advanced orthotics/prosthetics). Educational interests may also be pursued in academic programs leading to advanced master's and doctoral degrees in physical therapy. Such programs enable a physical therapist to develop further skills in research, education, and administration. Physical therapists also may obtain graduate degrees in related fields of interest (e.g., special education, developmental disabilities, motor learning, exercise physiology, or biological/anatomical sciences).

Licensure, Certification, and Continuing Education

Following graduation from an accredited physical therapy program, candidates seeking to practice physical therapy must pass state-administered examinations. These examinations are developed by the Committee of Licensure Examinations of the American Physical Therapy Association, in cooperation with Assessment Systems Incorporated (ASI), and evaluate both didactic and clinical knowledge. Licensure is required for the practice of physical therapy in all states, with specific requirements concerning successful completion of the examination varying among states. Physical therapists wishing to practice in a state other than the one in which they are licensed should contact the department of state government responsible for issuing professional licenses (American Physical Therapy Association, 1993a).

Clinical specialization within the field of physical therapy is obtained through demonstration of advanced expertise as recognized by the American Board of Physical Therapy Specialists (ABPTS). Areas currently recognized for specialization include cardiopulmonology, clinical electrophysiology, neurology, orthopedics, pediatrics, and sports medicine (American Physical Therapy Association, 1993b).

Continuing education is obtained through short-term coursework (in both clinical and academic settings) that meet the standards of the Continuing Education Committee for each state. These courses are awarded Continuing Education Units (CEU). The CEU requirements necessary to maintain current licensure vary from state to state.

Contributions to Interdisciplinary Practice

Physical therapists contribute their knowledge and understanding of human physiology, biomechanics, and motor development to an interdisciplinary team. Physical therapists (a) provide information concerning an individuals' physical condition; (b) recommend and provide therapeutic techniques that strengthen a person's physical status and decrease factors that diminish physical skills; (c) share their understanding of human movement and its influence on other aspects of skill or development; (d) furnish environmental modifications and assistive devices that offer alternatives for accomplishing functional skills; (e) assist individuals to realize their optimum performance; and (f) support the efforts of individuals (and their families) to integrate into society.

Physical therapists contribute information about an individual's abilities, and any limitations and precautions for involvement in various activities and situations. This includes information concerning the status of the musculoskeletal, neurodevelopmental, cardiopulmonary, and sensorimotor systems that impact on the functional capacity of persons with developmental disabilities. Therapeutic interventions that enhance physical conditions and promote function for individuals are suggested to interdisciplinary team members so that these techniques may be incorporated in other areas of care. Strategies are modified, based on information obtained through an interdisciplinary team process, enabling physical therapists to select or modify therapeutic interventions to meet the specific needs of the individual. Physical therapists explain the relationship between movement and associated developmental and functional areas that affect an individual's performance. For example, postural control may affect an individual's ability to communicate or socialize (Fetters, 1984; Robinson & Fieber, 1988).

Physical therapists contribute their knowledge of rehabilitation technology as a method of assisting people with developmental disabilities to attain functional goals. The physical therapist advises other team members about adaptive/assistive devices and environmental modifications which promote function, reduce pain, and prevent deformity. The physical therapist's knowledge and skills contribute toward comprehensive treatment plans that enhance an individual's ability to function at home, in school, at work, or during leisure activities.

All aspects of service among the various disciplines serving people with developmental disabilities must be interrelated. An understanding of postural control and motor skills is important in providing individualized programs that meet the specific needs of each person served. The combined skills and creativity of all concerned interventionists are aimed at allowing each person to achieve opportunities for integration into society.

Assessment

Physical therapy assessment combines interviews, clinical observations, and selected evaluation protocols that establish information pertaining to an individual's physical condition and functional abilities. Current concerns, review of pertinent medical information, and developmental history are obtained through interviews with the individual, family, or caregivers. Early intervention legislation (P.L. 99-457; P.L. 101-476) specifies that the resources, priorities, and concerns of the family be included in the assessment process (Chiarello, Effgen & Levinson, 1992; Kolobe, 1992). This concept also applies to the interview process for adults, including the personal concerns of the individual, the family, and caregivers. Thus, information obtained through interviews, combined with a review of medical records (yielding information about diagnoses, prognoses, indications, and contraindications), enables the physical therapist to (a) establish priorities for assessment and (b) plan therapeutic interventions that meet the needs of people with developmental disabilities.

Observational Assessments

Clinical observations of the individual performing varying activities, specific tasks, and interactions in different environments contribute comprehensive information relating movement within a developmental and functional framework (Montgomery, 1981; Robinson & Fieber, 1988). Analysis of observations are a significant component of the assessment, occurring throughout the entire evaluation process.

Posture analysis. A posture analysis combines the physical therapists' knowledge of anatomy and pathology to determine if musculoskeletal abnormalities compromise the individuals' functional or physical status. Postural concerns include observations of spinal deviations (scoliosis, kyphosis), limb length discrepancies, dynamics of muscle tone,and asymmetries (Bobath, 1971, 1980; Shumway-Cook & Woollacott, 1985; Tecklin, 1989). Based on observational assessment, further measurements are made to quantify the examination.

Gait analysis. Observation and appraisal of the components of ambulation provide clinical evidence of dynamic forces that decrease function and lead to joint damage. Gait analysis laboratories, utilizing computer technology to quantify the components of ambulation, are generally not available in situations serving people with developmental disabilities. However, standardization of observations using alternate measures is clinically available in order to document specific components of gait (Robinson & Smidt, 1981).

Cardiopulmonary observations. Primary pulmonary disorders or respiratory problems may be secondary to musculoskeletal deviations. Assessment combines observation and measurement of the shape and size of the thorax, pulse rate, respiratory rate, and auscultation (listening with a stethoscope). Cardiopulmonary observations concerning the person's general appearance, breathing patterns, ability to cough or sneeze effectively, and changes in endurance while performing movement skills, are additional components of a cardiopulmonary assessment (Clough, 1989; Hillegass, 1989; Tecklin, 1989).

Assessment Protocols

Physical therapists select from a variety of standardized clinical evaluation instruments which are designed to elicit specific musculoskeletal, sensory, developmental, functional, cardiopulmonary and neurological information. The specific protocol used to determine diagnostic or intervention information depends on the person's age, nature of disability, and developmental level.

Manual muscle testing (MMT). The MMT is a standard method of assessing muscle strength (Daniels, & Worthingham, 1986; Kendall, Kendall & Wadsworth, 1971). The ability of muscles to function in relation to gravity and resistance is documented. Information gathered through MMT provides a picture of functional abilities, helps to localize weakness, and assists in differential diagnosis (Canfield, 1989). An alternative method, used with young children or adults who are unable to follow directions, is to observe the individual's use of certain muscles during motor activities (Montgomery, 1981).

Range of motion (ROM). To assess range of motion, the arc of motion for each joint of the upper and lower extremities is measured with a protractor-like tool called a *goniometer*. The measurements for the individual are compared to established measures of normal joint ranges of motion (ROM) in order to determine the degree of restricted joint motion and the effect on functional skills. Goniometric (ROM) measurements are essential for assessing a person with muscular, neurological, or orthopedic impairment for documenting the effectiveness of interventions and quantifying loss or gain of joint mobility and function (Grohmann, 1983).

Reflex testing. Deep Tendon Reflexes (e.g., knee jerk) are commonly tested as an indication of increased, decreased, or normal muscle tone. Postural Reflex and Reaction evaluations, including tonic reflexes as well as righting and equilibrium reactions (Bobath, 1971; Fiorentino, 1972), are essential for determining neuromotor development and the effect on functional movement and activities (Bertoti, 1989; Easton, 1972; Montgomery, 1981). The Milani-Comparetti Motor Developmental Screening Test (Kliewer, Bruce & Trembath, 1977) and the Reflex Evaluation (Barnes, Crutchfield & Heriza, 1978) are frequently used postural reflex testing instruments.

Sensory testing. Sensory testing includes evaluation of a person's response to temperature, touch, deep pressure, and pain. Kinesthesia, proprioception (position sense), stereognosis, and two-point discrimination are also assessed. This provides information about an individual's neurological status and enables the physical therapist to incorporate precautions and contraindications into specific therapeutic interventions.

Volitional Movement

Volitional movement is the ability to control and organize motor responses in relation to various sensory stimuli. Volitional functional movement is viewed in the context of a sensory-motor-sensory feedback system, in which a sensory stimulus results in a motor response which, in turn, produces another set of sensory responses. Visual, auditory, tactile, proprioceptive, kinesthetic and vestibular sensory systems are also assessed in relation to a person's ability to accommodate motor responses in terms of

motor coordination, imitation of postures, and motor planning (Ayres, 1974; DeGangi & Greenspan, 1989; Rood, 1962; Stockmeyer, 1967).

Motor development. Developmental motor age-equivalents for children are determined by performance on either criterion-referenced or norm-referenced instruments. Assessment of motor development is used for diagnostic information, educational planning, and documenting the progress of a child. Frequently used norm-referenced instruments include the Peabody Developmental Motor Scales (Folio & Fewell, 1983), Miller Assessment for Preschoolers (Miller, 1982), Bruininks-Oseretsky Test of Motor Proficiency (Bruininks, 1978), Psychomotor Development Index (PDI), and Bayley Scales of Infant Development (Bayley, 1969). Criterion-referenced assessments include the Hawaii Early Learning Profile (Furuno, O'Reilly & Hosaka, 1985), the Carolina Curriculum for Handicapped Infants and Infants at Risk (Johnson-Martin, Jems & Attermeier, 1986), and the Early Learning Accomplishment Profile (Glover, Preminger & Sanford, 1978). These assessments provide quantitative information concerning motor skills, but do not indicate the quality of movement.

Movement assessment. For very young children, a criterion-referenced assessment of the quality of motor skills is the Motor Assessment of Infants (MAI) (Chandler, Andrews & Swanson, 1980). This assessment instrument is used for infants between the ages of one month and one year. The MAI provides a systematic method of qualifying movement in terms of muscle tone, primitive reflexes, automatic reactions, and volitional movement.

Oral-motor assessment. Oral-motor assessment involves an interdisciplinary evaluation, including participation of the parent (caregiver), occupational therapist, nutritionist and speech/language pathologist along with the physical therapist. The evaluation includes oral-motor reflexes, muscle tone, and postural control in relation to patterns of movement necessary for eating. Sensory reactivity in the mouth and respiratory competence during eating are assessed, along with components of the developmental and functional aspects of sucking, swallowing, and chewing (Linder, 1990; Morris, 1982; Scherzer & Tscharnuter, 1982).

Rehabilitation Technology

Assessment of the individual's requirements for orthotics, adaptive positioning equipment, assistive ambulation/mobility devices, and assistive technology are considered during physical therapy evaluations. Orthotics (i.e., splints and braces) prevent deformity or support limited physical ability. Assistive ambulation devices include canes, crutches, and walkers that support walking. Mobility devices (alternative methods for accessing the environment) include both power and manual wheelchairs, as well as various electric scooters. Adaptive seating and positioning equipment that enables the individual to sit comfortably, safely, and functionally are important assessment considerations for individuals with significant physical impairment (Hundertmark, 1985).

Assessments to determine appropriate assistive/adaptive equipment and environmental control devices are often fundamental to the successful mastery of skills for persons with developmental disabilities. Adaptive equipment assessment includes evaluation of feeding, bathing, and transfer devices that support both the individual and the family's ease of performance during activities of daily living (ADL). Devices that promote skills, reduce atypical movement, prevent deterioration of function, and allow for optimal function in various environments can then be obtained for persons with developmental disabilities.

Functional Motor Assessment

Motor skills are assessed, whenever possible, in the specific environment in which they are performed. The environment plus the resources needed to support an individual in that environment form components of a functional assessment. Functional motor assessment includes observations combining motor skills, assistive/adaptive resources and environmental influences that allow individuals to successfully play, work, engage in leisure activities, and perform activities of daily living (ADL) (Van Dillen & Roach, 1989).

Intervention

Physical therapists provide direct care, supervision, consultation, education, and advocacy services to people with developmental disabilities. Specific interventions are based on the priorities of the individual, family, and caregivers; the results of a physical therapy assessment; and information obtained through a comprehensive interdisciplinary evaluation. This results in a holistic approach, with physical therapy services provided directly to the individual or to the individual within the context of the family. Appropriate strategies should be devised and implemented in natural settings where the person lives, plays, and works (Cherry, 1991).

Direct Care Interventions

The specific physical therapy techniques used depend on a variety of factors including the person's age, the nature of the disability, indications and contraindications of various treatment methods and modalities, and the situation in which intervention is provided. Therapeutic interventions which enhance and encourage the acquisition of developmental skills and decrease pathological patterns of movement—along with rehabilitation techniques that prevent deformity, assist function, and maintain comfort—are applicable for persons with developmental disabilities.

Positioning and handling. Positioning and handling, as treatment modalities, are used to prevent deformity, decrease pathological patterns of movement, facilitate desired postural control, and promote attainment of skills. Positioning or handling techniques are incorporated into routine activities such as sleeping, eating, using the toilet, bathing, dressing, playing, and transportation (Copeland & Kimmel, 1989; Finnie, 1975; Scherzer & Tscharnuter, 1982). In addition to direct handling, physical therapists are instrumental in adapting, fabricating, and providing positioning devices that promote access and mobility, provide a safe and stable position, maintain postural alignment in different positions, improve respiratory status, and decrease progression of musculoskeletal deformities for persons with developmental disabilities (Alexander, 1985; Bergen, 1988; Fife, et al., 1991; Robinault, 1973; Staller, 1984a, 1984b, 1992; Stuberg, 1992).

Therapeutic exercises. Therapeutic exercise encompasses a wide range of treatment procedures aimed at increasing flexibility, strength, endurance and muscle power and improving cardiopulmonary function. Numerous exercises can be used to increase flexibility and mobility including passive and active stretching of the limbs and trunk, joint mobilization, traction, manipulation, and myofacial release. Isometric and isokinetic exercises are used to improve muscle strength, endurance, and power for a particular muscle or muscle group. General conditioning/aerobic exercises promote optimal muscular and cardiac capacity through carefully designed treatment programs that can incorporate such activities as walking, running, swimming, and bicycle riding. Balance and coordination exercises

include the development of specific activities that promote coordinated postural reactions in response to displacement of the center of gravity. Equipment that reduces stability and enhances postural mobility (e.g., balls, balance beams and tilt boards) is common in programs that serve people with developmental disabilities. Coordination activities involve increasing the speed, complexity, and duration of complicated motor skills (Crutchfield, Shumway-Cook & Horak, 1989).

Cardiopulmonary techniques. Physical therapists employ procedures to improve pulmonary hygiene, enhance respiratory capacity, and remove upper airway secretions for people with developmental disabilities. Postural drainage utilizes exact positions in order to drain bronchial secretions. Vibration and percussion are used to enhance the movement of secretions within the airways, and suctioning may be used to remove secretions from the upper air passages. Segmental breathing exercises and diaphragm support during coughing augment mobility of the thorax and allow for greater air exchange (Crane, 1989; Tecklin, 1989).

Neuromuscular facilitation methods. Neuromuscular treatment techniques include methods for individuals whose motor coordination and muscular difficulty are due to either musculoskeletal or central nervous system involvement. These treatment approaches are designed for individuals with pathological muscle tone (hypotonia, hypertonia, or fluctuating tone) as well as difficulties with muscle strength, coordination, and joint range of motion. The methods incorporate controlled sensory stimulation in order to gain a desired motor or adaptive response through specific technique of facilitation and inhibition. Examples of these approaches include Neurodevelopmental Treatment (NDT) (Bly, 1991; Bobath, 1971, 1980), Proprioceptive Neuromuscular Facilitation (PNF)

(Knott & Voss, 1968), and sensory integrative approaches (Ayres, 1974; DeGangi & Greenspan, 1989; Rood, 1962).

Application of physical agents and modalities. This intervention approach includes the therapeutic use of heat, cold, electric, and hydrotherapies. The indications concerning the use and method of application of a particular physical agent are based on the individual's diagnosis, clinical symptoms, and contraindications limiting any therapeutic effects. Heat is often used to decrease pain, reduce muscle spasms, and increase flexibility. Cold is used to decrease pain, reduce swelling, and decrease spasticity (Whitney, 1989). Hydrotherapy employs the properties of water as a therapeutic environment that allows nonresistant motion (without gravity), assisted motion (with buoyancy), or resisted motion (against buoyancy) in order to enhance muscle strength, joint range of motion, general conditioning, coordination, and relaxation. Electrical stimulation is used to activate primary muscle responses or facilitate action along a nerve that produces a muscle response.

Orthotic fabrication and management. A range of splinting and casting techniques are used by physical therapists to provide orthotic support for decreased muscle function, relieve painful motion, reduce or prevent limitations in motion, inhibit abnormal muscle tone, and promote postural control. Physical therapists fabricate orthotics, provide recommendations for orthotics made by other professionals, and teach the individual (or caregivers) methods of use and care of these devices. Orthotic fabrication and management are important elements of direct care for people with developmental disabilities (Bertoti, 1986; Cusick, 1988; Donatelli, Hurlbert, Conaway, & St. Pierre, 1988; Harris & Riffle, 1986; Lindsey & Drennan, 1981).

Mobility and ambulation training. Physical therapists are responsible for rec- ommending and selecting appropriate devices, instructing the individual (or caregivers) on the proper use and maintenance of equipment, and training the individual or caregiver in therapeutic applications of ambulation and mobility aides. The selection of specific devices is dependent on the neurodevelopmental, musculoskeletal, and functional requirements of the individual. Ambulatory and mobility devices can be used as a therapeutic intervention to encourage specific patterns of motion, as a supportive device to supplement limited skills, or as a functional device to substitute for skills not available to the individual (Alexander, 1985; Bergen & Colangelo, 1985; Robinault, 1973).

Rehabilitation technology. The use of technology to facilitate functional skills provides an enhancement of traditional methods of intervention. The physical therapist (a) uses assistive technology resources to change the environment in order to promote access for people with special needs or (b) recommends assistive devices that permit or enhance functional abilities otherwise not available to an individual. The use of micro-switch powered mobility is an example of rehabilitation technology that provides a functional alternative for persons with decreased motor skills.

Supervision

Supervision includes monitoring the effectiveness of individual therapeutic interventions, directing treatment programs for groups of people, planning the use, duration, and frequency of therapeutic procedures, and teaching and training others in specific skills needed to care for individuals with developmental disabilities. Physical therapists provide guidance to caregivers responsible for carry-over of specific therapeutic techniques. This enables therapeutic management to be incorporated into the daily routines of people with developmental disabilities, and serves to increase the frequency of therapeutic intervention provided in typical environments (Cherry, 1991). Physical therapists administer therapeutic strategies for groups of people, incorporating generalized principles of management (e.g., safety, prevention of injury for the individual and the caregiver), general conditioning, positioning, and handling in programs that serve specific populations of people with developmental disabilities.

Consultation

Physical therapists also contribute consultative services to people involved in the collaborative provision of services to individuals with developmental disabilities. Technical assistance and professional advice are contributed by physical therapists in educational environments, vocational centers, and residential/home settings. Physical therapists working in interdisciplinary settings participate in consultative efforts aimed at the development of comprehensive approaches that meet the medical, education, vocational, and social needs of individuals with developmental disabilities (American Physical Therapy Association, 1990; Idol & West, 1987).

Education

Physical therapists provide educational experiences to individuals, parents, community organizations, and professionals interested in the care of people with developmental disabilities. Physical therapists teach the individual (or family) about therapeutic procedures, developmental concerns, and functional alternatives critical to the attainment of goals. Community organizations are informed about the effects of motor impairments on educational/vocational experiences and how educational/vocational environments can be modified to permit optimal function for the individual. Educational experiences pertaining to physical therapy are provided as a component of professional training and include such topics as "safety requirements for the individual and caregiver," and "prevention of injury for the individual and the caregiver." Didactic and clinical instruction to trainees in physical therapy and other professional fields within an interdisciplinary setting expands the knowledge of practitioners. Physical therapists offer information on normal movement and development, atypical motor development, therapeutic procedures, the use of adaptive/assistive equipment, and resources available for individuals with developmental disabilities (American Physical Therapy Association, 1990).

Advocacy

Knowledge and understanding of the rights and services available to people with developmental disabilities enables physical therapists to advocate for individuals with developmental disabilities (Cherry, 1991). Physical therapists are able to advocate for infants and toddlers with developmental disabilities on issues concerning service delivery and program specifications as outlined in the Individual Family Service Plan (PL 99-457; PL 101-476). Physical therapists advocate for school-age children (Individuals with Disabilities Education Act, 1990) through participation in preschool and special education planning committees and, when necessary, acting as expert witness. The physical therapist is an integral part of the enactment of the American with Disabilities Act (1990), enabling resources in all environments to be provided for people with special needs.

Research

Physical therapists are involved with research activities pertaining to direct and indirect services for people with developmental disabilities. These include (a) investigations into the use of specific treatment techniques for specific problems; (b) the efficacy of specific therapeutic approaches to affect the physical or functional status of people with developmental disabilities; (c) the development and standardization of assessment instruments and procedures; (d) contributions made towards differences in a person's physical and/or functional competence with adaptive/assistive devices; and (e) identifying outcomes from "state of the art" programs for people with developmental disabilities.

Case Example

Referral

Tom M., a 5½-year-old boy, was initially referred to our university affiliated program's Child Assessment Team (CAT) by his mother, who was concerned about resources available for her son within his present school program. The family, along with the local school district's special education planning team, were seeking information concerning Tom's developmental status, and recommendations regarding appropriate support services.

History

A review of medical and educational records provided by the family and the school district contributed the following information. Tom was born following a full-term uncomplicated pregnancy and experienced a reportedly normal newborn period. Early childhood history evidenced slight delays in his attainment of developmental skills (i.e., he sat at 11 months, he walked at 14 months without ever crawling, and his speech emerged slowly so that at 2 years old he spoke only a few words). Additional information about his early development (obtained during an interview) included maternal concern over Tom's episodes of choking due to over-stuffing his mouth with fluids and edible and non-edible substances; difficulty holding him (during his infancy) because he arched his back; poor sleeping patterns, including his need to be held tightly before falling asleep; and apparent diminished response to pain (so that he rarely cried).

When Tom was 2 years old his mother brought him to Dr. C., a pediatrician at a local children's hospital. Dr. C. reported that Tom had a mild degree of neurological impairment manifested by short attention span with hyperactivity, delayed speech development, and some degree of clumsiness. Tom was then seen by an occupational therapist in private practice, who described him as having postural insecurity with low muscle tone. She further reported that he required tactile stimulation to promote appropriate motor responses and often used immature movement patterns during transitions from one position to another. Subsequent clinical evaluation by Dr. M., a neurologist at a large urban hospital, combined MRI findings of hypoplastic occipital lobes and increased cisterna magna (suggesting that the cerebellum might be small) led to a diagnosis of double hemiparesis, language disturbance, and possible mental retardation of unknown etiology.

When Tom was 3 years old, another occupational therapist at his preschool program reported motor problems. She described Tom as exhibiting low muscle tone, poor perception of his body in space, and precarious motor planning, although he could accomplish gross motor milestone skills.

An educational summary when Tom was 4 years old reported delays of at least one year in the acquisition of gross and fine motor skills. Reported scores on the Early Learning Accomplishment Profile showed: fine motor, cognitive, and expressive language skills scattered to the 33-36 months level; gross motor and social/emotional skills at the 36 months level; and self help-skills scattered to the 36-44 months level of development.

At age 5 the Dial-R screening assessment revealed motor scores at the 1st percentile. This report expressed additional concerns about Tom's eye-hand coordination and movement skills. Tom is described as appearing "not well coordinated" and to have "difficulty maintaining his balance." An additional occupational therapy assessment indicated areas of concern including: (a) weakness in visual-perceptual skills; (b) visual-motor integrative dysfunction; (c) deficits in tactile discrimination; (d) immature fine motor control; (e) inadequate postural control; (f) decreased strength; (g) poor integration of postural adjustment reactions; (h) decreased balance and equilibrium skills; and (i) poor trunk control.

Frequent references to visual problems led his mother to seek the services of an optometrist. He reported Tom achieved an age equivalent of 3 years 2 months on the Beery Test of Visual Motor Integration.

Tom attended a language-based preschool at 2 years of age and a special (Association for Retarded Citizens) preschool program from ages 3 to 4 years. He is currently attending his local elementary school in an inclusive program which provides occupational therapy and speech/language interventions.

It was of interest to Mrs. M. and our team that throughout Tom's early childhood there were frequent concerns about his motor skills and development, but physical therapy consultation had never been recommended. Mrs. M. felt that she would like to have a physical therapy assessment along with other assessments as part of the comprehensive evaluation she outlined in her initial screening interview with the team social worker. The interdisciplinary team that evolved to meet Tom's needs included a physical therapist, a developmental pediatrician, an occupational therapist, a speech/language therapist, an audiologist, an educational psychologist, and a clinical psychologist.

Mrs. M. accompanied Tom to all of the assessments and often came with her husband and Tom's brother. The family remained present and contributed to the individual evaluations.

In addition to determining the priorities for the assessment process, Mrs. M. also reported that she was particularly concerned about a number of Tom's behaviors and had a list of questions she would like the team to answer. This list became part of the team record and eventually all of the questions were addressed at the end of the comprehensive assessment process.

Findings

Tom was assessed by all members of the interdisciplinary team. The developmental pediatrician reviewed Tom's present physical and developmental status. The developmental and functional findings at this evaluation revealed speech and language delay, fine and gross motor coordination difficulties, deficits in visual-motor integration, decreased visual-perceptual skills, and decreased ability to perceive accurate spatial relationships. The physician also reported that Tom's behavior was distracted and impulsive, with a limited attention span and high activity level, and that symptoms were exacerbated with stress. The report by the psychologist was consistent with the findings of the pediatrician. She reported that Tom was a friendly, cheerful boy; however, his behavior and performance during the evaluation were immature and suggestive of a younger child. One of the most salient aspects of the evaluation was Tom's extreme distractibility, disorganization, impulsiveness, and compromised attention. He was a confused, frustrated and over-reactive youngster who tended to give up rather than risk failure. Results of standardized evaluations indicated that Tom was functioning at a pre-readiness level in academic achievement, achieving a score at the upper end of the borderline range of intelligence.

Evaluations were also conducted for speech/language, audiology, and occupational therapy. Tom demonstrated moderate to severe expressive language impairment with articulation disorder. Occupational therapy assessments indicated that Tom's acquisition of developmentally appropriate fine motor skills was compromised. Based on the results of the Peabody Developmental Fine Motor Scales, Tom scored in the 2nd percentile for age in the domains of eye-hand coordination and manual dexterity. This score represents a two-year delay in the acquisition of fine motor skills.

The Physical Therapy Evaluation

The physical therapy evaluation was of primary concern to this family. They were interested in specific physical, developmental and functional skills in relation to Tom's present level of performance. During the assessment, Tom often responded impulsively to test items, especially when he perceived that the task would be difficult. Intermittent oppositional behaviors emerged when activities challenged his abilities. His cooperation could easily be elicited when a turn-taking approach was used.

Musculoskeletal evaluations revealed low tone, ligamentous laxity, and muscle weakness, as evidenced by Tom's inability to attain and sustain an erect posture in sitting, the presence of scapula winging, palpation of his muscles, and decreased strength. Functional muscle testing demonstrated diminished muscle strength. For example, Tom could not do a sit-up or maintain a pivot-prone position. Tom also had difficulty using all muscles surrounding the shoulder joint in order to keep his arms straight out at his sides. Similar difficulty was noted in using the muscles around his hip in order to maintain a one-footed standing position. Range of motion assessment for all joints of both upper and lower extremities revealed decreased mobility.

Postural adjustment reactions were delayed with immature integration of tonic reflexes. Protective reactions were present and compensated for poor trunk control, decreased muscle tone, and diminished muscle strength. This resulted in minimal use of trunk righting reactions, tilting reactions, and inadequate sitting balance. Tom demonstrated poor standing balance as evidenced by a wide base of support in stance and his inability to maintain one-footed standing. His posture was compromised by compensatory arching of his back during standing and a rounding of his back during sitting.

Functional assessments indicated that Tom used a variety of compensations for decreased muscle tone. For example, he walked with a wide-based gait and a high-guard position of his arms. Movement patterns were done quickly in order to avoid maintained use of mid-range postures and balance. He had difficulty accessing all aspects of his environment in an independent fashion. For example, he resisted and had difficulty climbing onto benches in order to reach a toy. Mrs. M. reported that Tom "falls off the school bus step" and requires one hand held when he climbs stairs. During the assessment Tom walked down four flights of stairs. Initially, he went down the stairs quickly, without fear or awareness of potential dangers to himself. At first, he held on to one rail and descended in a step-to fashion; towards the end of this activity he began an alternating step pattern. He ascended the four flights holding onto one rail, using an awkward but alternating step pattern. He stamped his feet on each step, so that the whole process was most notable for the loud noise level.

Peabody Gross Motor Developmental Scales indicated that Tom was able to accomplish all skills at the 18-24 month level, demonstrating that he was functioning below his chronological age in gross motor skills. He manifested locomotor skills at the 24-29 month old level of gross motor development, with a scatter of skills to the 30-35 month old level in gross motor development. His strength was in the locomotor component of this evaluation, with his weakest area in balance, receipt, and propulsion. His performance was somewhat scattered due to his apparent lack of interest in particular tasks. For example, he completed child-directed activities, such as climbing stairs. However, in activities that required compliance to a set of directions (e.g., "Stand on one foot with your hands on your hips"), he was unable to gain a full score because the criteria required a specific behavior on the part of the child. Similar delays were noted in skills that required directed interactions with the examiner. For example, Tom did not want to engage in any ball-throwing tasks (e.g., "Throw the ball to me") which included criteria for both direction and distance.

Treatment Recommendations

As a result of the comprehensive interdisciplinary team assessment and collaborative meetings with the family, physical therapy was recommended for Tom. Mrs. M. requested that our team support her efforts

to gain PT services as part of Tom's individual educational plan. These recommendations included direct physical therapy interventions and consultative assistance to his teachers and others involved in his daily school routine. It was also recommended that a longer depth chair with sides or arms might assist Tom during tabletop activities. A meeting with Mrs. M. and members of the local elementary school resulted in provision of physical therapy as a related service in Tom's individual educational plan.

In order to meet these objectives in the least intrusive fashion, the members of the school district suggested that Tom start school early to receive individual services, enabling him to remain with his class during school hours. This avoided a large amount of pull-out from his regular activities. The direct physical therapeutic interventions and consultation that Tom had not received prior to this interdisciplinary assessment were now incorporated into his typical routine. Mrs. M. was relieved that this area was finally being addressed on both a specific level of one-to-one intervention as well as being incorporated into his school situation.

Outcomes

Tom was observed in his classroom as a follow-up after the interdisciplinary assessment. He was engaged in a readiness activity with his classmates and a teaching assistant. Tom remained seated although he hooked his feet around the legs of the chair to gain stability. He did not alter his position excessively during this task. The teaching assistant used a variety of verbal and gestural cues to keep Tom on task. Background noise and activity did not appear to affect his attention. When moving to another activity Tom was able to find his place (marked by a purple circle) unassisted. Visual cues structured and organized his environment. Tom went to music, library, and art without assistance but continued to have one-to-one assistance for stair-climbing activities.

Conclusions

Tom is a child who demonstrates delays in gross motor skills due to low muscle tone, poor postural control and compromised balance. The strategies which he has developed to deal with these delays have been inefficient. These limitations in function impact on all his developmental domains and his social, attention and behavior skills. Tom and his family found diagnostic and program planning resources through an interdisciplinary team process that provided comprehensive information pertaining to Tom's physical and functional status. The specific information from each team member (including the family) was integrated into an individualized strategy that supported Tom. The family gained assistance in their efforts to provide Tom with opportunities for optimum performance.

References

Alexander, M.A. (1985). Orthotics, adapted seating, and assistive devices. In G.E. Molnar (Ed.), *Pediatric rehabilitation* (pp. 158-175). Baltimore: Williams & Wilkins.

Americans with Disabilities Act (ADA), P.L. 101-336 (1990). 42 U.S.C. 12101.

American Physical Therapy Association (1990). *Physical therapy practice in educational environments: Policies and guidelines.* Alexandria, VA: Author.

American Physical Therapy Association (APTA) (1993a). *A future in physical therapy.* Alexandria, VA: Author.

American Physical Therapy Association (1993b). State licensing agencies. *Physical Therapy, 73,* 943.

Ayres, A.J. (1974). *The development of sensory integration theory and practice.* Dubuque: Kendall/Hunt.

Barnes, M.R., Crutchfield, C.A., & Heriza, C.B. (1978). *The neurological basis of patient treatment: Vol. II. Reflexes in motor development.* Atlanta: Stokesville Publishing.

Bayley, N. (1969). *Bayley scales of infant development.* New York: Psychological Corp.

Bergen, A. (1988). Putting the puzzle together: Using commercially available technology to create therapeutic seating. *Tot Line, 14*(2), 10-14.

Bergen, A.F., & Colangelo, C. (1985). *Positioning the client with central nervous system deficits: The wheelchair and other adapted equipment* (2nd ed.). Valhalla, NY: Valhalla Rehabilitation Publishers.

Bertoti, D.B. (1986). Effects of short leg casting on ambulation in children with cerebral palsy. *Physical Therapy, 66,* 1522-1529.

Bertoti, D.B. (1989). Physical therapy for the child with mental retardation. In J. S. Tecklin (Ed.), *Pediatric Physical Therapy* (pp. 237-261). Philadelphia: Lippincott.

Bly, L. (1991). A historical and current view of the basis of NDT. *Pediatric Physical Therapy. 3*(3), 131-135.

Bobath, B. (1971). *Abnormal postural reflex activity caused by brain lesions* (2nd ed.). London: William Heinemann Medical Books.

Bobath, K. (1980). *A neurophysiological basis for the treatment of cerebral palsy.* Philadelphia: Lippincott.

Bruininks, R.H. (1978). *Bruininks-Oseretsky test of motor proficiency.* Circle Pines, MN: American Guidance Service.

Canfield, J.S. (1989). The evaluation process. In R.M. Scully & M.R. Barnes (Eds.), *Physical therapy* (pp. 320-325). Philadelphia: Lippincott.

Chandler, L., Andrews, M., & Swanson, M. (1980). *The movement assessment of infants: A manual.* Rolling Bay, WA: Infant Movement Research.

Cherry, D. (1991). Pediatric physical therapy: Philosophy, science and technique. *Pediatric Physical Therapy, 3* (2),70-76.

Chiarello, L., Effgen, S., & Levinson, M. (1992). Parent-professional partnership in evaluation and the development of individualized family service plans. *Pediatric Physical Therapy, 4,* 64-69.

Clough, P. (1989). Respiratory causes. In R.M. Scully & M.R. Barnes (Eds.), *Physical Therapy* (pp. 258-288). Philadelphia: Lippincott.

Copeland, M.E., & Kimmel J.R. (1989). *Evaluation and management of infants and young children with developmental disabilities.* Baltimore: Paul H. Brookes.

Crane, L. (1989). Respiratory analysis. In R.M. Scully & M.R. Barnes (Eds.), *Physical therapy* (pp. 548-586). Philadelphia: Lippincott.

Crutchfield, C.A., Shumway-Cook, A., & Horak, F.B. (1989). Balance and coordination training. In R.M. Scully & M.R. Barnes (Eds.), *Physical therapy* (pp. 825-843). Philadelphia: Lippincott.

Cusick, B.D. (1988). Splints and casts: Managing foot deformity in children with neuromotor disorders. *Physical Therapy, 68,* 1903-1912.

Daniels, L. & Worthingham, C. (1986). *Muscle testing techniques of manual examination* (5th ed.). Philadelphia: W.B. Saunders.

DeGangi, G.A., & Greenspan, S.I. (1989). The development of sensory functions in infants. *Physical and Occupational Therapy in Pediatrics, 8*(4), 21-31.

Donatelli, R., Hurlbert, C., Conaway, D., & St. Pierre, R. (1988). Biomechanical foot orthotics: A retrospective study. *The Journal of Orthopaedic and Sports Physical Therapy, 10,* 205-212.

Easton, T.A. (1972). On the normal use of reflexes. *American Science, 60,* 591-599.

Fetters, L. (1984). Motor development. In M. Hanson (Ed.), *Atypical infant development* (pp. 313-358). Baltimore, MD: University Park Press.

Fife, S.E., Roxborough, L.A., Armstrong, R.W., Harris, S.R., Gregson, J.L., & Field, D. (1991). Development of a clinical measure of postural control for assessment of adaptive seating in children with neuromotor disabilities. *Physical Therapy, 71,* 981-993.

Finnie, N. (1975). *Handling the young cerebral palsied child at home.* New York: E.P. Dutton.

Firoentino, M.R. (1972). *Normal and abnormal development: The influence of primitive reflexes on motor development.* Springfield, IL: Charles C. Thomas.

Folio, M.R., & Fewell, R.R. (1983). *Peabody developmental motor scales.* Allen, TX: DLM.

Furuno, S., O'Reilly, K.A., & Hosaka, C.M., (1985). *Hawaii early learning profile.* Palo Alto, CA: VORT Corp.

Glover, M.E., Preminger, J.L., & Sanford, A.R. (1978). *Early learning accomplishment profile.* Winston-Salem, NC: Kaplan School Supply.

Grohmann, J.E.L. (1983). Comparison of two methods of goniometry. *Physical Therapy, 6,* 922-925.

Harris, S.R., & Riffle, K. (1986). Effects of inhibitive ankle-foot orthoses on standing balance in a child with cerebral palsy: A single subject design. *Physical Therapy, 65,* 663-667.

Hillegass, E. (1989). Cardiovascular analysis. In R.M. Scully & M.R. Barnes (Eds.), *Physical therapy* (pp. 515-547). Philadelphia: J.P. Lippincott.

Hundertmark, L.H. (1985). Evaluating the adult with cerebral palsy for specialized adaptive seating. *Physical Therapy, 65,* 209-212.

Individuals with Disabilities Education Act (1990). Education of the Handicapped Act Amendments, P.L. 101-476.

Idol, L., & West, J. (1987). Consultation and special education: Theory and practice. *Journal of Learning Disabilities, 20,* 474-479.

Johnson-Martin, N., Jems, K.G., & Attermeier, S.M. (1986). *The Carolina curriculum for handicapped infants and infants at risk.* Baltimore: Paul H. Brookes.

Kendall, H.O., Kendall, F.P., & Wadsworth, G.E.

(1971). *Muscles, testing and function* (2nd ed.). Baltimore: Williams & Wilkins.

Kliewer, D., Bruce, W., & Trembath, J. (1977). *Milani-Comparetti motor development screening test.* Omaha, NE: Meyers Children's Rehabilitation Institute.

Kolobe, T.H.A. (1992). Working with families of children with disabilities. *Pediatric Physical Therapy, 4*(2), 57-63.

Knott, M., & Voss, D. (1968). *Proprioceptive neuromuscular facilitation.* New York: Harper & Row.

Linder, T.W. (1990). *Transdisciplinary play-based assessment: A functional approach to working with young children.* Baltimore, MD: Paul H. Brookes Publishing.

Lindsey, R.W., & Drennan, J.C. (1981). Management of foot and knee deformities in the mentally retarded. *Symposium on orthopedic surgery in the mentally retarded: Orthopedic Clinics of North America, 12,* 107-112.

Miller, L.J. (1982). *Miller assessment for pre-schoolers.* Englewood, CO: Foundation for Knowledge in Development.

Montgomery, P.C. (1981). Assessment and treatment of the child with mental retardation: Guidelines for the public school therapist. *Physical Therapy, 61,* 1265-1272.

Morris, S.E. (1982). *Pre-speech assessment scale.* Clifton, NJ: J.A. Preston.

Pinkston, D. (1989). Evolution of the practice of physical therapy in the United States. In R.M. Scully & M.R. Barnes (Eds.), *Physical therapy* (pp. 2-30). Philadelphia: J.P. Lippincott.

Robinault, I.P. (1973). *Functional aides for the multiply handicapped.* New York: Harper & Row.

Robinson, C., & Fieber, N. (1988). Cognitive assessment of motorically impaired infants and preschoolers. In T.D. Wachs and R. Sheehan (Eds.), *Assessment of young developmentally disabled children* (pp. 127-161). New York: Plenum.

Robinson, J.L., & Smidt, G.L., (1981). Quantitative gait evaluation in the clinic. *Physical Therapy, 61,* 351-353.

Rood, M.S. (1962). *The use of sensory receptors in motor response approaches to the treatment of patients with neuromuscular disease.* International Therapy Congress. Dubuque, IA: W.C. Brown.

Scherzer, A.L., & Tscharnuter, I. (1982). *Early diagnosis and therapy in cerebral palsy: A primer on infant developmental problems (Pediatric Habilitation,* Vol. 3.) New York: Marcel Dekker.

Shumway-Cook, A., & Woollacott, M.H. (1985). Dynamics of postural control in the child with Down syndrome. *Physical Therapy, 65,* 1315-1322.

Staller, J. (1984a). An approach to adaptive seating. *Selective Proceedings from Barbro Salek Memorial Symposium.* Oak Park, IL: Neurodevelopmental Treatment Association.

Staller, J. (1984b). Choosing accessories to personalize a wheelchair. *Health Industry Today,* (July), 50-52.

Staller, J. (1992). Developing strategies of adaptive seating and positioning. Unpublished lecture notes.

Stockmeyer, S.A. (1967). An interpretation of the approach of Rood to the treatment of neuromuscular dysfunction. In *American Journal of Physical Medicine, 46*(1) 900-961.

Stuberg, W. (1992). Considerations related to weight-bearing programs in children with developmental disabilities. *Physical Therapy, 72,* 35-40.

Tecklin, J.S. (1989). Pulmonary disorders in infants and children and their physical therapy management. In J.S. Tecklin, (Ed.) *Pediatric physical therapy* (pp. 141-172). Philadelphia: J.P. Lippincott Co.

Van Dillen, L., & Roach, K.E. (1989). Analysis of activities of daily living. In R.M. Scully & M.R. Barnes (Eds.), *Physical therapy* (pp. 629-738). Philadelphia: Lippincott.

Whitney, S. L. (1989) Physical agents: Heat and cold modalities. In R.M. Scully & M.R. Barnes (Eds.), *Physical therapy* (pp. 844-875). Philadelphia: J.P. Lippincott Co.

13

Psychiatry

Joel D. Bregman, M.D., & John Gerdtz, Ph.D.

Psychiatrists are physicians with specialized training in the diagnosis and treatment of mental and emotional disorders. Psychiatrists are distinguished from other mental health professionals (for example, psychologists, social workers, or psychiatric nurses) by their education and licensure as physicians, a process which occurs prior to entering specialized psychiatric training. As physicians, psychiatrists have familiarity with medical conditions which either cause or influence the diagnosis and/or treatment of mental or emotional disorders. In addition, as licensed physicians, psychiatrists are able to prescribe and administer medication and other somatic treatments as part of a comprehensive treatment program for their patients. Other mental health professionals who are not licensed physicians are not expected, or able, to offer such treatment.

Physicians specializing in other fields of medicine, such as neurology, family practice, pediatrics, and others, sometimes become involved in the treatment of individuals suffering from mental and emotional disorders. Psychiatrists are distinguished from these other medical specialists by receiving intensive training and supervision in the diagnosis and treatment of mental and emotional disorders. This includes training in the use of specialized diagnostic instruments (e.g., structured and semistructured interviews, etc.) and treatment interventions (e.g., individual, family, and group psychotherapy, cognitive and behavioral interventions, medication, etc.). Well-trained psychiatrists are in a relatively unique position to synthesize the biological, psychological, and social factors involved in the development of mental and emotional disorders and to help coordinate a comprehensive treatment plan.

While there are clear differences between medical and non-medical disciplines involved in the treatment of mental and emotional disorders, and also among the various medical and non-medical specialties, some aspects of education and training are similar. Professionals from a variety of specialties often train together, learn from each other, and work together to provide optimal treatment. This is particularly relevant to the field of developmental disabilities. For example, the Emory Autism Resource Center (EARC) is an interdisciplinary program based in the Department of Psychiatry of Emory University. The EARC offers educational opportunities to students and trainees from various professional disciplines including psychiatry, pediatrics, psychology, social work, and special education.

Our experience at the EARC affirms that in the area of developmental disabilities, psychiatrists can function most effectively as members of a well-integrated interdisciplinary team. The needs of children and adults with developmental disabilities are often so complex and varied that no single profession could possibly provide all the necessary services. The interdisciplinary team at the EARC consists of professionals from psychiatry, psychology, special education, social work, and speech and language therapy. We find that each discipline has a unique and valuable perspective on the development of appropriate treatment programming.

Psychiatrists, like most professionals, undergo lengthy and rigorous training. After completing four years of medical school (at which time the M.D. degree is conferred), a physician planning a career in psychiatry enters a first year of residency training (formerly called internship), 6 to 12 months of which are based in either pediatrics or internal medicine. Some residents choose to complete two to three years of pediatric or medical training prior to beginning specialized training in psychiatry. This exposure to general pediatric or adult medicine includes a rotation in neurology (the diagnosis and treatment of medical conditions involving the brain). The resident then completes an additional three to four years of training in General Psychiatry, which takes place in both inpatient and outpatient settings. If the physician chooses to pursue a career in Child and Adolescent Psychiatry, two to three years of training in General Psychiatry is followed by an additional two years of subspeciality fellowship training in Child and Adolescent Psychiatry. This also includes clinical experiences in inpatient and outpatient settings. (Therefore, Child and Adolescent Psychiatrists are also trained in General Psychiatry.) Similar subspeciality

fellowship programs are available in Geriatric Psychiatry and Forensic Psychiatry.

Throughout the course of medical education and residency training, national examinations are conducted to supplement local medical school and residency examinations. In order to proceed with education and training, the physician must pass examinations administered by the National Board of Medical Examiners at the end of the second and fourth years of medical school and at the conclusion of the first year of residency (internship). Upon completion of specialty and subspeciality training, additional examinations are administered by the American Board of Psychiatry and Neurology. These examinations test theoretical knowledge as well as ability in formulating differential diagnoses and treatment recommendations for actual clinical cases. Board Certification in Psychiatry and the subspeciality disciplines is conferred for successful examination performance.

The practice of medicine is regulated by the licensing regulations of various licensing boards in all states in the U.S. Upon successful completion of medical school, internship, and the examinations administered by the National Board of Medical Examiners, physicians are eligible to apply for state medical licensure. Some states require additional examinations and interviews before a medical license is issued. In most states, medical licensing boards require that physicians obtain continuing medical education credits to ensure that clinical knowledge and skills are updated.

Psychiatrists, as physicians with specialized training in the treatment of mental and emotional disorders, have much to contribute to programs serving children and adults with developmental disabilities. These contributions are discussed below under the following headings: diagnosis, treatment, training, consultation, and research.

Diagnosis

An accurate and complete diagnosis is the foundation for an effective treatment plan for a person with developmental disabilities. The basic diagnostic system used by most psychiatrists in the United States is the *Diagnostic and Statistical Manual of Mental Disorders* published by the American Psychiatric Association. This manual, which is commonly known by the abbreviation DSM, is currently in its Fourth Edition (DSM-IV; American Psychiatric Association, 1994).

DSM-IV is organized in a hierarchy of five axes, and the clinician using the DSM is expected to evaluate a patient according to each axis, although it is not necessary to make a diagnosis or assessment in all five axes for all patients. This multiaxial system was developed to provide an assessment of various dimensions of an individual's functioning. Each axis is focused on different types of information about the past and current situation of the patient. Axis I is concerned with primary clinical syndromes (e.g. schizophrenia, major depression, alcohol dependence). Axis II refers to developmental disorders and personality disorders and syndromes. The developmental disabilities are coded on this axis. Each of the disorders included in Axes I and II are defined by specific criteria. Diagnostic algorithms have been developed for most of the disorders, based on the available research and the findings from clinical field trials. Axis III is used for physical or medical conditions which may influence the diagnosis or treatment of a psychiatric disorder. Axis IV is the clinician's assessment of the severity of all psychosocial stressors that may worsen the patient's psychiatric condition. Both acute and enduring adverse events and circumstances are rated on a six-level ordinal severity scale. Axis V is the clinician's assessment of the patient's overall psychological, social, and occupational functioning. Ratings are based on clinical anchor-points incorporated into a 90-point ordinal scale.

The DSM allows a clinician to indicate that a diagnosis may be preliminary or uncertain by referring to it as "provisional." In addition, more than one diagnosis can be given on Axes I and II (as long as exclusionary criteria are met). If this is the case, the clinician should indicate which condition is to become the principal focus of psychiatric treatment. DSM-IV (American Psychiatric Association, 1994) also includes a number of useful Decision Trees to assist clinicians in making an appropriate differential diagnosis.

As with all diagnostic systems, DSM has definite shortcomings and has received criticism in this regard. The DSM is nevertheless the most commonly accepted psychiatric diagnostic system in use in the U.S and is used by mental health professionals from various disciplines, including psychiatry, clinical psychology, social work, and psychiatric nursing, among others.

Accurate psychiatric diagnosis among persons with developmental disabilities follows from a comprehensive evaluation. The evaluation includes information obtained directly from the patient (through interviews, observations, and diagnostic tests); detailed medical, developmental, and social history; information supplied by parents, family members, and other caretakers; and the results of assessments provided by other professionals, including psychologists, speech and language therapists, educators, social workers, vocational counselors and job coaches, and others. For diagnostic purposes, the results of cognitive testing, speech and language evaluations, educational testing, a measure of current adaptive functioning, and a good developmental history, are especially important sources of information.

Many children and adults with mental

retardation and other developmental disabilities are at significant risk for developing psychiatric disorders in addition to their primary disability (Szymanski & Crocker, 1985). In fact, well-designed epidemiologial studies indicate that persons with developmental disabilities carry a substantially higher risk for the development of psychiatric disorders than individuals in the general population. An important diagnostic role for the psychiatrist, and the other members of the patient's interdisciplinary team, is to consider the possibility that a patient with mental retardation (with or without verbal skills) may *also* be suffering from a psychiatric condition (e.g., mood disorder, anxiety disorder, psychotic disorder, obsessive-compulsive disorder, etc.). The accurate diagnosis of psychiatric disorders in persons with developmental disabilities is especially difficult if the patient has limited verbal skills or is non-verbal. However, in these cases, it may be possible to develop behavioral indicators of psychiatric disorders (Bodfish & Madison, 1993; Charlot, Doucette, & Mezzacappa, 1993; Sovner & Lowry, 1990) and to obtain information regarding the presence of these behavioral indicators from various informants, such as family members or staff members of a residential program. Some laboratory tests, such as the Dexamethasone Suppression Test (DST) for depression, may also be useful in diagnosing possible psychiatric disorders among non-verbal patients with developmental disabilities. (See Greden, 1985 for a general overview, and Mattes and Amsell, 1993, for a discussion of the use of DST with adults with mental retardation.) The diagnosis of psychiatric conditions in persons with developmental disabilities is not just a matter of theoretical interest. If a psychiatric condition is diagnosed, it may be possible to treat the condition and significantly improve a patient's overall functioning and quality of life.

Important, yet sometimes neglected, components of the diagnostic process include the identification of possible medical conditions and medication interactions which may be causing, exacerbating, or otherwise influencing the person's psychiatric syndrome, and which require appropriate treatment intervention. Some studies have found that almost 10% of psychiatric patients have previously undetected medical conditions that require treatment (Torrey, 1993), and it is reasonable to expect that persons with developmental disabilities, especially those with limited or no verbal skills, may also have untreated medical conditions. It is also important to note that medication interactions and side-effects may present as psychiatric symptoms. Torrey (1993) reported the following case:

> A 34-year-old severely mentally retarded woman with a seizure disorder was referred because of lack of energy, sadness, irritability and increased low-level self-injury. Staff wondered if an antidepressant would help this "depression." A work-up revealed a toxic blood level of dilantin. Depressive symptoms resolved after her dilantin dose was adjusted. (p. 467)

A very important component of the diagnostic process is the reporting of evaluation results to the patient, his or her family, other caregivers, and (if possible) to the various professionals involved in the patient's plan of care. As Szymanski and Crocker (1985) noted, this diagnostic report by the psychiatrist should avoid theoretical speculations, and focus clearly on the diagnostic findings and the practical implications of these findings for the patient's plan of care. At the Emory Autism Resource Center, we have found that it is most effective to provide a verbal summary of the diagnostic findings and recommendations to the patient's family, caregivers, and other professionals, relatively soon after the actual diagnostic evaluation. A comprehensive written evaluation is then sent to the family and other involved professionals. The written evaluation includes a summary of test results and clinical findings, psychiatric diagnoses, and specific treatment recommendations (e.g., cognitive and behavioral treatment, medication, educational interventions, etc.). We have found that a detailed and integrated written report, in which specific treatment recommendations follow logically from the diagnosis, not only emphasizes the multidisciplinary nature of the diagnostic process, but also provides caregivers with a clear and reasoned treatment strategy.

Treatment

Psychiatrists typically provide a variety of treatments for their patients, the nature of which depends on the needs and circumstances of the individual patient. Psychiatrists are generally relied upon to provide psychopharmacological treatment, that is, the use of medications to treat psychiatric problems. While the appropriate use of medication is an important part of psychiatric training and professional practice, psychiatrists also have other treatment strategies available to them, which can be used alone or in conjunction with medication.

In the past, psychiatrists were generally known for providing long-term psychodynamic therapy based on one of the various theories of psychoanalysis. However, current psychiatric treatment approaches reflect the major advances which have taken place in the fields of neurobiology, psychology, and the social sciences during the past 40 years. Although long-term psychodynamic treatment continues to be offered, a variety of other treatment approaches have been adopted, including, among others, problem-focused, time-limited, and supportive psychotherapy, family therapy, cognitive therapy, behavioral interventions, and medication. Most psychiatrists are trained in the use of therapy with individuals, couples, families, and groups. Increasingly, psychiatrists in training are becoming exposed to, and learning, the various techniques associated with behavior modification or applied behavior analysis. A psychiatrist who specializes in services to children and adults with developmental disabilities will need a good understanding of various behavioral interventions used in developmental disabilities. Many psychiatrists also receive training in the use of various relaxation and desensitization procedures based on the principles of classical conditioning. Cognitive and cognitive behavioral procedures have also become an important part of psychiatric training.

Psychiatrists in clinical practice tend to be much like clinicians from other disciplines in adopting an eclectic approach to therapy with patients, rarely relying on a single modality or theoretical approach. Most psychiatrists, whatever their field of practice or specialization, now spend time working as members of a interdisciplinary team. Successful treatment outcomes for many psychiatric disorders requires the involvement of professionals from several disciplines, in addition to family members and other caregivers.

The use of psychotropic medication with persons with mental retardation and other developmental disabilities remains an area of controversy. Some studies (see Torrey, 1993, 471-472) have indicated that certain types of psychotropic medication, especially the antipsychotics, have been used at a high rate in residential programs for people with developmental disabilities. Most psychiatrists are well aware that medication may be part of a comprehensive treatment program and that, in many cases, medication should not be prescribed until appropriate educational and behavioral procedures have been implemented (Szymanski & Crocker, 1985).

Where a diagnosis of a psychiatric disorder has been made for a person with developmental disabilities, and there exists a medication which may be effective in treating that disorder, the use of medication can significantly improve the patient's quality of life and enhance the efficacy of behavioral and educational interventions. The prescription of an appropriate medication requires that the psychiatrist establish a correct diagnosis and explain the potential benefits and possible side-effects of the medication to the patient, the patient's legal guardian (if any), and caregivers (including family members, residential or day program staff, teachers, job coaches and others.) It is essential that caregivers understand the indications for prescribing the medication, the manner in which it is to be administered, and its potential side-effects. Patients, family members, and caregivers need to adopt realistic expectations regarding the benefits of a particular medication. Psychiatrists and other physicians have often been criticized for prescribing medications too readily, and in certain cases, no doubt, this criticism is justified. At the same time, it has been our experience that some caregivers, family members, and other professionals expect too much from a medication. It is very unlikely that a medicine, by itself, will improve a complex problem or situation without additional behavioral or educational interventions.

If a patient is prescribed medication, the psychiatrist needs to be closely involved in the patient's plan of care in order to assess clinical effectiveness and monitor for potential side-effects. Monitoring for side-effects requires special vigilance and increased

cooperation from family members or other caregivers when the patient is non-verbal (Szymanski & Crocker, 1985). Effective monitoring usually requires objective information on changes in the frequency and severity of problem behaviors, data on sleep and eating patterns, information on work or school productivity, and other general measures of functioning and patient well-being. Naturally, this type of information may be more readily available for a patient living in a residential program, while family members might not be able to provide as much objective information. Even for patients living with family members, however, it is generally possible to obtain some information regarding behavioral functioning at home (e.g., simple frequency counts). An alternative method of obtaining this information (as discussed in the case study at the end of this chapter) is to record family telephone contacts with the clinic to report behavioral crises.

Psychiatrists are trained to provide a variety of treatment interventions. Unfortunately, in the field of developmental disabilities, most patients have limited resources and rely largely on public mental health systems for services. The limited number of available psychiatrists often are overwhelmed with requests for consultation, and rarely are asked to provide more than medication management (cf. Ryan, 1993).

Comprehensive and appropriate psychiatric care can be provided to children and adults with developmental disabilities through a multidisciplinary team of professionals. This multidisciplinary team could be based within community mental health program (Torrey, 1993), a residential or day program or, as in the case of the Emory Autism Resource Center, a university or medical school (Ryan, 1993).

Psychotherapy can be an important component of treatment for patients with developmental disabilities. Szymanski and

Crocker (1985) have suggested that appropriate goals of psychotherapy include:

> Amelioration of affective discomfort, improvement in self-esteem, learning the skills of interpersonal relationships, developing realistic expectations of self, learning to express emotions appropriately, and resolving separation anxiety before moving away from the family (p. 1659).

Additional goals for psychotherapy or counseling include dealing with issues regarding a patient's serious or terminal illness, divorce or separation of parents or siblings, or the death of a parent or family member.

It is important to clarify the expectations of the patient, the patient's family, and other caregivers regarding the outcome of counseling or psychotherapy. Patients may be referred for counseling because of behaviors which disturb family members or caregivers, but which may not be particularly disturbing to the patient. Even in these situations, counseling may be appropriate for some patients, in conjunction with various behavior modification techniques in the patient's day program, job site, or residence. Ryan (1993) emphasized the importance of counseling or therapy focusing on the needs of the patient:

> Individual psychotherapy designed with the agency's, rather than the individual's agenda (e.g., to make the person "act nicer") will have cosmetic results at best, and will make the person feel worse in most cases (p. 480).

For counseling or psychotherapy to be effective, an initial comprehensive assessment of the patient's language and cognitive abilities is essential. For most patients with developmental disabilities, counseling or therapy needs to be concrete and focused,

and the therapist will have to be comfortable in setting appropriate limits (Szymanski & Crocker, 1985). It may be necessary to schedule frequent counseling sessions which are of relatively brief duration. In addition, regular evaluations should be conducted to ensure that treatment goals are being met and therapeutic efficacy is being achieved. At times, conflicts will arise regarding the balance between patient confidentiality and the need to appraise family members and/or other caregivers of serious concerns. This conflict is certainly not unique to therapy with patients with developmental disabilities, but additional complicating factors could be present with this population (for example, what information should be provided to the parents of an adult with developmental disabilities when the parents are not legal guardians?).

With appropriate modifications, supportive psychotherapy can be useful for some patients with developmental disabilities. Rockland (1993) summarized the basic techniques of supportive psychotherapy as follows:

> Strengthening the therapeutic alliance, instituting environmental interventions, offering education, advice, suggestion, encouragement and praise, establishing appropriate behavioral limits and prohibitions, undermining maladaptive defenses, strengthening adaptive defenses, and emphasizing strengths and talents (p. 1053).

The strengths of supportive therapy include a focused and concrete approach to problems, an emphasis on relatively brief therapy, the use of a variety of interventions (as described above), and empirical evidence indicating effectiveness of the approach with several patient populations. (See Rockland, 1993, for a good review of this research.)

Psychotherapy may also be an appropriate intervention for the families and siblings of a child or adult with developmental disabilities. It should not be assumed that all families of persons with developmental disabilities want or need counseling or therapy. Sometimes counseling or support groups are offered to a family as a way of defusing a conflict with professionals or in response to the family's request for other services (for example, respite). In these circumstances, the offer of therapy may weaken an already strained relationship. A straightforward discussion of disagreements and available services should be conducted first. However, when families and siblings do request therapy, a clear, focused, supportive psychotherapy would probably be the best option. Supportive psychotherapy could also be provided to families and siblings in a group setting.

In summary, effective psychiatric treatment for persons with developmental disabilities usually involves a number of treatment options including prescription and monitoring of medication, appropriate psychotherapy with individuals or groups, and recommendations for educational and behavioral interventions. These services are most effectively provided by a psychiatrist who is knowledgeable about developmental disabilities, and who is a member of a interdisciplinary team (Szymanski & Crocker, 1985).

Training

The Report of the American Psychiatric Association (APA) Task Force on Services to Adults With Mental Retardation and Developmental Disabilities (Szymanski, Madow, Mallory, Menolascino, Pace & Eidelman, 1991) emphasized the importance of training in developmental disabili-

ties for all psychiatrists. The members of the Task Force recognized that this training would not only prepare a psychiatrist to effectively serve patients with developmental disabilities, but would also help psychiatrists become better clinicians with all their patients.

Unfortunately, there are still relatively few psychiatric training programs offering opportunities for clinical experience in the field of developmental disabilities (Szymanski & Crocker, 1985; Torrey, 1993). As training opportunities increase, more psychiatrists in the general community will become willing and able to provide services to children and adults with developmental disabilities. A long-term follow-up study by Szymanski and Crocker (1985) found that psychiatrists trained in their specialized clinic continued to provide services to patients with developmental disabilities long after graduation from the program.

Psychiatrists are also important resources for training other medical and non-medical professionals to provide services to people with developmental disabilities and their families. Some professionals in the field of developmental disabilities have difficulty understanding the contributions that psychiatrists can make to clinical services, beyond prescribing and monitoring medications (Torrey, 1993). At the same time, some psychiatrists do not appear to understand or appreciate the contributions that other professionals make to clinical services for patients with developmental disabilities (Ryan, 1993). Multidisciplinary training programs and treatment clinics make it possible for professionals from a variety of disciplines and theoretical perspectives to gain experience in working together and developing effective treatment programs.

Continuing education programs are also important sources of training for psychiatrists and other professionals who are already in practice. The American Psychiatric Association and the Academy of Child and Adolescent Psychiatry have special interest groups or committees focusing on the needs of children and adults with developmental disabilities. Membership in these organizations and committees offers psychiatrists and other professionals regular opportunities for training and for obtaining current information on research and clinical practice in the field of developmental disabilities.

Consultation

Many psychiatrists are employed as consultants to various day and residential programs that provide services to people with mental retardation and other developmental disabilities. In many cases, the only role for the consultant psychiatrist is to make recommendations concerning medication. Even if the consultation role is confined to medication, a knowledgeable and experienced psychiatrist can still provide additional insights regarding the overall treatment plan for patients with mental retardation. Psychiatric consultants, along with other members of an interdisciplinary team, have been effective in reducing inappropriate uses of certain medications in residential programs for adults with developmental disabilities. (See Spreat, Serafin, Behar & Leiman, 1993, as an example.)

An effective psychiatric consultant needs considerable diplomatic skill in working effectively with members of the multidisciplinary team, particularly those who may have biases against psychiatry. In these situations, there is a strong tendency for personality and administrative conflicts to arise that may undermine aspects of the patient's treatment. Although the psychiatric consultant should be open and supportive with staff members and help to mediate

conflicts, it is also important that she or he avoid being drawn into the role of therapist for individual staff members. In these situations, appropriate referrals for treatment should be considered.

Effective consultation usually involves regular contact with staff members who are providing direct clinical, behavioral, and educational services. Szymanski and Crocker (1985) emphasize that staff members, especially those providing direct services, need to understand the rationale for a consultant's recommendations, and have the opportunity to meet with the consultant regularly to discuss difficulties which may arise with program implementation. A good consultant also encourages staff to persist in face of discouragement, and helps them to recognize even small improvements in a patient's situation.

Research

Psychiatric investigators have initiated research programs in developmental disabilities, often in collaboration with professionals from a variety of other disciplines. Such efforts have included basic research into the genetic and neurobiological processes which underlie developmental disabilities; studies focusing on the differential diagnosis of comorbid neuropsychiatric conditions and resultant treatment outcome; epidemiological investigations; and assessments of service needs, to name just a few (see Bregman, 1991; Bregman & Hodapp, 1991; Ballinger, Ballinger, Reid & McQueen, 1991).

Psychiatrists, equipped with medical training and knowledge regarding psychosocial interventions, have an important role to play in the development of effective educational and treatment programs for children and adults with developmental disabilities. Other important roles for psychiatrists in the field of developmental disabilities include professional training, program consultation, and research. In virtually all these roles, the psychiatrist will be most effective as a member of an interdisciplinary team.

Case Example

J.G. is an 18-year-old adolescent male with diagnoses of autism and severe mental retardation. J.G. is non-verbal and dependent on his family for assistance in meeting all his basic needs. He is short and stocky, and weighs over 250 pounds. J.G. is currently enrolled in a self-contained special education classroom in a local public school. A number of psychotropic medications had been prescribed for J.G. in the past, but the medications had not been effective in reducing problem behaviors. He was not on any psychotropic medication at time of referral.

J.G. was referred to the Emory Autism Resource Center (EARC) in a state of behavioral crisis. His family (consisting of both parents and a sibling) reported that their life at home had become unbearable. J.G. needed constant monitoring and redirection to keep him from breaking into kitchen cabinets and gorging himself with food. He frequently remained awake for most of the night, screaming and jumping up and down on his bed. His parents reported considerable property destruction in the home, as J.G. would often tear doors loose from their frames in an attempt to enter a room. Although behavioral difficulties were less severe at school, teachers called the family at least once a week requesting that they take J.G. home because he was "out of control." The family had been attempting for weeks to obtain emergency respite, without success.

A multidisciplinary assessment was performed, with direct observation of J.G., review of available school and medical records, and interviews with the family. Information was obtained from the family on the severity and frequency of the problem behaviors, and the behaviors appeared to increase in severity and frequency on a two- to three-week cycle: teacher observations confirmed the cyclical nature of the behaviors. The Vineland Adaptive Behavior Scales (Sparrow, Balla & Cicchetti, 1984), the Motivation Assessment Scale (Durand & Crimmins, 1992), and the Functional Analysis Interview Form (O'Neill, Horner, Albin, Storey & Sprague, 1990) were completed. These functional analysis instruments suggested that the problem behaviors were primarily motivated by sensory reinforcers, desire for tangibles, and desire for attention. There was a communicative function to much of this behavior, in that loud vocalizations and some forms of aggression appeared to serve to communicate J.G.'s protest or rejection of an activity.

Physical examination and laboratory testing did not suggest the presence of a direct medical etiology for J.G.'s affective and behavioral difficulties.

J.G. was diagnosed as manifesting an autistic disorder, severe mental retardation, and a cyclic mood disorder (atypical bipolar disorder). Based on the functional analysis noted above, a number of simple behavioral strategies were recommended for the family. The family was encouraged to keep J.G. occupied, and a list of suggested activities was compiled; basic crisis intervention strategies were developed; recommendations were made for some basic environmental changes in the home; and a program of planned ignoring and physical redirection was suggested. A home visit gave family members a clearer understanding of the environmental recommendations.

The family implemented a number of

recommendations, and began to see some improvement in behavior, especially with the systematic use of redirection. However, the problem behaviors were severe enough so that family members were calling the Center at least three to four times a week to report a behavioral crisis. J.G.'s school continued to ask the family to take him home at least once a week.

A medication (lithium carbonate) was prescribed to deal with some of the mood disorder symptoms. Within several weeks, the family quickly reported a positive clinical response, with a significant reduction in the frequency and severity of dyscontrol episodes (which included aggression and loud vocalizations). Family members reported that J.G. "looked happier," and for a period of four consecutive months there were no reports of behavioral crisis. During these four months, the daily report book from school indicated adaptive behavioral functioning, with no episodes of behavioral crises and no requests that the family take J.G. home from school.

J.G. still has many challenges in his life. While the behavioral improvement has continued, J.G. still needs intensive instruction in adaptive communication and functional living skills. The negative behaviors may well reoccur, even with medication, unless these important alternative skills are taught. The initial success in reducing problem behaviors brings with it a new challenge, the development of increased motivation among teachers and family members to teach the necessary alternative functional communication skills.

References

American Psychiatric Association (1994). *Diagnostic and statistical manual of mental disorders* (4th ed.). Washington, DC: Author.

Ballinger, B., Ballinger, C.B., Reid, A., & McQueen, E. (1991). The psychiatric symptoms, diagnoses and care needs of 100 mentally handicapped patients. *British Journal of Psychiatry, 158,* 251-254.

Bodfish, J.W., & Madison, J.T. (1993). Diagnosis and fluoxetine treatment of compulsive behavior disorder of adults with mental retardation. *American Journal on Mental Retardation, 98,* 360-367.

Bregman, J. (1991). Current developments in the understanding of mental retardation Part 2: Psychopathology. *Journal of the American Academy of Child and Adolescent Psychiatry, 30,* 861-872.

Bregman, J., & Hodapp, R. (1991). Current developments in the understanding of mental retardation Part 1: Biological and phenomenological perspectives. *Journal of the American Academy of Child and Adolescent Psychiatry, 30,* 707-719.

Charlot, L.R., Doucette, A.C., & Mezzacappa, E. (1993). Affective symptoms of institutionalized adults with mental retardation. *American Journal on Mental Retardation, 98,* 408-416.

Durand, V.M., & Crimmins, D.B. (1992). *The Motivation Assessment Scale (MAS).* Topeka, KS: Monaco.

Greden, J. (1985). Laboratory tests in psychiatry. In H.I. Kaplan & B.J. Sadock (Eds.), *Comprehensive textbook of psychiatry* (4th ed., pp. 2028-2033). Baltimore, MD: Williams & Wilkins.

Mattes, J.A., & Amsell, L. (1993). The Dexamethasone Suppression Test as an indication of depression in patients with mental retardation. *American Journal on Mental Retardation, 98,* 354-359.

O'Neill, R.E., Horner, R.H., Albin, R.W., Storey, K., & Sprague, J.R. (1990). *Functional analysis of problem behavior. A practical assessment guide.* Sycamore, IL: Sycamore.

Rockland, L.H. (1993). A review of supportive psychotherapy, 1986-1992. *Hospital and Community Psychiatry, 44,* 1053-1060.

Ryan, R. (1993). Response to "Psychiatric care

of adults with developmental disabilities and mental illness in the community." *Community Mental Health Journal, 29,* 477-481.

Sovner, R., & Lowry, M.A. (1990). A behavioral methodology for diagnosing affective disorders in individuals with mental retardation. *The Habilitative Mental Healthcare Newsletter, 9,* 55-61.

Sparrow, S.S., Balla, D.A., & Cicchetti, D.V. (1984). *Vineland Adaptive Behavior Scales.* Circle Pines, MN: American Guidance Service.

Spreat, S., Serafin, C., Behar, D., & Leiman, S. (1993). Tranquilizer reduction trials in a residential program for persons with mental retardation. *Hospital and Community Psychiatry, 44,* 1100-1102.

Szymanski, L.S., & Crocker, A. (1985). Mental retardation. In H.I. Kaplan & B.J. Sadock (Eds.). *Comprehensive textbook of psychiatry* (4th ed., pp. 1635-1671). Baltimore, MD: Williams & Wilkins.

Szymanski, L.S., Madow, L., Mallory, G., Menolascino, F., Pace, L., & Eidelman, S. (1991). *Report of the APA task force on services to adults with mental retardation and developmental disabilities.* Washington, DC: APA Press.

Torrey, W.C. (1993). Psychiatric care of adults with developmental disabilities and mental illness in the community. *Community Mental Health Journal, 29,* 461-476.

14

Psychology

George J. Vesprani, Ph.D., & Georgia Ann Pitcher, Ph.D.

Earlier definitions of psychology as a discipline evolved from the *study of mental activity* to the *study of behavior*. In current use, the study of behavior and mental processes includes both the objective study of observable behavior and the recognition that some mental processes cannot be directly observed; they must be inferred. Major fields of study are experimental and physiological psychology; clinical and counseling psychology; and social, personality, and developmental psychology. Areas of specialization, such as rehabilitation, pediatric, and neuropsychology, invite further study.

Experimental and *physiological psychologists* study the measurement and control of psychological phenomena of both human and animal reactions to auditory, visual, tactile, and kinesthetic stimuli; learning and remembering; and other behavioral responses. *Psychoneurobiologists* investigate the relationship of behaviors to events taking place inside the body, particularly within the brain and nervous system, such as the structural location of language, memory, and emotions. Comparisons between animal and human studies are a major interest to these investigators. *Industrial* and *engineering psychologists* are concerned with the study of human beings in the work force, human

resources, motivation, morale, and related technological areas.

Developmental psychologists study the factors in normal human behavior and their changes throughout the life span, while some psychologists are interested in studying only one aspect of human development such as personality or social behavior.

The application of psychological principles to the diagnosis and treatment of emotional and behavioral problems is the *clinical* and *counseling psychologists'* major area of study. Mental illness, juvenile delinquency, criminal behavior, mental retardation, marital and family conflict, health, physical illness, and addictive behaviors are some of the areas of interest to this group of professionals.

Educational psychologists are specialists in learning and teaching, with school psychology a very important subspeciality. Educational psychologists oversee a very broad domain. They can teach at universities and colleges, develop training programs for vocational enterprises and industry, and/or conduct research in learning and teaching strategies. *School psychologists* work with individual children and youth in diagnosing specific learning problems for special education programs, counseling individuals and groups in social skills and problem solving, and consulting with teachers and parents on a variety of issues concerning learning and behavior.

About one-half of the psychologists who have advanced degrees are employed in teaching, research, and counseling in colleges and universities. Others hold positions in public schools, hospitals, clinics, research institutes, government agencies, business, industry, and in private practice.

Historically, psychology has been one of the core disciplines within University Affiliated Programs (UAPs). The majority of psychologists who work within UAPs have emerged from psychology training programs implicit in the "Boulder Model." This paradigm, whose name is derived from the conference held in 1949 in Boulder, Colorado, trains psychologists to become knowledgeable contributors to and consumers of research literature, *as well as* practitioners of psychological theories and methodologies. Thus the scientist–practitioner concept of training in psychology was developed.

Since psychology is a broad field with many specialty areas, each has its unique contribution to the understanding of developmental disabilities. Psychologists who have a variety of professional specializations and interests and serve on interdisciplinary teams will be encountered within the UAP system. Roberts and Magrab (1991) presented an ecological framework for the changing roles of the psychologist from a clinic-based to a family-centered, community-based approach to service delivery for young children. In many parts of the United States, this systems change extends to individuals throughout their life span and to their families as well. This broader approach integrates psychology with other health and education disciplines and, along with the client and the family, serves to develop individualized therapeutic plans and goals.

Educational and Training Requirements

A bachelor's degree with a major in psychology can be earned at the college or university level. It signifies that the student has fulfilled a required course of study in psychology developed by the faculty and approved by the board of trustees. Introductory and basic courses in development, research methods, personality, learning, and tests and measurement are usually included in four years of study.

Colleges and universities with graduate programs can offer a major in psychology. The student takes advanced courses in a basic core program and begins to specialize in one of the fields described above, such as experimental, educational, or clinical. At the end of two years or with about 30 to 36 hours of course work—and often a thesis—the student is awarded a master's degree in psychology.

The Educational Specialist degree is offered by some institutions of higher learning to include advanced course work approximately a year or 30 hours beyond the master's degree and includes requirements for state and national licensure in school psychology.

The next level of study leads to the doctoral degree. Approximately 60 hours of study beyond the bachelor's degree or 30 beyond the master's degree is common. Some programs do not require formal attainment of the master's degree, but the hours remain about the same: 60 hours including both levels. At the doctoral level, students are required to further specialize. In professional psychology programs (clinical, counseling, and school psychology), courses in theory are often combined with practical or practicum experiences. Students are placed at sites for supervised practice. School psychology majors typically are placed in practica in educational settings such as day care, preschools, and elementary and high schools. Clinical and counseling majors gain experiences at mental health centers, hospitals, clinics, and/or criminal justice agencies.

Predoctoral internship programs are required for clinical, counseling, and school psychologists by the American Psychological Association and the National Association of School Psychologists. From 1500 to 2000 hours (two semesters or about one calendar year) of supervised practice are required for the doctoral degree.

The American Psychological Association grants approval for programs that follow strict guidelines for doctoral degrees in psychology that have been developed by members of the organization. Realistically, job opportunities are best for individuals who have completed APA-approved programs.

Doctoral level psychologists can be trained in Departments of Psychology or Education, or within professional schools of Psychology. Degrees such as Doctor of Philosophy (Ph.D.), Doctor of Education (Ed.D.), and Doctor of Psychology (Psy. D.) respectively reflect these different backgrounds.

Granted from college or university programs in psychology or education, degrees at the master's level may include Master in Education (M.Ed.), Master of Arts (M.A.), and Master of Science (M.S.), depending on the nature of the training program. Unless licensed or certified by the state in which the individual practices, professional limitations and supervision are to be expected upon first employment. Psychology majors at the bachelor's degree level are not yet sufficiently trained to practice within the field without considerable structure and supervision. They serve as aides to psychologists and/or technicians and, as such, are service extenders.

The UAP model provides preservice training for individuals seeking the master's and/or doctoral levels of professional practice. Some UAP's provide pre- and postdoctoral training programs in psychology. A number of these sites are accredited by the American Psychological Association (APA). The APA neither accredits master's degree programs nor grants full membership to master's level psychologists, even though some colleges and universities offer master's degrees in psychology.

Licensure, Certification, and Continuing Education

The American Psychological Association is an excellent source of information regarding requirements for licensure/certification of psychologists (APA, 1994). The practice of psychology is regulated by law in all 50 states, the District of Columbia and eight of the Canadian provinces. State and provincial laws for the regulation of psychology refer to either licensure or certification. Certification limits the use of the title *psychologist*. Licensure laws control the title and also list activities which comprise the practice of psychology for which a license is required. Most psychology licensure and certification laws are general, granting the same license for practice to psychologists regardless of their field of specialization. The APA's Ethical Principles of Psychologists (1981), referenced by many state laws, limit the psychologist's practice to his or her particular area of competence. This is a self-regulating obligation of the profession.

Requirements for licensure and certification differ by state. The Association of State Psychology Boards and the Council for the National Register of Health Service Providers in Psychology have worked together to identify doctoral programs in psychology which meet their guidelines for professional psychology programs. The APA accredits doctoral training programs in three recognized fields of psychology: clinical, counseling, and school psychology.

The doctoral degree is the necessary level of training for licensure/certification in nearly all of the states. A majority of states mandate that this degree be granted in an APA-approved program. Training below the doctoral level is recognized in some states by the use of the terms *psychological assistant* or *psychological associate*. However, these designates must function under the supervision of a psychologist who is licensed/certified for independent practice. Laws governing psychological practice ordinarily affect only individuals identifying themselves as *psychologists* to the public in a fee-for-service setting. Academic and research activities are usually exempt from regulation. Federal civil service standards parallel state requirements for practice at the present time.

School psychologists who are not trained at the doctoral level are often certified for service within educational settings by state departments of education. Department of education certification as a school psychologist does not constitute a license or certificate for the independent general practice of psychology. The National Association of School Psychologists has established requirements, standards, ethics, and examinations for national certification.

State examining boards in psychology administer, promulgate rules and regulations, and conduct examinations for licensure/certification. Some state boards require continuing education as one of the conditions of licensure or certificate renewal. The requirements are either in the licensing/certification law itself or are part of the administrative regulations adopted by the board.

Contributions to Interdisciplinary Practice

Assessment

A significant contribution of the discipline of psychology to the interdisciplinary practice for persons with developmental disabilities is the development and application of assessment tools and methodologies reflecting the empirical and scientific orientation in a psychologist's training. The assessment process itself reflects the application of clinical skills and expertise. The methodologies used in assessment depend on a number of factors, including the age of the individual being assessed as well as the questions being asked by the evaluator. Literally thousands of assessment tools have been developed, each designed to measure some subset of a broad range of behavior for study as part of a comprehensive evaluation.

In spite of the numerous assessment tools available, clinical practice dictates that only a few of these assessment tools will emerge as the optimum available in any given assessment area. The literature contains several excellent attempts to characterize the psychologist's role as assessor and evaluator in dealing with populations of individuals with developmental disabilities. For example, Erickson (1980) speaks of specific assessment methods traditionally used with children who are developmentally disabled. Johnston and Magrab (1978), in an earlier attempt to deal with assessment issues in populations of children with developmental disabilities, focus clearly on the interdisciplinary process and the team approach as a framework from which to view the child. Magrab (1982) summarized how these assessment tools can be understood and utilized by individuals without a major background in psychology. Witt & Covell (1986) present issues of psychological assessment with individuals who are mentally retarded or who present major learning disabilities from the viewpoint of a multidisciplinary approach. They present information regarding the background and training of psychologists along with detailed discussion of issues related to test design. They also discuss specific assessment tools which find frequent application with individuals with developmental disabilities, although not necessarily reflecting an integrated or interdisciplinary approach as practiced within UAPs.

Not all assessment is accomplished within highly structured and formal environments which parallel laboratory conditions. While this might reflect more traditional approaches to assessment, there has been a growing trend to carry the process of assessment into less-structured and less-traditional environments reflecting the *real world* in which the individual with developmental disabilities functions.

Just as factors such as age of the individual being assessed can guide the use of a particular assessment tool, various philosophies have also had an impact on how a psychologist shapes the assessment process. For example, there is a current philosophical emphasis on *family-centered and community-based* approaches to assessment which dictate that traditional mechanisms may be inappropriate if they do not adequately reflect the needs of the family or the environment in which the individual with developmental disabilities operates. Basically, this philosophical approach sensitizes the psychologist to the fact that assessment should not occur in a vacuum, that it recognizes reality and is of necessity linked to the intervention procedures which follow as a natural outcome of the assessment process. A body of literature is emerging in this area. For example, Roberts and Magrab (1991) spell out the psychologist's potential role within this model. In particular, it suggests that traditionally formal assessment approaches are a part of a mix of assessment

data to be gathered and that both the environment and levels of assessment are broadened to reflect reality. Further, the investigators argue for a competency-based versus pathology-based model as a framework from which to view families in order to promote *healthy* development of the family and the individual with developmental disabilities.

In the following discussion, assessment methodologies and tools have been grouped into areas reflecting particular kinds of behavior and their corresponding data.

Developmental Evaluation

Developmental tests focus on measurement of basic language, motor, and related skills that emerge on a predictable developmental schedule. Evaluation tools such as the Bayley Scales of Infant Development II (Bayley, 1993), when applied to infants and toddlers, can provide normative data about the development of motor skills as well as mental functioning. These instruments are not typically good measures of later cognitive skills, since they measure a domain of skills that is largely sensorimotor in nature without many of the language skills which are better predictors of later cognition. Nonetheless, the skills measured by developmental tests may reflect the presence or absence of early building blocks necessary for later cognitive development. Developmental assessment has taken on particular importance and relevance because of growing concern for early interventions with families and their children who may be developmentally disabled or delayed. Such an early intervention approach would be consistent with provisions and mandates of P.L. 99-457 and a specific focus on children 0–3 years of age. These assessments can lead to interventions which are truly family-centered and community-based.

Cognitive Assessment

Cognitive tests, such as measures of general intelligence with older clients, help psychologists to understand the strengths and weaknesses of the individual's problem solving skills as well as to determine the overall level or degree of his intellectual skills. The Stanford-Binet Intelligence Scale, now in its fourth edition (Thorndike, Hagen, & Sattler, 1986), represents one of the oldest, most valid, and most frequently used instruments in the assessment of general intelligence. The Wechsler Intelligence Scale for Children (Wechsler, 1949), now in the third edition, along with the Kaufman Assessment Battery for Children (Kaufman & Kaufman, 1983), represent widely accepted measures of cognitive functioning of children, each with specific strengths in measuring aspects of cognitive development. The Wechsler Adult Intelligence Scale-Revised (Wechsler, 1981) is the adult counterpart. In using these instruments, the psychologist's goal is to ascertain the individual's overall level of cognitive functioning using a standardized test that allows comparison of the individual's performance to a previously obtained normative sample. Further, such measurement also allows the psychologist to understand patterns of development that may be somewhat outside the range of normal development. In such an analysis, various aspects of cognitive style, strengths and weaknesses, etc., are better understood.

Behavioral Assessment

Behavioral assessment reflects a broad diversity of tools developed by the psychologist, both within the laboratory and in clinical practice, to quantify various aspects of behavior demonstrated by the individual. In basic terms, it represents the counting or quantification of target behaviors, i.e., the establishment of base rates. Circumstances surrounding the production of base rate behaviors also need to be understood. These include reinforcers or other ecological factors that maintain or deter the presentation of the target behavior. Once these factors are understood, a natural consequence of behavior assessment is the application of behavioral management techniques in order to modify the production of the behaviors.

Assessment of Personality and Emotional Functioning

The measurement of personality assumes that the individual typically presents styles of behavior or traits which are relatively stable over a period of time. These behaviors include temperament, attitudes, feelings, and interests which reflect the individual's typical response patterns to the environment. Personality tests and inventories have been developed to measure these traits, particularly in older children and adults. Because many of these instruments require the individual to read in order to provide a self-report, they are not readily applicable to younger children or adults with mental retardation. In these instances, parents or caregivers might respond to inventory items which they view as characteristic of the child's typical response patterns. The Personality Inventory of Children (Wirt, Lachar, Klinedinst, & Seat, 1982) and the Minnesota Multiphasic Personality Inventory (Hathaway & McKinley, 1943) are typical instruments of this category. Behavior rating scales such as the Child Behavior Checklist and the Youth Self Report (Achenbach, 1988) represent another avenue of approach to quantifying typical behavior patterns of children and youth as perceived by themselves, their parents and their teachers. Yet another approach to understanding personality and emotional functioning is found in projective tests. Although not as psychometrically rigorous and objective as are inventories and checklists, these tests also attempt to sample the individual's behavior, as reflective of attitudes, feelings, and emotional states.

Assessment of Social and Adaptive Skills

Social adaptability is crucial in the identification of developmental disabilities. The ability to meet various roles demanded by society is not directly dictated by a specific level of cognitive function but by the capacity to respond to environmental and community needs. For example, the ability to demonstrate personal self-sufficiency, as in meeting basic needs such as eating, drinking and toileting, mandates consideration. Community self-sufficiency might reflect an individual's ability in traveling about the neighborhood and performing simple economic activities. The appropriateness of a person's behavior in a social context such as relating to other individuals and assuming a social role in conjunction with other individuals is paramount. The Vineland Adaptive Behavior Scales (Sparrow, Balla, & Cicchetti, 1984) and the American Association on Mental Retardation Adaptive Behavior Scale (Nihira, Leland, & Lambert, 1993) are examples of instruments which have been designed to quantify various aspects of social/adaptive functioning. Data for these assessments are typically acquired through the interview of a third-party informant.

Assessment tools which focus on social/adaptive functioning have been variously successful, in part depending on the definition of competencies within this broader area of functioning. One thing is clear: More theoretical analysis and the development of new assessment tools are needed in this area. This is especially relevant to the changes in the definition of mental retardation as espoused by the American Association on Mental Retardation (1992) which expresses an increased emphasis on functional elements, with particular concentration on aspects of social/adaptive skills.

Assessment of Neuropsychological Functioning

Perhaps the most rapidly developing area in the field of psychological assessment is derived from neuropsychology. Although neuropsychological assessment methodologies represent the development of new and unique measurement tools, they generally reflect the use of already established techniques within a unique theoretical and conceptual framework from which to view these assessment data. The focus is on understanding various brain/behavior relationships, particularly as manifest in children who demonstrate clear or suspected evidence of central nervous system involvement. Thus, children with manifest or suspected brain trauma, various symptoms of neurological deficits, learning disabilities, and attentional problems may warrant specific neuropsychological assessment. The Luria-Nebraska Neuropsychological Battery: Children's Revision (Golden, 1987) is but one example of several test batteries in the realm of neuropsychological assessment. Psychologists with specialized information and training on brain/behavior relationships may also interpret the findings of some of the traditional assessment instruments within a neuropsychological framework.

Assessment of Academic Achievement

Measuring academic achievement represents another body of standardized and normatively based assessments which can be applied by psychologists in an interdisciplinary setting. Because this group of instruments focuses specifically on school-related activities, school psychologists, by virtue of their training, may be more knowledgeable in approaching this body of data. In some IDTs, educational assessment data may be the responsibility of special educators. In any case, to understand children of school age who manifest diverse learning problems, information from this domain is frequently required.

Assessment of Vocational Functioning

Not all UAPs utilize assessment tools and methodologies which focus on vocational functioning. This is due in part to issues such as age and social expectations as they apply to the work environment. In many UAPs the focus is on evaluation and treatment of children as opposed to adults. In those UAPs with an adult component, issues of aptitude and interests need to be considered, along with limitations placed on an individual's ability to function in the work place by virtue of their developmental disability. Specialty areas such as habilitation, rehabilitation, or neuropsychology can have specific contributions to make with regard to vocational assessment and programming.

Assessment Using the Clinical Interview

Interviewing and observational skills with both family and clients round out the broad range of skills necessary to assess an individual with developmental disabilities. While interviews can be as rigorous and as structured as many of the instruments designed to measure cognition, they are generally less structured and less formal. In fact, naturalistic observations of the family and/ or client, whether at home, school, play, or work, may be the most informal assessment approach of all. Yet this information adds breadth as well as depth to the continuum of data, which may be vital in a family-centered and community-based process of understanding and planning for the needs of a family with a member who has developmental disabilities.

Intervention

In many IDTs psychologists act in the capacity of case managers or evaluation coordinators, with the responsibility for designing and monitoring the interdisciplinary process of evaluation as well as designing the most appropriate treatment plan. At the very least, they are vital participants in the interdisciplinary team process. By virtue of their training in development, they are able to provide not just discipline-specific information, but information from a broader perspective. In that regard, they are generalists and may be uniquely valuable participants on the team. Intervention is fundamentally linked to the process of assessment and evaluation.

In some practice environments, the psychologist does not provide direct service to a client. Instead, consultative services are provided by utilizing already existing data as a basis for participating in the team process. This contrasts with other practice environments in which the psychologist is also a direct service provider. Once the necessary data are in hand, the IDT shares its respective data pools, and service delivery can be planned and carried out.

Following the assessment or evaluation process, the psychologist can be involved in other applied activities, including designing and implementing recommendations as part of the IDT process. Various psychological treatment modalities or interventions may be offered directly to the client and family as part of the UAP training and service delivery programs. In some instances, referral will be made to community programs external to the UAP when this best meets the family needs. For example, psychologists, as part of the IDT, participate in the design of individual family service plans (IFSP's) for implementation of P.L. 99-457 (1986). They recommend treatment for psychological adjustment and/or emotional problems and assist in referral to the appropriate community resources if the client is not treated within the UAP itself. There is often liaison with community agencies, including schools, to insure that educational recommendations regarding the client's learning skills and behavior are understood and that the environment is responsive to the client's needs. In addition to the design of individual family service plans, which may represent the best opportunity to put family-centered and community-based strategies in place, psychologists provide a broad range of intervention strategies which typically include the following approaches:

Behavior Management

Naturally linked to *behavioral assessment*, a treatment program based on behavioral principles can be designed using data gathered as part of the behavior assessment process. This has been a particularly productive approach to changing behavior in younger children or in individuals with limited cognitive abilities. Because behavioral approaches, in contrast to more traditional *talk therapies*, do not require high levels of exchange of verbal information, they sidestep one of the major limitations—lack of communication skills, which may typify some persons who have developmental disabilities. In many instances, the psychologist applies behavioral methods directly to an individual client. In most instances, however, the psychologist acts in the capacity of consultant and facilitator, teaching the parents and caregivers to apply behavioral

strategies within a much broader arena than just the psychologist's office. Once again, the philosophy of family-centered and community-based services finds appropriate expression in this intervention arena.

Behavioral methodologies assume that behavior is in large part a function of its consequences. Behavior that is reinforced will likely occur again, at an increased rate or otherwise strengthened. During the behavior assessment phase, target behaviors are identified and base rates are established. During the treatment phase, appropriate reinforcers are defined, and schedules are developed and implemented. Evaluation of change is an ongoing process and contributes to decisions regarding new target behaviors or changes in reinforcement schedules. It should be noted that psychologists have developed ethical standards for the use of reinforcers with emphasis on use of positive reinforcers to guide or develop appropriate behaviors.

Counseling/Psychotherapy

This group of more traditional methods of intervention is highly reliant on interactive communication skills. These methods not only can be applied to individuals but in many instances find application within the context of the family. A broad range of philosophies and theoretical approaches can be reflected within the context of the training received by the psychologist, the relative success of certain strategies as reported in the research literature, as well as the personal preferences of the psychologist applying these methodologies. The use of play therapy, i.e., use of traditional toys and play materials designed to enable a child to play out otherwise unverbalized ideas and feelings, may be particularly useful with young children or individuals with limited verbal capacity.

Crisis Intervention

Crisis intervention has as its focus the timely application of intervention strategies, from whatever source, to assist the family and individual with developmental disabilities to cope with some immediate stressor. These therapeutic approaches are usually in response to unpredictable stressors which threaten to destabilize the coping abilities of the individual or family. Not only must they be timely, but these strategies are likely to be highly focused and often time-limited. Thus, a family may receive immediate supportive services from the psychologist over several continuous days or weeks to assist them in coping with an immediate crisis. Crisis, of course, can be defined in many ways and is a relative term defined in part by the individual family resources in dealing with that source of stress.

Group Therapy

Not all traditional psychotherapeutic or counselling methods take place within individual or family settings. Rather, they may encompass groups of individuals who share common problems and experiences. Thus, group therapy may focus on a number of areas or conditions as well as common areas of interest. It is not uncommon for example, for groups to coalesce around issues of sexuality, social skills development, or problems related to conditions such as Attention-Deficit Hyperactivity Disorder. The availability of these services within UAPs is highly individualized and thus may vary greatly from setting to setting. An important attribute of group therapy is that it allows for the application of treatment strategies to a larger number of people by a single professional. In addition, group therapy allows individuals with common difficulties to gain a perspective that may not otherwise be available within an individual therapy approach.

Consultation/Community Liaison

There appears to be a growing need to carry many of the services currently available within IDT settings into the community in order to meet the individual's needs in those settings. In this regard, psychologists often act in the role of consultants to community agencies as they provide services to individuals with developmental disabilities. This is a perfect paradigm for application of principles consistent with the philosophy of family-centered, community-based practice. Models of consultation differ, of course, and vary from workshops, lectures, and teaching of courses to more individualized liaison approaches wherein the psychologist relates to service providers on a continuing basis, where the focus may be on specific individuals. Individuals with developmental disabilities have by definition developmental problems which may be manifest over an extended period, perhaps lifelong in nature. It is imperative, then, that there be a continuum of services available throughout the life span, and that the services be available in the broadest environmental context, consistent with a family-centered, community-based approach.

Summary

Within the broad field of psychology, psychologists who work in the field of developmental disabilities typically have doctoral degrees in clinical, counseling, educational, school, developmental psychology, obtained from accredited universities or professional schools. The psychologist on the IDT provides direct services to clients in a family-centered situation, acts as the case coordinator, and/or renders consultative services to other professionals in a community-based setting.

Direct services include assessment and evaluation of intellectual, academic, social, emotional, and adaptive development and/

or behavior. Observations, interviews, psychometric, and projective testing also are used in the evaluation process. As the case coordinator, the psychologist is responsible for guiding the evaluation, staying in contact with the client and family, making certain that the recommendations are carried through. The psychologist in the role of consultant can interpret the evaluation findings and interventions to the local professionals who are responsible for carrying out the recommendations. Recommendations for therapeutic interventions can be carried out by the evaluator, by other members of the interdisciplinary team, or professionals in the client and family's community.

Developmental disabilities, which by definition occur before age 22, are life-long conditions which require on-going assessment and interventions. Therefore, as generalists, psychologists as well as the other professionals on the interdisciplinary team can follow individuals and their families from birth throughout the life span. Psychologists also can specialize in one or more developmental areas such as infancy, preschool, school age, youth, or adults. Elderly persons with developmental disabilities have become of special interest to some psychologists.

Case Example

The following example is adapted from an authentic interdisciplinary team report with the customary efforts taken for the confidentiality of the client and family.

Referral

Mary (age 11 years/11 months) was referred by her parents through her physician for behavior problems and poor achievement test scores. Mary's parents have concerns about her learning, memory, attention, and below-average weight. Her teacher notes that she is achieving below expectations.

Background Information

Mother had regular medical care and an uncomplicated pregnancy. Mary was born at 7 lbs., 3 oz. Mary had slow development and difficulty eating as an infant. She also had multiple ear infections. Developmental milestones include sitting at 9 months, crawling at 10 months and walking at 13 months. She began to combine words at 1½ years and used sentences at 3 years.

Mary currently is in the 6th grade. She received special tutoring services and counseling before moving to her present school. In November, 1989, her performance on the Wechsler Intelligence Scale for Children-Revised (Wechsler, 1974) resulted in a Verbal IQ in the low-average range, a Performance IQ in the borderline range, and a Full Scale IQ in the low-average range. The Peabody Picture Vocabulary Test-Revised (Dunn & Dunn, 1981) yielded a scaled score in the borderline range of ability. The standard scores from the Woodcock-Johnson Tests of Achievement-Revised (Woodcock & Johnson, 1989) and the Wide Range Achievement Test-Revised (Jastak, Jastak & Wilkinson, 1984) were also within the borderline range of ability. The Peabody Individual Achievement Test-Revised (Markwardt, 1989) also revealed a scaled score in the borderline range. Mary was recommended for retention in the 1st grade, but did go on to 2nd grade. It was noted that Mary had vision problems and glasses were prescribed, although she does not need to wear them now. It was also noted that she may have learning difficulties.

Mary lives with her parents and 10-year-old brother. Her brother has a complicated medical history including seizures and asthma.

Procedures Administered

Physical examination; audiological evaluation; psychological testing; speech and language assessment; psychological/social parent interview; and mental status examination.

Summary of Findings

Mary has a normal developmental history with the exception of delayed language. Her coordination appeared normal to the mother. There has been no regression or loss of developmental skills. Mary has a history of seizures, which include staring spells about every five seconds, with three episodes witnessed by the social worker today. There is a strong family history of learning disabilities and seizures. Mary is currently on 10 mgs. of Ritalin twice a day, although her mother wonders if increasing the dose would be appropriate. Mary's height was 151 centimeters which is on the 50th percentile. Her weight was 36.6 kilograms, which is on the 25th percentile. Her head circumference was 53.2 centimeters, which is within +1 standard deviation of the mean for her age. Upon examination, Mary was cooperative and had some spontaneous speech. Her skin revealed no lesions. Head, eyes, ears, nose, and throat, and lung exams were within normal limits. Upon neurological evaluation the muscle stretch reflexes were generally 3+ in the upper extremities and 2+ in the lower extremities. The cranial nerves appeared to be intact. Her coordination appeared to be somewhat slow, and movements appeared slightly awkward. Heelcords were not tight. No rigidity or spasticity was observed. No compulsive activity or dysmorphic features were noted during the physical examination. Mary's audiometric evaluation resulted in normal tympanograms bilaterally. Normal hearing was demonstrated bilaterally.

During the psychological evaluation, Mary's performance on the Wechsler Intelligence Scale for Children-III (Wechsler, 1991) resulted in a Full Scale IQ of 77, within the borderline range of intellectual functioning. This performance places Mary at the 6th percentile when compared to others her age in the general population. Mary did not demonstrate any significant difference between her performance on manipulative tasks as compared to the verbal tasks. Mary performed best when she used visual memory and visual motor coordination to copy a code within a time limit. She had significant difficulty with the ability to copy a two-dimensional design with blocks. This task requires organizational skills, reasoning, planning and visual-motor skills. The Peabody Individual Achievement Test – Revised (Markwardt, 1989) was administered as a measure of academic performance. Mary read words at the mid-3rd grade level, for a standard score in the borderline range of ability (SS=78). Reading comprehension was a beginning 2nd grade level (SS=59). Mathematical computation and reasoning was measured at the end-2nd grade level (SS=65), and spelling was her strength at a mid-5th grade level (SS=96). When asked to write a story, Mary printed neatly. Her story was shorter in length and had more grammar errors than that expected of others her age.

During the speech/language evaluation Mary was functioning at an 8-year, 9-month-old level in expressive naming vocabulary. She rarely used collective terms in naming groups of pictures. She typically named the function of each object or an associated term on pictures she did not successfully recall. The Expressive One Word Picture Vocabulary Test – Revised (Gardner, 1990) was administered to probe her vocabulary usage and ability to grasp the meanings of words. Strengths were identified in the areas of oral definitions, multiple meaning words, and recognizing semantic absurdities. Weaknesses were noted in naming synonyms and opposites. Marked delays were noted in making verbal associations and rationalizing why. Mary is currently functioning at the 9 year old level on vocabulary usage, placing her at the 5th percentile. Skills are currently commensurate with her ability level. Mary is presently functioning with a language age of 5 years, 10 months on the Clinical Evaluation of Language Fundamentals – Revised (Semel, Wiig, & Secord, 1987). Receptive language (SS=50) is significantly lower than expressive language skills (SS=64). Marked delays were noted in following oral directions, associating words by classes, and comparing vocabulary by semantic relationships. Mary does not have left/right progression. Sequencing skills (first, next, etc.) were extremely weak. She could not successfully complete any three-level directions. Associating words by their category was a strength. Opposites, spatial and temporal relations were areas of concern. Expressively, Mary demonstrated strengths in the areas of sentence assembly. She performed best with visual cues and was fairly successful grouping words into the correct order to make meaningful utterances. Her memory for sentences was poor. Mary struggled with formulating sentences: conjunctions were hard for her, and she did not seem to have the concept of combining information. Language skills were significantly delayed, compared to her ability level.

Adaptive behavior was evaluated using the Vineland Adaptive Behavior Scale (Sparrow, Balla, & Cicchetti, 1984), in an interview with Mary's mother. Communication skills were reported at a 3-year-old level, for a standard score of 37. Her mother reported that Mary has difficulty following instructions with two actions, listening to a story for thirty minutes or more, and remembering material that is four lines in length. She is able to address an envelope, writes beginning letters and reads books at a 2nd grade

level. Daily living skills were assessed at a 6-year-old level for a standard score of 49. Her mother reported that Mary needs help putting her shoes on the correct feet, bathing, using tableware, and washing her hair. She is able to take care of her fingernails and dry her hair. Mary has not helped with housecleaning or putting things away. She attempts to make her own bed when asked and can use the stove or microwave. Mary has difficulty making change and using emergency telephone numbers, although she can use a pay telephone and tell time.

On the Child Behavior Checklist (Achenbach, 1988), it was reported again by the parent that Mary enjoys basketball, skating, bike riding, singing, and crafts. She participates in the Red Cross. The behaviors that were of most concern to the mother centered around attention and depression. It is also reported that Mary has some aggressive behaviors such as arguing, bragging, demanding attention, and destroying other people's property. Her teachers do not note any significant behavior problems. They report that she gets along fairly well with her peers and with other adults.

Mary lives with her parents and 10-year-old brother on the west side of the city. She and her brother ride the bus to school. The school system transferred them to another school this year because they were using the address of a relative to attend a school in that district. Her mother feels that Mary did better in the first school, where she received special tutoring services. Mary's parents have maintained a relationship since she was born; they married in May, 1993. Mary's mother felt that this was a happy occasion and is working out well. She is concerned about some of Mary's "new friends" in her new school, her "closing in" when she is upset, her need for supervision for personal hygiene, and her developing sexuality. Mary's maternal grandmother, who was living in their home, died two years ago after an illness.

Mary was observed to go willingly with the examiners. She was cooperative, though very quiet and mild-mannered throughout the evaluation. She rarely initiated conversation.

Summary

Mary is an 11-year, 11 month-old girl in the sixth grade who was cooperative and polite. She currently is taking Ritalin. Mary previously had special tutoring services; however, she is not in any program this year. Mary's intellectual functioning is within the borderline range of ability. Achievement scores are below that of others her age. Adaptive behavior was also rated below that of others her age. According to the speech/language evaluation, Mary is presently functioning with a language age of 5 years, 10 months. Receptive language is significantly lower than expressive language skills. Mary does not appear to have difficulty with hearing or vision. It does appear that she may have seizures. Emotionally, Mary appears to be sensitive, sad, and angry at times. She appears to perceive her mother and teachers as being supportive.

Diagnostic Impressions

1. Expressive and receptive language disorder.
2. Borderline intellectual ability.
3. History of staring episodes daily.
4. Attention problems.

Recommendations

1. Continue Ritalin at present dose of 10 mgs. bid or increase to 15 mgs. bid only if necessary. Recommend drug holidays on Saturday and Sunday, holidays, and during the summer.
2. An EEG was scheduled for November 23, 1993. (This was a normal awake and drowsy EEG. There were no localizing or epileptiform features seen. If staring episodes continue, a repeat EEG was suggested.)
3. A Case Conference Committee should convene to discuss Mary's eligibility to receive special services, to include speech/language therapy one hour each week.
4. Specific information for the speech pathologist and classroom teachers will be shared at the Case Conference.
5. Mary may benefit from her teacher grading her with positive remarks to enhance self-esteem. For example, mark Mary's paper with the number of problems correct rather than those wrong.
6. Watch for opportunities to praise and positively reinforce Mary. An opportunity to have her earn a special activity with someone in the family or another adult would be beneficial.
7. Counseling for Mary and her family is very important. Referral to their local mental health center is encouraged.
8. When Mary exhibits inappropriate behavior:
   a. Remain calm, state rule and avoid arguing and debating.
   b. Avoid ridicule and criticism.
   c. Tell her exactly what she needs to do to improve her behavior.
   d. Model appropriate behaviors.
   e. Give frequent feedback on how her behavior affects others.
   f. Have pre-established consequences for misbehavior.
   g. Enforce rules consistently.
   h. Make sure disciplinary action is appropriate.
9. Mary is encouraged to continue being involved in groups of other children her age such as Girls' Club, Girl Scouts, church, etc. She may be interested in joining clubs or organized sports at school.

Case Discussion

The psychologist in the illustrative case made contact with the family as soon as the case was scheduled. She met with the IDT and made out the assessment schedule. On the day that Mary and her family were seen, the psychologist conducted the assessment and made sure that the schedule for the day ran smoothly. At the end of the day, she met with the family, explained the findings of the day, and went over the recommendations from the team. The psychologist collected all of the information from the other IDT members and developed the report. After the report was sent, the psychologist called the parent to find out how the immediate recommendations were working. The psychologist joined the parent and the case conference committee at Mary's school and together they developed an Individual Educational Plan (IEP) for Mary. The psychologist continued to follow the case periodically and was available to the parent and school for further consultation as needed.

References

Achenbach, T.M. (1988). *Child Behavior Checklist* and *Youth Self-Report*. Burlington, VT: Author.

American Association of Mental Retardation (1992). *Mental retardation: Definition, classification, and systems of support* (9th ed.). Washington, DC: Author.

American Psychological Association (1981). Ethical principles of psychologists. *American Psychologist, 36,* 633-638.

American Psychological Association (1994). *Legal and regulatory affairs* (pamphlet). Washington, DC: Author.

Bayley, N. (1993). *Bayley Scales of Infant Development - II*. San Antonio, TX: The Psychological Corporation.

Dunn, L.M., & Dunn, L.M. (1981). *Peabody Picture Vocabulary Test - Revised*. Circle Pines, MN: American Guidance Service.

Erickson, M.T. (1980). Psychological assessments methods. In S. Gabel & M.T. Erickson (Eds.). *Child development and developmental disabilities* (pp. 203-222). Boston, MA: Little, Brown & Company.

Gardner, M.F. (1980). *Expressive one word picture vocabulary Test-Revised*. Novato, CA: Academic Therapy Publications.

Golden, C.J. (1987). *Luria-Nebraska neuropsychological battery-Children's revision*. Los Angeles, CA: Western Psychological Services.

Hathaway, S., & McKinley, J.C. (1943). *Minnesota multiphasic personality inventory*. Minneapolis, MN: NCS Assessments.

Jastak, J.F., Jastak, S., & Wilkinson, G.S. (1984). *Wide range achievement test-Revised*. Wilmington, DE: Jastak Associates.

Johnston, R.B., & Magrab, P.R. (1976). *Developmental disorders: Assessment, treatment, education*. Baltimore, MD: University Park Press.

Kaufman, A.S., & Kaufman, N.L. (1983). *K-ABC: Kaufman Assessment Battery for Children*. Circle Pines, MN: American Guidance Service.

Magrab, P. R. (1982). A primer for integrating psychological test results. *Pediatric Annals, 11,* 470-479.

Markwardt, F.C., Jr. (1989). *Peabody individual achievement test-Revised*. Circle Pines, MN: American Guidance Service.

Nihira, K., Leland, H., & Lambert, N. (1992). *AAMR adaptive behavior scales* (2nd ed.). Washington, DC: American Association on Mental Retardation.

Roberts, R.N., & Magrab, P.R. (1991). Psychologists' role in a family centered approach to practice, training, and research with young children. *American Psychologist, 46,* 144-148.

Semel, E., Wiig, E.H., & Secord, W. (1987). *Clinical evaluation of language fundamentals-Revised*. San Antonio, TX: The Psychological Corporation.

Sparrow, S.S., Balla, D.A., & Cicchetti, D.V.

(1984). *Vineland Adaptive Behavior Scales*. Circle Pines, MN: American Guidance Service.

Thorndike, R.L., Hagen, E.P., & Sattler, J.M. (1986). *Guide for administering & scoring the Stanford-Binet Intelligence Scale* (4th ed). Chicago, IL: Riverside Publishing.

Wechsler, D. (1949). *Wechsler Intelligence Scale for Children*. San Antonio, TX: The Psychological Corporation.

Wechsler, D. (1974). *Wechsler Intelligence Scale for Children-Revised*. San Antonio, TX: The Psychological Corporation.

Wechsler, D. (1981). *Wechsler Adult Intelligence Scale-Revised*. San Antonio, TX: The Psychological Corporation.

Wechsler, D. (1991). *Wechsler Intelligence Scale for Children-III*. San Antonio, TX: The Psychological Corporation.

Wirt, R.D., Lachar, D., Klinedinst, J.K., & Seat, P.D. (1982). *Personality Inventory for Children-Revised Format*. Los Angeles, CA: Western Psychological Services.

Witt, J.C., & Covell, T.A. (1986). Psychological assessment. In D.L. Wodrich & J.E. Joy (Eds.), *Multi-disciplinary assessment of children with learning disabilities and mental retardation* (pp. 31-75). Baltimore, MD: Paul H. Brookes Publishing Co.

Woodcock, R.W., & Johnson, M.B. (1989). *Woodcock-Johnson Psycho-Educational Battery-Revised*. Allen, TX: DLM Teaching Resources.

15

Social Work

Judith M. Levy, M.S.W.

The practice of offering humane service to individuals dates back to biblical times. Its development into a profession is more recent and can be traced to the late nineteenth century and the Progressive Era. At this time, social work was carried out from the base of *settlement houses*: programs begun in Great Britain in the 1880's as part of an effort to mediate the negative effects of urbanization and industrialization on human beings. Humanists, more fortunate and frequently wealthy people, and university students would move into the poorest sections of a city to share their education, experience, cultural activities, and ideas about social reform. They served as enablers and organizers. The settlement house movement came to the United States in the late 1800's, when the first settlement house was set up in the Lower East Side of New York City. This idea caught on quickly in the U.S. because of the waves of immigrants entering the country, and the coincidental urbanization and industrialization which was occurring (Loavenbruck & Keys, 1987).

Although social workers today do not necessarily move into a community in order to help people, the purpose and values of those humanists who worked in the settlement houses are consistent with the basic purpose and values of the social work pro-

fession today. Social work is committed to the enhancement of human well-being and to the alleviation of poverty and oppression (Council on Social Work Education [CSWE], 1992, 1993). According to Meyer (1987), the central purpose of social work is to effect the best possible adaptation among individuals, families, and groups, and their environments. This may also be accomplished through direct practice with organizations and communities. Social workers are involved in the formulation and implementation of new social policies and programs to meet human needs and develop human capacities, as well as social or political action to empower groups at risk and promote social and economic justice (CSWE, 1992, 1993).

Values emphasizing concern for clients' well-being, and their rights to self-determination and choice, to participate in their own decision making, and to confidentiality, fairness and justice, are the hallmarks of social work practice (Meyer, 1987). Self-determination is limited by the parameters of the law and professional ethics, which do not permit a social worker to knowingly allow a client to hurt himself or someone else. Equally important in the social work value system is the acceptance of the individual, as he is, as a person of worth regardless of his or her circumstance (Hollis, 1967; Perlman, 1957).

Regardless of where and with what population social workers practice, a common history, purpose and values undergird and define the profession of social work. Social work is practiced in a wide variety of settings, including public and private family service agencies such as religious organizations, community mental health clinics, public social service agencies, hospitals, and private practice. Today social workers provide more than half of all mental health services in the United States.

The practice of most social workers consists mainly of direct service to individuals, sometimes within their family group, or within a group of people experiencing similar life circumstances, such as depression, divorce, financial instability, or a life-threatening illness. Other social workers may engage in indirect practice such as community organizing, social action, policy practice, administration and management, research, and professional education (Briar, 1987). These latter social workers might be involved in advocating for the homeless, helping people with disabilities organize themselves to obtain needed services, testifying before state and federal legislators about issues pertaining to a particular population or the need for national health insurance, or developing policies and programs to enable welfare recipients to become self-sufficient.

Clinical social work focuses on individuals, families, and groups, and has always been a primary method for the delivery of social work services. The National Association of Social Workers defines clinical social work as:

The professional application of social work theory and methods to the treatment and prevention of psychosocial dysfunction, disability, or impairment, including emotional and mental disorders. It is based on knowledge of one or more theories of human development within a psychosocial context ... includes interventions directed to interpersonal interactions, intrapsychic dynamics, and life-support and management issues. Clinical social work services consist of assessment; diagnosis; treatment, including psychotherapy and counseling; client-centered advocacy; consultation; and evaluation. (NASW, 1989, p. 4)

The uniqueness of the social work approach lies in its expertise in recognizing the dynamic relationship between intrapersonal factors and environmental circumstances (Hopps & Pinderhughes, 1987). This is commonly referred to as the 'person-in-situation' perspective, which conceptualizes human functioning on individual, interactional, familial, group, neighborhood, and community levels. Social casework has drawn heavily on psychodynamic perspectives, such as the developmental theories of Erik Erikson and the ego psychology of Anna Freud, as well as the social and cultural perspectives of sociology, social psychology and anthropology (Briar, 1987). Although this has been the historical framework for social work practice, it is now popularly referred to as the ecological systems perspective. This supports the notion that individuals are influenced by internal as well as external forces, and identifies the individual's perceptions of the environment as a critical element. Social workers presently use a variety of theoretical approaches including object-relations, cognitive-behavioral, and behavior-analytic perspectives, all of which involve the conscious use of self in forming therapeutic relationships. This combination of individual, social and environmental theories is the foundation of social work.

Educational and Training Requirements

There are three levels of social work education taught at colleges and universities in the fifty United States and Puerto Rico, involving over 400 bachelor's (B.S.W.), over 110 master's (M.S.W.), and 50 doctoral (Ph.D. or D.S.W.) programs. B.S.W. and M.S.W. programs must be accredited by the Council on Social Work Education (CSWE), established in 1952. Doctoral programs are not subject to external professional accreditation, but they are approved and periodically reviewed by the university offering them.

Education at the baccalaureate level is expected to prepare for beginning generalist social work practice and provides the professional foundation. Social work education at the master's level includes professional foundation and one or more concentrations or specialized fields of practice which prepare an advanced practitioner. Graduates at these levels differ from one another in the depth, breadth, and specificity of knowledge and skill that they are able to apply to practice. Doctoral level work trains graduates for careers in research, teaching, advanced practice, administration, planning and policy analysis (Khinduka, 1987). Significant undergraduate training in the liberal arts is a prerequisite for admission into professional social work degree programs.

The professional foundation includes coursework in the following areas: social work values and ethics, diversity, social and economic justice, populations-at-risk, human behavior and the social environment, social welfare policy and services, social work practice, research, and field practicum.

The student's field practicum or internship provides supervised social work practice and an opportunity to apply theory in the work setting. The bachelor's level requires 400 hours of field practicum experience, while the master's level requires 900 hours. The foundation practicum permits students to develop an awareness of self in the helping process, to practice social work in a supervised setting, to use and develop oral and written communication skills in the professional work setting, and to analyze and evaluate agency policy in the context of social work ethics.

Licensure, Certification, and Continuing Education

The practice of social work is legally regulated in all fifty states, the District of Columbia, Puerto Rico and the U.S. Virgin Islands. The major reason to require the legal regulation of practice is to protect the client by assuring professional competence through the establishment of minimum criteria for practice. At the same time, this provides protection for social workers by establishing a forum for addressing charges of malpractice and unethical conduct. Finally, it facilitates the inclusion of social workers in the insurance reimbursement system for the provision of mental health treatment to the public (Hopps & Pinderhughes, 1987).

Interestingly, all states do not require licensure for all social workers. Eleven states specify "clinical" social workers, or those diagnosing and treating people with mental illness, or those social workers in private practice receiving reimbursements for their services. Sixteen states provide only for title protection.

Although the states and territories vary in their approach to regulating professional practice, certain trends do exist. Most states have enacted laws rather than regulations. In the majority of states the regulatory agency is a board having both social work and consumer members.

Over half of the states regulate the practice of social workers at both the baccalaureate and master's degree levels. Seven states even regulate persons serving in social work assistant or technician capacities having A.A. or B.A. degrees in fields which are unspecified. No state requires a doctoral degree for any level of licensure. The number of levels of certification varies from one to five, with most jurisdictions having three or four. The categories relate to education, experience and, in some cases, the nature of an individual's practice.

All but a few states and territories require the passage of a written examination for licensing of social workers at the M.S.W. level. Almost half of the states exempt federal, state, and other public employees, or certain non-profit agencies, from legal regulation. This practice is most likely related to issues of liability and availability of personnel to fill critical positions. Many so-called social workers do not have degrees in social work. This is particularly true in public agencies. In many states, when licensing was originally implemented, it was difficult to imagine how to retain public employees in crucial positions if they were forced to comply with the criteria for licensure. Additionally, it was not deemed necessary for individuals in administrative positions to be licensed. In recent years this has changed, with twenty-six states having no exempt employee groups other than supervised students and numerous others exempting only federal employees. In all but nine states, the laws include privileged communication protection for clients. Only fifteen states do not mandate continuing education credits for renewal of licensure.

Over 30 states and the District of Columbia dictate that insurance policies with mental health coverage must reimburse for services provided by licensed or certified social workers to beneficiaries in those jurisdictions. These states have vendorship laws which mandate licensure to receive reimbursement. In certain states, additional clinical experience, examination, or professional certification is required also. Social workers in most of these states are reimbursed for providing mental health treatment without a referral from a physician.

Obviously, the system of licensure or regulation is not uniform across the states and territories. Because of this and the need for leadership and accountability, the National Association of Social Workers (NASW) has developed standards of practice for numerous specializations. These include clinical social work, case management, and social work in health-care settings, in long-term care facilities, in child protection, in schools, and for the functionally impaired.

In the 1960s, prior to the existence of laws legally regulating the practice of social work in most states, the NASW established the Academy of Certified Social Workers (ACSW) to serve as a credential indicating that the M.S.W. has attained competence for independent practice. Membership in the ACSW requires passing a written examination, two years of post-M.S.W. supervised work experience, and letters of endorsement. A related credential for B.S.W.s (ACBSW) has recently been developed by NASW, but is not intended to convey competence for independent practice.

There are two separate diplomate credentials available to clinical social workers. The NASW offers the 'Diplomate in Clinical Social Work,' and the independent American Board of Examiners in Clinical Social Work provides the 'Board Certified Diplomate.' Both diplomate programs are only available to M.S.W.s licensed at the highest level of clinical practice in their state; both involve passing an examination, providing letters of endorsement, and several years of post-M.S.W. *clinical* practice under supervision. The diplomate programs differ from the ACSW in that the latter does not require demonstrated *clinical* competence, but rather is a more generic certification.

Contributions to Interdisciplinary Practice

The Council on Social Work Education (CSWE) specifically requires that schools of social work train professionals who are competent to serve the poor, the oppressed, and those experiencing discrimination. In 1976, the President's Committee on Mental Retardation reported that 70% of mentally handicapping conditions have poverty as their root cause. Begab, Haywood and Garber (1981) noted the following poverty-related factors, among others: malnutrition; the use of tobacco, alcohol, and other drugs during pregnancy; teenage pregnancies; the lack of early screening programs; lead poisoning; child abuse; nutritional deprivation in the early developmental years; and lack of stimulation. While these factors are perhaps more prevalent in families with low income, it is obvious that they are not unique to poor families. It is clear that historically, people with developmental disabilities, whether or not they are poor, have experienced oppression and discrimination in all aspects of their lives, and despite current trends in philosophy and service delivery, do so even now.

Horejsi (1979) noted that social work contributions to interdisciplinary practice have been made in the provision of psychosocial evaluations as part of the interdisciplinary process; the provision of brokerage and case advocacy services in order to assist families in obtaining needed services; and in intake, discharge planning and case management activities related to placement and movement within a service system. Additionally, the social worker may provide individual and group counseling to persons with mental retardation, their parents and siblings; assist in the development of alternative living arrangements such as foster or group homes; and provide protection and advocacy services when necessary. The social worker may be therapist, ombudsman, and teacher.

Social Work Assessment

A critical aspect of the psychosocial assessment of people with disabilities and their families is the prevention of labeling the entire family as disabled. Parents should not be labeled "C.P. parents" or "spina bifida parents". The literature on families and disabilities has reflected the tendency of professionals to view the family from the perspective of the medical model and to "pathologize" them (Gartner, Lipsky & Turnbull, 1991). In the words of one parent who protests this,

> Jeff is neither my burden nor my chastisement, although his care requires more than I want to give at times. He is not an angel sent for my personal growth or my future glory; he is not a punishment for my past sins. He is a son. (Pieper, n.d., p. 88)

Information gathered for the psychosocial assessment should assist the team in remembering that these families have more similarities to other families than differences, and that all families experience difficult periods. According to Gartner et al. (1991), the family's role in the development of the child with a disability has gained considerable attention, with the current focus being an exploration of the relationships within the family system. They point out that the "sophistication and professionalization ... of this new focus" may be approaching "overkill" (p. 65). As an example, they cite the research design of a study with families whose children have suffered traumatic brain injuries, which included at least eight measures of individual and family functioning.

Bearing the latter danger in mind, this author notes that Gartner et al. (1991) provide a comprehensive inventory of family assessment measures. Any of these measures may used by social workers in the field of developmental disabilities. The measures include the following: Minuchin's (1974) enmeshment and disengagement; Moos's (1976) relationships, personal growth, and system maintenance; Olson, Russell, and Sprenkle's (1979); family cohesion, family adaptability, and family communication; Olson, Portner, and Lavee's (1985) FACES (Family Adaptability and Cohesion Scales); McCubbin and Thompson's (1991) CHIP (Coping Health Inventory for Parents).

Friedrich, Greenberg and Crnic (1983) proposed a model for understanding the range of possiblepositive and negative familial adaptations to the perceived stress associated with the presence of a retarded child. They described the family's coping resources and ecological environments as interactive systems that serve to mediate the family's response to stress. These authors factor-analyzed Holroyd's (1974) Questionnaire on Resources and Stress and found four distinct factors which were most reliable: Parent and Family Problems, Pessimism, Child Characteristics, and Physical Incapacitation. On the basis of this analysis they reduced the size of the original Holroyd questionnaire to 52 items, now the QRS-F (1983). The advantage of this measure, besides its brevity and readability (sixth-grade level), is that it points to the multidimensional nature of the issues facing families who have children with disabilities or chronic illness.

Social workers emphasize a normal developmental framework. According to

O'Hara and Levy (1984):

Proponents of the life cycle approach to understanding individual dynamics suggest that intersections of biological and psychological development mark important life milestones. Erikson (1963) has suggested that the tasks and needs facing individuals at a particular time can be understood in terms of an interactive process through which individuals seek to balance their own intrinsic drive toward self-actualization with the expectations placed on them by the society in which they live. Similarly, within a family, there are average expectable milestones characterized by phase-specific tasks and needs (Rhodes, 1977). Tasks of a given life stage are accomplished through utilizing opportunities and available resources. When there is a deficit in opportunities and/or resources, tasks cannot be accomplished.....This model promotes a perspective which permits diagnosis of a problem distinguishing normal family tension from that originating from or exacerbated by, a handicapping condition (p. 66).

Somewhat more recently, perhaps since P.L.99-457 made it imperative that parents direct the course of treatment for their children, many authors have designed questionnaires to ask parents what their preferences and needs are. Bailey & Simeonsson (1990) designed a survey for parents to identify areas of need such as information, family and social support, financial, how to explain disability to others, child care, professional support, and community services.

The Family Needs Scale developed by Dunst, Trivette and Deal (1988) represents an even broader array of needs, certainly related to anyone in the family and again reflecting the intent of the Individual Family Service Plan (IFSP) of P.L.99-457. On this scale parents are asked to identify the extent to which they need help in a number of areas, including, as a few examples: *having money to buy necessities and pay bills;paying for special needs of my child; feeding my child; getting a place to live; getting furniture, clothes, toys;* and so forth.

Social workers may also use other established and reliable measures of individual functioning, such as the Beck Depression Inventory, Achenbach's Child Behavior Checklist, or structured clinical interviews for psychiatric diagnoses. Although numerous formal measures of family functioning do exist, the majority of social workers in interdisciplinary teams, in UAPs and in the field of developmental disabilities generally do not use formal procedures, but rather rely on the psychosocial assessment and social history. Henry, DeChristopher, Dowling and Latham (1983) point out that:

> The gathering of information for the social history is a process that requires the sensitivity and skills of a person with training in interpersonal relationships .... The interpretation of this information requires a knowledge of people and systems as well as of laws and regulations....The result of the gathering of this information is a dynamic impression of what influences the child's learning and functioning on the interpersonal, familial, and environmental levels. (p. 77)

The process of completing the psychosocial assessment/history begins the foundation of the therapeutic relationship which is intended to continue to support the patient/family through the continuum of care over the life cycle. The nature of the relationship that is established will influence the willingness of the patient or family to ask for assistance in the future from the same or a different social worker.

The assessment should include information about the patient or family's goals, expectations, and perception of the issue for which they are asking help. What do they want from professionals? Is the issue diagnostic, or is it a particular problem related to the disability which is already diagnosed? What diagnostic information have they received previously? What do they understand about the etiology of the problem? Do they perceive that the problem is their fault, beyond their control, curable? Do the parents blame each other or professionals? What do the parents believe about the child's ability to influence the problem? Do they have previous history with this disability in their family or friendship network which is influencing their reaction? If the individual with the disability is cognitively aware of and able to understand the disability, how does he or she perceive the problem or disability and the response of his or her family to the situation? Is the entire family "handicapped" as the result of this circumstance, or have they learned to function "around" it? Do either the person with the disability or the family see the disability as all-encompassing, or as one area of limitation in a person with other strengths?

The assessment of psychosocial functioning should address the functional and relational aspects of the individual and family, i.e. housing, neighborhood, finances, employment, health, mental health, education, involvement in the court system, nuclear and extended family relationships, religion, organizational membership, leisure time activities, and how each of these areas affects or is affected by the disability or the specific problem being addressed. The social worker can be expected to use good interviewing and communication skills to obtain this very sensitive but important information.

The concept of reciprocity between individuals and their environments was mentioned previously. Bearing in mind the person–environment configuration, the social worker on an interdisciplinary team must know an individual's or family's coping style, history, and supportive resources in order to help the team understand their reaction to the handicapping condition and the treatment recommendations.

Finally, the social worker should make some prediction about the family/patient's response to the evaluation information as well as their ability and willingness to follow through on the proposed treatment recommendations.

Social workers beginning with families referred for ongoing treatment need to assess four areas initially: Can the family accept differences in family members and promote the growth of individuals as well as the family as a whole? Can the family perform necessary roles while supporting each other emotionally? Is there a leadership hierarchy in the family? Does the family communicate clearly? (O'Hara & Levy, 1984)

Social Work Intervention

The social worker can be expected to be an advocate for the person with the disability and for the family. Involving the individual and family in the evaluation and treatment process is essential to the success of any program. Moxley, Raider, & Cohen (1989, p. 306) identified three categories of barriers to family involvement:

1. *Resource Barriers*: lack of time, opportunity, and supports to make it possible for family members to become involved
2. *Training and Skill Barriers:* lack of concrete knowledge and skills family members require to successfully carry out involvement roles
3. *Communication Barriers:* lack of knowledge and understanding families and

professionals may have of each other's subjective experience, which can result in divergent views and expectations of involvement.

Whereas the social worker will not personally resolve all of these barriers, it is reasonable to assume that he or she will identify them and help the family and team to work them out. This may involve problem solving and negotiation to look for new solutions or recommendations, acting as educator or liaison to obtain necessary training for family members, or helping team members and family see the perspectives of one another and communicate with one another.

As the result of gathering information for the psychosocial assessment, the social worker can educate the team about the strengths as well as the limitations of the patient and family.

Sometimes it is necessary to reframe the perspective of team members who view an individual's behavior in a particularly negative way. For example, when a parent doesn't visit a hospitalized child daily, staff may need to be reminded that the parent is working in order to retain his or her employment so that the child has a safe, financially stable home to which to return. The parent is not neglecting the child. Another parent may cope with a difficult diagnosis such as mental retardation by openly disagreeing with it and refusing to use the label. That same parent may, however, be following through on recommendations for a school placement which meets the child's needs appropriately.

Informing people of difficult information is an area where the social worker can be very helpful to team members. Based on the assessment, the social worker has some idea of how particular individuals cope with difficult situations. This information will help in preparing the presentation. Additionally, social workers are trained to distinguish when and how to confront situations rather than avoid them, and to value a person's right to be informed so that he or she can make informed choices. Some IDTs always involve both the physician and social worker in the informing interview, in order to provide advocacy and support for the family and to promote a fuller discussion of the information including the family's emotional reactions.

Some IDTs provide the family with written documentation of the informing interview so that they can review it at home with each other or relatives and friends. This is done by the social worker during the discussion so that it accurately reflects what was said, and uses correct terminology with explanations in lay terms. A copy is maintained in the record so that other team members can review the content as well.

Sometimes it may be necessary to take action to protect a child who is being neglected or abused by the parents. This is only done when absolutely necessary; it should not be done when the problem is a disagreement between parents and team members over a particular treatment which is not required. The social worker can utilize conflict resolution skills and, if necessary, can be instrumental in involving the appropriate child protection resources in the community and in facilitating communication between the two systems.

Case management is a basic social work skill, taught at all levels of social work education and valued since the time of the settlement workers when they advocated for the needs of poor people and facilitated their obtaining services to which they were entitled. The *NASW Standards for Social Work Case Management* (1992, p. 5) provides the following definition of case management:

A method of providing services whereby a professional social worker assesses

the needs of the client and the client's family, when appropriate, and arranges, coordinates, monitors, evaluates, and advocates for a package of multiple services to meet the specific client's complex needs....Distinct from other forms of case management, social work case management addresses both the individual client's biopsychosocial status as well as the state of the social system in which case management operates...is both micro and macro in nature: intervention occurs at both the client and system levels.

The social worker may therefore provide case management within the UAP interdisciplinary system, within the community, or between the two. Related to this is a critical skill noted by Horejsi (1979) called *boundary work*, or intervention at the interface of social systems. For example, a social worker might intervene to help a family obtain Supplemental Security Income. Here, the systems are the family and the social security bureaucracy. Helping a person with a disability transition from his family home to a group home involves the boundaries of the individual, the family and the group home residents, and perhaps direct care and administrative staff. Coordinating several community agencies which have services to offer a family involves boundary work with each of the agency systems.

The social worker can be expected to provide families with information about disabilities, service systems, and entitlements. Depending on the desires and capabilities of the individuals involved, this information may be in written or verbal form, or printed materials. The information should cover the spectrum of resources generally available to the population and those specific to people with disabilities.

Social workers commonly provide counseling and psychotherapy to individuals and families. According to Wikler and Berkowitz (1983), although prior to the 1970's individuals with mental retardation were thought to be incapable of benefiting from psychotherapy, "recent clinical research indicates that psychotherapeutic approaches can be effective with the mildly retarded adult when there is an understanding of the cognitive impairments" (p. 9). Supportive therapy with persons with mental retardation, whether adults or children, can mediate stress and facilitate the individual's adjustment to personal differences or limitations, a common problem for people with mild handicapping conditions. Behavioral approaches are often used alone or in conjunction with other approaches, depending on the client's needs. Group therapy is often used to enhance social skills, encourage verbal skills, teach sexuality, and model appropriate behaviors. Group therapy is frequently very useful in developing social support networks, especially since people with mental retardation and other developmental disabilities are frequently socially isolated.

Individual, family, or couples counseling may be provided to help parents or other family members deal with their emotional response to a diagnosis, a particularly upsetting life event related to a handicapping condition, or to understand how a disability in the family may be impacting on relationships or role performance. For example, the presence of cerebral palsy may affect the development of mutuality between parent and child—without understanding the persistence of primitive reflexes and stiffening, the parent may think that the baby is actually pulling away or rejecting the parent's advances. Parents may not understand why they are unable to support one another during the crisis of diagnosis but, through counseling, may learn that they have different coping styles. Parents may be very disappointed that the teenage sib-

lings of the child with a disability seem intolerant all of a sudden. Counseling may reveal that this is a normal part of their need to disengage from the family and identify with their peers.

Social workers may help parents learn how to integrate their child with a disability into the mainstream of the family without neglecting the needs of other family members or giving special preference to the child with a disability. This involves discussions about values, child-rearing practices, and discipline. The social worker may teach the parents basic principles of behavior modification.

Siblings often benefit from individual or group counseling with other siblings to address issues related to family and peer relationships, responsibilities, guilt, anger, and future plans for their own families and career choices. Group counseling can be very useful if provided in a normalizing and supportive atmosphere. This will encourage parents or siblings to hear that others share some of their seemingly unspeakable thoughts and fears and to receive encouragement and ideas from others who have similar experiences.

Parents whose children have become disabled traumatically need help in adjusting to the "new" child, with different strengths and limitations. The child, depending on cognitive capabilities, will need assistance in accepting the changes in physical and mental capabilities, limitations, future choices, and relationships.

Sometimes parents need help dealing with uncertainty or lack of a diagnosis. For example, children who have had a difficult birth experience and have spent time in a neonatal intensive care unit (NICU) may be at greater risk for developmental disabilities than other children. They may develop slowly or have minor abnormalities which are not diagnosable at first. The children may not be diagnosed with a learning disability until school age, although their parents may have suspected that something was different about their child all along. Supportive counseling and honest appraisals from professionals who monitor the child's development will go a long way toward helping the parents cope with the anxiety provoked by uncertainty.

Case Example

The following case example is adapted from Levy (1988). Jeremy was born to a middle-income, intelligent couple in their twenties. They had been married 6 years, had a 4-year-old son, Brad, owned a house, and planned to have two children. The mother stayed home with the children in a development of single family homes about a 45 minutes' drive from the university hospital where Jeremy was born. The couple described a good, mutually supportive relationship but very little contact with extended family members on either side. This couple felt strongly that they had only themselves to rely on. At birth, Jeremy did not do well, and a heart problem was detected. His feeding was difficult and he would not nurse. He went home with his family after several weeks in the NICU taking formula. A follow-up visit was scheduled with the cardiologist. Jeremy's parents became concerned because he was not progressing normally. Their pediatrician said that because of the problems at birth and the heart problem, it was expected that he would lag a little initially. Finally, at 1 year, Jeremy was still not eating well, gaining weight, or sitting up. The parents had experienced a year of sleepless nights, uncertainty, and anguish. The mother insisted that their pediatrician recommend a specialist who might be able to give them answers about Jeremy. The pediatrician recommended a hospital that specialized in the diagnosis, evaluation, and treatment of developmentally disabled children.

During the evaluation period, the social worker spoke with both parents and learned that although their relationship was basically solid, their efforts to cope with Jeremy's deficits took quite different paths. The father, who participated less in Jeremy's care than he had in Brad's care, was able to intellectualize about the slowness of Jeremy's milestones by pointing to his birth history and physical problems as well as to their pediatrician's counsel that Jeremy would probably lag a little initially. He did not want to discuss his fears and anxieties about Jeremy's condition, even with his wife, and accused her of exaggerating. The mother, now raising her second child, was acutely aware that something was wrong, could not deny it to herself, and needed to be able to verbalize her fears. She confided to the social worker that the marital relationship was under great strain. They were not able to share their thoughts with each other, and they had not gone out without the children since Jeremy's birth because they were afraid to leave him with anyone. With the exception of the paternal grandmother, most of their extended family was unaware of Jeremy's status since birth. Although their friends were sympathetic, this couple really did not share their worst fears with anyone and would not ask their friends for moral support or even babysitting help. No one on either side of the family had any experience with children with disabilities.

At the IDT meeting, other team members voiced concern about the father's seemingly angry demeanor and reluctance to give developmental information to the therapists. They expressed anger at the way he spoke to his wife when he disagreed with her and worry over how he would deal with the diagnosis and recommendations for special interventions. The social worker gave the team information about the parents and their very different methods of coping with this crisis. She talked about their relative isolation from friends and family and the lack of supportive contacts outside of the marriage. Additionally, the father was in the process of changing jobs and was worried about coverage for a pre-existing condition. Although neither parent had actually mentioned the word *fear*, the social worker hypothesized that the father in particular was probably fearful about raising this child to be independent.

Jeremy was diagnosed as having a rare, genetically transmitted syndrome that involved cardiac deficits, mental retardation, and metabolic problems. Counseling with the parents included the developmental pediatrician and the social worker. In addition to providing accurate diagnostic information, they talked with this couple about normal parental reactions to having a child with a disability, reassuring them that what they were experiencing was to be expected. The difference in parental coping styles was brought into the open so they could begin to understand what prevented them from supporting one another. The father maintained that Jeremy was not mentally retarded but slow due to the physical problems he had. He refused to discuss the recommended therapy or school programs. The physician and social worker did not argue with the father but reiterated that this was their best professional judgement. They advised the couple to take time to listen to one another, to identify the value dilemma they were facing, and to begin to ask for some support from friends or family by sharing information with them. They were asked to call the physical and occupational therapists to set up appointments when they were ready and were advised that the team would follow up with them. The social worker gave them information about a parent association for

Jeremy's disorder.

The social worker offered to help the father look into insurance coverage for Jeremy under the new policy and investigated the provisions for children with handicaps in the new school jurisdiction. Although the parents had not come to any conclusions about intervention through the school system, they did agree that they would accept help from the team related to Jeremy's feeding and his next physical milestone, sitting up. The team members working with them were able to empathize with the father and ultimately formed good working relationships with him during follow-up visits to the hospital. Eventually, this family decided to introduce Jeremy to the school system where they continued to see him make progress. They were beginning to understand and to share their thoughts and feelings with each other, although they continued to be somewhat isolated from outside contacts with family or friends.

Summary

Social work brings certain values, knowledge and skills to interdisciplinary practice. The concepts of normalization and individual and family-centered practice which are central to the standards of best practice with persons with developmental disabilities are clearly consistent with social work's central values. These are concern with the client's well-being, the right to self-determination and to participate in one's own decision-making, and acceptance of the individual as a person of worth regardless of circumstance. Social workers see persons within their environment, whether that is the family, community, or society as a whole. They understand the dynamics of individual growth and development, and can provide interventions to enhance the coping of individuals within their environment. Social workers are trained to advocate for persons within the political and service systems. The education of a social worker includes the ability to appreciate diversity and to recognize and treat at-risk populations.

Because social workers see individuals holistically, that is, biopsychosocially, they are particularly well suited to interdisciplinary teamwork. They understand that the complexity of the needs of persons with developmental disabilities requires a team of experts to meet the gamut of those needs using a unified, coordinated and respectful approach.

References

Bailey, D., & Simeonsson, R. (1990).*Family needs survey*. Chapel Hill, NC: University of North Carolina, Frank Porter Graham Child Development Center.

Battle, M.G. (1987). Professional associations: National Association of Social Workers. In A. Minahan (Ed.). *Encyclopedia of social work* (18th ed., Vol 2, pp. 333-341). Silver Spring, MD: National Association of Social Workers.

Begab, M., Haywood, C., & Garber, H. (1981). *Psychosocial aspects of mental retardation theory* (Vol. 1). Baltimore, MD: University Park Press.

Briar, S. (1987). Direct practice: Trends and issues. In A. Minahan (Ed.), *Encyclopedia of social work* (18th ed., Vol.2, pp. 681-695). Silver Spring, MD: National Association of Social Workers.

Council on Social Work Education. (1992). *Curriculum policy statement for master's degree programs in social work education*. Washington, DC: Author.

Council on Social Work Education. (1993). *Curriculum policy statement for baccalaureate degree programs in social work education*. Washington, DC: Author.

Dunst, C.J., Trivette, C.M., & Deal, A.G. (1988). *Enabling and empowering families: Principles and guidelines for practice*. Cambridge, MA: Brookline Books.

Erikson, E.H. (1963). *Child and society* (2nd ed.). New York: Norton.

Ferguson, P.M., & Asch, A.(1989). What we want for our children: Perspectives of parents and adults with disabilities. In D. Biklen, D. Ferguson, & A. Ford (Eds.), *Schooling and disability* (pp. 181-203). Boston, MA: Little, Brown.

Friedrich, W.N., Greenberg, M.T., & Crnic, K. (1983). A short-form of the Questionnaire on Resources and Stress. *American Journal on Mental Deficiency, 88*, 41-48.

Gartner, A., Lipsky, D.K., & Turnbull, A.P. (1991). *Supporting families with a child with a disability: An international outlook*. Baltimore, MD: Brooks/Cole.

Henry, D.L., DeChristopher, J., Dowling, P., & Lapham, E.V. (1983). Using the social history to assess handicapping conditions. In L. Wikler & M.P. Keenan (Eds.). *Developmental disabilities: No longer a private tragedy* (pp. 76-82). Washington, DC: National Association of Social Workers and American Association on Mental Deficiency.

Hollis, F. (1964). *Casework: A psychosocial therapy*. New York: Random House.

Holroyd, J. (1974). The questionnaire on resources and stress: An instrument to measure family response to a handicapped family member. *Journal of Community Psychology, 2*, 92-94.

Hopps, J.G., & Pinderhughes, E.B. (1987). Profession of social work: Contemporary characteristics. In A. Minahan (Ed.), *Encyclopedia of social work* (18th ed., Vol.2, pp.351-366). Silver Spring, MD: National Association of Social Workers.

Horejsi, C.R. (1979). Developmental disabilities: Opportunities for social workers. *Social Work, 24*, 40-43.

Khinduka, S.K. (1987). Social work and the human services. In A. Minahan (Ed.), *Encyclopedia of social work* (18th ed., Vol.2, pp. 681-695). Silver Spring, MD: National Association of Social Workers.

Levy, J.M. (1988). Family response and adaptation to a handicap. In J.P. Gerring & L. McCarthy (Eds.). *The psychiatry of handicapped children and adolescents.* Boston, MA: Little, Brown.

Loavenbruck, G., & Keys, P. (1987). Settlements and neighborhood centers. In A. Minahan (Ed.). *Encyclopedia of social work* (18th ed., Vol. 2, pp. 556-561). Silver Spring, MD: National Association of Social Workers.

McCubbin, H.I., & Thompson, A.I. (Eds.) (1991). *Family assessment inventories for research and practice.* Madison, WI: University of Wisconsin.

Meyer, C.H. (1987). Direct practice in social work: Overview. In A. Minahan (Ed.). *Encyclopedia of social work* (18th ed., Vol. 1, pp. 409-422). Silver Spring, MD: National Association of Social Workers.

Moxley, D.P., Raider, M.G., & Cohen, S.N. (1989). Specifying and facilitating family involvement in services to persons with developmental disabilities. *Child & Adolescent Social Work Journal,* 6, 301-312.

National Association of Social Workers (1989). *NASW standards for the practice of clinical social work.* Washington, DC: Author.

National Association of Social Workers (1992). *NASW standards for social work case management.* Washington, DC: Author.

National Association of Social Workers (1993). *State comparison of laws regulating social work.* Washington, DC: Author.

O'Hara, D.M., & Levy, J.M. (1984). Family adaptation to learning disability: A framework for understanding and treatment. *Learning Disabilities,* 3(6), 63-77.

Olson, D.H., Portner, J., & Lavee, Y. (1985). *FACES-II.* St. Paul, MN: Family Social Science, University of Minnesota.

Olson, D., Russell, C.S., & Sprenkle, D.H. (1979). Circumplex model of marital and family systems II: Empirical studies and clinical intervention. In J. Vincent (Ed.), *Advances in family intervention, assessment and theory.* Greenwich, CT: JAI.

Perlman, H.H. (1957). *Social casework: A problem-solving process.* Chicago, IL: University of Chicago Press.

Pieper, E. (n.d.). *Sticks and stones: The story of loving a child.* Syracuse, NY: Human Policy Press.

Rhodes, S.L. (1977). A developmental approach to the life cycle of the family. *Social Casework,* 58, 301-304.

Wikler, L., & Berkowitz, N.N. (1983). Social work, social problems, and the mentally retarded. In L. Wikler & M.P. Keenan (Eds.), *Developmental disabilities: No longer a private tragedy* (pp. 8-11). Washington, DC: National Association of Social Workers and American Association on Mental Deficiency.

16

Special Education

Dianne L. Ferguson, Ph.D., & Ginevra Ralph, M.S.

Special education emerged as a field in the twenty years or so spanning the turn of the century in conjunction with the emergence of compulsory education laws. The increasing student diversity that resulted from the requirement that *all* children attend school so challenged teachers, school systems, and educational conventions that "special" education emerged to accommodate those students who did not seem to "fit" current practices (Ferguson, 1987; Hoffman, 1975; Sarason & Doris, 1979). That essential responsibility has remained largely unchanged until now. Special education quickly became a parallel discipline and organizational structure within American public education, designed to provide adapted curriculum and teaching to students who had either failed—or were likely to fail—in the "mainstream" of compulsory public education. Over time, special education created its own specialized curriculum approaches which came to support a burgeoning number of subspecialties, each matching curriculum and teaching strategies to ability and performance characteristics of an identifiable group of children or youth. The more unusual the student's characteristics, the more specialized the intervention and the teacher that provided that intervention (Sarason & Doris, 1979).

As a field, special education received full professional legitimacy and procedural power with the passage of comprehensive federal legislation in 1974. The landmark Education for All Handicapped Children Act (EHA, P.L. 94-142), reauthorized and updated as the Individuals with Disabilities Education Act (IDEA, P.L. 101-476) in 1990, mandated a free, appropriate, public education for *all* children and youth, regardless of the type or severity of their disability. Until 1974, many potential students with more severe and multiple developmental disabilities had been "excused" from the requirements of compulsory education because they were believed incapable of learning; believed to require primarily custodial care; and believed to need protection from the eyes and possible taunts of nondisabled or less disabled peers (Berry, 1931; Hoffman, 1975; Kirk & Johnson, 1951; Wallin, 1966). These newest members of the school community, like their more able predecessors early in the century, challenged the current teachers in both general and special education, spawning still more specializations within the field (Perske & Smith, 1977; Thomas, 1977). In current times, special education in the 1990s faces dramatic changes. Like American public education in general, recent and current schooling reform agendas challenge the discipline of special education to reinvent itself.

Education and Training

The current climate of reform in education has included a focus on changes in teacher preparation, especially for general education teachers. Proposals, and critiques, range from changing the status of teacher preparation from undergraduate to graduate (The Holmes Group, 1986; Tom, 1985), to alternatives for university preparation (Grossman, 1990; The Holmes Group, 1986) to having university teacher educators who are also responsible for area classrooms of public school students. Perhaps the most comprehensive of the teacher preparation reform proposals is that of John Goodlad and colleagues (Goodlad, 1990; Goodlad, Soder, & Sirotnik, 1990a; Goodlad, Soder, & Sirotnik, 1990b) whose lengthy analysis offers 19 postulates for improving the preparation of teachers.

In both special education and general education, recommendations involve a broadened definition of teacher roles and capacities, including multi-theoretical fluency, creative problem-solving, self-management, peer cooperation and collaboration, and ongoing professional growth (Baumgart & Ferguson, 1991; Goodlad, 1990). Teachers must be better prepared and supported to become technically competent and reflective educators, able to work with wider student diversity and to achieve more and more complex student outcomes (Grimmett & Erickson, 1988; Sarason, 1993; Schön, 1983).

Special educators involved in the blending of general and special education reforms find their roles shifting from designated provider of specialized knowledge and services to a more generic teacher of diverse groups of students working in collaboration with other teachers to share areas of expertise and interest toward the learning benefit of all the students (Ferguson, 1993; Roach, 1993). In order to support these changes in teacher roles, universities are restructuring their initial preparation programs to better integrate content from the traditionally separate fields. Some programs accomplish this by requiring teachers to take courses and field-based experiences in both general and special education, usually ending with some kind of dual certification. In a small number of more experimental programs, however, students receive preparation that is more integrated into a single focus on meeting the learning needs of the full range of students, including students who are currently labeled *gifted and talented* or *disabled*.

Licensure, Certification, and Continuing Education

Consistent with the overriding categorical approach of special education organization and practice, the licensure of practitioners has been largely categorical in nature. For each identified disability requiring special education services, the field has created a matching teacher. Thus, teachers were typically certified to teach a single disability category (unless, of course, they collected multiple certificates or endorsements). Thus, special educators were certified to teach students with learning disabilities, orthopedic impairments, visual impairments, emotional disturbance, or mental retardation. Within some of these disability categories, licenses were further delineated according to level, generating *teachers of students with mild mental retardation* as well as *moderate, severe, profound* retardation or *severe emotional disturbance*. The assumption that service should be tied to person and place naturally created difficulties for a small number of students who possessed multiple disabilities. Should the student with both significant orthopedic impairments and cognitive impairments be taught by the "physically handicapped teacher" or the "mentally retarded teacher" (as educators came to label themselves in day-to-day conversation)? What should be done with the student who has both severe retardation and severe behavioral and emotional disorders?

Some states are restructuring their licensure systems, moving away from categorical systems toward licenses that focus on working with a full range of students within particular age-ranges. Thus the traditional K-12 special education license is becoming reconceptualized as an endorsement on an elementary, middle years, or secondary basic teaching license.

In addition to basic licensure according to disability category, special education has also developed a system of further specialization, also tied to specific disabilities or conditions. Teachers with "emotional disturbance" or "mental retardation" certificates might later acquire additional specialization in autism or behavioral intervention, giving rise to the itinerant consultant, who might be a "behavior consultant," "autism specialist," or "vision specialist."

Although preparation programs have differed somewhat, depending upon the state granting the license, generally speaking, special education personnel preparation has been solidly grounded in the psychology of disability and learning difference. Although a variety of theoretical approaches have been available and popular at various times in the history of special education, the field has been dominated by behavioral theory, especially applied behavioral analysis (Ferguson, 1987). Preservice students typically take a variety of courses focused on student characteristics and different disability categories, followed by a series of methods courses. Once licensed, special educa-

tors, like their general education counterparts, continue to take focused courses and attend special education inservices on the expectation that their knowledge and skills are thereby continuously updated.

Contributions to Interdisciplinary Practice

In a specific sense, then, the contributions of special education to interdisciplinary practice for persons with developmental disabilities only slowly emerged in relatively recent history. Prior to public education assuming responsibility for students with developmental disabilities—especially those with moderate and severe developmental disabilities—special education for such students, when it existed at all, more frequently occurred in special schools and clinics administered by other branches of social service, such as medicine or health and human services.

Assessment

In a very real and powerful sense, special educators have always borne the responsibility of educating those students deemed not to "fit" general education. Prior to EHA, the procedures for identifying students shifted from being idiosyncratic and phenomenological to more scientific and precise approaches. The emergence of intelligence testing in the early decades of the century greatly aided this effort (Anderson, 1917; Gesell, 1925; Gould, 1981). More important, however, was the pattern of identification established: precise identification of a student's abilities and deficits was necessary in order to identify both the corresponding curriculum and teaching objectives, and the expected learning accomplishments (Goddard, 1920; Mitchell, 1916;

Wallin, 1924). Thus, one popular textbook (Perry, 1960) devoted to educating the "trainable" student urged development of programs that emphasized self-care, socialization, and expressive skills. Follow-up studies during the same period revealed that nearly half of such students entered institutions immediately after leaving school (Scheerenberger, 1983).

After the passage of EHA, the essential pattern for identification of both students eligible for special education, and the services they required, remained largely unchanged. The identification of a student's abilities and disabilities must be determined by more than intelligence testing alone, students must be assessed with regard to all areas of possible deficit, and they must be tested with instruments that are both culturally and racially sensitive and do not punish them for known disabilities. Thus, for example, a student with an obvious motor impairment should not be assessed with intelligence tests that require motor performance. In the years since EHA, special educators have developed a range of other supporting assessment strategies designed not only to confirm the presence of a disability that is interfering with learning, but to direct special educators more precisely in the kinds of curriculum and teaching approaches that will best serve the remediation effort. These assessment forms range from criterion-referenced instruments to curriculum-based assessment approaches (Guess, Horner, Utley, Holvoet, Maxon, Tucker & Warren, 1978), and various kinds of functional assessment (O'Neill, Horner, Albin, Storey & Sprague, 1990; Ferguson, Willis, Rivers, Meyer, Young & Dalman, in press). There is also a growing number of home-, community-, and peer-referenced assessment approaches (e.g., Ferguson & Meyer, 1991; Hunt, Cornelius, Leventhal, Miller, Murray & Stoner, 1990; Turnbull, 1991).

Despite the dramatic range of disabilities—and abilities—possessed by special education's students, especially after the implementation of EHA, the overriding purpose of special education remained constant: Try to remediate deficits in development and performance, repair pathologies, and otherwise ameliorate the effects of impairment and disability so that students might function as normally as possible and learn to their fullest potential. This logic is most clearly captured in the requirements of the Individual Education Plan (IEP) which requires a description of a student's current abilities and a detailed plan of how special educators will change that ability in the direction of the general education requirements and typical peer performance.

Curriculum

The overriding logic of special education— to identify those students who do not fit, figure out what is wrong, and fix the problem—naturally led to the development of a separate, parallel system of special education. Previously, the categorical nature of the assessment process (Does the child have a disability? What is it? Does it interfere with the child's ability to benefit from general education?) further elaborated the special education system into separate classrooms and schools, frequently physically distant from public schools, that were staffed by special education teachers, assistants, and related professional staff (Whipple, 1927). Districts without the resources to create segregated schools typically offered, as an alternative, self-contained classrooms and parallel use of other school facilities (such as the library, gym, cafeteria, and even playground).

Despite repeated critiques of separate education, beginning with the efficacy studies of the 1960s (Dunn, 1968; Lilly, 1970; Reynolds, 1962; Taylor, 1988; Shapiro, Loeb

& Bowermaster, 1993), the practical interpretation of "appropriate education" quickly became "appropriate placement on the continuum of services" where each service was tied to a particular location. The more intense the services required to remediate or ameliorate disability, the more distant from general education environments, and the greater distance needed to travel to eventually return to that environment (Taylor, 1988).

Once identified and placed, whether locally or regionally, the services offered special education students were as closely tied to their determined disability as was their placement in the educational system. Each location along the continuum of special places "matched" a set of curricular objectives, specialized teaching and management strategies, and preferred materials.

Along with these shifts in curriculum and teaching came new calls to reconsider where special education services should be housed within public education. Efforts to "mainstream" during the 1970s, driven in large part by the disproportionate number of poor, nonwhite, and non-English-speaking students in special education classrooms (Dickie, 1982; Mercer, 1973), had not substantially altered the separate special education service delivery system (Macmillan, Jones & Meyers, 1976). The 1980s revisited mainstreaming with new calls to integrate all special education services into the mainstream of public education (Certo, Haring & York, 1984; Stainback & Stainback, 1985).

Later initiatives in special education have called for the integration of students with disabilities into the general education classrooms. Current reforms in special education have rapidly shifted to calls for "rethinking" (Wang, Reynolds, & Walberg, 1986), "restructuring" (Reynolds, Wang, Walberg, 1987; Skrtic, 1987), and moving "beyond special education" (Gartner & Lipsky, 1987). Integration and mainstreaming—resulting all too often in mere physical presence of students with disabilities and their teachers—has led to new calls for full learning membership and *inclusion* of both special educators and students with disabilities into the life of the broader school community (Ferguson, in press; Forest & Pearpoint, 1991; Fullwood, 1990). The experience of *integration* taught some special educators the limits of tolerated presence for producing the educational outcomes sought for children and youth with any kind of disability. To be an effective learning context—if full inclusion and membership are ever to be realized—schools themselves must be dramatically reformed (Pearman, Huang, Barnhart & Mellblom, 1992).

The agenda for special education in the 1990s is to increase efforts to achieve inclusion of children and adolescents who have disabilities. Not only will inclusion involve all levels of the educational system, but individuals at each level must engage in the "phenomenology of change" (Fullen, 1991), in both what they do and what they experience in schools (Peck, 1993), in order to avoid such incomplete results as "class within a class" (Salisbury, Palombar & Hollowood, 1993) or "bubble kids" (Ferguson et al., 1993; Schnorr, 1990). Despite some continuing debates about student outcomes (Buswell & Schaffner, 1992; Strully & Strully, 1989), there is an emerging consensus that successful inclusion must address *both* learning and the social experiences of students in a balanced way (Brown, Schwartz, Uduari-Solner, Kampschroer, Johnson, Jorgensen & Gruenwald, 1991; Ferguson, Meyer, Jeanchild, Juniper & Zingo, 1992; Giangreco, Dennis, Cloninger, Edelman & Schattman, 1993; Jorgenson, 1992; Salisbury et al., 1993; Stainback & Stainback, 1992).

One theme in the current reform discussion involves moving away from the connection between disability category and service. Some states (e.g., Vermont and Oregon) have changed special education funding patterns in order to begin disassociating funding from disability categories. General and special educators are working together to integrate and include students previously receiving services in pull-out or entirely separate educational environments. They are developing a new appreciation for the applicability of many traditional special education curricula and teaching strategies to a wide variety of children and youth who do not meet special education eligibility requirements. Conversely, special educators are becoming more familiar with effective general education curriculum and teaching practices that well complement their own familiar tools and approaches.

This gradual erasing of distinctions between effective general- and special-education teaching approaches, as well as the newly emerging blends of these traditionally separate approaches, may eventually change how the field thinks about the "special education student." Already in some schools and classrooms, children and youth do not have to demonstrate a disability in order to "qualify" to receive benefit from either special educators or their special knowledge and teaching tools. In countries like Iceland and Denmark, the shift away from tying resources to categories of disability toward making resources available to students according to their learning needs, preferences, and achievement has already been formalized in national policies.

Of course, there will always be labels—naming differences seems to be an established human pattern. What may be emerging in education, however, is a situation in which labels do not determine where students can learn or the kinds of resource supports, curriculum, or teaching approaches that are available to them. Whether or not this direction becomes dominant is impos-

sible to predict. There are other strong movements to legitimize new disability categories and maintain separate environments for some classes of students (especially students identified as severely emotionally disturbed or deaf).

Having demonstrated that special education's newest students could indeed learn, proponents and practitioners of the resultant instructional technology began to question whether learning was enough of an accomplishment for schools to achieve for students. New calls to make school relevant to students' future lives (Brown, Nietupski, & Hamre-Nietupski, 1976; Thomas, 1977) led to new "functional" curriculum approaches that focused more on ensuring that students could actually use their learning in their lives outside of school (Guess & Helmstetter, 1986; Sailor & Guess, 1983; Wilcox & Bellamy, 1982), sometimes by moving the activity of teaching and learning to community environments and naturally occurring times (Hamre-Nietupski, Nietupski, Bates & Maurer, 1982; Horner, McDonnell & Bellamy, 1986; Sailor, Halvorsen, Anderson, Goetz, Gee & Doering, 1986).

Case Example

This account of Alex's involvement with special education, although occurring in the very recent past, captures the kinds of changes that typify special education in the 1990s. Not all students with developmental disabilities experience either the same constellation of educational needs as Alex or the changes in delivery of services. Nevertheless, in various ways, more and more of special education's students, regardless of their label, are experiencing changes in how school happens and what it accomplishes.

History

While playing on the beach at age 2, Alex was caught by an unexpectedly large wave and almost drowned. After a period of recuperation, Alex and his family discovered the experience had left him with multiple impairments and disabilities. He has very limited voluntary movement, uses a gastrointestinal tube for nutrition, and requires intermittent suctioning to sustain adequate breathing. He acquired a number of official labels, including *profound mental retardation, severe orthopedic impairment,* and *functional blindness.* He is also nonverbal and has very limited communication using other modes of expression.

Despite efforts to incorporate Alex and his care into their family life, by age 6 the challenges were too great for Alex's family to manage his care alone. Options available at the time, however, precluded hiring in-home assistance, and there were no foster homes available in Alex's rural coastal town that could manage his level of care. With profound reluctance, Alex's parents agreed to allow Alex to move into a geriatric nursing home in a city ninety miles away. The facility met criteria for funding and served eighty senior citizens in addition to four other children.

Intervention

Alex attended school for the first time in his new community. School district assessments confirmed that he was disabled in ways that were likely to affect his ability to benefit from school and recommended placement in a self-contained classroom of similarly labeled primary-aged students operated by a county-wide intermediate school district. The classroom was located in a nearby elementary school, but not the school located a block from the nursing facility; this necessitated special transportation. Alex was also assigned the services of

a number of support staff who worked either for the county-wide district or a multi-county regional program. Specialists included a physical therapist, speech therapist, augmentative communication specialist, and a vision specialist. A third educational assistant was assigned to the classroom, in addition to the two already there, in order to provide the extra supports everyone believed Alex required. Alex's home county reimbursed his new county for his educational costs.

Because of the drip tube feeding schedule at the nursing facility, Alex arrived at school mid-morning, usually when his classmates were on their way to recess. When there was time, one of the assistants would take Alex to join his classmates. Recess was followed by an hour of stimulation activities for Alex in a special corner of the room while his classmates pursued other learning activities. After the stimulation activities were completed, Alex typically joined one of the other learning groups, sometimes participating, sometimes just watching. After a session of switch practice on the computer, Alex remained in the classroom while his classmates went to lunch at their special table in the cafeteria. Early on, Alex also went to the cafeteria to sit at the class table and taste some of the foods, but the special education teacher believed his participation not to be very image-enhancing or productive. She arranged for Alex to have his schedule of physical therapy activities and time on the supine stander in the quiet classroom while the rest of the class went to lunch.

Alex rejoined his classmates for after-lunch toothbrushing, grooming, and other personal hygiene needs. The last hour and a half of the day typically involved art activities with fourth-grade peer tutors who came to the self-contained classroom, followed by a mail delivery job Alex shared with two other classmates, and then twenty minutes of language during a closing circle time. Alex left school at two o'clock, returned home, was changed into pajamas, and attached to his drip feeder until nine the next morning. Occasionally, Alex was taken to the sitting room to visit with other residents and participate in the various opportunities arranged by the activities director.

During his three years at this nursing facility and school, Alex's family tried to visit at least twice each month, but they began to feel more and more distant from Alex. Although they missed Alex deeply, and wanted him to be nearer home, they believed they were making the best decisions they could within the current resource constraints and service options. Still, at IEP-related meetings Alex's mother reported feeling that the nursing facility and school staffs were coming to know her son better than she did, and she deferred all educational decisions to them.

Three years after beginning school, some of the adults in Alex's daily life began asking different questions: Why does he always have to be late to school? Why can't he spend more time in general education classrooms? Is his educational program effective? What is the quality of his life outside of school? Does his schooling relate to his life? Does he have any friends? Is his family interested or is he a ward of the state? Why does he have to live so far from home? Is school really "working" for Alex?

Answers began to emerge. Encouraged by Alex's teacher and parents, a graduate student investigated what might have changed during the three years of Alex's residence in the city, in hopes of discovering new options, and possibly even resources, that might result in a change for Alex. Although much had not changed, there had been one important change in personnel in Alex's home community. A new case manager not only listened to the questions, but asked more. The combined result of different people questioning both the status quo and imagining new possibilities resulted in Alex returning to a nursing facility near his parents' home and the neighborhood elementary school.

The school district had a longstanding policy of supporting all students' learning in general education classrooms and assigned Alex to Ms. Peters' class. They also provided an educational assistant. Ms. Peters taught a multi-age, mixed ability classroom, using a wide variety of teaching strategies—from tested to innovative—to implement an activity-rich curriculum. District administrators expected to have to plead Alex's case with Ms. Peters, but she surprised all involved with her genuine excitement about including Alex in her room. She prepared classmates for his arrival in mid-spring by explaining his accident, but mostly by emphasizing that as a result he had been away from home for three years. By the time he arrived, everyone was eager to celebrate his return.

Ms. Peters was a confident and creative teacher who was already skillful at tailoring her teaching to all 27 different students already in her room. Still, she realized Alex would be a unique challenge and eagerly accepted the support and assistance of the district special education support teacher and a university-sponsored special project focusing on validating innovative educational practices for children like Alex. These specialized supports complemented Ms. Peters' basic teaching approaches and strategies. The team began by trying to incorporate Alex in all classroom activities as an assessment approach to discover what he liked, how to best assist him physically, what he could do without assistance, how peers and other adults might react to him, and which school and community activities he might best be able to participate in actively.

Quickly information began to emerge.

Alex seemed happiest and most alert when surrounded by the chatter and hubbub of other students. Classmates in his cooperative learning groups became adept at creating meaningful participation for Alex in class projects and activities, responding to differences in his facial expressions, sounds, and smiles. They also discovered how best to assist him when it was necessary. They competed to bring snacks that Alex might share and became efficient at assisting Alex to use his extra equipment and supports. The assistant explored ways to use dial-a-ride services so that Alex could join classmates on weekend outings and taught his classmates the route to his nursing facility so they could visit him on weekends and after school. By the end of the school year Alex surprised everyone by reliably raising his hand to indicate a definite "yes" and moving his hand sideways to indicate "no" when presented with choices. His response to and understanding of things people were saying also seemed to be considerably greater than previously thought, leading Ms. Peters and the specialist support team to design new assessments and information systems to validate their hunches.

Shortly after entering fourth grade the following fall, Alex needed major spinal surgery, resulting in many weeks of missed school. His teacher and classmates continued to design learning projects that included him. The classroom assistant escorted rotating small groups to the nursing home, bringing ongoing classroom projects to Alex until his recuperation was complete. Nursing facility staff agreed to help Alex with his homework and other homebound assignments, keeping him as connected as possible with both the classroom and his unique learning agenda.

Alex's return to his home community has rekindled the family membership and community caring that supported him during the first four years after his accident. His involvement in the fourth grade is one important aspect of the community caring and support that Alex, and many other students, sorely need. His classmates think of him as part of the class and miss him when he is absent.

Alex is working on many of the same learning goals he began in the special education classroom: communicating what he knows, wants, and dislikes; improving the consistency and quality of his motor abilities so he can participate in more ways in all kinds of routines and learning activities; making and communicating his choices; and maintaining his general health and fitness. Perhaps as important as what Alex is doing is the context. Fourth grade is quite different from his self-contained classroom. Ms. Peters is his teacher, despite not being officially licensed to teach students with the kinds of differences Alex brings to her classroom. (She "stepped up" with her class in order to follow all of them, including Alex, through another year of growth and achievement.) She accomplishes this role only with the assistance of the additional technical information offered by special educators, therapists, and other specialists on the interdisciplinary team and with the firm conviction and permission to be the leader in synthesizing these differing bits of information and knowledge into the activities and agendas of her fourth grade class. Alex, like his classmates, also benefits from the teaching of the 27 other fourth graders in the class. Ms. Peters, the assistant, and the special educator together pursue professional development opportunities offered by their district, the state department, and the local university, to better serve this most diverse group of students.

Summary

As educational reform continues to pursue a variety of agendas designed to improve both the responsiveness and effectiveness of public education, the discipline of special education is also undergoing substantive and systemic change. Historically, reforms in special education emphasized the development of more specialized services and subspecialities designed to respond to more and more categories of disability among school children and youth. While this pattern continues in some subfields of the discipline, other increasingly dominant reforms emphasize the merging of special and general education disciplinary knowledge and practice, reinventing special education and special educators in the process. Although many debates continue, and it is impossible to predict all the outcomes of current change efforts, it does seem clear that special education in the 21st century will have acquired new meanings and special educators new roles in American public education.

References

Anderson, M. (1917). *Education of defectives in the public schools.* New York: World Book Company.

Anderson, R., & Greer, J. (1976). *Educating the severely and profoundly retarded.* Baltimore, MD: University Park Press.

Anderson, V. (1921). Education of mental defectives in state and private institutions and in special classes in public schools in the United States. *Mental Hygiene, 5,* 85-122.

Aronowitz, S., & Giroux, H. (1985). *Education under siege: The conservative, liberal, and radical debate over schooling.* South Hadley, MA: Bergin & Garvey Publications.

Baumgart, D., & Ferguson, D. (Eds.) (1991). *Personnel preparation: Directions for the future.* Baltimore, MD: Paul H. Brookes.

Berry, C. (1931). *Special education: Report of the White House Conference on Child Health and Protection.* New York: The Century Co.

Biklen, D. (1985). *Achieving the complete school: Strategies for effective mainstreaming.* New York: Teachers College Press.

Boyer, E. (1983). *High school: A report on secondary education in America.* New York: Harper and Row.

Brinker, R. (1985). Curricula without recipes: A challenge to teachers and a promise to severely mentally retarded students. In D. Bricker & J. Filler (Eds.), *Severe mental retardation: From theory to practice* (pp. 208-229). Lancaster, PA: Lancaster Press.

Brown, L., Nietupski, J., & Hamre-Nietupski, S. (1976). Criterion of ultimate functioning. In M. Thomas (Eds.), *Hey, don't forget about me!* (pp. 2-15). Reston, VA: Council for Exceptional Children.

Brown, L., Schwartz, P., Udvari-Solner, A., Kampschroer, E., Johnson, F., Jorgensen, J., & Gruenewald, L. (1991). How much time should students with severe intellectual disabilities spend in regular education classrooms and elsewhere? *The Journal of the Association of Persons with Severe Handicaps, 16,* 39-47.

Buswell, B., & Schaffner, B. (1992). Building friendships: An important part of schooling. *OSERS News in Print, 4*(4), 4-8.

Certo, N., Haring, N., & York, R. (Eds.). (1984). *Public school integration of severely handicapped students: Rational issues and progressive alternatives.* Baltimore, MD: Paul H. Brookes.

Cohen, M., Gross, P., & Haring, N. (1976). Developmental pinpoints. In N. Haring & L. Brown (Eds.), *Teaching the severely handicapped* (pp. 35-110). New York: Grune & Stratton.

Conley, D. (1991). *Restructuring schools: Educators adapt to a changing world.* Eugene, OR: University of Oregon, ERIC Clearinghouse on Educational Management.

Council of Administrators of Special Education [CASE] (1993). *Future agenda for special education: Creating a unified educational system.* Bloomington, IN: Indiana University.

Danielson, L., & Bellamy, G. (1989). State variation in placement of children with handicaps in segregated environments. *Exceptional Children, 55,* 448-465.

Darling-Hammond, L. (1990). Achieving our goals: Superficial or structural reform? *Phi Delta Kappan, 72,* 286-295.

Davis, S. (1992, October). *Report card to the nation on inclusion in education of students with mental retardation.* Arlington, TX: The ARC.

DeVore, S. (1977). *Individualized learning program for the profoundly retarded.* Springfield, IL: Charles C. Thomas.

Dickie, R. (1982). Still crazy after all these years: Another look at the question of labeling and non-categorical conceptions of exceptional children. *Education and Treatment of Children, 5,* 355-363.

Dunn, L. (1968). Special education for the mildly retarded: Is much of it justifiable? *Exceptional Children, 35,* 5-22.

Eisner, E. (1991). What really counts in schools. *Educational Leadership, 48*(5), 10-17.

Elmore, R. (1990). *Restructuring schools: The next generation of educational reform.* San Francisco: Jossey-Bass.

Ferguson, D. (1987). *Curriculum decision making for students with severe handicaps: Policy and practice.* New York: Teachers College Press.

Ferguson, D. (1989). Severity of need and educational excellence: Public school reform and students with disabilities. In D. Biklen, D. Ferguson, & A. Ford (Eds.), *Schooling and disability* (pp. 25-58). Chicago, IL: University of Chicago Press and The National Society for the Study of Education.

Ferguson, D. (1993). Policy Issues: Certification practices. Paper presented at the Association for Persons with Severe Handicaps Annual Conference. Chicago, IL: November 5, 1993.

Ferguson, D. (in press). Persons with severe developmental disabilities: "Mainstreaming" to

supported community membership. In T. Husen & T. Postlethwaite (Eds.), *The international encyclopedia of education.* Great Britain: Pergamon Press.

Ferguson, D., & Meyer, G. (1991). *The elementary/secondary system: Supportive education for students with severe handicaps. Module 1c: Ecological assessment.* Eugene, OR: Specialized Training Program, University of Oregon.

Ferguson, D., Meyer, G., Jeanchild, L., Juniper, L., & Zingo, J. (1992). Figuring out what to do with the grownups: How teachers make inclusion "work" for students with disabilities. *The Journal of the Association for Persons with Severe Handicaps, 17,* 218-226.

Ferguson, D., & Searl, S. (1982). *The challenge of integrating students with severe disabilities.* Syracuse, NY: Special Education Resource Center, Syracuse University.

Ferguson, D., Willis, C., Boles, S., Jeanchild, L., Holliday, L., Meyer, G., Rivers, E., & Zitek, M. (1993). *Regular class participation system (RCPS): A final report.* Eugene, OR: University of Oregon, Specialized Training Program.

Ferguson, D., Willis, C., Rivers, E., Meyer, G., Young, M., & Dalmau, M. (in press). Widening the stream: Ways to think about including "exceptions" in schools. In D. Lear & F. Brown (Eds.). *Students with profound disabilities* (2nd ed.). Baltimore, MD: Paul H. Brookes.

Finn, C. (1991). *We must take charge: Our schools and our future.* New York: Free Press.

Forest, M., & Pearpoint, J. (1991). Two roads: Exclusion or inclusion? *Developmental Disabilities Bulletin, 19*(1), 1-11.

Fredericks, H., Riggs, C., Furey, T., Grove, D.W.M., McDonell, J., Jordan, E., Hanson, W., Baldwin, V., & Wadlow, M. (1976). *The teaching research curriculum for moderately and severely handicapped.* Springfield, IL: Charles C. Thomas.

Fuchs, D., & Fuchs, L. (1994). Inclusive schools movement and the radicalization of special education reform. *Exceptional Children, 60,*

294-309.

Fullen, M. (1991). *The new meaning of educational change* (2nd ed.). New York: Teachers College Press.

Fullen, M., & Miles, M. (1992). Getting reform right: What works and what doesn't. *Phi Delta Kappan, 74*, 745-752.

Fullwood, D. (1990). *Chances and choices: Making integration work*. Baltimore, MD: Paul H. Brookes.

Gartner, A., & Lipsky, D. (1987). Beyond special education: Toward a quality system for all students. *Harvard Educational Review, 57*, 367-395.

Gersten, R., & Woodward, J. (1990). Rethinking the regular education initiative: Focus on the classroom teacher. *Remedial and Special Education, 11*, 7-16.

Gesell, A. (1925). *The retarded child: How to help him*. Bloomington, IL: Public School Publishing Co.

Giangreco, M., Dennis, R., Cloninger, C., Edelman, S., & Schattman, R. (1993). "I've counted on Jon": Transformational experiences of teachers educating students with disabilities. *Exceptional Children, 59*, 359-372.

Goddard, H. (1920). *Feeblemindedness: Its causes and consequences*. New York: Macmillan.

Goodlad, J. (1984). *A place called school: Prospects for the future*. New York: McGraw-Hill.

Goodlad, J. (1990). *Teachers for our nation's schools*. San Francisco: Jossey-Bass.

Goodlad, J., & Lovitt, T. (Eds.). (1993). *Integrating general and special education*. New York: Merrill.

Goodlad, J., Soder, R., & Sirotnik, K. (1990b). *Places where teachers are taught*. San Francisco: Jossey-Bass.

Goodlad, J., Soder, R., & Sirotnik, K. (Eds.). (1990a). *The moral dimensions of teaching*. San Francisco: Jossey-Bass.

Gould, S. (1981). *The mismeasure of man*. New York: W.W. Norton.

Grimmett, P., & Erickson, G. (Eds.). (1988). *Reflection in teacher education*. New York: Teachers College Press.

Gross, B., & Gross, R. (1985). *The great school debate: Which way for American education?* New York: Simon & Schuster, Inc.

Grossman, P. (1990). *The making of a teacher: Teacher knowledge and teacher education*. New York: Teachers College Press.

Guess, D., & Helmstetter, E. (1986). Skill cluster instruction and the individualized curriculum sequencing model. In R. Horner, L. Meyer, & H. Fredericks (Eds.), *Education of learners with severe handicaps: Exemplary service strategies* (pp. 221-248). Baltimore, MD: Paul H. Brookes.

Guess, D., Horner, D., Utley, B., Holvoet, J., Maxon, D., Tucker, D., & Warren, S. (1978). A functional curriculum sequencing model for teaching the severely handicapped. *AAWSPH Review, 3*, 202-215.

Hamre-Nietupski, S., Nietupski, J., Bates, P., & Maurer, S. (1982). Implementing a community-based educational model for moderately/severely handicapped students: Common problems and suggested solutions. *Journal of the Association for the Severely Handicapped, 7*, 38-43.

Hoffman, E. (1975). The American public school and the deviant child: The origins of their involvement. *Journal of Special Education, 9*, 415-423.

Holmes Group, The. (1986). *Tomorrow's teachers: A report of the Holmes Group*. Lansing, MI: Author.

Horner, R., McDonnell, J., & Bellamy, G. (1986). Teaching generalized skills: General case instruction in simulation and community settings. In R. Horner, L. Meyer, & H. Fredericks (Eds.), *Education of learners with severe handicaps: Exemplary service strategies* (pp. 289-314). Baltimore, MD: Paul H. Brookes.

Hunt, M., Cornelius, P., Leventhal, P., Miller, P., Murray, T., & Stoner, G. (1990). *Into our lives*. Akron, OH: Children's Hospital Medical Center.

Jorgensen, C. (1992). Natural supports in inclusive schools. In J. Nisbet (Eds.), *Natural supports in school, at work, and in the community for people with severe disabilities* (pp. 179-216). Baltimore, MD: Paul H. Brookes.

Kauffman, J., & Hallahan, D. (1993). Toward a comprehensive delivery system for special education. In J. Goodlad & T. Lovitt (Eds.), *Integrating general and special education* (pp. 73-102). New York: Macmillan.

Kirk, S., & Johnson, G. (1951). *Educating the retarded child.* Boston, MA: Houghton Mifflin.

Kozol, J. (1991). *Savage inequalities: Children in America's schools.* New York: Crown Publishing.

Lilly, M. (1970). Special education: A teapot in a tempest. *Exceptional Children, 37,* 43-48.

Lovitt, T. (1993). Recurring issues in special and general education. In J. Goodlad & T. Lovitt (Eds.), *Integrating general and special education.* New York: Macmillan.

Macmillan, D., Jones, R., & Meyers, C. (1976). Mainstreaming the mildly retarded: Some questions, cautions, and guidelines. *Mental Retardation, 14,* 3-10.

Meisels, S., & Provence, S. M. (1989). *Screening and assessment: Guidelines for identifying young disabled and developmentally vulnerable children and their families.* Washington, DC: National Center Clinical Infant Programs.

Mercer, J. (1973). *Labeling the mentally retarded.* Berkeley, CA: University of California Press.

Mitchell, D. (1916). *Schools and classes for exceptional children.* Cleveland, OH: Survey Committee of the Cleveland Foundation.

National Association of State Boards of Education. (1990). *Today's children, tomorrow's survival: A call to restructure schools.* Alexandria, VA: Author.

National Commission on Excellence. (1983). *A nation at risk: The imperative for educational reform.* Washington, DC: U.S. Government Printing Office.

O'Neill, J. (1991). Drive for national standards picking up steam. *Educational Leadership, 48*(5), 4-8.

O'Neill, R., Horner, R., Albin, R., Storey, K., & Sprague, J. (1990). *Functional analysis of problem behavior: A practical assessment guide.* Sycamore, IL: Sycamore Publishing Company.

Oakes, J., & Lipton, M. (1990). *Making the best of schools: A handbook for parents, teachers, and policy makers.* New Haven, CT: Yale University Press.

Passow, A. (Eds.). (1990). *How it happened wave by wave: Whither (or wither) school reform?* Boston, MA: Allyn & Bacon.

Pearman, E., Huang, A., Barnhart, M., & Mellblom, C. (1992). Educating all children in school: Attitudes and beliefs about inclusion. *Education and Training in Mental Retardation, 27,* 176-182.

Peck, C. (1993). Ecological perspectives on the implementation of integrated early childhood programs. In C. Peck, S. Odom, & D. Bricker (Eds.), *Integrating young children with disabilities into community programs* (pp. 3-15). Baltimore, MD: Paul H. Brookes.

Perry, N. (1960). *Teaching the mentally retarded child.* New York: Columbia University Press.

Perske, R., & Smith, J. (1977). *Beyond the ordinary: The preparation of professionals to educate severely and profoundly handicapped persons.* Parsons, KS: Words & Pictures Corp.

Popovich, D., & Laham, S. (1981). *The adaptive behavior curriculum* (Vol. 1). Baltimore. MD: Paul H. Brookes.

Pugach, M., & Lilly, S. (1984). Reconceptualizing support services for classroom teachers: Implications for teacher education. *Journal of Teacher Education, 35,* 48-55.

Reynolds, M. (1962). A framework for considering some issues in special education. *Exceptional Children, 28,* 367-370.

Reynolds, M., Wang, M., & Walberg, H. (1987). The necessary restructuring of special and regular education. *Exceptional Children, 53,* 391-398.

Roach, V. (1993). "Winners all". *Colloquium,* October 18, 1993. Eugene, OR: University of Oregon.

Sailor, W., Anderson, J., Halvorsen, A., Doering, K., Filler, J., & Goetz, L. (1989). *The comprehensive local school: Regular education for all students with disabilities*. Baltimore, MD: Paul H. Brookes.

Sailor, W., & Guess, D. (1983). *Severely handicapped students: An instructional design*. Boston, MA: Houghton Mifflin.

Sailor, W., Halvorsen, A., Anderson, J., Goetz, L., Gee, K., & Doering, K.H.P. (1986). Community intensive instruction. In R. Horner, H. Meyer, & H. Fredericks (Eds.), *Education of learners with severe handicaps: Exemplary service strategies* (pp. 251-288). Baltimore, MD: Paul H. Brookes.

Salisbury, C., Palombaro, M., & Hollowood, T. (1993). On the nature and change of an inclusive elementary school. *The Journal of the Association of Persons with Severe Handicaps, 18*, 75-84.

Sarason, S. (1990). *The predictable failure of educational reform*. San Francisco: Jossey-Bass.

Sarason, S. (1993). *The case for change: Rethinking the preparation of educators*. San Francisco: Jossey-Bass.

Sarason, S., & Doris, J. (1979). *Educational handicap, public policy, and social history*. New York: Free Press.

Scheerenberger, R. (1983). *A history of mental retardation*. Baltimore, MD: Paul H. Brookes.

Schnorr, R. (1990). "Peter? He comes and goes...": First graders' perspectives on a part-time mainstream student. *The Journal of the Association of Persons with Severe Handicaps, 15*, 231-240.

Schön, D. (1983). *The reflective practitioner: How professionals think in action*. New York: Basic Books.

Shapiro, J., Loeb, P., & Bowermaster, D. (1993). Separate and unequal: How special education programs are cheating our children and costing taxpayers billions each year. *U.S. News and World Report*, Dec. 13, 1993, pp. 46-60.

Shearer, D. (1972). *The Portage guide to early education*. Portage, WI: Cooperative Educational Agency Bulletin No. 12.

Sizer, T. (1992). *Horace's school: Redesigning the American school*. Boston: Houghton Mifflin.

Skrtic, T. (1987). An organizational analysis of special education reform. *Counterpoint, 8*(2), 15-19.

Smull, M., & Bellamy, G. (1991). Community services for adults with disabilities: Policy challenges in the emerging support paradigm. In L. Meyer, C. Peck, & L. Brown (Eds.), *Critical issues in the lives of people with severe disabilities* (pp. 527-536). Baltimore, MD: Paul H. Brookes.

Snell, M. (1978). *Systematic instruction of the moderately and severely handicapped*. Columbus, OH: Charles E. Merrill.

Snell, M. (1983). *Systematic instruction of the moderately and severely handicapped* (2nd ed.). Columbus, OH: Charles E. Merrill.

Sontag, E. (Eds.). (1977). *Educational programming for the severely and profoundly handicapped*. Reston, VA: Council For Exceptional Children.

Stainback, S., & Stainback, W. (Eds.) (1985). *Integration of students with severe handicaps into regular school*. Reston, VA: Council for Exceptional Children.

Stainback, S., & Stainback, W. (1992). *Curriculum considerations in inclusive classrooms*. Baltimore, MD: Paul H. Brookes.

Stainback, W., Stainback, S., & Moravec, J.S. (1992). Using curriculum to build inclusive classrooms. In S. Stainback & W. Stainback (Eds.), *Curriculum considerations in inclusive classrooms: Facilitating learning for all students* (pp. 65-84). Baltimore, MD: Paul H. Brookes.

Strully, J., & Strully, C. (1989). Friendship as an educational goal. In S. Stainback, W. Stainback, & M. Forest (Eds.), *Educating all students in the mainstream of regular education* (pp. 59-68). Baltimore, MD: Paul H. Brookes.

Switzky, H., Rolatori, A., Miller, T., & Freagon, S. (1979). The developmental model and its implications for assessment and instruction for the severely/profoundly handicapped. *Mental retardation, 17*, 167-170.

Taylor, S. (1988). Caught in the continuum: A critical analysis of the principle of the least restrictive environment. *Journal of The Asso-*

ciation for Persons with Severe Handicaps, 13, 41-53.

The Association for Persons with Severe Handicaps. (1994, February). Resolution on inclusive education. *TASH Newsletter* (pp. 4-5). Seattle, WA: Author.

Thomas, M. (1977). *Hey, don't forget about me!* Reston, VA: Council for Exceptional Children.

Tom, A. (1985). Inquiring into inquiry-oriented teacher education. *Journal of Teacher Education, 36*(5), 35-44.

Turnbull, A. (1991). Identifying children's strengths and needs. In M. McGonigel, R. Kaufmann, & B. Johnson (Eds.), *Guidelines and recommended practices for the individualized family service plan* (pp. 1-5). Bethesda, MD: Association for the Care of Children's Health.

Wallin, J. (1924). *The education of handicapped children.* Boston: Houghton Mifflin.

Wallin, J. (1966). Training of the severely retarded, viewed in historical perspective. *Journal of General Psychology, 74,* 107-127.

Wang, M., Reynolds, M., & Walberg, H. (1986). Rethinking special education. *Educational Leadership, 44*(1), 26-31.

Whipple, H. (1927). *Making citizens of the mentally limited.* Bloomington, IL: Public School Publishing Co.

Wilcox, B., & Bellamy, G. (1982). *Design of high school programs for severely handicapped students.* Baltimore: Paul H. Brookes.

Will, M. (1986). Educating children with learning problems: A shared responsibility. *Exceptional Children, 52,* 411-415.

17

Speech-Language Pathology

Billy T. Ogletree, Ph.D., CCC-SLP, Yvonne N. Saddler, Ed.S., CCC-SLP,

& Linda S. Bowers, M.S., CCC-SLP

The speech–language pathologist offers a wide range of services to persons with communication variations and disorders across the lifespan. The American Speech-Language-Hearing Association (ASHA), in its latest scope of practice statement (1990), recognizes the "dynamic and continuously developing" nature of the field and the multifaceted job of the speech and language professional (p. 97). For example, the speech-language pathologist (SLP) of today may serve individuals with disorders of communication, cognition, and oropharyngeal functioning. In addition, they will be expected to possess knowledge of hearing impairment and assistive technology and may be requested to provide assistance to persons who do not have disordered communication, but desire to enhance their communicative effectiveness.

In an effort to address these varied needs, the SLP must present a broad knowledge base specific to the assessment and treatment of communication differences and disorders. In cases where a communication deficit is only a part of an individual's service needs, the SLP must also possess the ability to consult with other professionals, make appropriate referrals, and coordinate care. In addition to these traditional roles, SLPs are often required to assume other professional responsibilities. For example, SLPs frequently serve as counselors and advocates for persons with communication deficits and their families, function as technicians and troubleshooters for people in respect to assistive technology, and serve as educators, supervisors, and researchers.

As the scope of practice continues to expand, SLPs will be called upon to assume even more diverse roles in service delivery. According to Marge (1993), one such role will be disability prevention. Although prevention will provide new opportunities in the areas of employment and research, it will create significant challenges given our nation's cultural diversity, the profession's current emphasis upon crisis intervention, and concerns over financial compensation for preventive efforts.

Whereas SLPs were once limited in their choice of work settings, current employment opportunities are broadening. In an effort to address the profession's ever-growing scope of practice, SLPs can now choose from a variety of employment options ranging from traditional to unique.

The traditional work site for SLPs has been the public schools, where a typical caseload consists of children with speech, language, and hearing deficits (Silverman, 1984). Common speech problems encountered in the schools include articulation, fluency, and voice disorders. Disorders of language might include problems with language form, content, and use. A traditional service delivery model for the public schools has been direct therapy. However, recent federal legislation (P.L. 99-457) has created the need for alternate models, including consultation, to extend services for three- to five-year-olds.

SLPs are also employed in health care facilities such as hospitals, nursing homes, and rehabilitation centers (Silverman, 1984). Caseloads vary by site but may include children or adults with organically-based communication disorders and vegetative oropharyngeal dysfunction (i.e., feeding/ swallowing disorders). These individuals' problems may be acute or long-term. In any event, the SLP will most likely be a member of a team operating from a medical model of service delivery.

Other, more unique work settings include university training programs, community-based service centers, and residential schools or institutions (Silverman, 1984). Caseloads and service delivery models vary tremendously in these settings. In university programs and community-based service centers, a full range of clinical populations are typically served either directly or through consultation. In contrast, residential schools or institutions tend to provide services specific to populations with exceptionality, such as persons with hearing impairment or mental retardation.

Some SLPs forego the typical employment settings to establish private practices. The private speech–language clinician can make decisions about addressing either a narrow spectrum or broad range of communicative disorders. A small percentage accept non-traditional challenges and become consultants to persons without disability. These clients are often seeking to alter their dialects or improve their skills as communicators.

Education and Training Requirements

The professional organization, ASHA, mandates specific academic and clinical training prior to the unrestricted practice of speech–language pathology. Minimally, SLPs must hold a master's degree with a course of study including 75 semester credit hours (undergraduate/graduate) in: (a) the biological/physical sciences and mathematics; (b) the behavioral and/or social sciences including normal aspects of human behavior and communication; and (c) the nature, prevention, evaluation, and treatment of speech, language, hearing and related disorders. In addition, course work should include information pertaining to human development and behavior across the life span and culturally diverse populations (American Speech-Language-Hearing Association, 1993).

The SLP's clinical training includes observations and clinical practicum experiences which must be supervised by individuals holding current and appropriate certification. Requirements include at least 25 hours of supervised observations prior to participation in practica. These hours should include the evaluation and treatment of children and adults with disorders of speech, language, and hearing. Upon completion of observations, 350 hours of supervised practica are required. Clinical practicum experiences are designed according to ASHA's Scope of Practice (American Speech-Language-Hearing Association, 1990) and minimally include evaluation and treatment experiences specific to speech, language, and hearing disorders in children and adults. As of January 1, 1994, graduate course work and clinical practica must be completed at accredited institutions and conform to standards set by the Educational Standards Board (ESB). Graduates from accredited programs will receive automatic approval of course work and practica, providing application for certification is made within three years of graduation.

Post-Education Requirements

A Certificate of Clinical Competence is awarded to all individuals who meet professional standards established by the association for SLPs (American Speech-Language-Hearing Association, 1993). The standards have been designed to insure that SLPs meet requirements for independent service provision. Requirements include specific academic and clinical achievement (described in the previous section), satisfactory performance on a national examination, and completion of a clinical fellowship.

After completing educational requirements, the next step in the certification process is the National Examination in Speech-Language Pathology and Audiology (NESPA). This exam assesses specific professional knowledge, concepts, and issues. Candidates must pass the examination within two years from their initial date of testing. Failure at this juncture results in a re-initiation of the complete certification process.

The final phase of the certification process is the completion of the clinical fellowship. The fellowship occurs over a minimum of 36 weeks of full-time professional employment or a designated part-time equivalent. The clinical fellow must submit a plan for approval and be supervised by a certified SLP. The supervisor provides on-site observations across a variety of clinical service activities. At the end of the fellowship, the supervisor conducts a formal evaluation and makes recommendation for cer-

tification, if appropriate.

Either concurrently or upon completion of national certification, many SLPs also pursue certification from state education agencies (American Speech-Language-Hearing Association, 1993). Requirements vary widely for state certification and renewal (Goddard, 1993). While some states issue original certificates that are valid for life, the majority specify periods of time after which renewal must occur. State-level certification is most applicable to SLPs working in public schools.

Although continuing education is not necessary to renew national certification, the American Speech-Language-Hearing Association has long supported post-degree educational programs. In 1979, a program was initiated to offer continuing education credits on a voluntary basis to professionals in the field (Cornett & Chabon, 1988). Sponsors for continuing education programs were approved, and the Award for Continuing Education (ACE) was established. The ACE is awarded to SLPs who complete specified activities and pay designated fees. Possible activities include attending training seminars, completing course work from accredited programs, retaking the national exam, and participating in independent studies, journal studies, teleseminars, and conferences. ASHA maintains a permanent record of continuing education units earned and confirms each SLP's participation in approved activities (Fagan, 1992).

Thirty-six states require continuing education for the renewal of licensure (Lynch & Welsh, 1993). Requirements range from 50 continuing education hours in a two- to three-year period to 15 hours per year. Florida requires continuing education not only for practicing SLPs but also for speech and language assistants. Some state education agencies also require specific continuing education experiences for renewal of state certification. Individual states approve various activities/experiences for renewal credit, such as college or university classes, work experience, and local workshop participation.

The practice of speech–language pathology is regulated in most states by licensure requirements. Licenses are granted in forty-one states, and one state, Minnesota, has a registration process (American Speech-Language-Hearing Association, 1993). In most cases licensure and national certification requirements are comparable; however, many states have yet to modify licensure according to the most current national standards (Lynch & Welsh, 1993).

The structure and organization of licenses differ widely by state. Costs for licenses vary from $10 to $100 per year, and depending upon the state, licenses are renewed annually, biennially, or triennially. All but two states (California and New York) practice reciprocity, accepting licenses from other states as suitable proof of eligibility for licensure in that particular state. Exemptions and qualifications also vary widely. Typical exemptions include SLPs credentialed by state agencies, physicians and those in their employment, and government employees including university personnel. There are also differences between states about the licensing of persons completing the clinical fellowship or postgraduate professional experiences. Some states simply require supervision, while others also require temporary licenses. Temporary licenses are also often required of professionals who move from one state to another.

Contributions to Interdisciplinary Practice

According to the ASHA's Committee on Mental Retardation/Developmental Disabilities (MR/DD) (1990), the diverse needs of persons with MR/DD are ideally met within an interdisciplinary team (IDT) model. Interdisciplinary practice is best defined as collaborative goal-setting from a "whole-person" perspective (Bagnato & Neisworth, 1991; David & Smith, 1987; Golin & Ducanis, 1981). The successful implementation of an interdisciplinary model depends on the integrated efforts of numerous team members, each of whom brings unique contributions to the assessment and treatment of persons with disabilities.

During the past decade, the SLP's contributions to this model have increased, becoming less discipline-specific and more team-oriented. In contrast to previous position statements, ASHA's 1991 Committee on Language identified 85 knowledge bases or skills needed by SLPs serving persons with language, socio-communicative, and/or cognitive-communicative impairments. Over half (53) of these bases or skills addressed interprofessional collaboration and could be considered vital contributions to successful interdisciplinary practices. Table 17-1 provides a sample of these organized into three categories: general knowledge, collaboration, and communication.

The SLP possesses general knowledge in a variety of areas that is critical to optimal team functioning. For example, knowledge of typical and atypical communication development provides the IDT with communicative expectations necessary for appropriate assessment and intervention decisions for persons with disabilities. Likewise, understanding of how communication and language interact with other developmental domains contributes to a holistic view of individuals served by the interdisciplinary team. Furthermore, the SLP's knowledge of professional positions, family roles, and joint assessment and intervention strategies facilitates the IDT's integrated service

Table 17-1.

The Speech-Language Pathologist's knowledge bases and skills contributing to interdisciplinary practices (ASHA, 1991).

General Knowledge	Collaboration	Communication
Knowledge of typical and atypical socio-communicative development	Skill in reviewing medical, developmental, and educational history and other available diagnostic information	Skill in interviewing parents and other caregivers and educational personnel to obtain relevant background information
Knowledge of the interactional influences of developmental/ educational domains (e.g., language, self-help, psycho-social, cognitive, motor, reading, writing, spelling)	Skill in designing and implementing an intervention plan that is coordinated or integrated with other services	Skill in communicating assessment and intervention outcomes to families and other professionals
Knowledge of the roles that other professionals may assume in delivering services	Skill in assisting families in the transition from one service setting to another	

provision.

The SLP makes a major contribution to interdisciplinary team functioning by assisting with the collection and dissemination of communication-related information. This process occurs throughout assessment and treatment as the SLP works to create communicative environments that encourage information and collaborative decision-making between persons with disability, their families, and members of the team. The SLP's knowledge and modeling of strategies to encourage communication from persons with disability can have the outcome of improving overall team effectiveness. For example, Mirenda and Donnellan (1986) reported that a facilitative style of interaction such as the use of comments, expectant pause, and following the lead of partners helps to elicit representative behaviors from persons with disability. The use of facilitative interaction by all members of the IDT could contribute to more accurate assessment and effective intervention.

Assessment of Individuals and their Families

One of the SLP's major contributions to the interdisciplinary team is the assessment of communication. Success is dependent upon numerous factors, not the least of which is the integration of ever-changing assessment principles and practices. In the past two decades, assessment principles have changed from exclusionary, one-time, client-focused practices to those which are more inclusive, ongoing, and ecologically valid. Four major principles which support the assessment process are outlined and discussed (Beukelman & Mirenda, 1992).

Principle I: All people communicate. Acceptance of this principle is vital if communication assessments are to be generally accessible. Prior to being embraced by most SLPs, however, there was an informal assumption of assessment candidacy. When implemented, more severely impaired individuals may have been denied or given cursory assessments on the grounds that they were "noncommunicative." This principle specifies that communication is a characteristic of all people, regardless of functional ability.

Principle II: Assessment should be a process. If intervention efforts are to meet the changing needs of persons with developmental disability, assessment cannot be a static or fixed event. This is particularly true with respect to the assessment of a dynamic developmental domain such as communication. To implement this principle, SLPs must incorporate assessment into all phases of service delivery. Assessments need to be performed early in the service delivery process to identify problems, determine directions for intervention, evaluate treatment effectiveness, and project future treatment needs.

Principle III: Assessment should be functional. Communication assessment must provide functional information needed to meet the needs of persons with disability. In a description of "past practices" and "best practices," McLean (1990) encouraged SLPs to be as functional as possible. She advocates the use of functional communication skills (e.g., verbal and nonverbal communicative abilities needed in everyday settings) over procedures which make comparisons of a person with a disability to existing norms or standards.

Principle IV: Assessments should involve more than the person with disability. In the past, SLPs and other professionals have been guilty of assessing persons with disability without assessing their communicative partners and environments. Once again, McLean (1990) argues against focusing solely upon the performance of an individual within an isolated "testing" context. Instead, assessment needs to be structured to evaluate the person with disability, people with whom they communicate, and their multiple communicative environments.

Assessment Practices

Viewing assessment as a process has generated new reasons for assessing persons with developmental disability. Assessments are no longer solely conducted to confirm the existence and identify the causes of communication problems (Duchan, 1988). This information can be either obvious or unattainable and may fail to provide clear directions for intervention. In contrast, communication assessments for persons with disability currently focus upon identifying functional abilities, needs, and treatment effectiveness.

New reasons for assessments have resulted in new assessment procedures. Prior to their discussion, however, a review of traditional communication assessment is warranted.

Historically, communication assessments for persons with developmental disability have begun with an evaluation to determine hearing status, typically conducted by a certified audiologist (simple screenings can be administered by the SLP). Findings have been used to either identify or rule out hearing loss. Subsequent to hearing assessments, SLPs have assessed communication through the administration of standardized norm-referenced tests and structural analyses of speech and language. Findings have been compared to "normal" standards to identify discrepancies and ultimately generate diagnoses of communication impairment. These methods have been best suited for one-time, center-based use; applied mostly to oral communicators; emphasized weaknesses rather than strengths; and provided little insight into the functional communicative needs or abilities of persons with disability. Furthermore, the validity of discrepancy-based criteria for identifying communication impairments has recently been questioned (Aram, Morris & Hall, 1992).

An evaluation of communication and needs and interaction with communication partners are vital components of the assessment process for a person with a developmental disability. Current assessment processes have been modified to be less artificial and more representative of contexts in which communication actually occurs. To be more representative, SLPs have included observation of communicative partners to supplement direct assessment findings. For younger children and persons with more severe disabilities, informant-based tools designed for infants and toddlers [e.g., the *Receptive Expressive Emergent Language Scale-Revised* (Bzoch & League, 1990); the *Infant Toddler Language Scale* (Rossetti, 1990)] have been used. For persons with lesser degrees of disability, SLPs have frequently generated informal partner questionnaires including items such as "How does John let you know he wants something?," "When John talks, do most people understand him?" and related questions.

Aside from assisting with the generation of representative findings, informancy can be paired with SLP observations across settings to evaluate communicative environments and partners. Partners can be questioned regarding the everyday communicative opportunities and performances of persons with disability and responses can be used to determine treatment needs and effectiveness. This information can be integrated with data from direct observations of the SLP. Interaction patterns between a person with a disability and a partner can be assessed to determine the need for partner-directed interventions, such as instruction in the implementation of interactions styles which facilitate rather than inhibit communication.

Norm-referenced tests and structural speech and language analyses have historically been included in the assessment of persons with disability. Norm-referenced measures are comprised of relevant and valid items which have been administered to a large sample representative of a target population (Haynes, Pendzola, & Emerick, 1992). Persons performing significantly below the sample population (e.g., two standard deviations below the mean) are considered to present problems significant enough to warrant concern. Structural speech and language analyses are similar in that findings regarding the use of specific speech and language forms are compared to developmental standards in an effort to identify delayed or deviant speech and language emergence. Table 2 presents a non-exhaustive list of norm-referenced communication-related tests frequently used with persons with developmental disability.

As an alternative to norm-referenced testing, many SLPs are now using criterion-referenced measures. Rather than indicating the relative status of peoples' performances, these tests measure mastery of specific skills (Salvia & Yesseldyke, 1991). Criterion-referenced measures are particularly useful as the SLP attempts to identify the communication-related abilities and needs of persons with disability and determine treatment effectiveness. Unfortunately, there are few such measures commercially available.

A final supplement to traditional communication assessment has been structured communication sampling which allows the SLP to observe persons with disability in real world communication systems. Such a situation might include eating in front of a person without offering food. Structured communication sampling protocols have proven useful as a means of assessing the functional communicative abilities of young children and persons with severe to profound developmental disabilities (McLean, McLean, Brady & Etter; 1991; Ogletree, Wetherby & Westling, 1992; Wetherby, Yonclas & Bryan, 1989).

Table 17-2.

Common norm-referenced speech and language measures.

Speech	*Arizona Articulation Proficiency Scale*	(Fudala & Reynolds, 1986)
	Goldman-Fristoe Test of Articulation	(Goldman & Fristoe, 1986)
	Khan-Lewis Phonological Analysis	(Khan & Lewis, 1986)
	Templin-Darley Test of Articulation	(Templin & Darley, 1969)
Language	*Clinical Evaluation of Language Fundamentals-Revised*	(Semel & Wiig, 1987)
	Language Processing Test	(Richard & Hanner, 1985)
	Peabody Picture Vocabulary Test-Revised	(Dunn & Dunn, 1981).
	Test for Auditory Comprehension of Language-Revised	(Carrow-Woolfolk, 1988)
	Test of Adolescent Language-2	(Hammil, Brown, Larsen & Weiderholt, 1987)
	Test of Language Competence	(Wiig & Secord, 1985)
	Test of Language Development-2	(Newcomer & Hammill, 1988)
	Test of Problem Solving	(Zachman, Jorgensen, Huisingh & Barrett, 1984)

Methods of Service to Persons with Developmental Disabilities

Treatment Goals

The selection of treatment goals was once primarily based upon developmental information. Assessment data were used to identify unattained developmental milestones which were selected as treatment targets. Although developmental information is a critical component to current decision-making, it should be only one factor in the decision-making process. Other factors should include priorities of persons with developmental disability and their families, immediate and future communicative needs, functionality, and chronological age appropriateness.

Persons with developmental disabilities and their families are currently assuming greater responsibility with respect to determining directions for allied health and educational service delivery (Dunst, Trivette & Deal, 1988). This is particularly true in the area of goal setting for very young children, but is also is applicable to persons of all ages with disability. Treatment decisions— once made and owned by "professionals"— now should be made by and in the best interests of individuals and their families. The SLP, then, must know the priorities of persons with disabilities and their families before generating treatment goals.

The selection of goals should also be influenced by the immediate and future communicative needs of persons with developmental disability. In addition to communication assessment results, information about communication needs can come from typical peers. Interviewing and observing peers can provide performance discrepancy information vital to the selection of treatment goals (Buekelman & Mirenda, 1992). For example, if peers have to ask questions to participate in school or work activities, and John cannot ask questions, question forms would appear to be a reasonable treatment target for him.

Individuals' future communicative needs can be determined from informants and from the SLP's participation in transitional planning. Knowledge of transitions assists the SLP in the selection of goals relevant to individuals' future placement settings. For example, the SLP might select goals specific to the acquisition of work-related vocabulary for a young adult transitioning to a competitive work opportunity.

An additional factor influencing the selection of treatment goals should be functionality. For the SLP, this means moving away from targeting specific linguistic forms, focusing entirely upon the speech mode, and only emphasizing changing the performance of persons with disability (McLean, 1990). Functional communication training should emphasize all communication modes and improving the communicative abilities and environments of persons with disability.

Finally, treatment goals should be age-appropriate. SLPs and other professionals working from a developmental perspective have frequently selected goals according to functioning level. According to this perspective, a goal for a 12-year-old with profound mental retardation might read "Pam will turn her head upon hearing the sound of a rattle." Although this may appear appropriate given Pam's functioning, the use of the rattle could contribute to undesirable perceptions that limit her inclusion with typical peers.

Treatment approaches

SLPs can choose from at least three treatment approaches to structure communication intervention for persons with developmental disability. Fey (1986) describes these options as (a) trainer-oriented, (b) child-oriented, or (c) hybrid. While these training approaches are described below with reference to children, they are certainly applicable to adults with disability.

In trainer-oriented approaches, the trainer attempts to control all aspects of treatment sessions (Fey, 1986). The "trainer" may be a professional such as the SLP; however, parents, educators, or significant others may also assume this role. Many of these types of approaches make use of operant procedures where the trainer presents specific stimuli (physical or verbal), prompts responses, and provides reinforcement. If the child's performance is deemed inadequate, the trainer may also attempt to shape responses to approximate desired treatment targets. Gradually, trainers fade prompts and shaping procedures to encourage independence.

Other trainer-oriented approaches emphasize the use of modeling where the child's primary role is to listen and subsequently process training stimuli (Fey, 1986). After hearing several modeled examples of target forms, the child participates by attempting to replicate the model.

Although trainer-oriented approaches have proven effective with persons with developmental disability (Blank & Milewski, 1981; Jeffree, Wheldall & Mittler, 1973; Schumaker & Sherman, 1970) limitations do exist. For example, due to the controlled nature of training, learned skills may not generalize easily across trainers or settings

(Costello, 1983; Guess, Keogh & Sailor, 1978). Furthermore, these approaches appear to be most appropriate for the training of specific linguistic forms rather than functional communication.

Fey (1986) characterizes child-oriented treatment approaches as those allowing the child to determine the "whats," "whens," and "hows" of learning. In contrast to tightly controlled trainer approaches, learning occurs as the child participates in unstructured interactions with significant others. During these interactions, trainers typically implement specific training strategies. Some of these include: (a) following the child's lead, where the trainer waits for the child to initiate behavior and responds in a manner thought to facilitate communication; (b) "self" and "parallel" talk, where the trainer verbalizes about events as they occur in an effort to model appropriate communicative behaviors; (c) expansion, where the trainer expands the child's communicative efforts by repeating them using greater complexity; and (d) expatiation, where the trainer responds contingently to the child, adding new information (Fey, 1986).

Child-oriented approaches have intuitive appeal to SLPs serving persons with developmental disability. They are more natural than trainer approaches and appear more useful in the training of functional communicative abilities. Unfortunately, strong empirical support for their use has been limited (Seitz & Hoekenga, 1974; Seitz & Marcus, 1976).

Finally, hybrid communication training represents a middle ground between trainer- and child-oriented approaches (Fey, 1986). That is, trainers assume responsibility for the directions and procedures associated with training, yet maintain a naturalness conducive to generalizable learning. Fey (1986) describes four examples of hybrid training: *focused stimulation, vertical structur-*

ing and expansion, incidental teaching, and *mand-model.*

When using *focused stimulation,* trainers both arrange the environment in a way to increase the likelihood of target responses and frequently model targets themselves. This occurs in the absence of specific efforts to make the child respond. *Vertical structuring and expansion* training differs in that stimuli are presented under less natural conditions and efforts are made to encourage responses. In contrast, *incidental teaching* and *mand-model training* are procedurally more like trainer-oriented approaches (e.g., they use prompts and cues), yet they occur in natural training environments during daily activities. Incidental teaching differs from trainer-oriented approaches in that the child initiates training episodes and, if necessary, reinforcers are administered prior to the production of "ideal" responses. For example, an episode may begin when a child reaches for an object which is out of reach. The trainer may subsequently model/prompt a response which would allow the child to obtain the desired object. If the child fails to produce the target after two attempts, the object would be provided in an effort to maintain its value as a reinforcer and reduce the child's frustration. A mand-model approach differs from incidental teaching in that the trainer initiates the training sequence. In the example above, as the child moved toward the object, the trainer would request a response (e.g., "Tell me what you want.") and model/prompt if necessary.

Although the development of hybrid training is in its infancy, these approaches appear to hold significant promise for SLPs serving persons with developmental disabilities. In fact, studies conducted to date have yielded positive results (Goldstein & Hockenberger, 1991; Warren & Kaiser, 1986; Warren, Yoder, Gazdag, Kim & Jones, 1993).

Decisions regarding the selection of specific treatment approaches are influenced by a variety of factors, including the communication impairments of persons with disabilities and the potential level of involvement of significant others. With the selection of a treatment approach, SLPs must determine their role within service delivery. While some children might benefit from direct services, others may be better served through consultation. For example, direct services are most appropriate for persons whose treatment emphasis is remedial (designed to eliminate or mitigate the long-term effects of deficits), while consultative service delivery is more appropriate if treatment emphases are more preventative or compensatory (Ogletree & Burns Daniels, 1993).

Case Example

Referral

Lewis, a 13-year-old child with severe mental retardation, was referred to the interdisciplinary team (IDT) of his public school. The process was initiated by his mother, the SLP, and the special education teacher, who requested information regarding current functioning and assistance with future programming. The referral was originated after a period of regression in communication and other developmental skills. In addition, Lewis had become violent in the classroom, often injuring himself and others.

Given the referral concerns, the SLP from the IDT was selected to serve as the case manager. She began by reviewing information in Lewis' public school chart to construct a chronology of his development and the services he had received to date. To obtain case history data, the SLP spoke with each of the referring parties to clarify their concerns and validate information obtained. Lewis' mother suggested that her primary concern was his behavior at school. She had heard reports of outbursts, but had not seen them in the home setting. The school SLP was concerned with his skill regression, especially his lack of using his communication board. In addition, she was concerned that there might be a larger pattern of regression across other skill domains. Finally, Lewis' teacher stated that behavior was her primary concern since Lewis was partially integrated with typical peers. She expressed worry that his outbursts might jeopardize his future placements and the placements of others.

History

As an infant, Lewis had been hospitalized several times and had participated in a team developmental evaluation at 18 months of age. Complete records of these events were requested and received. Early hospitalizations had been the result of seizure activity (currently controlled by medications), while the developmental evaluation had resulted in a diagnosis of mental retardation. The IDT SLP also learned that Lewis had participated in early intervention services and was transitioned to an integrated regular education setting in the first grade. He was moved to a segregated classroom for persons with severe disabilities in the third grade but has had limited regular education activities such as art, music, lunch, and physical education.

Until one year prior to his referral, Lewis had made steady progress on his Individualized Education Program (IEP) goals. At that time, however, skill regression was noted, especially in the area of communication. Specifically, he had reverted to physically pulling people around him to request attention and objects rather than using his object board. In addition, data suggested that he had not made progress with fine motor and self-help goals. Finally, over the past year, Lewis had been engaging in violent outbursts consisting of self-injurious and aggressive behavior.

Findings

The IDT SLP briefly provided an overview of Lewis' history and the concerns of referring parties to the interdisciplinary team. Team members suggested possible causes for the types of outbursts Lewis was experiencing and recommended evaluations by a developmental physician, pediatric neurologist, psychologist, physical therapist, occupational therapist, and special educator. The SLP also suggested that Lewis receive a communication assessment to determine if his behavior was serving communicative purposes. A hearing evaluation was recommended by the team's audiologist in response to the initial referral concern regarding Lewis' current status. Finally, the team social worker requested some time with Lewis' mother to evaluate his family's status and determine family priorities regarding his education. The SLP then requested that team members be certain to address all referral concerns, including Lewis' current status, possible regression, behavioral outbursts, and future needs.

The SLP began her assessment by interviewing those with whom Lewis interacted most frequently, including his mother, special education teacher, paraprofessional, and school SLP. General questions were posed regarding his communicative abilities and needs across setting. Questions were also asked about Lewis' behavior and the "more typical" interaction patterns of individuals in his class. Findings suggested that Lewis had been communicating in a less sophisticated manner over the past year in the classroom. Furthermore, his behavioral outbursts seemed to occur most often during group activities in regular classrooms. The

typical interaction patterns of his peers in those settings were described as serving informative and social purposes. That is, students in Lewis' regular classes needed to respond to questions and participate in social interaction, especially in group situations. The SLP concluded her interviews with Lewis' mother and teacher by administering the *Receptive Expressive Emergent Language Scale-Revised* (Bzoch & League, 1990), an informant-based measure of receptive and expressive language. Findings were consistent, revealing 18- to 24-month abilities.

The SLP then invited the team psychologist to view videotapes of Lewis filmed in his home and at school. Frequent nonsymbolic communicative behaviors (e.g., reaching, pointing, and vocalizing) were observed in both settings. Observations of partner interactions suggested that Lewis' regular education teachers and peers frequently used question forms and attempted to physically manipulate Lewis. Furthermore, Lewis was often excluded from classroom activities and seldom had his object board within reach when he was included. Only two examples of outbursts were recorded, both occurring when Lewis was not included in a classroom activity. These consisted of face-slapping episodes and ended when the teacher and peers directed their attention toward Lewis. The videotape from home revealed that Lewis was capable of recognizing environmental symbols. For example, he frequently requested food items by pointing to boxes only marked with photographs and written words. As in the school setting, Lewis' parents were frequently directive, and his object board was often unavailable during communicative opportunities.

After viewing the videotapes, the SLP prepared for her hands-on assessment of Lewis by consulting with the audiologist and observing the psychologist's session with Lewis. The audiologist, who was the first team member to evaluate Lewis, reported that he was compliant and cooperative. Her findings suggested normal hearing for speech. During the psychologist's session, Lewis was observed to make requests through reaches and vocalizations. Although his object board was available throughout the session, he only used it twice. He appeared capable of following simple requests.

The SLP's session began with the administration of a structured communication-sampling protocol. Since Lewis had already been observed to request, the expression of other communicative functions was emphasized (e.g., protesting, greeting, and commenting). During sampling, Lewis protested and greeted with gestures and vocalizations. Structured sampling was followed by simple probes to evaluate Lewis' symbolic abilities and comprehension. He was observed to recognize and match simple color photographs of food items and favorite activities. In fact, Lewis was quickly trained to select some photographs to request food. Comprehension probing revealed the ability to follow simple functional commands (e.g., Lewis gave objects upon command). The session ended with the inspection of Lewis' current object board. Objects were noted to provide limited requesting choices. In addition, some were inappropriate given Lewis' chronological age, such as toys that were more appropriate for younger children.

Treatment Recommendations

Representatives of all disciplines who evaluated Lewis and the referring parties attended the post-assessment staffing. As case manager, the SLP convened the meeting by restating referral concerns for Lewis. Discipline representatives then reported findings specific to each concern. With regard to current status, Lewis was determined to be a generally healthy, post-pubescent male with a controlled seizure disorder. His overall developmental functioning was reported to approximate the 24-month level. Lewis' current special education programming was considered functional and appropriate, with the exception of a lack of meaningful integration opportunities.

Lewis' medical and motor evaluations revealed no clear evidence of regression. These team members suggested instead that his rate of skill acquisition might be slowing down, contributing to the appearance of lost skills. The SLP agreed, stating that rather than skill regression, Lewis' reluctance to use his communication board was possibly more the result of limited opportunity and the limitations of the board.

Team members proposed numerous hypotheses to explain Lewis' behavioral outbursts. The developmental physician questioned the onset of puberty in his behavioral change. The special educator suggested that Lewis' limited ability to engage in meaningful activities could be a contributing factor. The SLP and psychologist mentioned that behaviors seemed to occur somewhat consistently and might serve communicative purposes. They noted that episodes from the videos could be interpreted as serving attention-getting functions. Opinions of the special educator, SLP, and psychologist were particularly appealing to the referral parties given that outbursts were not observed in all settings.

The staffing ended with a discussion of Lewis' future needs. The team social worker and Lewis' mother conveyed family priorities specific to his education and long-term care. These included as much exposure as possible to typical peers and educational emphases directly addressing functional needs. All staffing participants agreed that meeting these priorities necessitated increasing meaningful regular education experiences, while continuing to stress functional skill instruction. Consistent with these efforts, the SLP suggested numerous communication-related needs including: (a) increasing facilitative partner interactions; (b) increasing meaningful communicative opportunities in the classroom; (c) evaluating the potential communicative value of Lewis' behaviors; (d) upgrading his current communication device; and (e) training in using the device. To facilitate the treatment process, the SLP assumed a coordinator role to mobilize the interdisciplinary team as a treatment group. After the staffing, the SLP summarized findings for the referral parties and assisted with treatment planning designed to implement IDT recommendations.

Specific to communication-related treatment, SLPs from the interdisciplinary team and the public school worked collaboratively to select goals. Primary factors influencing selection included the priorities of Lewis' family and his immediate and future communicative needs. An additional factor was Lewis' chronological age.

Goals were selected to address Lewis' communicative environment and personal communicative needs. Environmental goals included teaching Lewis' communicative partners: (a) to use facilitative interaction styles; (b) to recognize Lewis' nonsymbolic communicative efforts as communication; (c) to create meaningful communicative opportunities for Lewis; (d) to familiarize themselves with his communication board and make it available during communicative opportunities; and (e) to encourage Lewis' participation in group activities. Goals related to Lewis' personal needs included: (a) expanding/adapting his board by adding photographs and removing inappropriate objects; (b) encouraging a broader expression of communicative functions (i.e., communicating to express more than requesting) with or without his board; and (c) monitoring behavioral outbursts to determine if communicative purposes were being served.

Prior to treatment, videotapes at home and the school setting were analyzed to obtain baselines for environmental treatment goals. Subsequently, environmental goals were implemented through a consultative treatment model. The school SLP worked directly with Lewis' regular classroom teachers and peers. Inservice training was provided in addition to in-class modeling and coaching. After three weeks, new videos of Lewis' regular class experiences revealed improvement in all targeted areas.

While working on environmental goals, the school SLP modified Lewis' board to include pictures of common objects, activities, and communicative partners. In addition, a buzzer was mounted on his board for use as an attention-getting device. The occupational therapist served as a consultant for all of Lewis' board modifications, providing input regarding optimal picture and buzzer placement.

Once the board was modified, the SLP implemented a hybrid training approach to facilitate Lewis' symbolic (i.e., communication board) and nonsymbolic (i.e., gestures and vocalizations) communication. Training occurred in regular education classrooms and included Lewis' paraprofessional. Finally, an observation chart was initiated to monitor Lewis' behavioral outbursts. The chart allowed for descriptions of behaviors and events that immediately preceded and followed them.

To provide a measure of treatment effectiveness, data were collected each week on Lewis' use of communication in his regular education classrooms. Videotapes which were recorded during classroom activities were analyzed to determine the frequency and range of communicative behaviors he expressed. Within three months, Lewis was communicating twice as frequently as noted at the initiation of treatment. Most often, he communicated with his board, although he continued to use some nonsymbolic gestures and vocalizations. Furthermore, his range of communicative functions had expanded to include requests for participation, comments, and greetings. During the initial three months of treatment, Lewis' behavior chart revealed a dramatic decline in outbursts. This decrease appeared to coincide with his mastery of the buzzer mounted on his board for attention-getting. Evaluation of charting data suggested that when outbursts continued to occur after introduction of the buzzer, Lewis' board was typically out of reach.

References

American Speech-Language-Hearing Association (1982, March). Serving the communicatively handicapped mentally retarded individual. *ASHA,* 547-553.

American Speech-Language-Hearing Association (1990). The role of speech-language pathologists and audiologists in service delivery for person with mental retardation and developmental disabilities in community settings. *ASHA, 32,* (2), 5-6.

American Speech-Language-Hearing Association (1990). Scope of practice, speech–language pathology and audiology. *ASHA, 32* (2), 1-2.

American Speech-Language-Hearing Association (1993). Implementation procedures for the standards for the certificates of clinical competence. *ASHA, 35,* 76-83.

Aram, D.M., Morris, N., & Hall, N.E. (1992). The validity of discrepancy criteria for identifying children with developmental language disorders. *Journal of Learning Disabilities, 25,* 549-554.

Bagnato, S.J., & Neisworth, J.J. (1991). *Assessment for early intervention: Best practices for professionals.* New York, NY: Guilford Press.

Beukelman, D.R., & Mirenda, P. (1992). *Augmentative and alternative communication: Management of severe communication disorders in children and adults.* Baltimore, MD: Paul H. Brookes.

Blank, M., & Milewski, J. (1981). Applying psycholinguistic concepts to the treatment of an autistic child. *Applied Psycholinguistics, 2,* 65-84.

Bzoch, K., & League, R. (1990). *Receptive-Expressive Emergent Language Scale-Revised.* Austin, TX: Pro-Ed.

Carrow-Woolfolk, E. (1988). *Test for Auditory Comprehension of Language-Revised.* Allen, TX: DLM Teaching Resources.

Cornett, B.S., & Chabon, S.S. (1988). *The clinical practice of speech-language pathology.* Columbus, OH: Merrill Publishing Co.

Costello, J. (1983). Generalization across settings: Language intervention with children. In J. Miller, D. Yoder, & R. Schiefelbusch (Eds.), *Contemporary issues in language intervention.* Rockville, MD: American-Speech-Language Hearing Association.

David, R., & Smith, B. (1987). Preparing for collaborative working. *British Journal of Special Education, 14*(1), 19-23.

Duchan, J.F. (1988). Assessment principles and procedures. In N.J. Lass, L.V. McReynolds, J.L. Northern, & D.E. Yoder (Eds.), *Handbook of speech–language pathology and audiology* (pp. 356-376). Philadelphia, PA: B.C. Decker.

Dunn, L., & Dunn, L. (1981). *Peabody Picture Vocabulary Test-Revised.* Circle Pines, MN: American Guidance Service.

Dunst, C.J., Trivette, C.M., & Deal, A. (1988). *Enabling and empowering families: Principles and guidelines for practice.* Cambridge, MA: Brookline Books.

Fagan, E.C. (1992). ASHA's continuing education: What is new in '92. *ASHA 34,* 47-48.

Fey, M.E. (1986). *Language intervention with young children.* Austin, TX: Pro-Ed.

Fudala, J.B., & Reynolds, W.R. (1986). *Arizona articulation proficiency scale* (2nd ed.). Los Angeles, CA: Western Psychological Services.

German, D. (1986). *Test of word finding.* Allen, TX: DLM Teaching Resources.

Goldman, R., & Fristoe, M. (1986). *Goldman-Fristoe test of articulation*. Circle Pines: MN: American Guidance Service.

Goldstein, H., & Hockenberger, E.H. (1991). Significant progress in child language intervention: An 11-year retrospective. *Research and Developmental Disabilities, 12*, 401-424.

Golin, A.K., & Ducanis, A.J. (1981). *The interdisciplinary team: A handbook for the education of exceptional children*. Rockville, MD: Aspen.

Goddard, R.E. (1993). *Teacher certification requirements in all 50 states* (11th ed.). Sebring, FL: Teacher Certification Publications.

Guess, D., Keogh, W., & Sailor, W. (1978). Generalization of speech and language behavior. In R. Schiefelbusch (Ed.), *Bases of language intervention*. Baltimore, MD: University Park Press.

Hammill, D., Brown, V., Larsen, S., & Weiderhold, L. (1987). *Test of adolescent language-2*. Austin, TX: Pro-Ed.

Hammill, D., & Larsen, S. (1983). *The test of written language*. Austin, TX: Pro-Ed.

Haynes, W.O., Pendzola, R.H., & Emerick, L.L. (1992). *Diagnosis and evaluation in speech pathology*. Englewood Cliffs, NJ: Prentice-Hall.

Jeffree, D., Wheldall, I., & Mittler, P. (1973). Facilitating two-word utterances in two Down's syndrome boys. *American Journal on Mental Deficiency, 78*, 117-122.

Khan, L.M.L., & Lewis, N.P. (1986). *Khan-Lewis phonological analysis*. Circle Pines, MN: American Guidance Service.

Lynch, C., & Welsh, R. (1993). Characteristics of state licensure laws. *ASHA, 35*, 130-139.

Marge, M. (1993). Disability prevention: Are we ready for the challenge? *ASHA, 35*, 42-44.

McLean, L.K.S. (1990). Transdisciplinary issues in early communication intervention. Paper presented at the *Social Use of Language: Pathways to Success* Conference, Nashville, TN.

McLean, J., McLean, L.K.S., Brady, N.C., & Etter, R. (1991). Communication profiles of two types of gestures using nonverbal persons with severe to profound mental retardation. *Journal of Speech and Hearing Research, 34*, 294-308.

Mirenda, P.L., & Donnellan, A.M. (1986). Effects of adult interaction style on conversational behavior in students with severe communication problems. *Language Speech and Hearing Services in the Schools, 17*, 126-141.

Newcomer, P., & Hammill, D. (1988). *Test of language development-2*. Austin, TX: Pro-Ed.

Ogletree, B.T., Wetherby, A.M., & Westling, D. (1992). Profile of the prelinguistic intentional communicative behaviors of children with profound mental retardation. *American Journal on Mental Retardation, 97* (2), 186-196.

Ogletree, B.T., & Burns Daniels, D. (1993). Communication-based assessment and intervention for prelinguistic infants and toddlers: Strategies and issues. *Infants and Young Children, 5 (3)*, 22-30.

Richard, G., & Hanner, M. (1985). *Language processing test*. East Moline, IL: LinguiSystems.

Rossetti, L. (1990). *Infant-Toddler Language Scale*. East Moline, IL: LinguiSystems.

Salvia, J., & Yesseldyke, J.E. (1991). *Assessment* (5th ed.). Boston, MA: Houghton-Mifflin.

Schumaker, J., & Sherman, J.A. (1970). Training generative verb usage by imitation and reinforcement procedures. *Journal of Applied Behavior Analysis, 3*, 273-278.

Seitz, S., & Hoekenga, R. (1974). Modeling as a training tool for retarded children and their parents. *Mental Retardation, 12*, 28-31.

Seitz, S., & Marcus, S. (1976). Mother-child interactions: A foundation for language development. *Exceptional Children, 42*, 445-449.

Semel, E., & Wiig, E. (1987). *Clinical evaluation of language fundamentals-Revised*. San Antonio: The Psychological Corporation.

Silverman, F.H. (1984). *Speech-language pathology and audiology: An introduction*. Columbus, OH: Merrill Publishing Company.

Templin, M.C., & Darley, F.L. (1969). *Templin-Darley Tests of Articulation*. Iowa City, IA: University of Iowa Bureau of Educational Research and Service.

Warren, S.F., & Kaiser, A.P. (1986). Incidental language teaching: A critical review. *Journal of Speech and Hearing Disorders, 51*, 291-299.

Warren, S.F., Yoder, P.J., Gazdag, G.E., Kim, K., & Jones, H.A. (1993). Facilitating prelinguistic communication skills in young children with developmental delay. *Journal of Speech and Hearing Research, 36*, 83-97.

Wetherby, A.M., Yonclas, D.G., & Bryan, A.A. (1989). Communicative profiles of preschool children with handicaps: Implications for early intervention. *Journal of Speech and Hearing Disorders, 54*, 148-158.

Wiig, E., & Secord, W. (1985). *Test of language competence.* San Antonio, TX: The Psychological Corporation.

Zachman, L., Jorgensen, C., Huisingh, R., & Barrett, M. (1984). *Test of problem solving.* East Moline, IL: LinguiSystems.

18

The Changing Nature of Interdisciplinary Practice

Zolinda Stoneman, Ph.D., & D. Michael Malone, Ph.D.

The individual with disabilities needs to be the conductor of a symphony of support that changes in intensity, frequency, and tempo with his or her ever-changing world, instead of being an object of service provision. (Dufresne & Laux, 1994, p. 279)

We are in the dawn of a new era in the provision of services and supports to individuals with disabilities and their families. Indeed, professionals who, heretofore, held dominion over the treatment and care of these individuals and their families have been charged with the challenge of rethinking the *who, what, where, why,* and *how* of service delivery. Professionals who work with individuals with disabilities have been challenged to set aside their belief that determining the best interests of their constituents is solely within their jurisdiction. Professionals are being asked to open their minds and change their approach to doing business to include, as partners, a wider circle of persons and options than was previously the case. As this new era evolves, we must examine closely that which has become the hallmark of contemporary service de-livery, the interdisciplinary team. It is our premise that teams will undergo radical change as society embraces full inclusion of people with disabilities into all aspects of community life.

This chapter examines the future of teams within a paradigm of inclusive, community-based supports for individuals with disabilities and their families. We will begin with a description of the classic team model and move to a discussion of the shift from a service to a support paradigm. We will address changes in society and in the disability field that will impact teams of the future. Finally, we will discuss attitudes and skills that will be needed by professional and nonprofessional personnel as we move into a new era of supporting people with disabilities and their families.

Authors' Note: Support for the preparation for this chapter was provided by Grant No. 90DD0276 from the Administration on Developmental Disabilities, Administration on Children, Youth, and Families, U.S. Department of Health and Human Services to the University Affiliated Program, The University of Georgia. The opinions expressed herein do not necessarily reflect the policy of the granting agencies and no official endorsement by these agencies should be inferred.

Description of the Classic Interdisciplinary Team

As discussed in the opening chapter of this volume, the efficacy of the team-based model of providing services to persons with disabilities has been examined since the early 1900s. The contemporary design of interdisciplinary teams reflects little change since Whitehouse (1951) described three basic assumptions underlying teamwork:

1. The human organism is dynamic and is an interacting, integrated whole.
2. Treatment must be dynamic and fluid to keep pace with the changing person, and must consider all that person's needs.
3. Teamwork, an interacting partnership of professions specializing in these needs and dealing with the person as a whole, is a valid method of meeting these requirements (pp. 45-46).

Early efforts to coordinate services using a multidisciplinary approach brought professionals together for diagnostic and planning meetings but was limited in the extent to which true integration or coordination of services could be achieved. Whitehouse (1951) noted that positive team outcomes are not the result of the compilation of individual reports, but the assimilation of information from contributing disciplinary observations and assessments. It is from such realizations over the course of the last 40 years that an interdisciplinary approach to service delivery was born. (See also Brill, 1976; Farrell, 1991; Garner, Uhl & Cox, 1992; Golin & Ducanis, 1981; Horwitz, 1970.)

One schematic representing the interdisciplinary team is presented in Figure 18-1. The team members strive to make the collective team identity supersede the individual identities associated with independent disciplines. Interaction processes are vital since the team, not the separate disciplines, is primarily responsible for program design and implementation. Thus, the team, with members working interdependently, is believed to be equipped with the knowledge to make informed collaborative decisions and to develop integrated goals and service

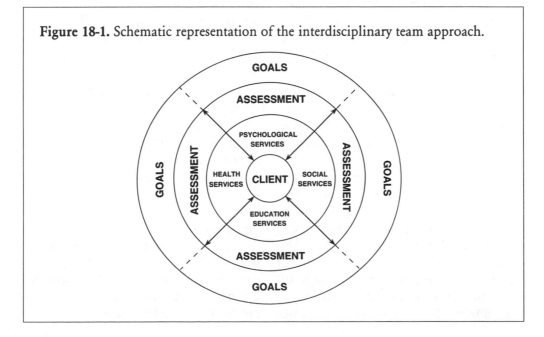

Figure 18-1. Schematic representation of the interdisciplinary team approach.

programs based on all available information.

Although the interdisciplinary team represented significant improvement over the unidisciplinary and multidisciplinary approaches, this model is inadequate in the face of current trends toward a community-based support paradigm. At the very least, the strong professional focus evident in this model will have to undergo substantial revision.

Current and Future Trends

Shift to a Support Paradigm

It is not an overstatement to suggest that the disability field is in the midst of a conceptual revolution, not unlike the major paradigm shifts in science described by Kuhn (1962). Paradigm shifts are accompanied by a need to change how things are done. In this instance, there is a need to transform the manner in which services for people with disabilities are designed and delivered (Bradley, 1994). For many years, the disability field has utilized a ideological paradigm that focuses on the importance of each individual in society achieving as much independence and self-sufficiency as their capabilities allow (Schwartz, 1992; Turnbull & Brunk, 1990). The process through which this goal is actualized emphasizes skill development and reduction of behavior that interferes with learning and self-sufficiency.

In the current paradigm, important life decisions concerning the focus individual are controlled by an interdisciplinary team, functioning ideally through team collaboration and consensus. One important team responsibility is to make placement recommendations. The person with a disability is placed in a setting (e.g., a group home or special education classroom) believed by the team to best fit his or her current level of functioning. In general, the most norma-

tive placement is selected from a continuum of settings that range from most to least restrictive. Placement in typical settings, such as a regular education classroom or a home in the community, is deferred until the person can develop skills believed by the team to be prerequisite for successful community functioning.

Unfortunately, this model represents a dead end for many people with disabilities. Once they are removed from their homes, classes, or communities, they never return. The child moved to a residential facility stays until adulthood, or even until death. The child in a special education class remains in a segregated educational setting until leaving school. Adults in sheltered workshops never enter competitive employment.

The support paradigm departs rather dramatically from current practices. Rather than independence, the focus is on the *interdependence* of all members of the community, including the community member with a disability (O'Brien & O'Brien, 1993; Racino, Taylor, Walker & O'Connor, 1993; Walker & Racino, 1993). Development and maintenance of quality friendships and social relationships are valued as the most important outcome (Bradley, 1994; Schwartz, 1992; Turnbull & Brunk, 1990). There are no prerequisites to living in your own home or to being included in your community (Klein, 1992). Supports are provided to the individual in the typical community settings where her or she lives, works, plays, and goes to school. This change is accompanied by an increased appreciation of what ecological psychologists have argued for many years: "environments effect change more powerfully than training can" (O'Brien & Lovett, 1992, p. 3).

The support paradigm emphasizes collaborative community partnerships. "The current reform effort seriously challenges the interdisciplinary team as the dominant model for decision-making" (Knoll &

Racino, 1994, p. 307). Interdisciplinary teams have sometimes endorsed practices that have segregated people from communities and limited their life options (Racino, O'Connor, & Walker, 1993). Children and adults in institutions, for example, often continue to reside there with the endorsement of an interdisciplinary team. Other teams have moved people from institutions, transitioning them into nursing homes. Teams have not always been effective at implementing best practices or at insuring a positive quality of life.

The support paradigm fosters a move from a professionally-dominated interdisciplinary team to a team that includes family, friends, and community members. Highly trained disability professionals, however, are not discredited or minimized. Specialized personnel are valued as guiding diagnosis and intervention in technical areas of life functioning. When an adaptive chair needs to be customized, experienced, trained professionals are called upon. Rather than negating technical services, the support paradigm places these services in balanced perspective. Indeed, basic tenets of the support paradigm have been incorporated into the revised definition of mental retardation published by the American Association on Mental Retardation (Luckasson, Coulter, Polloway, Reiss, Schalock, Snell, Spitalnik & Stark, 1992). This prominent endorsement by the leading professional association concerned with mental retardation all but insures that the major changes in values and practices sponsored by this paradigm will continue in the future.

Self-Advocacy

In addition to the shift to a support paradigm, a strong self-advocacy movement is changing the political landscape related to disability issues. People with disabilities have emerged as powerful advocates for their rights and needs. After a long history of dependence, self-advocates have demonstrated that—through organized political action at the community, state, and national level—they can affect the laws, regulations, and practices that influence their lives (Sutherland, 1981). These efforts have culminated in the Americans With Disabilities Act of 1990 (P.L. 101-336). Even people with intellectual disabilities, through organizations such as People First, have learned to speak and advocate for themselves. Although not every person with a disability is able (or desires) to be a self-advocate, the number of people taking this empowered role has forever changed the relationship between the consumers of services and those who plan and provide those services.

Person-Centered Approaches

In the past decade, a variety of approaches have been developed that fit under the general rubric of Person-Centered Planning (Forest & Lusthaus, 1989; Forest & Pearpoint, 1992; Mount & Zwernick, 1988; O'Brien, 1987; Pearpoint, 1990; Vandercook & York, 1989). In many ways, person centered planning teams offer an alternative to the classic interdisciplinary team. Useful for both children and adults, person-centered approaches begin by asking focus persons what they want for their lives and then engage in joint problem-solving to try and make those desired outcomes happen. The process draws upon the knowledge of people who know and care about the person with a disability in order to understand (rather than assess or diagnose) the person (Smull & Danehey, 1994). The focus is on whole-life planning, centered around the person's dreams for a desirable future (Kiracofe, 1994).

Natural and Informal Supports

New approaches to interventions emphasize the importance of natural and informal supports for persons with disabilities. These supports include friends, family members, neighbors, and community members. Team members work together to create "a network of people who care" (Nisbet, 1992, p. 4). These people are then drawn upon to assist the focus person in his or her day-to-day activities. Such assistance might include a classmate who helps a child in a wheelchair get to the playground or a coworker who assists an employee to learn aspects of the job. Bradley (1994) noted that surrounding people with paid staff can inadvertently isolate them from friends and family. Informal support networks reconnect people with their communities.

Family-Focused, Family-Driven Supports

It is increasingly accepted that all children, regardless of the severity of their disability, should live in families (Taylor, 1991). The recognition of the centrality of families in the lives of people with disabilities across the lifespan combines with a strong parent advocacy movement (Dybwad, 1990) to produce a climate of family empowerment. Families are demanding increased decision-making roles.

Much has been written about family-centered approaches to intervention (e.g., Bailey & Simeonsson, 1988; Brewer, McPherson, Magrab & Hutchins, 1989; Dunst, Trivette & Deal, 1988). These approaches recognize the basic right of families to decide what services and resources they need and want (Covert, 1992; Dunst, Trivette, Starnes, Hamby & Gordon, 1993; Taylor, 1991; Taylor, Knoll, Lehr & Walker, 1989), leading to flexible, family-driven models of support which shift control from professionals to families (Singer & Powers, 1993).

Full Community Inclusion and Inclusive Education

The movement toward full community inclusion means that people with disabilities work, live, learn, recreate, go to church, shop, and live day to day in the communities of their choice, taking part in all aspects of community life that are available to nondisabled community members. O'Brien (1987) wrote of the importance of *community presence*, "sharing of the ordinary places that define community life" (p. 177). Provision of highly intense, pervasive supports does not of necessity demand that the person with a disability spend time in segregated, restrictive settings. Full inclusion includes the provision of intensive supports in typical community contexts.

A parallel trend, *inclusive education*, calls for all children to be educated in regular education classrooms alongside their nondisabled peers. Segregated educational placements are eliminated and, in their place, a system of supports is developed that provides children with whatever they need to achieve success in regular education. Inclusive schools demand a high degree of team collaboration in order to be effective; professionals from both the regular education and special education systems must expand roles to provide support (Jorgensen, 1992). In addition to assuring that the educational needs of the child are met, the team is responsible for working toward a more holistic goal, namely, that the child becomes a valued member of the school community.

Blurring of Professional Roles and "Turf"

The reconceptualization of team practice will undoubtedly result in a blurring of professional roles. Skill areas that were once clearly the domain of a single discipline are now incorporated into training of personnel from multiple disciplines. Employment issues, for example, have been traditionally addressed by rehabilitation professionals. Today, those specializing in employment may be special educators, psychologists, social workers, or business graduates. Family issues, once the domain of social workers, are being addressed by nurses, special educators, psychologists, and gerontologists, among others.

Although the blurring of professional roles is confounded by disciplinary regulation (e.g., American Psychological Association, American Speech-Language-Hearing Association, and American Academy of Pediatrics) that serves to protect professional "turf", the inclusive team model moves beyond such regulation and presents the field with challenges not previously acknowledged by many professionals. The composition of the inclusive team is based not on perceived requisite disciplinary representation, but on the identified needs of the team's constituent. Members with specific skills may be essential on a given team, but no one discipline is indispensable. As noted by Rokusek (Chapter 1, this volume) and Pappas and Knoll (1994), teams may include extended family, friends, community planners, clergy, engineers, architects, attorneys, coworkers, business owners, and human service providers. Each team member contributes expertise (be it therapy or carpentry) to support the personal vision of the constituent.

Cost Containment

One strong societal theme for the coming decade is the demand that human service providers do more with less. Human need is increasing, but fiscal resources to support that need are finite. Smull and Danehey (1994) suggested that the primary mechanism for controlling the costs of community services has been progressive under-

funding. Interdisciplinary teams are very expensive. Teams comprised of numerous highly paid professionals drive up budgets and can force cutbacks in other service areas. Are interdisciplinary teams worth the cost?

Future reliance on teams can be justified only if they create better outcomes for people with disabilities than less-expensive service delivery modes. Switching to an individual support model will decrease the amount spent for most people, but, for a few, may cause a cost increase (Smull & Danehey, 1994). Future teams will be driven by fiscal concerns.

Accountability

It would seem that after years of implementation there would be an answer to the question of whether interdisciplinary teams make a difference in the lives of people with disabilities. Unfortunately, research does not exist on which to base an informed answer to this question. Theoretically, and intuitively, interdisciplinary teams provide a relatively good fit with holistic models of human development. However, as noted in the opening chapter of this volume, empirical support for these theories and intuitions is scarce. This is particularly true of outcome data that are directly related to the service system designed for individuals with disabilities. Few, if any, published studies exist which document that interdisciplinary teams are better than other modes of service delivery in creating positive outcomes for children or adults with disabilities. Given the widespread support of interdisciplinary team practice, this paucity of research is surprising and distressing.

Swap (1984) suggested that the values, attitudes, and backgrounds of team members may be the most powerful determinants of group decisions. Further, team members' "buying into" the team philosophy is considered critical to team functioning (Given & Simmons, 1977; Spencer & Coye, 1988). Effective outcomes have been characterized as a function of a membership-wide understanding of group process and dynamics (Brill, 1976; Garner, 1988; Golin & Ducanis, 1981; Horwitz, 1970). However, empirical support for these claims is scarce.

Interdisciplinary teams have proliferated and been codified into numerous regulations with little or no empirical support for their effectiveness. In a future where cost containment drives service delivery, this lack of accountability for a highly expensive service delivery mode will not be acceptable. Similarly, if practices derived from the support paradigm are not documented as being effective, they too will not withstand the coming emphasis on fiscal and programmatic accountability.

Competencies Required to Be an Effective Team Member

In the remainder of this chapter, we will examine the competencies that will be required of team members as the field moves to a support paradigm. We will begin by reviewing the skills that are needed to work effectively on teams as they currently exist and will then explore the additional team competencies that we believe will be required in the future.

Skills Needed for Contemporary Team Model

Much has been written about the organization of teams and the requisite abilities and roles of team members. At the most basic level, a healthy team atmosphere is a function of the extent to which individual members can work with one another. Underly-

ing this skill is the ability to effectively communicate. Indeed, while certain individual traits such as initiative, an appropriate attitude, and a base set of values (Garner, 1988; Spencer & Coye, 1988) are also necessary, many of the skills that have been identified as highly desirable are associated with the ability to communicate. Garner, Uhl and Cox (1992) discuss the "10 C's" of teamwork: communication, cooperation, collaboration, confronting problems, compromise, consensus decision-making, coordination, consistency, caring, and commitment. Each "C" may be viewed as an individual skill or team characteristic.

Other skills identified as essential to effective team work include the ability to initiate discussion, to facilitate a structured team meeting, to convey congruent messages (e.g., matching of words, tone of voice, and nonverbal cues), to listen, to coordinate individual efforts with those of other team members, to participate in the resolution of problems, to make decisions, and to give and receive feedback (Garner, 1988; Garner et al., 1992). Team members must bring to the team expertise in their respective disciplines (Spencer & Coye, 1988). In addition, they must understand and appreciate the unique contributions of others on the team. Finally, team members must adapt to various roles, of which some are task-related and some are related to building and maintaining the team (Landerholm, 1990; Neugebauer, 1984).

Skills Needed for Future Team Model

"All change involves learning" (Nisbet, Jorgensen & Powers, 1994, p. 222). Changing to a support paradigm will demand new skills. In the following sections, we examine some of the additional skills and attitudes that will be needed by team members of the future.

Relinquishing professional power. Sutherland (1981) wrote that the question of who does and does not have a disability is "essentially a question of power" (p. 79). The move to a support paradigm brings with it a profound change in the power relationships between people with disabilities and their service providers (Bradley, 1994; Forest & Pearpoint, 1992). Evidence of a power shift is already emerging. In person-centered teams, individuals with disabilities are directing the development of their own plans (Dufresne & Laux, 1994). Personal assistants, and sometimes other staff as well, are hired and fired by the person with a disability.

Family support programs are directed by families with assistance from professionals, rather than the other way around (Taylor et al., 1989). In the past, for many people with severe disabilities, power over service providers has been limited to expressing opposition through noncompliance (O'Brien, 1987; O'Brien & O'Brien, 1991). In the future, finding effective ways of sharing power with persons with pervasive cognitive disabilities will challenge even the most responsive teams.

Negotiating with people with disabilities and with their families and friends, instead of imposing professional will, calls for new attitudes and skills. Dilemmas will emerge as choices made by the focus person are deemed to be self-destructive or unwise. There will be times when the team will act in the "best interests" of the person with a disability, even if the action taken is against the person's will. But these situations will be fewer in number and will create greater moral perplexity for team members. Respecting the family's right to self-determination, while acknowledging that families do not always make the best choices for the family member with a disability, requires a difficult blend of compromise and advocacy.

The period of transition to a new way of doing things is always threatening; this is the case with power shifts that accompany the support paradigm (Bradley, 1994). Most resistance to change is coming from professionals who have invested many years in education and training to become experts in a given field (Dufresne & Laux, 1994). With this expertise came an implicit expectation of power. Professional training programs have concentrated on teaching students how to exercise this power in a competent fashion. A challenge that traditional disciplines face is that their future role is not likely to be that of all-knowing expert.

Shared dreaming. It may at first seem odd to think about the ability to dream as a needed professional skill. The gift of dreaming has been extinguished in all too many professionals. Dreams are often labeled as unrealistic, whether they originate from individuals with disabilities, their families, or service providers. Dreams of a fulfilling future for persons with disabilities have been commonly viewed as evidence of denial or lack of reality orientation. Professionals who have dared to dream have encountered ridicule, and sometimes laughter, from their colleagues. To envision a child with a severe cognitive disability playing with friends in a neighborhood school, or to imagine a woman who needs pervasive supports living in her own home, requires team members to dream about a quality future for these individuals. Implementing the support paradigm requires a willingness to create visions with people and to listen to and share their dreams. To be effective, team members must learn to see a range of possibilities in the lives of people with disabilities similar to that which they see in their own lives, or in the lives of their own children (Racino & Walker, 1993). In many instances, traditional team planning has focused on developing a list of goals and objectives that, even if accomplished, would not bring the focus person's dream closer to reality (Mount, 1994). The aim is not to engage in fantasy or fictional expectations, but to learn to dream with a strong base in reality.

Some people, for a variety of reasons, cannot articulate their dreams. For these persons, team members need to spend time talking to those who know the person well and learning about the person from observation. For people with disabilities whose lives have been extremely restricted, it is hard to dream about things never experienced (Racino & Walker, 1993). Team members must learn how to create opportunities for new learning without violating the person's sense of control. The ability (and the willingness) to listen is critical (Nisbet, 1992; Racino & Walker, 1993), as is respect for the person's cultural heritage (Racino, Taylor, Walker & O'Connor, 1993).

Holistic thinking. A disability does not reside in the individual; it results from the interaction between a person and the environment (Institute of Medicine, 1991; Luckasson et al., 1992). This recognition compels a focus on the total person (Bradley, 1994; Taylor et al., 1989). As Bogdan (1991) exclaimed, "Look at the life, not just at the behavior" (p. 248). This holistic approach is inconsistent with the traditional interdisciplinary team model and requires a different set of assessment and evaluation attitudes and skills.

"Our society has created a billion dollar industry to fix people who are not fixable. It is destined to failure. It doesn't work, and there are tremendous costs both to society and to the people who cannot be fixed" (Judith Snow, cited in Forest & Pearpoint, 1992, p. 68). Holistic thinking shifts from an exclusive focus on "fixing" the individual to a focus on adapting the settings where the person lives, works, and goes to school (Smull & Danehey, 1994). One important strategy is the use of community, or *ecologi-*

cal, assessments (Racino, Taylor, Walker & O'Connor, 1993). Ecological assessment is required in the new diagnostic procedures for mental retardation (Luckasson et al., 1992) and is central to holistic life planning for children and adults with other disabilities as well. Community-based assessments demand that those conducting the evaluation spend extensive time with the individual to understand the interaction between the person's competencies and the specific demands of multiple community environments in which the person spends time. Holistic and ecological assessment skills will be crucial for team members of the future.

Community-building. Another set of skills lacking in the repertoire of most professionals is that of community-building (Mount, 1994). In holistic life planning, community members are viewed as partners in designing solutions to the problems faced by persons with disabilities (Knoll & Racino, 1994). Rather than focusing on how resources can be found within the existing service system, new solutions are found by developing partnerships with generic service providers, neighbors, community organizations, and individual citizens (Mount, 1994).

Forest and Pearpoint (1992) caution that communities should not be romanticized. The field is turning to communities, not as utopia, but as a lesser evil than institutions and other congregate residential placements. "Building intentional community" (Forest & Pearpoint, 1992, p. 70) is difficult, complex, time-consuming work. It often requires confronting the devalued roles that people with disabilities occupy in society (Kendrick, 1994). Communities do not always welcome all people. Advocacy and leadership skills, coalition-building, conflict resolution, resource management, and negotiation strategies are only a few of the community-building skills seldom taught to aspiring human service professionals and rarely seen as key competencies for members of traditional teams.

Building systems of natural supports. An important aspect of community-building is the development of systems of natural support for people with disabilities and their families. Natural, or informal, supports are those provided by unpaid community members, such as family, friends, neighbors, coworkers, or classmates. For some people, natural support does not happen spontaneously. People with severe disabilities, in particular, face barriers in developing support networks in their own behalf (O'Brien & O'Brien, 1992). Jorgensen (1992) suggests using a "least intrusive supports first" (p. 210) planning process in which specialized supports are accessed as a last resort. Informal supports cannot replace public investment in assisting people with disabilities. Paid personnel usually must perform the work of developing and sustaining systems of support. As with other aspects of community-building, developing informal supports is a complex, difficult task for which most human service providers are ill-prepared.

In developing informal supports, there is a risk of professionalizing friendships (O'Brien & O'Brien, 1992). Friendship interventions must be subtle. We do not choose other people's friends and cannot predict which people will become friends and which will regard each other with disinterest or dislike (Perske, 1993). "Supporting friendships can be fragile, delicate, magical, and sensitive work. It is not work that easily fits into formalized systems and agency patterns" (Amado, 1993, p. 373). It is also not work for which team members are generally trained or skilled.

Providing supports to people where they are. In the past, it was standard practice to remove people with disabilities from their community in order to remediate skill deficits or maladaptive behavior. In this tradi-

tional model, the level of needed support and the type of intervention setting are packaged together, often requiring a person to live in a certain type of facility to receive specific services (Racino, Taylor, Walker & O'Connor, 1993). In the support paradigm, the objective is to provide quality community life for the person *now*, rather than at some point in the future (O'Brien, 1987; Strully & Strully, 1992). Decisions about settings and services are separated. People receive needed supports wherever they live, work, play, or go to school. In the future, team members will need to implement effective, respectful interventions in everyday community settings, which is very different from most interventions implemented today.

Taking responsibility for finding a solution. In contrast to the diagnostic team model, the support team of the future will not develop plans for others to implement; responsibility for implementing change will reside with the team. It is not enough for team members to learn to dream with the focus person, they must also assume responsibility for taking action to implement those dreams. The team cannot determine that no appropriate supports exist and then stop.

Providing support is a lifelong process that can, at times, carry with it the very survival of the person being supported (Forest & Pearpoint, 1992; Knoll & Racino, 1994). Time must be spent getting to know the person, listening, gaining trust and building a relationship (Forest & Pearpoint, 1992; Racino & Walker, 1993; Smull & Danehey, 1994). The demands placed on team members far exceed those that are commonplace today. The responsibilities are great—but if done well, the reward is also great: a substantially enhanced quality of life for the focus individual.

Creativity in problem-solving. In addition to an increased demand for team responsibility, the support paradigm also creates an expanded need for creativity and innovation in addressing and overcoming problems and barriers. Team skills needed in the future will include openness to non-traditional solutions, brainstorming, and resilience in the face of failure (Forest & Pearpoint, 1992). Professionals must learn to actively problem-solve *with* people with disabilities and their families, rather than *for* people with disabilities (Taylor et al., 1989). Team leadership will include helping others listen to people with disabilities, acting as a broker, obtaining desired supports and resources, and finding mutual solutions (Nisbet, 1992; O'Brien & O'Brien, 1992, 1994).

One major challenge will be the need to overcome decades of bureaucracy that has developed in support of the current paradigm. Teams sometimes feel compelled to focus on insuring that the proper paperwork is completed, rather than focusing on insuring that the quality of life of the focus person is improved. To implement the support paradigm, teams must be willing to break free of the standard way of doing things, bend rules, and change basic practices of service agencies and organizations in order to get the needed work done (O'Brien & O'Brien, 1992; Racino, O'Connor, & Walker, 1993; Racino & Walker, 1993; Walker & Racino, 1993).

Summary

Limitations of the current system—including the poor fit between services and individual needs, lack of accessibility to programs and knowledge, lack of equity, lack of empowerment of constituents, a monopoly of state-run services, and too few resources that promote community inclusion—will require multiple changes to overcome. New skills must be developed; basic

attitudes and beliefs must be transformed. The challenge is exciting, but resistance is strong.

Although the support paradigm is gaining momentum, some aspects of change happen slowly. Institutions, discredited over three decades ago, still exist. Monetary and personnel investments of the past create inertia and strong opposition to change. Potential job loss takes precedence over the needs and desires of people with disabilities. Segregated group homes, day activity centers, special education classrooms, and sheltered workshops are still expanding. Funding policy lags behind paradigm shifts; so does the preparation of personnel. Academic institutions, like the rest of society, are resistant to change. Faculty develop set ways of teaching and, all too often, perpetuate a fixed belief system over the course of a career.

People with disabilities and their families are making demands on the system for dramatic change. The power achieved by these constituents will not be easily relinquished. It is too late for professionals to lead the way, the path is already being blazed by people with disabilities and their families. It is now our task as professionals to catch up and to develop new partnerships to assist people with disabilities and their families to get to where they want to be. As we do that, the interdisciplinary team will undergo radical change. Our role as disability professionals will undergo fundamental change as well.

References

Amado, A.N. (1993). Afterword. In A.N. Amado (Ed.), *Friendships and community connections between people with and without disabilities* (pp. 373-376). Baltimore: Paul H. Brookes.

Bailey, D.B., Jr., & Simeonsson, R.J. (1988). *Fam-

ily assessment in early intervention. Columbus, OH: Merrill.

Bogdan, R. (1991). We care for our own. In S.J. Taylor, R. Bogdan, & J.A. Racino (Eds.), *Life in the community: Case studies of organizations supporting people with disabilities* (pp. 215-226). Baltimore: Paul H. Brookes.

Bradley, V.J. (1994). Evolution of a new service paradigm. In V. J. Bradley, J.W. Ashbaugh, & B.C. Blaney (Eds.), *Creating individual supports for people with developmental disabilities* (pp. 11-32). Baltimore: Paul H. Brookes.

Brewer, E.J., McPherson, M., Magrab, P.R., & Hutchins, V.L. (1989). Family-centered, community-based, coordinated care for children with special health care needs. *Pediatrics, 83,* 1055-1060.

Brill, N.I. (1976). *Teamwork: Working together in the human services*. Philadelphia, PA: J.B. Lippincott Company.

Covert, S.B. (1992). Supporting families. In J. Nisbet (Ed.), *Natural supports in school, at work, and in the community for people with severe disabilities* (pp. 121-164). Baltimore: Paul H. Brookes.

Dufresne, D., & Laux, B. (1994). From facilities to supports: The changing organization. In V.J. Bradley, J.W. Ashbaugh, & B.C. Blaney (Eds.), *Creating individual supports for people with developmental disabilities* (pp. 271-280). Baltimore: Paul H. Brookes.

Dunst, C.J., Trivette, C.M., & Deal, A.G. (1988). *Enabling and empowering families*. Cambridge, MA: Brookline Books.

Dunst, C.J., Trivette, C.M., Starnes, A.L., Hamby, D.W., & Gordon, N.J. (1993). *Building and evaluating family support initiatives: A national study of programs for persons with developmental disabilities*. Baltimore, Paul H. Brookes.

Dybwad, R.F. (1990). *Perspectives on a parent movement: The revolt of parents of children with intellectual limitations*. Cambridge, MA: Brookline Books.

Farrell, S.E. (1991). The interdisciplinary team process in developmental disabilities. In A.J. Capute & P.J. Accardo (Eds.), *Developmental*

disabilities in infancy and childhood (pp. 209-217). Baltimore: Paul H. Brookes.

Forest, M., & Lusthaus, E. (1989). Promoting educational equality for all students: Circles and MAPS. In S. Stainback, W. Stainback, & M. Forest (Eds.), *Educating all students in the mainstream of regular education* (pp. 43-57). Baltimore: Paul H. Brookes.

Forest, M., & Pearpoint, J. (1992). Families, friends, and circles. In J. Nisbet (Ed.), *Natural supports in school, at work, and in the community for people with severe disabilities* (pp. 65-86). Baltimore: Paul H. Brookes.

Garner, H. (1988). *Helping others through teamwork: A handbook for professionals*. Washington, DC: Child Welfare League of America.

Garner, H.S., Uhl, M., & Cox, A.W. (1992). *Interdisciplinary teamwork training guide*. Richmond, VA: Virginia Institute for Developmental Disabilities.

Given, B., & Simmons, S. (1977). The interdisciplinary health-care team: Fact or fiction. *Nursing Forum, 16,* 165-184.

Golin, A.K., & Ducanis, A.J. (1981). *The interdisciplinary team: A handbook for the education of exceptional children*. Rockville, MD: Aspen Publication.

Horwitz, J.J. (1970). *Team practice and the specialist: An introduction to interdisciplinary teamwork*. Springfield, IL: Charles C. Thomas.

Institute of Medicine (1991). *Disability in America: Toward a national agenda for prevention*. Washington, DC: National Academy Press.

Jorgensen, C.M. (1992). Natural supports in inclusive schools: Curricular and teaching strategies. In J. Nisbet (Ed.), *Natural supports in school, at work, and in the community for people with severe disabilities* (pp. 179-216). Baltimore: Paul H. Brookes.

Kendrick, M. (1994). Public and personal leadership challenges. In V.J. Bradley, J.W. Ashbaugh, & B.C. Blaney (Eds.), *Creating individual supports for people with developmental disabilities* (pp. 361-373). Baltimore: Paul H. Brookes.

Kiracofe, J. (1994). Strategies to help agencies shift from services to supports. In V.J. Bradley, J.W. Ashbaugh, & B.C. Blaney (Eds.), *Creating individual supports for people with developmental disabilities* (pp. 281-298). Baltimore: Paul H. Brookes.

Klein, J. (1992). Get me the hell out of here: Supporting people with disabilities to live in their own homes. In J. Nisbet (Ed.), *Natural supports in school, at work, and in the community for people with severe disabilities* (pp. 277-340). Baltimore: Paul H. Brookes.

Knoll, J.A., & Racino, J.A. (1994). Field in search of a home: The need for support personnel to develop a distinct identity. In V.J. Bradley, J.W. Ashbaugh, & B.C. Blaney (Eds.), *Creating individual supports for people with developmental disabilities* (pp. 299-324). Baltimore: Paul H. Brookes.

Kuhn, T. (1962). *The structure of scientific revolutions.* Chicago: University of Chicago Press.

Landerholm, E. (1990). The transdisciplinary team approach in infant intervention programs. *Teaching Exceptional Children, 23,* 66-70.

Luckasson, R., Coulter, D.L., Polloway, E.A., Reiss, S., Schalock, R.L., Snell, M.E., Spitalnik, D.M., & Stark, J.A. (1992). *Mental retardation: Definition, classification, and systems of supports* (9th ed.). Washington, DC: American Association on Mental Retardation.

Mount, B. (1994). Benefits and limitations of personal futures planning. In V.J. Bradley, J.W. Ashbaugh, & B.C. Blaney (Eds.), *Creating individual supports for people with developmental disabilities* (pp. 97-108). Baltimore: Paul H. Brookes.

Mount, B., & Zwernik, K. (1988). *It's never too early; it's never too late.* St. Paul, MN: Metropolitan Council.

Neugebauer, R. (1984, January). Who's responsible for making your team work? *Child Care Information Exchange,* pp. 4-6.

Nisbet, J.A. (1992). Introduction. In J. Nisbet (Ed.), *Natural supports in school, at work, and in the community for people with severe disabili-*

ties (pp. 1-10). Baltimore: Paul H. Brookes.

Nisbet, J.A., Jorgensen, C., & Powers, S. (1994). Systems change directed at inclusive education. In V.J. Bradley, J.W. Ashbaugh, & B.C. Blaney (Eds.), *Creating individual supports for people with developmental disabilities* (pp. 213-236). Baltimore: Paul H. Brookes.

O'Brien, J. (1987). A guide to lifestyle planning using The Activities Catalog to integrate services and natural support systems. In B. Wilcox & G.T. Bellamy (Eds.), *A comprehensive guide to The Activities Catalog: An alternative curriculum for youth and adults with severe disabilities* (pp. 175-189). Baltimore: Paul H. Brookes.

O'Brien, J., & Lovett, H. (1992). *Finding a way toward everyday lives: The contribution of person centered planning.* Harrisburg, PA: Pennsylvania Office of Mental Retardation.

O'Brien, J., & O'Brien, C.L. (1991). Sustaining positive changes: The future development of the residential support program. In S.J. Taylor, R. Bogdan, & J.A. Racino (Eds.), *Life in the community: Case studies of organizations supporting people with disabilities* (pp. 153-168). Baltimore: Paul H. Brookes.

O'Brien, J. & O'Brien, C.L. (1992). Members of each other: Perspectives on social support for people with severe disabilities. In J. Nisbet (Ed.), *Natural supports in school, at work, and in the community for people with severe disabilities* (pp. 17-64). Baltimore: Paul H. Brookes.

O'Brien, J. & O'Brien, C.L. (1993). Unlikely alliances: Friendships and people with developmental disabilities. In A.N. Amado (Ed.), *Friendships and community connections between people with and without disabilities* (pp. 9-40). Baltimore: Paul H. Brookes.

O'Brien, J. & O'Brien, C. L. (1994). More than just a new address: Images of organization for supported living agencies. In V.J. Bradley, J.W. Ashbaugh, & B.C. Blaney (Eds.), *Creating individual supports for people with developmental disabilities* (pp. 109-140). Baltimore: Paul H. Brookes.

Pappas, V., & Knoll, J. (1994, February). *Meeting the challenge of inclusive communities: New conceptions of interdisciplinary education at UAPs.* Paper presented at the Second Annual National Forum on Inclusive Communities, Kansas City, Missouri.

Pearpoint, J. (1990). *From behind the piano: The building of Judith Snow's unique circle of friends.* Toronto: Inclusion Press.

Perske, R. (1993). Introduction. In A.N. Amado (Ed.), *Friendships and community connections between people with and without disabilities* (pp. 1-6). Baltimore: Paul H. Brookes.

Racino, J.A., O'Connor, S., & Walker, P. (1993). Conclusion. In J.A. Racino, P. Walker, S. O'Connor, & S.J. Taylor (Eds.), *Housing, support, and community: Choices and strategies for adults with disabilities* (pp. 355-366). Baltimore, Paul H. Brookes.

Racino, J.A., Taylor, S.J., Walker, P., & O'Connor, S. (1993). Introduction. In J.A. Racino, P. Walker, S. O'Connor, & S.J. Taylor (Eds.), *Housing, support, and community: Choices and strategies for adults with disabilities* (pp. 1-32). Baltimore, Paul H. Brookes.

Racino. J.A., & Walker, P. (1993). "Whose life is it anyway?": Life planning, choices, and decision making. In J.A. Racino, P. Walker, S. O'Connor, & S.J. Taylor (Eds.), *Housing, support, and community: Choices and strategies for adults with disabilities* (pp. 57-80). Baltimore, Paul H. Brookes.

Schwartz, D.B. (1992). *Crossing the river: Creating a conceptual revolution in community and disability.* Cambridge, MA: Brookline Books.

Singer, G.H.S., & Powers, L.E. (1993). Contributing to resilience in families: An overview. In G.H.S. Singer & L.E. Powers (Eds.), *Families, disability and empowerment* (pp. 1-26). Baltimore: Paul H. Brookes.

Smull, M.W., & Danehey, A.J. (1994). Increasing quality while reducing costs: The challenge of the 1990s. In V.J. Bradley, J.W. Ashbaugh, & B.C. Blaney (Eds.), *Creating individual supports for people with developmental disabilities* (pp. 59-78). Baltimore: Paul H. Brookes.

Spencer, P.E., & Coye, R.W. (1988). Project BRIDGE: A team approach to decision-making for early services. *Infants and Young Children, 1,* 82-92.

Strully, J.L., & Strully, C. (1993). That which binds us: Friendship as a safe harbor in a storm. In A.N. Amado (Ed.), *Friendships and community connections between people with and without disabilities* (pp. 213-226). Baltimore: Paul H. Brookes.

Sutherland, A.T. (1981). *Disabled we stand.* Bloomington: Indiana University Press.

Swap, W.C. (1984). *Group decision-making.* Beverly Hills, CA: Sage.

Taylor, S. J. (1991). Families and their children. In S.J. Taylor, R. Bogdan, & J.A. Racino (Eds.), *Life in the community: Case studies of organizations supporting people with disabilities* (pp. 15-18). Baltimore: Paul H. Brookes.

Taylor, S.J., Knoll, J.A., Lehr, S., & Walker, P.M. (1989). Families for all children: Values-based services for children with disabilities and their families. In G.H.S. Singer & L.K. Irvin (Eds.), *Support for caregiving families: Enabling positive adaptation to disability.* Baltimore: Paul H. Brookes.

Turnbull, H.R. III, & Brunk, G.L. (1990). Quality of life and public philosophy. In Schalock, R.L. (Ed.), *Quality of life: Perspectives and issues.* Washington: American Association on Mental Retardation.

Vandercook, T., & York, J. (1989). The McGill Action Planning System (MAPS): A strategy for building the vision. *Journal of the Association for Persons with Severe Handicaps, 14,* 205-215.

Walker, P., & Racino, J.A. (1993). "Being with eople": Support and support strategies. In .A. Racino, P. Walker, S. O'Connor, & S.J. Talor (Eds.), *Housing, support, and community: Choices and strategies for adults with disabilities* (pp. 81-106). Baltimore, Paul H. Brookes.

Whitehouse, F.A. (1951). Teamwork: A democracy of professions. *Exceptional Children,* November, 45-52.

Index

About the Editors

Bruce A. Thyer is Professor of Social Work and Adjunct Professor of Psychology at the University of Georgia, and Associate Clinical Professor of Psychiatry and Health Behavior at the Medical College of Georgia. Dr. Thyer holds the M.S.W. degree from the University of Georgia and the Ph.D. in social work and psychology from the University of Michigan. Dr. Thyer has published over 130 professional journal articles, 25 book chapters, and 7 books in the human services. In addition, he is the editor of *Research on Social Work Practice*, a quarterly peer-reviewed journal produced by Sage Publications, Inc.

Nancy P. Kropf is an assistant professor in the School of Social Work and the assistant director of the Gerontology Center at the University of Georgia. She holds an M.S.W. degree from Michigan State University and a Ph.D. in social work from Virginia Commonwealth University. Her publications include research on older adults in care provider roles and older people with lifelong disabilities. In addition, she is co-editor of the text *Gerontological Social Work: Knowledge, Skills and Special Populations*.